Global Piracy

Global Piracy

A Documentary History of Seaborne Banditry

JAMES E. WADSWORTH

BLOOMSBURY ACADEMIC
LONDON • NEW YORK • OXFORD • NEW DELHI • SYDNEY

BLOOMSBURY ACADEMIC
Bloomsbury Publishing Plc
50 Bedford Square, London, WC1B 3DP, UK
1385 Broadway, New York, NY 10018, USA

BLOOMSBURY, BLOOMSBURY ACADEMIC and the Diana logo are trademarks of
Bloomsbury Publishing Plc

First published in Great Britain 2019

Copyright © James E. Wadsworth, 2019

James E. Wadsworth asserted his right under the Copyright,
Designs and Patents Act, 1988, to be identified as Author of this work.

For legal purposes the Acknowledgements on p. ix
constitute an extension of this copyright page.

Cover design by Dani Leigh
Cover image: A lithographic Victorian illustration of a pirate ship preparing for an attack,
London, England, 1880. (© Transcendental Graphics/Getty Images)

A catalogue record for this book is available from the British Library.

A catalog record for this book is available from the Library of Congress.

ISBN: HB: 978-1-3500-5819-4
           PB: 978-1-3500-5818-7
           ePDF: 978-1-3500-5821-7
           eBook: 978-1-3500-5820-0

Typeset by Integra Software Services Pvt. Ltd.
Printed and bound in Great Britain

To find out more about our authors and books visit www.bloomsbury.com
and sign up for our newsletters.

CONTENTS

LIST OF ILLUSTRATIONS

Figures

Tables

ACKNOWLEDGEMENTS

It is, perhaps, cliché to state that no author ever writes a book alone, but this couldn't be truer of the book you now hold in your hands. The germ of the idea began when I first started teaching my Global History of Piracy class, which I entitled 'Beneath the Skull and Crossbones'. Because I am a world historian at heart, I wanted to teach a course that was truly global in its reach, that avoided Western stereotypes and that was honest about who and what pirates were. I wanted to push my students to reconsider the pirate myths of their youths by confronting them with documents that went beyond the run-of-the-mill pirate stories.

In trying to gather material for that class, I ran into the insurmountable problem that no one had yet put together a truly global history of piracy. There were many exceptionally well-researched books for specific regions and periods. Yet, no one had created a book that combined the excellent modern research with primary documents that let students have access to real pirates and their victims. I struggled for years with unwieldy reading packets until I finally grew weary of them and began compiling sources and collecting secondary works as I began to consider how I might approach the book.

I was only into the third chapter and thought I had several years to work on the book, when Emma Goode, my first editor with Bloomsbury Publishing, contacted me. She mentioned that a historian at a conference had lamented the lack of a good global history of piracy that avoided the overly romanticized narratives we usually encounter and asked if I knew anyone who might be interested in writing one. I told her I had already started doing just that and she asked me to send her a proposal. I hesitated since I hadn't yet identified all the documents I needed and I still had a lot of research to do, but I drafted a proposal and sent it away. Helpful comments from the reviewers of the proposal and later reviewers of the completed draft have made this a much better book. Thank you, Emma, for pushing me to get this project finished and to all the reviewers for your insightful comments and suggestions.

I also need to thank Dian Murray for her invaluable guidance years ago when I first started teaching about piracy. She shared her syllabus and assignments with me. She also helped me with Chinese orthography. She is an example of generosity and collegiality. The reference librarians at Stonehill College spent countless hours helping me locate primary sources and tracking down copyright owners. Nancy Dunsing lent her time and skill in helping me get all the permissions and maps paid for in a timely manner. Her patience and good-natured approach to a potentially frustrating experience was unmatched. Maria Curtin helped me track down financing and has consistently given her support to this project. Barry Levely worked with me closely over a period of months to create the maps and patiently revised over and over again until we had them just right. The copyeditor, proofreader and indexer did a fabulous job and their work has made this book more accessible. Creating a documentary history requires considerable financial resources, and Stonehill College has generously supported this project financially at every step. Without their generous assistance, this book could not have been compiled.

To all of you and many more who I cannot name individually, I say thank you. You have made this voyage through the oceans of pirate history possible.

A NOTE TO INSTRUCTORS

Pirates represent some of the most popular and yet least understood figures in history. It has proven too easy, and too entertaining, to homogenize and stereotype them. Most students will have very romantic notions of piracy and very little exposure to primary sources about piracy. They will often hold the incompatible view that modern pirates are simple thugs and villains to be feared and suppressed, while believing that the Caribbean buccaneers were dignified bandits, worthy of emulation and admiration.

This documentary history seeks to address these contradictions by forcing readers to confront their preconceived notions and to provide them with access to 'real' pirates unfiltered, as much as possible, by the distractions of authorial voice and interpretation. This book cannot present a definitive account of piracy in world history. Such a work would be a massive undertaking and would fill many library shelves. I have also intentionally departed from the run-of-the-mill narratives and primary source collections that offer very little new information or insights and that tend to use the same sources.

Too often, our studies of piracy privilege Western piracy and pirates. Western pirates are portrayed as the most dangerous, the most effective, the most brutal, the most feared, etc. I have tried to correct these self-serving misconceptions by giving equal treatment, as far as possible to the range of global piracy from the ancient Greeks to modern Nigeria. I have tried very hard to provide a balanced and nuanced documentary history based on recent scholarship with each region and era set in its own unique global context.

In selecting and editing the primary sources, I have endeavoured to choose sources that are interesting and that illustrate the complexity and variety of piratical activity. I have edited the sources, sometimes considerably, to make them accessible to a modern English-reading audience while still preserving the flavour and colour of the original writing. Where possible, I have also tried to find sources from the perspective of both the pirates or privateers themselves and their victims.

Not everyone will agree with my selections, my interpretations or my approach. I have had to leave out regions, episodes and figures that many readers may hope to find. For example, I have not explored in detail pirates who operated off the Canadian coast, nor have I examined Irish pirates or the pirates operating in the Caribbean in the nineteenth century. I do not have a chapter on female pirates, though I considered including one.

The challenge is that, when viewed from a global perspective, female pirates were rare, few in number and historically insignificant. When women were involved in piracy or privateering, they are discussed in the regions and eras where they appeared. I also have not spent time retelling pirate tales that are already available to the public. This book makes original arguments about global piracy based on recent scholarship and seeks to place seaborne banditry in a truly global context.

I have devised this book with a global history of piracy course in mind, which is what I teach. But the book can be used either in its entirety or in pieces, depending on your needs. The maps, glossary and questions should help your students contextualize and think about piracy as a global phenomenon. But feel free to set your own course through the oceans of history. There is no one way or even best way to approach this vast topic. What you have here is my way. Feel free to tinker with it and to help your students engage and/or challenge the arguments this book presents.

CHAPTER ONE

Enemies of All Nations

If you are a student of history, either by inclination or by coercion, you will have encountered pirates. You may even have joined the throngs of children who wielded cardboard cutlasses and sported eye patches and pencilled-in beards on some stage for the benefit of your parents. You may have sung 'pirate' songs, which were really nothing more than regular sea shanties all Western sailors sang. You may even have downed a mug of apple juice and called it pirate grog. Pirates also probably populated the cartoons you watched, the books you read and the films you viewed. They may even have found their way onto your pillowcases and bedsheets. Pirates form an essential part of the imaginative childhood experience in many Western countries.

Yet, when Somali pirates began hijacking ships at the beginning of the twenty-first century, most Westerners were shocked and scandalized. This apparently sudden appearance of Somali piracy stimulated a media storm. Western audiences sat enthralled to the coverage of the sensational 2008 hijacking of the *Maersk Alabama* and the dramatic rescue of Captain Phillips by US Navy SEALs.

These acts of piracy so shocked many in the West because we had convinced ourselves that pirates were a thing of the past. In the United States, we still pat ourselves on the back because we 'stood up' to the Mediterranean pirates in 1805 when Thomas Jefferson sent ships to attack Tripoli and then in the 1820s when we 'eradicated' pirates from the Caribbean.[1] Our collective ignorance and amnesia of ongoing episodes of piracy elsewhere in the world allowed us to fabricate the lie that Western powers had suppressed piracy by the middle of the nineteenth century. We imagined that a temporary regional decline in piracy meant that piracy ceased to exist everywhere in the world. To us, pirates had become semi-fictional, heroic characters that populated our fantasies. They had become innocuous rebels that excited our envy and admiration.

Despite our collective ignorance, the upsurge in piracy in the early twentieth century was no aberration, no departure from normal sea-bound commerce – quite the contrary. Piracy has long been the normal state of affairs for seaborne traffic. The truly global decline in piracy following the Second World War was the real aberration when piracy reached an historical low point. But it was only a decline – a low tide in the history of global piracy. There has never been a time in human history since ocean-going merchants first carried valuable goods in the holds of their ships in which seaborne banditry has not existed. Since this is true, we have to ask ourselves: Where did we miss the boat?

Making heroes out of villains

Pirates crop up everywhere and inhabit our imaginations year round. 'National Talk-Like-A-Pirate Day' comes around every September 19 in the United States. On that day, otherwise rational people run around shouting, 'Ahoy Mate' and 'Avast ye land lubber'. Every Halloween, hordes of swashbuckling, eye-patch-wearing and sword-toting pirates swarm our streets to beg for candy. Store shelves bend under the weight of pirate ships, pirate swords, pirate games and pirate figurines. Over 160 pirate films have been produced since 1908. Dozens of comics, video games and books have been written to celebrate pirates. The Pittsburgh Pirates, the Tampa Bay Buccaneers and the Oakland Raiders have capitalized on piracy themes. Everywhere their fans live, crossed swords and bats, earrings, skeletons and bandanas are put on proud display. For $45, you can take a ride on the 'pirate' ship *Formidable* in Boston Harbor. You can take tours in North and South Carolina out to pirate havens such as Ocracoke Island, where Blackbeard reputedly spent his last night alive. The 'pirate' ship *Revenge*, of Beaufort South Carolina, invites us to 'unleash our inner pirate' and join them on a cruise.[2] For $400, you can send your child to a pirate-themed summer camp. No one seems to catch the irony of a pirate-themed Cub Scout day camp that seeks to 'help the boys to become a part of another time and place and to be able to play-act in a safe, structured environment'.[3] Play-act what, precisely? Hijacking? Kidnapping? Robbery? Murder? And *safe*? Do we want these activities to be safe? Do we want children to perceive them as play?

The point is that pirates and piracy have infiltrated just about every corner of our popular culture and entertainment industry. Everyone knows what pirates looked like, how they talked, what motivated them, what kinds of weapons they used, etc. – or, at least, they think they do. A Google search will quickly reveal several websites that will teach you 'pirate speak' as if all pirates the world over spoke a common language. In fact, the Atlantic and Caribbean pirates who supposedly spoke this way spoke every European language and several Native American and African languages. They even used a distinct maritime pidgin that most Western sailors used. Robert Louis Stevenson, in his book *Treasure Island,* gave his pirates a Devonshire accent. But the actor Robert Newton, who played Long John Silver in the 1950 Disney film *Treasure Island*, used a West Country accent. His portrayal was so compelling that the West Country accent still dominates our representations of pirate language.[4] This is the form of pirate speech you will most likely find on the web. And yet, pirates spoke a babel of languages, including Greek, Arabic, Latin, Malayalam, Mandarin, Japanese, Somali, Portuguese, Spanish, Turkish, Tausug, Malay, French, English, Dutch, Danish, Finnish, Yoruba, Izon, Ibibio and Tagalog. Likewise, pirates are almost always portrayed in extravagant, fictionalized, late-seventeenth-century European dress – long coats, peg legs, earrings, head bandanas, tattoos, curved knives, missing teeth, scars on the face, eye patches, the ever-present talking parrots and the occasional hook. Though some of this is certainly accurate for late-seventeenth-century Caribbean buccaneers, it is not representative of pirates or pirate cultures everywhere. Most of our 'knowledge' about pirates is only loosely based on authentic primary sources. It is almost always filtered through Disneyland, books, movies, toys, birthday parties and sports. Much of the modern Western imagery of pirates originates from Charles Johnson's 1724 *A General History of the Pyrates* because this has been the most influential source on pirate lore in the Western world.[5] His depictions have been filtered through our popular media so effectively that they have become the standard by which all pirates are measured.

As the pirate myths have evolved, our perceptions have evolved with them. In early-twentieth-century popular culture, pirates were seen either as villainous cutthroats or as comic buffoons. The Second World War generation read books like *Treasure Island* and watched films like Errol Flynn's *Sea Hawk*. They saw pirates as adventuresome and glamorous.[6] By the 1950s, pirates became true heroes in the Robin Hood fashion. The baby boomer generation drew inspiration from Disney's *Peter Pan* and *Treasure Island*. They created fraternities that used the skull and crossbones and treasure maps in their initiations. This generation associated pirates with the heroic rescue of beautiful women and perceived them as misunderstood, noble bandits who robbed from the rich and gave to the poor. The belief that pirates were social bandits has been supported by some scholars who have noted that pirates rebelled against the constraints of their oppressive societies and sought vengeance on their oppressors. Though some pirates may have been social bandits in this sense, one is hard-pressed to find a pirate who willingly delivered his ill-gotten gains to the poor.[7] The modern college student of the early twenty-first century grew up inundated with pirate-based Disney films, such as *Muppet Treasure Island, Treasure Planet* and *Pirates of the Caribbean*. If nothing else, Johnny Depp proved that a permanently half-drunk, crude, womanizing, swaggering, slightly effeminate pirate who cavorts with zombies and mermaids can still make a lot of money for film producers – though Johnny Depp's statement that pirates were like the rock stars of their times is not accurate.[8]

Privateers and pirates in the Western world occupied a distinctly ambiguous and complicated space. Those who preyed on someone else could be quite popular among local communities because they often brought in much-needed supplies and money. Their activities were 'justified on grounds of religion, maritime defense, war, and political independence'.[9] They could claim to be patriotic heroes fighting for the fatherland. But when pirates or privateers raided local shipping, they were seen more like modern drug cartels and organized criminals. They became rock stars only to modern audiences.[10]

The problem with our modern Western stereotypes is that we have taken a very small group of men that operated for only about 300 years in only one part of the world (granted it is a large geographical area), and we have frozen them in time. We have frozen them in a late-seventeenth-century context in terms of technology, dress, culture and politics. In the process, we have acted as if these pirates were somehow distinct from other sailing men of their times. In fact, they were not. Most pirates belonged to the sailing classes of the societies from which they came and moved back and forth from fishing and commerce to piracy with great alacrity. No observer could have distinguished a pirate from a sailor simply by his dress or his speech.[11] To put it bluntly, the Atlantic and Caribbean pirates that dominate the Western imagination seem insignificant when compared to the massive fleets of Chinese pirates of the early nineteenth century and with the range, effectiveness and brutality of Southeast Asia pirates of the same era. All of this begs the questions: 'What happened? How did pirates move into mainstream society as the rehabilitated heroes we laugh at and admire?'

A brief review of the relevant history suggests an answer. In colonial America, pirates and privateers found ready acceptance as suppliers of exotic goods, currency and food. When they returned with shiploads of plunder that infiltrated the local economy, they could enjoy considerable fame. Popular opinion began to shift in the eighteenth century as the government became more intent on reining in private plundering in favour of non-violent trade and as European nations became more effective at imposing their concepts of sovereignty on the high seas.[12] This contraction of private plunder and the extension of state sovereignty coincided with the suppression of piracy in the West and the rise of the modern industrialized nation state. European nations began to exert greater control over pirates and privateers of all kinds in the later part of the seventeenth century. By the early nineteenth century, they joined forces to suppress the Barbary corsairs of North Africa. The United States used the Monroe Doctrine to pursue pirates in the Caribbean. Commodore David Porter employed his 'special squadron of pirate killers', to clear the bays and harbours of Texas, Florida, Cuba and Puerto Rico of pirates.[13] After the US annexation of the Philippines in 1898, the US Navy engaged in a prolonged and bloody campaign against people they called pirates of the Southern Philippines. All around the world in the nineteenth century, Western powers aggressively suppressed what they perceived as piracy to protect their vast seaborne empires.[14]

This nineteenth-century decline in global maritime predation coincided with the rise of mid-nineteenth-century nation states, increased industrialization and the growing power of employers. Both the nation states and the employers sought to discipline the working class to make them better taxpayers, better soldiers and better industrial workers. Workers lost access to land and to leisure time. They often found themselves crammed into fetid slums, breathing putrid air and drinking filthy water. There were very few laws to protect them from abuse and exploitation. All of this, of course, left workers with a greater sense of dependence and oppression – longing for the freedom of a more unregulated world that had once seemed so full of potential.[15]

The bandits and outlaws who had dared to fight the system, to take life by the throat and ride the waves to adventure and glory, became very alluring. And, if the bandits robbed the rich – made them pay at least a token price for their abuse of the poor – so much the better. It did not even matter if the pirates never redistributed their ill-gotten gains to the less fortunate. At least they had had the courage to take them. In this context, bandits of all types came to be glorified as Robin Hood-like heroes. Pirates were no exception. As soon as they ceased to be a threat, we dummied them down, romanticized, homogenized and stereotyped them so much that we are now completely incapable of taking pirates seriously, either as real historical actors or as the modern menace to global shipping that they are.

Historians have also contributed to this perspective. They have portrayed pirates as an easily identifiable archetype – rebels operating outside the bounds of the law who sought to escape the sexual and social constraints of land-based societies.[16] This perspective assumes that all land-based societies shared a common set of standards, moral values, concepts of sovereignty and the legitimate application of violence.[17] This was never true for a country as small as England, let alone the entire world. Recent scholarship has shown that pirates and privateers were deeply embedded in land-based communities from which they drew support and to whom they sold their loot.[18] The growth of scholarly analysis of piracy in the last thirty years has challenged our long-standing stereotypes of Western piracy and requires a new more global analysis of seaborne banditry.

What is piracy? Working towards a definition

Our historical amnesia about global piracy is partly a symptom of our confusion over what constitutes true piracy. This question plagued the early Greeks, who were the first to leave us written accounts of piracy. They used the terms *leistes* and *peirates*. *Leistes* referred to plunder or booty, while *peirates* was a pejorative term for raider or plunderer and is the origin of the Latin word *pirata* and our modern English word 'pirate'.[19] The Greeks did not make hard and fast distinctions between pirates who operated at sea using ships and bandits who always operated on land. But they did eventually make the distinction. Strabo (64 BCE–24 CE) described the Bosporan peoples near Colchis as 'they who live by plundering at sea'. The Greeks did develop a phrase that translated only as pirate and not as bandit, which was *kata-pontistes* (one who throws into the sea). The Romans used *Praedo* and *Pirata*. *Praedo* could mean either bandit or pirate, while *pirata* referred to maritime plunderers.[20] The Romans called them the *hostis humani generis* (enemies of all nations) to assert sovereignty over seas that they did not really control. It has never been true that pirates were the enemies of all nations because pirates always acted with the support of communities and states. They had to have havens or bases where they could resupply and sell their loot.[21]

Given the heated debates about what constitutes piracy today, it is unlikely that we will arrive at any agreement. As Peter Shapinsky argues, and despite what some pretend, 'The term pirate does not constitute a stable, objective category that a simple legal definition can make comprehensible. In most cases, the meaning of "pirate" depends on its representations in various historical and cultural contexts'.[22] I am interested in defining piracy in historical terms not for legal purposes. States have long debated what constituted legal (state-sanctioned) and illegal (non-state-sanctioned) maritime predation.[23] The Roman Republic, post-Viking-era Scandinavia and Northern Europe, North Africa, China and Southeast Asia all had states who struggled to exert sovereignty over the seas – which meant that they had to claim a monopoly on extraterritorial violence.[24] To claim a monopoly, states had to impose their own sovereignty and exclude those who did not recognize it. The debate was not finally settled until the twentieth century. Consequently, modern legal definitions of piracy make little sense historically and so muddy the waters that we are left unable to discuss piracy in any meaningful terms prior to the seventeenth century.

The 1982 United Nations Convention on the Law of the Sea, Part VII, Article 101 defines piracy as follows:

> Piracy consists of any of the following acts: (a) any illegal acts of violence or detention, or any act of depredation, committed for private ends by the crew or the passengers of a private ship or a private aircraft, and directed: (i) on the high seas, against another ship or aircraft, or against persons or property on board such ship or aircraft; (ii) against a ship, aircraft, persons or property in a place outside the jurisdiction of any State; (b) any act of voluntary participation in the operation of a ship or of an aircraft with knowledge of facts making it a pirate ship or aircraft; (c) any act of inciting or of intentionally facilitating an act described in subparagraph (a) or (b).

According to this definition, a pirate is only someone who commits or participates in armed robbery or violence in international waters against another ship using a private ship for private ends. By this definition, robbery and violence in territorial waters is not piracy. Mutiny and the seizure of one's own ship is not piracy. Hijacking or robbing a ship while at anchor in a harbour or port is not piracy. Naval ships of any state cannot commit piracy. Attacking and pillaging a town, village or city by sea is not piracy. In fact, this definition is so narrow that it defines away most commercial raiders or seaborne bandits from the early Greeks to the Sulu Sea to the present day.[25] For example, since Somali pirates are using inflatable motorboats rather than ships to approach their victims, by this definition they cannot technically be considered pirates. Nigerian pirates who attack ships at anchor in Nigerian waters are not pirates. Bandits who attack a vessel from canoes on the Amazon River would also not be pirates. The Barbary corsairs who worked for Muslims states in North Africa would not be pirates. The Chinese who raided villages in the Pearl River Delta would not be pirates. This legal definition was created to clarify and simplify prosecutions of maritime crimes according to modern international law, but it is of little use in a global study of piracy.[26]

The uncritical acceptance by modern scholars of this twentieth-century legal definition of piracy confuses the historical record and distorts the way piracy was perceived and practised prior to the twentieth century. As Guy Chet has argued, the distinction between legal and illegal predation may be 'legally valid' in some cases in the seventeenth- and eighteenth-century Atlantic where it developed, but it was and is 'culturally untrue' and ahistorical virtually everywhere else.[27] Legality and legitimacy are not the same and peoples around the world frequently challenged the perceived illegitimacy of piracy and commerce raiding.[28] In the eighteenth and nineteenth centuries as Europeans attempted to export and impose this definition of piracy around the world, they found that the peoples of Asia, Southeast Asia, India and Saudi Arabia did not agree with or even understand the distinction. The East India Company had to continually 'instruct' Asian and Indian rulers that piracy was illegitimate armed robbery.[29]

This distinction made little sense to Southeast Asian societies dependent on control of the seas and on control of people, not land. Anthony Reid has argued that in Southeast Asia 'forcing or encouraging trade to come to one's port exemplified the essence of statecraft, and the ability to protect such trade from attack by enemies, the proof of accomplishment. The path to statehood often began with violent seizures at sea'.[30] Southeast Asian languages, such as Malay and Javanese, do not contain a word for piracy. Yet European states insisted on declaring any act of defence or conquest by these states as piracy in an attempt to delegitimize and negate native claims to sovereignty of the seas.[31]

Obviously, pirates seldom self-identified as criminals in need of repression. For most of them, piracy was, or is, a job. They preferred euphemisms such as 'to take purchase', 'to go roving', 'to do an exploit' or 'to go on account'.[32] Some seafarers, such as Blackbeard, understood that 'land-based authorities depicted them as pirates and engaged with those depictions in

order to craft identities'.[33] Whether we perceive someone as a pirate or not
depends on which end of the sword or gun we are looking at. One man's
legally sanctioned privateer is another man's pirate. One man's legal tax is
another's robbery. One man's legitimate trade is another man's smuggling.
The pirate Samuel Bellamy illustrated this problem when he reportedly said,
'They vilify us, the Scoundrels do, when there is only this Difference, they
Rob the Poor under the Cover of Law ... and we plunder the Rich under the
Protection of our own Courage.'[34]

Who, then, gets to decide what constitutes legal/legitimate trade, plunder
and warfare? The victims? The perpetrators? The state? Merchants? State
attempts at controlling the discourse resulted in legal distinctions between
legitimate maritime predation and illegitimate predation that began to
emerge in the fifteenth and sixteenth centuries when European states sought
to extend their claim to a monopoly on violence beyond their territories.
During the 'medieval period, violence was democratized, marketized, and
internationalized'.[35] States sought to 'escape feudalism's restraints on the
exercise of violence and [were] intent on amassing wealth and military
power autonomous from their subjects and other rulers'.[36] They unleashed
non-state actors in the form of mercenaries, privateers and mercantile
companies, but found that they could not always control them.

Our modern definition of piracy was created by nation states intent on
both regulating warfare and trade and seizing control of the high seas. Those
who resisted or did not participate in this endeavour were labelled pirates. By
the mid-seventeenth century, anyone performing an act of maritime violence
with some legal cover from land authorities was termed a corsair.[37] By the
eighteenth century, the sea dogs from England called themselves privateers.[38]
The Portuguese declared their exclusive right to control the shipping lanes
of the Indian Ocean on the lie that no native state had ever tried to regulate
them. When local states and merchant communities resisted, the Portuguese
'confiscated' their goods as trespassers.[39] The Europeans were happy to call
the peoples of Borneo and the Malabar Coast of India pirates when they
attacked European ships. But when the Dutch and the Portuguese attacked
the shipping of native peoples in Southeast Asia, it was considered legitimate
warfare. We have become too accepting of these self-serving European state
narratives.

The late-seventeenth-century reaction against privateers and pirates in
Europe occurred as states began to attempt to regain control of the non-
state actors they had unleashed. To do so, they had to convince merchants
that trade with state interference was more profitable than trade without
it. Merchants had to agree to set aside their weapons and accept the
protection of the state in exchange for the state's right to regulate and tax
their businesses. Not until the nineteenth century did European states agree
that they should prevent private individuals or companies from waging
their own wars and making maritime trade a military target. Only then did
formal navies replace privateers.[40]

Indeed, piracy could not be defined as illegal and stateless until all the forms of 'legal' predation were eliminated and states asserted a monopoly on the use of violence, which happened only when European powers agreed to abandon privateering and corsairing. That is when pirates came to be defined as stateless criminals.[41] The historian Guy Chet describes the problem succinctly:

> Most scholars of piracy assume an *essential* difference between piracy and privateering: whereas pirates preyed on the commerce of all nations, privateers were 'commissioned' by governments (through letters of marque) to carry out similar attacks solely on enemy merchant vessels. Thus, historians suggest that the close of the seventeenth century saw a passage from an age of Atlantic and Caribbean piracy to an age of privateering; outright piracy was forcefully suppressed and replaced by state-sanctioned, state-regulated, and targeted commerce raiding. In fact, however, the eighteenth-century distinction between piracy and privateering was a semantic novelty that did not enjoy universal acceptance. This semantic and legalistic distinction was meaningless in practice as well – privateers were rarely mindful of the restrictions of their commissions, attacking neutral, allied, and British shipping. Moreover, privateering commissions attracted more individuals to commerce raiding and made Atlantic shipping more risky and violent. These commerce raiders, many of whom were former pirates, utilized the same types of vessels and tactics as pirates, and often targeted the same prizes.[42]

Likewise, pirates and privateers of all stripes not only captured and plundered ships at sea, they raided and looted coastal towns, villages and cities, and even conquered territories and bases from which to operate.[43]

Ultimately, what distinguishes piracy from all other forms of banditry is the use of watercraft as the vehicle with which to travel from place to place and to carry out attacks. Ships offer far greater scope for pirates than land-based bandits enjoy, while also requiring a higher commitment in resources.[44] Pirates may be employees of the state or of private institutions. They may be social and political renegades. They may be merchants and fishermen seeking new economic opportunities. They may be cutthroats and thieves. They may operate during times of war or peace. They may belong to the social elite, or they may be social outcasts. Pirates are a complex, heterogeneous group that defy easy definitions, but they all use watercraft of some kind.

Still, to write about them, we have to define them. Common definitions of piracy based on twentieth-century sensibilities are much too narrow to be useful.[45] Piracy as a pure modern legal abstraction, unadulterated by historical reality and complexity, would be **non-state-sanctioned predation emanating from the sea**. The problem here is the inherent state bias of this definition. Even the European states who championed this idea did not adhere to it in practice. They routinely accused the states of Southeast Asia of piracy. The Brunei state of Borneo or the Sulu State in the Philippines could not by this definition engage in piracy and yet every European nation active in Southeast Asian waters accused them of it.[46] Likewise, if pirates form their own state, then, by the legal UN definition, they are no longer pirates. This is not mere hyperbole. Pirate states have emerged in Taiwan, the Malabar Coast and even perhaps on Madagascar. And yet, the Chinese and the English refused to acknowledge the legitimacy of those states. A simple nod and a wink from a state can turn a pirate into a privateer overnight while his behaviour, victims, tools, purpose and motivations remain utterly unchanged. The reality is that piracy was not clearly defined as non-state violence until the nineteenth century when European states agreed to make it so.[47] This definition of piracy in its purist form may work for some areas and at some times, but it does not work everywhere.

My working definition of piracy is quite simply **seaborne banditry**. I do not use the term 'banditry' to refer to outlawry, but to plunder, which may or may not be seen as legitimate by one or both parties. The concept of legality or illegality is far too nebulous to be of use here. In many ways, it was simply a state's way of delegitimizing its enemies.[48] If we remove the state and legitimacy from discussions of seaborne banditry, we can speak of three broad types of maritime predation that exist along a continuum from parasitic to episodic to intrinsic.[49] First, pirates can act as macroparasites that thrive where trade flourishes. They infest the trade networks of their host communities and drain off a portion of the wealth for themselves. If they are efficient, they may debilitate their host. But it is not in their interest to destroy it, though they could do so. For example, when faced with the rise of Atlantic nations and Islamic power in the Mediterranean, Venice proved unable to withstand the pirate attacks of the Uskoks, Algerians, Tunisians, Dutch, English and Turkish corsairs of the sixteenth century and so began to turn away from the sea.

Second, episodic piracy can occur during a weakening of local or regional political power such as the seventeenth-century decline of 'Iberian, Ottoman, Mughal, and Ming empires [that created] a "great pirate belt" … from the Caribbean to the South China Sea'.[50] Disruption of trade or the close of formal wars can leave seamen and ships idle with few alternatives for employment. It is no accident that piracy surged after the end of hostilities between England and Spain in 1603 or after the Treaty of Utrecht in 1713 or after the Napoleonic wars in 1815. It is also no accident that cries for the suppression of piracy from American businessmen surfaced only as the nineteenth-century American cities increased domestic production, expanded their trade networks and discovered new opportunities for employment, trade and capital. In this sense, piracy can be seen as an economic activity driven by shifts in the demand and supply of labour caused by political and economic changes.[51]

Third, when seaborne banditry becomes an accepted part of economic, commercial or state institutions, it can be said to be intrinsic. Despite the propaganda of northern European Christian nations to the contrary, there was little difference between the activities of the corsairs of Tripoli, Algiers and Salé and those of their own privateers or the Knights of St. John from Malta or of St. James from Livorno. For all involved, piracy had become an intrinsic part of commerce, private enterprise, state formation and public finance.[52] By seeing seaborne banditry on a continuum from parasitic through episodic to intrinsic, we can account for the wide variety of piratical activities, avoid anachronism and evade becoming bogged down in sterile debates over legality and legitimacy. For our purposes in this book then, **piracy is seaborne banditry that can manifest itself as parasitic, episodic, intrinsic or some combination of the above, given the specific historical and cultural context in which it was practised.**

I am well aware that my solution to this problem of defining piracy will not satisfy everyone – perhaps no one. However, it does allow us to examine the myriad forms of maritime predation and commerce raiding that have been such an important part of world history. Some may argue that the definition is too broad and that even naval warfare could be included as piracy. I grant them the point with the caveat that piracy was very often warfare by other means, and so any attempt to make nice, neat distinctions will always get bogged down in the details. Although we can accept that in the minds of some practitioners of seaborne banditry there was a distinction between state-sanctioned and non-sanctioned plunder, those lines were not always well defined or universally accepted. In the end, I think we must be satisfied with a useful working definition rather than demand one that is stable, uncomplicated, uncontroversial and accepted by all. The definition must, in fact, reflect the unstable and contextual nature of seaborne banditry.

Given the confusion surrounding what a pirate is, we should not be surprised that there is little agreement about what constitutes a pirate attack in the modern world. The International Maritime Organization (IMO) and the International Maritime Bureau (IMB) count pirate attacks differently. The IMO follows the international legal view of piracy that excludes attacks in territorial waters and requires that pirates use privately owned ships for private purposes. The IMB does not require the attack to be in international waters or that pirates use a ship. In the IMB criteria, naval craft can engage in acts of piracy and pirates can attack from a raft or even a dock.[53] Consequently, the IMB numbers are probably more accurate for our purposes. Even so, reporting probably woefully undercounts real pirate attacks by more than half. States do not always report pirate attacks against their ships because they see it as an internal matter that could be dangerous to the country's reputation. Ship owners do not report attacks because they worry about bad publicity, reprisal of port authorities against ships who complain about port security, crews demanding higher salaries, increased insurance premiums, loss of clients, and the risk of having their vessels and their cargoes delayed for an investigation. Attacks on fishing boats are also rarely reported.[54]

Piracy is one of those human activities constructed on the long underlying waves of geologic time.[55] It is no accident that piracy flourished in certain places for thousands of years and resurfaces again and again in the same locations – even after desperate attempts to eradicate it. Oceans and seas, like mountains, have proven difficult for states and empires to dominate. Everywhere piracy flourishes, rugged coastlines fragmented by mountains, harbours, bays, rivers and islands provide havens for pirates and pathways for their depredations. Piracy also flourishes where widespread poverty, or perceived economic deprivation, coincides with political fragmentation or the absence of strong unified rule and the corruption or acquiescence of government officials.[56] But none of these together or alone would foster piracy without the presence of vibrant trade along predictable sea-lanes and the existence of markets willing to buy and sell pirate loot. When all of these conditions combine, piracy will flourish, and it will persist so long as these conditions endure.

Why study piracy?

The simplest answer to the question of why we should study piracy is that pirates are interesting. Anyone who has dressed up as a pirate for Halloween or who has obsessed about *Pirates of the Caribbean* will probably agree. But there are other reasons – more important reasons. Piracy has played and continues to play a significant role in the development of the modern world. Pirates have pushed states towards increased centralization and have helped create codified international laws.[57] They also have contributed to the spread of global commerce, the creation and decline of global empires and the movement of commodities and money over large distances. It is difficult to imagine how England could have risen to the level of a global maritime power without its pirates and privateers. The piratical ransacking of the Portuguese and Spanish Empires by just about every European nation that could put a boat on the water contributed to the decline of both empires. Pirates not only preyed upon global commerce, they facilitated it. The Dutch pirates who fought under the flags of the Dutch East India Company or the Dutch West India Company secured vast wealth and treasure for the companies' stockholders. Pirates also pioneered sea-lanes and established cities. They created informal economies and subcultures that defined entire regions and eras in world history.

A study of piracy also allows us to examine the process of state formation, social and gender hierarchies, globalization, naval warfare, commerce, imperialism, terrorism, marginalization, international law, colonialism, racism, labour and underdevelopment from a different perspective. The simple truth is that, if we wish to understand the development of the modern global economy, international law and modern nation states, we must have a clear understanding of piracy as a global phenomenon.

Notes

1 Turner, 'President Thomas Jefferson and the Barbary Pirates', 157–168. Konstam, *Piracy*, 275–278.

2 http://beaufortpiratesrevenge.com/index.html

3 http://circleten.org/sites/circle10.org/files/captains_cove_element.pdf

4 Babits, 'Pirate Imagery', 271–272.

5 Johnson, *A General History*.

6 Showronek, 'X Marks the Spot', 290–293.

7 See Hobsbawm, *Bandits*; Wagner, 'Thuggee and Social Banditry Reconsidered'; Antony, 'Peasants, Heroes, and Brigands'; Rediker, 'The Seaman as Pirate'.

8 http://www.dnaindia.com/entertainment/report-pirates-were-rock-stars-of-the-18th-century-1100331

9 Hanna, *Pirate Nests*, 167.

10 Lunsford, *Piracy and Privateering*, 2–3.

11 Babits, 'Pirate Imagery', 274–276.

12 See Hanna, *Pirate Nests*; Chet, *The Ocean Is a Wilderness*; and Thomson, *Mercenaries*.

13 Konstam, *Piracy*, 277–278.

14 Ritchie, 'Government Measures against Piracy and Privateering', 23–25; Showronek, 'X Marks the Spot', 283–286.

15 Kooistra, 'Criminals as Heroes', 217–239.

16 Cowley, 'The Sea Jacobins', 327–329; Rediker, *Villains of All Nations*; Linebaugh and Rediker, *The Many-Headed Hydra*; Rediker, *Between the Devil and the Deep Blue Sea*. On sexuality and gender, see Turley, *Rum, Sodomy, and the Lash*; Burg, *Sodomy and the Perception of Evil*; Burg, *Sodomy and the Pirate Tradition*; Rediker, 'Liberty beneath the Jolly Roger'; Klausmann, *Women Pirates and the Politics of the Jolly Roger*; Stanley, *Bold in Her Breeches*.

17 Hanna, *Pirate Nests*, 7.

18 See for example, Ritchie, *Captain Kidd*; Burgess, *The Pirate's Pact*; Burgess, *The Politics of Piracy*; Hanna, *Pirate Nests*; McDonald, *Pirates, Merchants, Settlers, and Slaves*.

19 Souza, *Piracy in the Graeco-Roman World*, 3–9.

20 Souza, *Piracy in the Graeco-Roman World*, 3–9, 13.

21 McDonald, *Pirates, Merchants, Settlers and Slaves*, 12–13.

22 Shapinsky, 'From Sea Bandits to Sea Lords', 27; Lunsford, *Piracy and Privateering*, 6.

23 Heller-Roazen, *The Enemy of All*.

24 Thomson, *Mercenaries*; Amirell and Müller, 'Introduction', 3.

25 Warren, 'Trade for Bullion to Trade', 152.

26 Campbell, 'A Modern History of the International Legal Definition of Piracy', 19–32.

27   Chet, *The Ocean Is a Wilderness*, 49.

28   Chet, *The Ocean Is a Wilderness*, 6.

29   Risso, 'Cross-Cultural Perceptions of Piracy'.

30   Reid, 'Violence at Sea', 16.

31   Gaynor, 'Piracy in the Offing', 840.

32   Senior, *A Nation of Pirates*, 13.

33   Shapinsky, 'From Sea Bandits to Sea Lords', 27.

34   Johnson, *General History*, 587.

35   Thomson, *Mercenaries*, 4.

36   Thomson, *Mercenaries*, 6.

37   Rodger, 'The Law and Language of Private Naval Warfare', 5–16.

38   Hanna, *Pirate Nests*, 46.

39   Prange, 'The Contested Sea', 9–10.

40   Pérotin-Dumon, 'The Pirate and the Emperor', 41–45; Thomson, *Mercenaries*.

41   Thomson, *Mercenaries*, 143–144.

42   Chet, *The Ocean Is a Wilderness*, 5.

43   Antony, 'Introduction', 7–8.

44   Souza, *Piracy in the Graeco-Roman World*, 11.

45   Showronek and Ewen, *X Marks the Spot*, xv; Cordingly, *Under the Black Flat*, xvii; Antony, *Pirates in the Age of Sail*, 7; Souza, *Piracy in the Graeco-Roman World*, 1.

46   Thomson, *Mercenaries*, 114–115.

47   Thomson, *Mercenaries*, 117–118, 140.

48   Souza, 'Piracy in Classical Antiquity', 25, 43.

49   The discussion that follows is drawn from Anderson, 'Piracy and World History', 82–106; Lunsford, *Piracy and Privateering*, 3.

50   Anderson, 'Piracy and World History', 94.

51   Starkey, 'Pirates and Markets', 107–124.

52   Anderson, 'Piracy in the Eastern Seas', 88.

53   Elleman et al., 'Introduction', 10–11.

54   Eklöf, *Pirates in Paradise*, 91–92; Elleman, 'Introduction', 11–12.

55   See Braudel, *The Mediterranean and the Mediterranean World*.

56   Souza, *Piracy in the Graeco-Roman World*, 202.

57   See Thomson, *Mercenaries*.

CHAPTER TWO

Bandits of the Wine Dark Sea: Piracy in the Classical World

It is tempting to trace the origins of piracy to the second millennium BCE in the Mediterranean, but we should not yield to the temptation. We know that ships carrying valuable cargoes traversed the waters of the Mediterranean from Egypt to the Aegean Sea and that the Red Sea and Persian Gulf were also sea-lanes. We also know that fighting at sea took place because we have scenes depicting it on temple walls or engraved or painted on various artefacts. The problem is, quite simply, that there was no such concept. No distinction was made between warfare and piracy.[1] Some have pointed to the migration of the 'sea peoples' around 1200 BCE as one of the earliest examples of large-scale piracy.[2] We know very little about these people, but they probably originated in Anatolia and swept through the eastern Mediterranean. The problem with seeing them as pirates is that, even though the sea peoples used ships and fought on board ships, their raids were more about migration and conquest than simple plunder.

We cannot find the concept of piracy that was distinguished from warfare and trade until roughly the period 800–500 BCE in the Homeric poems of the *Iliad* and the *Odyssey*. These poems were composed around 750–700 BCE and so should not be construed as depicting Greek society of the 1200s, as some have done, but of the society of the period in which they were composed. Though Homer differentiates between pirates and heroes, their actions and motives are exactly the same. The only thing that distinguishes a hero from a pirate appears to be the approval of the gods.[3] Three things emerge from a study of piracy in this period. First, pirates were regarded with a certain amount of disapproval, but they could also achieve high status. Philip de Souza argues that 'in the Homeric world, piracy was not necessarily a shameful or deplorable activity'.[4] Second, the methods and goals of both piracy and warfare were so similar that it is virtually

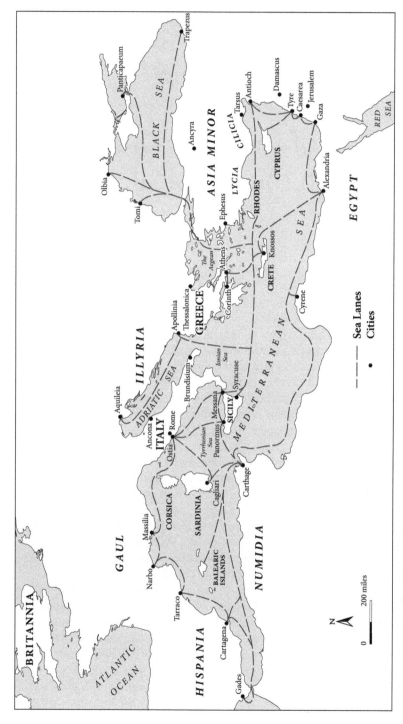

FIGURE 2.1 *Map of ancient sea-lanes.*
Source: Map produced by Barry Lively, Cartographer.

impossible to tell them apart. Third, the Homeric pirates and heroes did not attack ships at sea.[5] They attacked settlements on land.[6]

These early raiders shared similar sailing and fighting technology, methods and motives. They used fighting ships that were about forty to ninety feet long with steeply curved ends, low gunwales and no decks. The ships had both oars and sails and were light and manoeuvrable, but they were also fragile. Consequently, most raiders put in to shore at night or during foul weather. The warriors who sailed these ships were equipped with bronze swords, spears and axes and with bows, clubs, slings and leather armour. They preferred to strike fast at dawn or by trickery in the classic ambush that all raiders favour.[7] The heroes and villains of the Homeric era who embarked on their adventurous exploits all sought wealth in the form of precious metals, cattle, slaves or other objects of value because then, as now, wealth created status and status created power.

Still, it can be difficult or impossible to distinguish piracy from warfare and armed trade in this period. Piracy appears to have differed from warfare in both the scale and the importance attributed to the activity. For example, the siege of Troy was much more important than a single coastal raid. It could yield much greater wealth, it was organized by a polity instead of private individuals and it bestowed much greater prestige.[8] Though trade and piracy both share the same motive, they differ in that piracy necessarily includes violence where trade thrives much better without violence.

As states of the classical period c. 500–330 BCE became better organized with citizen armies and/or mercenaries the distinction between piracy and warfare becomes much clearer.[9] This is because city-states like Athens came to perceive piracy paradoxically as an impediment to the growth of long-distance trade upon which they depended for their wealth and their food, and, at the same time, they viewed it as a useful tool in their competition with other Aegean states. The Hellenistic city-states of the eastern Mediterranean regularly deployed pirates as naval auxiliaries and sometimes engaged in piracy themselves.[10] During the Peloponnesian War (431–404 BCE), piracy became a regular part of the conflict as Athens become evermore desperate for funds and resources. The famous Athenian general Iphikrates used pirates during the Corinthian War (395–387 BCE). A Spartan general, Teleutias, seized ships and plundered the coasts of Attica to get slaves and cargoes he could sell so that he could pay his sailors and keep his army afloat.[11] Seaborne banditry was no longer the province solely of small privately funded groups. It had become an intrinsic part of warfare and state formation.

Sea bandits of the classical period gained access to iron weapons and stronger ships that could serve as fighting platforms. The penteconter had fifty oars, a ram and a deck. Over time, these ships grew larger with greater numbers of oarsmen for ramming power. Ramming an enemy could send it to the bottom; but if the purpose was to capture it, boarding was still the only option.[12] Bows and arrows and catapults that launched combustibles

FIGURE 2.2 *Roman trireme warship.*
Source: Photo by Rischgitz/Hulton Archive/Getty Images.

or even venomous snakes and scorpions onto the enemy ship were used to soften the enemy as the ships closed for hand-to-hand combat.[13]

With the rise of Macedonia in the middle of the fourth century BCE, the history of piracy took a new turn. Both Philip of Macedon and the Athenians began to claim the right to destroy pirate bases in the interests of all Greeks. But the reality is that they each condoned and practised piracy against their enemies while condemning it when it was practised against them. Both polities saw piracy as 'an opportunity to justify aggression and military expansion in terms of suppressing piracy'.[14] Neither group, however, was serious about suppressing piracy for at least four reasons. First, no Greek state made hard and fast distinctions between piracy and warfare in the fourth century. Piracy was simply warfare by other means. Second, without their pirates Athenian efforts to remain the dominant power in the Greek world would have been crippled. Third, no one in the Greek world at the time possessed the enormous fiscal or military power necessary to suppress piracy. Fourth, piracy was also a form of trade that depended on markets to dispose of its loot. Most Greek city-states benefitted economically from the pirate trade.[15] In this context, the term 'pirate' was often thrown around to insult enemies, to justify warfare and used by victors to describe the vanquished.[16]

One of the primary objectives of piratical activity in the Greek world was human slaves, who were sold at one of the slave markets on Rhodes, Delos or Crete. Slaves were disposed of according to their status and the chances that someone might be willing to pay a ransom for them. Free men and women, who were captured, relied on the commercial and political influence of their cities or the kindness of strangers to save them from slavery. Representatives from their cities might be able to negotiate their release. Indeed, cities maintained special treaties to protect free persons from being enslaved. Wealthy merchants near the slave markets also sometimes purchased a slave's freedom as a way of accumulating prestige and honour through acts of charity.[17] Pirates probably sold non-Greek slaves more frequently than Greek ones and would have preferred the system of ransom payments for Greek slaves. Ransom usually brought in more revenue since people were valued by their status in their home communities rather than at the going rate for slaves in the market. It also freed the pirates from the trouble of having to transport the slaves to market in the first place.[18]

Though the Romans complained loudly about pirates, they did not become involved in pirate suppression until the second and first centuries BCE.[19] Pirates come to play a complex role in Roman political, economic and military thought. Romans wanted to protect trade with their allies in places like Rhodes in the eastern Mediterranean where piracy was rampant. Anti-pirate propaganda became useful in garnering the support of the social and political elite in the eastern Mediterranean where Rome hoped to extend its influence. Rome also needed to protect Roman colonists abroad from marauding pirates and to justify the extension of their military control over the seas. Victorious Roman generals also sought prestige and influence in Rome through successful campaigns against pirates. And, perhaps most importantly, Rome needed to secure its food supplies – especially grain – which pirates threatened. Consequently, the Romans were the first to define pirates as the enemy of all. Indeed, Cicero in his first-century work, *On Duties,* argued that since pirates could not be considered lawful enemies, no one needs to keep an oath made to a pirate.[20]

This self-serving bit of propaganda continues to inform many of our legal and cultural ideas about pirates.[21] Rome, from about 100 BCE to 200 CE, constructed an 'image of pirates as violent, flamboyant, seafaring outlaws' that lives with us still. They 'took the idea of piracy and fashioned it into a flexible, pejorative label, which they used for political purposes. Roman campaigns against maritime enemies were presented as the suppression of piracy because that suited contemporary political needs, especially when the Roman aristocracy wanted to convince reluctant allies that they should fight with or for the Roman cause'.[22]

When they could, the Romans imposed the burden of suppressing piracy on their allies and their allies' subjects. But this was not always possible. By 70–60 BCE, Rome itself seemed to be threatened by piratical activity. Even Julius Caesar had been kidnapped by the Cilician pirates and had to be ransomed.[23] After he was released, Caesar turned pirate himself. He gathered some ships on his own account and attacked the pirates while they still lay in harbour. He crucified all the pirates he captured and took their plunder for himself.[24]

Rome decided to send Pompey in 67 BCE to clear the seas of pirates and much has been made of this campaign as the first truly successful attempt to suppress piracy. Some authors have uncritically accepted this second bit of Roman propaganda, but the evidence does not support this conclusion.[25]

Pompey spent only forty days in the Western Mediterranean before moving off to the eastern Mediterranean, where it appears that the pirates simply gave up without a fight. The truth is that, unlike other Roman generals who had come to kill pirates, Pompey had come to negotiate with them. He declared his willingness to come to terms if the Cilician pirates would exchange their ships for land. Most of them did, and he settled them in cities along the coast. What he apparently hoped to do was convert the pirates into farmers.[26] In this way, he was able to end what was expected to be a three-year campaign in three months, thus gaining a reputation as a military genius that he later exploited when he returned to Rome.[27]

Pompey's plan, however, was nonsense. The cities he settled the pirates in were better suited for piracy than for farming, which explains why the pirates were so keen to surrender to him. He simply relocated them to better ports. Consequently, despite the much-vaunted *pax romana* (Roman peace), piracy remained a constant problem in the Mediterranean, though the new Roman navy did keep piracy to tolerable levels for the next two centuries.[28] The problem with Pompey's swift campaign was that truly defeating pirates required the conquest and occupation of territory. To do that, they had to attack pirate bases from land and defeat them on land. Then they had to hold that land to keep the pirates from returning to their old ways. Pompey simply avoided the whole mess by offering them better bases and integration into the Roman state in return for a temporary hiatus to their activities.[29] Roman control over much of the Mediterranean world helped discourage piracy until the slow collapse of the empire in the third and fourth centuries CE.

The progressive weakness of Roman power can be seen in the rise of piracy in the English Channel. In the last half of the third century, Rome built a series of forts along both sides of the English Channel to form what has been called the Saxon Shore System, whose purpose appears to have been the suppression of Saxon and Frankish pirates who raided the coasts of East Anglia, Britain and Gaul. This system may have used 'signaling stations and scouting ships' to catch pirates on their predictable routes to and from their raids.[30] The rise of the Vandals in the early fifth century brought a renewed upsurge in piracy in the Mediterranean. The new Vandal Empire that stretched across North Africa was built by a combination of raids for booty and larger, more extended expeditions to acquire territory and bases.[31]

The political changes heralded by the rise of Islam in the seventh century CE brought a new kind of piracy to the Mediterranean. As the Arab armies advanced across North Africa and into Spain, Egypt became a base for piratical operations against Christians in the Mediterranean. The Caliphate sponsored these raids, called *koursa,* and so initiated what would become a long tradition of Islamic state-sponsored piracy in the Mediterranean. As Arab *koursas* began rampaging around the Greek, Anatolian and Aegean islands, the Byzantines struggled to deal with them. But they lacked the manpower to attack the pirates in their bases and so could make very little headway. The realignment of the Mediterranean world with the Christians in the north and the Muslims in the south would eventually evolve into the broad corsairing tradition that became endemic in the Mediterranean in the sixteenth century.[32] The slow collapse of the Roman Empire also left the coasts of England exposed to invasion by the Picts and Scots and raids from the Northmen. The cry that would soon be heard throughout the British Isles, Ireland and the coasts of Western Europe was, 'From the fury of the Northmen, O Lord, deliver us'.

As you read the following documents, consider the following questions:

1 What, if anything, distinguished piracy from warfare in the ancient world?

2 What appears to be the primary objective of pirates in the early Mediterranean? What motivated them?

3 How did piracy serve the interests of the Mediterranean city-states?

4 What role did ransom play in piracy?

5 Why was suppression of pirates so difficult in the ancient Mediterranean?

6 How did piracy contribute to the creation of an empire in the Mediterranean and assertions of sovereignty over the seas?

7 How was piracy, as practised in the ancient Mediterranean, both parasitic and intrinsic?

Homer, the *Odyssey*, translated by Samuel Butler (1898). Odysseys 14 and 17.

Odysseys

I did not care about farm work, nor the frugal home life of those who would bring up children. My delight was in ships, fighting, javelins, and arrows – things that most men shudder to think of; but one man likes one thing and another another, and this was what I was most naturally inclined to. Before the Achaeans went to Troy, nine times was I in command of men and ships on foreign service, and I amassed much wealth. I had my pick of the spoil in the first instance, and much more was allotted to me later on. My house grew apace and I became a great man among the Cretans. (Odyssey 14)

But it pleased Jove to take all away from me. He sent me with a band of roving robbers to Egypt; it was a long voyage and I was undone by it. I stationed my ships in the river Aegyptus, and bade my men stay by them and keep guard over them, while I sent out scouts to reconnoitre from every point of vantage. But the men disobeyed my orders, took to their own devices, and ravaged the land of the Egyptians, killing the men, and taking their wives and children captives. The alarm was soon carried to the city, and when they heard the war-cry, the people came out at daybreak till the plain was filled with soldiers, horse and foot, and with the gleam of armour. Then Jove spread panic among my men, and they would no longer face the enemy, for they found themselves surrounded. The Egyptians killed many of us, and took the rest alive to do forced labour for them. (Odyssey 17)

Philip de Souza, *Piracy in the Graeco-Roman World* (Cambridge, Cambridge University Press, 1999), 46–47, 61, 83, 116–117. Used with permission.

Ainetos, the Greek general of Ephesos in 287 BCE, used local pirates under Andron to attack his enemies under Lykon. Since these men owed no allegiance to either side, Lykon successfully bribed them to betray Ainetos and help him take Ephesos.

When Ainetos, the general of Demetrios, was defending Ephesos and ravaging the environs with many pirates, Lykon, the general of Lysimachos, bribed the archpirate Andron with money and took possession of Ephesos. The archpirate led into the city some of Lykon's soldiers, unarmed, in cloaks and rough garments and with their hands bound, as though they were prisoners, and getting near to the citadel he issued them with daggers, which they kept hidden under their arms. Having killed the gatekeepers and the guards on the acropolis, he raised the signal to those with Lykon. These men marched in, laid hold of Ainetos and occupied Ephesos. And, having given the pirates their reward, straightaway escorted them out of the city, believing that their faithlessness towards their former friends made it unsafe to have them around.

Though the following account from the third century BCE Aegean island of Amorgos suggests that the pirates willingly released their prisoners, it is more likely that a ransom had been agreed upon.

Resolved by the council and the people; Soterides, son of Phidias, of Kosyllos was president, Philoxenos, son of Philothemis of Alsos moved: since, when pirates made an incursion into the countryside at night and captured a total of more than thirty girls, women, and other persons, free and slave, and scuttled the ships in the harbor and captured the ship of Doreaio, in which they sailed off with their captives and the rest of their booty; when all this had happened Hegesippos and Antipappos, the sons of Hegesistratos, who were themselves prisoners, persuaded Sokleides, the captain of the pirates to release the free persons and some of the slaves, and volunteered to act as hostages on their behalf, and showed great concern that none of the citizen women should be carried off as booty and be sold, or suffer hardship. And that no free person should perish; thanks to these men the prisoners were saved and returned home without suffering harm.

The Illyrians were a Hellenized group of tribes living along the eastern coast of the Adriatic who sought to carve out an empire in the Adriatic through large-scale raids. The episode recounted below led to the first Illyrian war and the defeat of the Illyrians by the Romans in 229 BCE.

For some time previously it had been the custom of this people to prey upon vessels sailing from Italy, and at this moment, while they were occupying Phoinike, a number of them, operating independently of the Illyrian fleet, attacked Italian traders; some of these they had robbed, some they had murdered. And a large number were carried off into captivity. In the past, the Roman government had always ignored complaints made to them about the Illyrians. But now, as more and more people approached the senate on this subject, they appointed two commissioners, Gaius and Lucius Coruncanius, to travel to Illyria and inquire into what was happening.

A 200 BCE treaty between Rhodes and Hierapytna provided Rhodes with assistance in its ongoing war with the Cretan pirates.

(X) And if pirates establish bases in Crete and the Rhodians wage war at sea against the pirates or those who provide shelter or assistance to them, the Hierapytnians shall take part in the operations by land and sea with all possible strength and at their own expense. The pirates who are captured shall be handed over to the Rhodians together with their ships, while each of the allies shall take half of the rest [of the booty].

(XVII) And if during a campaign which the Hierapytnians are waging with the Rhodians to destroy a pirate base, any of those who provided shelter or assistance to the pirates wage war on the Hierapytnians because of this campaign, the Rhodians shall come to the help of the Hierapytnians with all possible strength, and anyone who acts in this way shall be an enemy of the Rhodians.

Mithridates VI, king of Pontos (120–63 BCE), proved to be a determined enemy of Roman expansion into the eastern Mediterranean. He actively cooperated with Cilician pirates to assist him in his efforts to fend off Roman aggression.

When Mithridates first went to war with the Romans and conquered Asia (Sulla being busy with Greece), believing that he could not hold on to Asia for long, he despoiled it one way and another, as I have mentioned, and sent out pirates on the sea. At first, they harassed people by sailing around in a few small boats, as pirates do, but as the war dragged on, they became more numerous and sailed in larger ships. Having acquired a taste for rich plunder, they still did not cease their activities when Mithridates was defeated, made peace and retreated. For, having been robbed of their living and their homeland on account of the war, and having fallen into hardship and poverty, they harvested the sea instead of the land, first in *myoparones* and *hemioliai*, then in biremes and triremes, cruising around in squadrons, under the command of archpirates just like generals in a war.

Plutarch, *The Parallel Lives: Agesilaus and Pompey. Pelopidas and Marcellus*, vol. V. Translated by Bernadotte Perrin (Cambridge, MA: Harvard University Press, 1917), Pompey, 24–30, 173–193.

Pompey and Piracy in the Eastern Mediterranean [67–66 BCE]
    The power of the pirates had its seat in Cilicia at first, and at the outset it was venturesome and elusive; but it took on confidence and boldness during the Mithridatic war, because it lent itself to the king's service. Then, while the Romans were embroiled in civil wars at the gates of Rome, the sea was left unguarded, and gradually drew and enticed them on until they no longer attacked navigators but also laid waste islands and maritime cities. And presently men whose wealth gave them power, and those whose lineage was illustrious, and those who laid claim to superior intelligence, began to embark on piratical craft and share their enterprises, feeling that the occupation brought them a certain reputation and distinction. There were also fortified roadsteads and signal-stations for piratical craft in many places, and fleets put in here which were not merely furnished for their peculiar work with sturdy crews, skillful pilots, and light and speedy ships; nay, more annoying than the fear which they inspired was the odious extravagance of their equipment, with their gilded sails, and purple awnings, and silvered oars, as if they rioted in their iniquity and plumed themselves upon it. Their flutes and stringed instruments and drinking bouts along every coast, their seizures of persons in high command, and their ransomings of captured cities, were a disgrace to the Roman supremacy. For, you see, the ships of the pirates numbered more than a thousand, and the cities captured by them four hundred. Besides, they attacked and plundered places of refuge and sanctuaries hitherto inviolate, such as those of Claros, Didyma, and Samothrace; the temple of Chthonian Earth at Hermione; that of Asclepius in Epidaurus; those of Poseidon at the Isthmus, at Taenarum, and at Calauria; those of Apollo at Actium and Leucas; and those of Hera at Samos, at Argos, and at Lacinium. They also offered strange sacrifices of their own at Olympus and celebrated there certain secret rites, among which those of Mithras continue to the present time, having been first instituted by them.
    But they heaped most insults upon the Romans, even going up from the sea along their roads and plundering there, and sacking the neighboring villas. Once, too, they seized two praetors, Sextilius and Bellinus, in their purple-edged robes, and carried them away, together with their attendants and lictors. They also captured a daughter of Antonius, a man who had celebrated a triumph, as she was going into the country, and

exacted a large ransom for her. But their crowning insolence was this. Whenever a captive cried out that he was a Roman and gave his name, they would pretend to be frightened out of their senses, and would smite their thighs, and fall down before him entreating him to pardon them; and he would be convinced of their sincerity, seeing them so humbly suppliant. Then some would put Roman boots on his feet, and others would throw a toga round him, in order, forsooth, that there might be no mistake about him again. And after thus mocking the man for a long time and getting their fill of amusement from him, at last they would let down a ladder in mid ocean and bid him disembark and go on his way rejoicing; and if he did not wish to go, they would push him overboard themselves and drown him.

This power extended its operations over the whole of our Mediterranean Sea, making it unnavigable and closed to all commerce. This was what most of all inclined the Romans, who were hard put to it to get provisions and expected a great scarcity, to send out Pompey with a commission to take the sea away from the pirates. Gabinius, one of Pompey's intimates, drew up a law which gave him, not an admiralty, but an out-and-out monarchy and irresponsible power over all men. For the law gave him dominion over the sea this side of the pillars of Hercules, over all the mainland to the distance of four hundred furlongs from the sea. These limits included almost all places in the Roman world, and the greatest nations and most powerful kings were comprised within them. Besides this, he was empowered to choose fifteen legates from the senate for the several principalities, and to take from the public treasuries and the tax-collectors as much money as he wished, and to have two hundred ships, with full power over the number and levying of soldiers and oarsmen.

... For five hundred ships were manned for him, and a hundred and twenty thousand men-at-arms and five thousand horsemen were raised. Twenty-four men who had held command or served as praetors [magistrate] were chosen from the senate by him, and he had two quaestors [revenue officials]. And since the prices of provisions immediately fell, the people were moved to say in their joy that the very name of Pompey had put an end to the war.

However, he divided the waters and the adjacent coasts of the Mediterranean Sea into thirteen districts, and assigned to each a certain number of ships with a commander, and with his forces thus scattered in all quarters he encompassed whole fleets of piratical ships that fell in his way, and straightway hunted them down and brought them into port; others succeeded in dispersing and escaping, and sought their hive, as it were, hurrying from all quarters into Cilicia. Against these Pompey intended to proceed in person with his sixty best ships. He did not, however, sail against them until he had entirely cleared of their pirates the Tyrrhenian Sea, the Libyan Sea, and the sea about Sardinia, Corsica, and Sicily, in forty days all told. This was owing to his own tireless energy and the zeal of his lieutenants.

... Some of the pirate bands that were still rowing at large begged for mercy, and since he treated them humanely, and after seizing their ships and persons did them no further harm, the rest became hopeful of mercy too, and made their escape from the other commanders, betook themselves to Pompey with their wives and children, and surrendered to him. All these he spared, and it was chiefly by their aid that he tracked down, seized, and punished those who were still lurking in concealment because conscious of unpardonable crimes.

But the most numerous and powerful had bestowed their families and treasures and useless folk in forts and strong citadels near the Taurus mountains, while they themselves manned their ships and awaited Pompey's attack near the promontory of Coracesium in Cilicia; here they were defeated in a battle and then besieged. At last, however, they sent suppliant messages and surrendered themselves, together with the cities and islands of which they were in control; these they had fortified, making them hard to get at and difficult to take by storm. The war was therefore brought to an end and all piracy driven from the sea in less than three months, and besides many other ships, Pompey received in surrender ninety which had brazen beaks [i.e. prows]. The men themselves, who were more than twenty thousand in number, he did not once think of putting to death; and yet to let them go and suffer them to disperse or band together again, poor, warlike, and numerous as they were, he thought was not well. Reflecting, therefore, that by nature man neither is nor becomes a wild or an unsocial creature, but is transformed by the unnatural practice of vice, whereas he may be softened by new customs and a change of place and life; also that even wild beasts put off their fierce and savage ways when they partake of a gentler mode of life, he determined to transfer the men from the sea to land, and let them have a taste of gentle life by being accustomed to dwell in cities and to till the ground. Some of them, therefore, were received and incorporated into the small and half-deserted cities of Cilicia, which acquired additional territory; and after restoring the city of Soli, which had lately been devastated by Tigranes, the king of Armenia, Pompey settled many there. To most of them, however, he gave as residence Dyme in Achaea, which was then bereft of men and had much good land.

Well, then, his maligners found fault with these measures, and even his best friends were not pleased with his treatment of Metellus in Crete. Metellus, a kinsman of the Metellus who was a colleague of Pompey in Spain, had been sent as general to Crete before Pompey was chosen to his command; for Crete was a kind of second source for pirates, next to Cilicia. Metellus hemmed in many of them and was killing and destroying them. But those who still survived and were besieged sent suppliant messages to Pompey and invited him into the island, alleging that it was a part of his government, and that all parts of it were within the limit to be measured from the sea. Pompey accepted the invitation and wrote to

Metellus putting a stop to his war. He also wrote the cities not to pay any attention to Metellus, and sent them one of his own officers as general, namely, Lucius Octavius, who entered the strongholds of the besieged pirates and fought on their side, thus making Pompey not only odious and oppressive, but actually ridiculous, since he lent his name to godless miscreants, and threw around them the mantle of his reputation to serve like a charm against evil, through envy and jealousy of Metellus.

Plutarch, *The Parallel Lives: The Life of Julius Caesar*, vol. 7. Translated by Bernadotte Perrin (Cambridge, MA: Harvard University Press, 1919), 445–447.

Caesar among the Cilician Pirates [75 BCE]

Caesar … went down to the sea and sailed to King Nicomedes in Bithynia. With him he tarried a short time, and then, on his voyage back, was captured, near the island Pharmacusa, by pirates, who already at that time controlled the sea with large armaments and countless small vessels.

To begin with, then, when the pirates demanded twenty talents for his ransom, he laughed at them for not knowing who their captive was, and of his own accord agreed to give them fifty. In the next place, after he had sent various followers to various cities to procure the money and was left with one friend and two attendants among Cilicians, most murderous of men, he held them in such disdain that whenever he lay down to sleep he would send and order them to stop talking.

For eight and thirty days, as if the men were not his watchers, but his royal body-guard, he shared in their sports and exercises with great unconcern. He also wrote poems and sundry speeches which he read aloud to them, and those who did not admire these he would call to their faces illiterate Barbarians, and often laughingly threatened to hang them all. The pirates were delighted at this, and attributed his boldness of speech to a certain simplicity and boyish mirth.

But after his ransom had come from Miletus and he had paid it and was set free, he immediately manned vessels and put to sea from the harbor of Miletus against the robbers. He caught them, too, still lying at anchor off the island, and got most of them into his power. Their money he made his booty, but the men themselves he lodged in the prison at Pergamum, and then went in person to Junius, the governor of Asia, on the ground that it belonged to him, as praetor of the province, to punish the captives.

But since the praetor cast longing eyes on their money, which was no small sum, and kept saying that he would consider the case of the captives at his leisure, Caesar left him to his own devices, went to Pergamum, took the robbers out of prison, and crucified them all, just as he had often warned them on the island that he would do, when they thought he was joking.

E. W. Brooks, 'The Arabs in Asia Minor (641–750), from Arabic Sources', *The Journal of Hellenic Studies*, vol. 18 (1898): 187.

Muslim capture of the Island of Rhodes in 673 CE as recorded by the Arab chronicler Al Tabari.

And among the events of this year was the wintering of Abd Al Rachman, the son of Urn Al Chakham, the Thakafi, in the land of the Romans. And in it Rudus (Rhodes), an island in the sea, was taken; and its captor was Gunada, the son of Abu Umayya, the Azdi; and he settled the Moslems in it, as recorded by Mahomet the son of Umar; and they sowed seed and acquired flocks and herds in it, which they pastured all round it: and, when men approached, they took them into the fortress; and they had watchmen who gave them warning of anyone upon the sea who wished to make war upon them, and they were on their guard against them. And they were the greatest annoyance to the Romans, and they attacked them on the sea and cut off their ships. And Mu'awiya supplied them plentifully with provisions and pay; and the enemy were afraid of them.

Notes

1   Souza, *Piracy in the Graeco-Roman World*, 15–16.
2   Konstam, *Piracy*, 15–16; Ormerod, *Piracy in the Ancient World*, 82–88; Ward, *Pirates in History*, 7.
3   Souza, *Piracy in the Graeco-Roman World*, 17–20.
4   Souza, *Piracy in the Graeco-Roman World*, 17–18.
5   Little, *Pirate Hunting*, 25.
6   Souza, *Piracy in the Graeco-Roman World*, 17–18. The quote is from these pages.
7   Little, *Pirate Hunting*, 22–26.
8   Souza, *Piracy in the Graeco-Roman World*, 19–21.
9   Souza, *Piracy in the Graeco-Roman World*, 25.
10 Gabbert, 'Piracy in the Early Hellenistic Period', 156–163.
11 Souza, *Piracy in the Graeco-Roman World*, 34.
12 Little, *Pirate Hunting*, 41–42.
13 See Mayor, *Greek Fire*, 41–97; Little, *Pirate Hunting*, 54–55.
14 Souza, *Piracy in the Graeco-Roman World*, 38.
15 Souza, *Piracy in the Graeco-Roman World*, 38–41.
16 Souza, 'Rome's Contribution to the Development of Piracy', 71–96.
17 Souza, *Piracy in the Graeco-Roman World*, 60–65.
18 Souza, *Piracy in the Graeco-Roman World*, 65–67.

19 Dell, 'The Origin and Nature of Illyrian Piracy', 344–358.

20 Souza, *Piracy in the Graeco-Roman World*, 76–80, 134–136.

21 See, for example, Heller-Roazen, *The Enemy of All*.

22 Both quotes are from Souza, 'Rome's Contribution to the Development of Piracy', 71.

23 Ward, 'Caesar and the Pirates', 267–268.

24 Canfora, *Julius Caesar*, 9–11.

25 Little, *Pirate Hunting*, 65–68; Konstam, *Piracy*, 20–22.

26 Souza, *Piracy in the Graeco-Roman World*, 167–172.

27 Tröster, 'Roman Hegemony and Non-State Violence', 32.

28 Souza, *Piracy in the Graeco-Roman World*, 167–172, 175–178.

29 Souza, 'Piracy in Classical Antiquity', 175–178.

30 Pearson, 'Piracy in Late Roman Britain', 337–353.

31 Souza, *Piracy in the Graeco-Roman World*, 229–238.

32 Souza, *Piracy in the Graeco-Roman World*, 238–240.

CHAPTER THREE

Vikings: The Scourge from the North

The monk, Alcuin of York, who was living in Charlemagne's court at the time, described the 793 CE Viking attack on the monastery of St. Cuthbert on the island of Lindisfarne.

> Never before has such terror appeared in Britain as we have now suffered from a pagan race, nor was it thought that such an inroad from the sea could be made. Behold, the church of St. Cuthbert spotted with the blood of the priests of God, despoiled of all its ornaments; a place more venerable than all in Britain is given as prey to pagan people.[1]

If we accept the desperate clamour of the victims of the Viking raids, it is easy to exaggerate their numbers, fighting prowess, savagery and the suddenness of their arrival. After all, the victims needed to inflate Viking power to justify their own impotency in the face of the raids. Their embellishments could also lead us to accept that the attacks came out of nowhere – that the Vikings simply surged onto the scene with unprecedented and irrational brutality. We do not have to exaggerate the Viking attacks to appreciate the historical significance of the raids. But we do need to understand the context that produced the raids if we are to understand them at all. The Scandinavian and Danish societies from which raiders emerged between the seventh and eleventh centuries experienced considerable transformations that resulted in a long period of folk wandering.

The long, fragmented Scandinavian and Danish coastlines marked by deep fjords 'made political unity difficult' and competition fierce.[2] Increased social stratification began with the emergence of chieftains who governed ever-larger domains and who sought to centralize power in their own hands. This centralization of power coincided with a steady growth

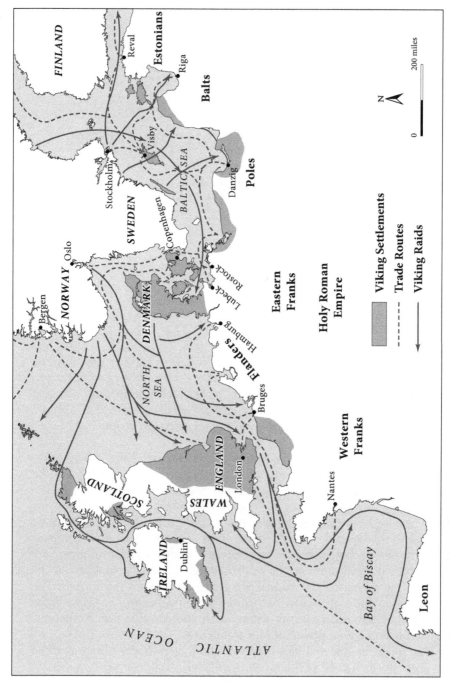

FIGURE 3.1 *Map of Viking raids and settlements.*
Source: Map produced by Barry Levely, Cartographer.

in population and the creation of fortified trading towns and powerful kings that exacerbated social tensions and stimulated migration out of Scandinavia – especially of young men seeking opportunity. Those young men who were not satisfied with farming had two choices – trading or raiding.[3]

The raid at Lindisfarne did not come out of nowhere. Trading had flourished in the seventh century between England and the Continent. Scandinavian and Danish traders had long visited England and Ireland and the coasts of France. They exchanged whetstones, honey, walrus ivory, whalebones, amber, furs and other forest products extracted as tribute from Saami, Finns and Balts for glass, textiles, weapons, spices, slaves and grindstones.[4] The promise of rich trading opportunities in the south and east lured many out of their homelands. Traders followed the rivers of northwestern Europe all the way to the Black Sea, across the channel to the newly stabilized English Kingdoms, and down the coasts of the expanding Frankish Empire. Walrus ivory, honey, furs and amber were much sought after in southern markets. Those who controlled the Nordic trade could amass great riches and become powerful lords. The path to status and power had to be paved with gifts of 'weapons, gold, silver, ships and feasts'.[5] Kings and chieftains needed to acquire a reputation of being successful in war and plundering to attract the best warriors and most powerful lords to their retinues.[6] Those who found themselves excluded from this trade could always turn to piracy. It offered both status and wealth, which could be used to challenge chieftains at home. A leader of successful raids was able to acquire followers and the wealth necessary to retain their loyalty. Raiding could also allow them to open new markets and settle new lands.[7]

Of course, none of this could have happened without the availability of light, manoeuvrable ships that could carry heavy cargos and crews of raiders. Using both square-rigged sails and oars, these ships could sail the high seas and navigate close inland and up coastal rivers. These capabilities gave the Vikings a real advantage in speed and manoeuvrability, making it easy for them to come in close and quick and escape if the battle went against them. The ships could also be tied together and used as floating fighting platforms.[8]

Despite the myths, Viking raiders were not simply vicious hordes of ignorant rabble. Their bands tended to be small, limited by the need to supply them with food and weapons, especially on extended expeditions and they used the common and time-tested tactics of raiders. Most Viking raiders probably did not have access to the famed Viking swords because steel was expensive. Only a wealthy Viking could afford a sword, mail armour and a steel helmet. Most Vikings probably used the axe or the spear as their primary weapon and wore hardened leather helmets. Vikings often began an engagement with a shower of stones, arrows, small hatchets and

FIGURE 3.2 *Viking longboat.*
Source: Photo by Keystone/Getty Images.

javelins, then closed in for hand-to-hand fighting with axes, knives, spears and swords. Most Vikings carried round shields constructed from planks of wood and sometimes covered or rimmed in rawhide. The shields could be used in both defence and offense but were not built to last. These round shields explain why most injuries found on Viking skeletons occur on the legs and the head. The rest of the body was well protected by the shield. Vikings did wear leather or mail armour and leather or metal helmets, but there is no evidence that Vikings wore horned helmets. This probably developed from Christian propaganda that sought to portray Vikings as demonic.[9] Some good evidence now suggests that Viking women may also have joined in the raids and the fighting. Viking sagas sometimes portray women as warriors[10] and female skeletons have been found among the mass burials of Viking raiders in Repton, England.[11] Viking women have also been buried with weapons, which may suggest that they used them in life.[12]

Vikings did not limit their activities to raiding. The Swedes, who went east up the rivers that fed the Baltic, found thinly populated, dense forests occupied mostly by poor forest dwellers with little wealth. So, there was no point in pillaging them.[13] Instead, the Swedes created a system of long-distance trade that brought the goods of the forest to the wealthy Byzantine and Arab peoples to the south. Those Vikings who turned west and south to Ireland, England and France found acquisitive Christian people whose wealth proved tempting to the restless, opportunistic and ambitious migrants from the north.

The reason for Viking success had little to do with their supposed superiority in battle, though there is no reason to doubt their martial prowess. Their real tactical advantage lay in their mobility and their hardiness. The sea gave them a refuge into which they could retreat and from which they could appear with little warning. The first raids were small affairs, but their success generated interest back home and produced a momentum on their own. When speed and surprise failed and the Vikings met real resistance, they usually left in search of softer targets. They were raiders and collectors of portable wealth, not suicidal maniacs. They avoided pitched battles, and they were vulnerable in open country. As Viking power grew and interest in the lands across the sea increased, so did the size of the raiding parties until we find large Viking armies moving inland on campaigns of territorial conquest in the ninth and tenth centuries. These Viking armies were seldom professional armies, but that does not mean that they were simply an undisciplined rabble. Vikings raids had leaders and were frequently led by kings or *jarls* in search of territorial acquisitions. Still, despite popular legend, Viking armies probably lost more battles than they won. They were, after all, usually outnumbered and in hostile territory.[14]

We should, of course, remember that Viking piracy was a method of trade by other means and Vikings had complex motives. It was a forced exchange, it is true, but it was a form of economic activity that redistributed wealth and helped circulate it throughout northern Europe. To maximize their potential returns, Vikings often chose to raid on festival days when populations and their wealth converged on pilgrimage sites or when the population was preoccupied with religious devotions. They could also use the threat of violence to extract tribute. For example, in the Carolingian Empire in what is modern France, Vikings extracted 14 per cent of the 'monetary economy' as protection money 'over a 100 year period'.[15] Despite our popular imaginations, Vikings sought more than gold and silver. They also raided for food and drink, for human beings to be ransomed or sold as slaves and for land to settle.[16]

The victims of Viking raids could and did mount effective resistance. When they did, this response included laws that treated the Vikings as pirates and navies that could defeat Viking fleets on the water and carry out naval patrols along the coast. These navies were expensive and when they declined, merchants and towns had to expend their own resources in defence. The age of Viking sea raiders began to fade in the tenth century to be replaced by raiders linked more securely to national and economic powers. The potential targets for Viking raids had hardened, as the peoples of northern Europe became more effective at counteracting the raids. The increased frequency of the raids also led to over-plundering and decreased profits. Vikings then began to settle down to exploit the people through taxation and tribute. They protected their new clients from raids by other Vikings and asserted a monopoly on the use of violence. Eventually, they carved out new homelands in Ireland, England and Normandy.[17]

In the Viking raids:

> We can perceive something individually motivated and guided by charismatic leadership, with a mercenary ethic that was highly adaptable to circumstance. This in turn was fueled by an intense but mutable sense of identity, characterized by inter- and intra-group competition. Viking piracy was subject to periodic state sponsorship within the wavering factions in the civil conflicts of their victims, but primarily operated through independent pirate polities in the form of the great fleets, with regional and chronological variation.[18]

In the North Atlantic, after the Viking era had already faded to distant memory, piracy again became a tool of the state as the Danes resisted the Hanseatic League (founded in 1358) that struggled to maintain a monopoly on trade from the Baltic Sea to the North Sea. This collection of merchant guilds and market towns stimulated vibrant trade, which struggled against pirate organizations like the Victual Brothers who were employed by the King of Sweden to attack Hanseatic shipping. The League also encouraged piracy against the Danes. The Victuallers were not defeated until 1402 CE when Simon of Utrecht smashed or dispersed the pirate fleet and captured the pirate commander, Stertbeker, who was executed in Hamburg. The Viking age may have come to an end by the thirteenth century, but the raiding and trading by sea had not.[19]

As you read the sources that follow, consider these questions:

1 What does Egil's saga reveal about the Viking sense of honour?
2 What do the documents reveal about Viking tactics?
3 How did Viking methods and goals shift over time? Why?
4 Do the documents support the perception that the Vikings were invincible warriors? Why or why not?
5 Why would the inhabitants of the British Isles agree to pay tribute to the Vikings, and why would the Vikings accept it?
6 What evidence can you find that the Vikings alternated between trading and raiding, even on the same expedition?
7 How well does Viking activity align with the modern legal definition of piracy?
8 Why might it be appropriate to see Viking raids as a complex interplay of parasitic, episodic and intrinsic piracy?
9 How were Viking raids driven by geography?

The sources below come from Viking Sagas and Christian chronicles. In many cases, these are the only sources we have for Viking raids, but they can be tricky sources to use. The sagas were passed down orally for many generations before being written down. Egil's saga purports to narrate events from about 850 to 1000 CE but was probably not written down until about 1220 or 1240 CE. Obviously, this means that errors could be introduced. The sagas are a mix of the historical fact and fanciful stories. The supernatural material they contain often reflects the beliefs and values of the times in which they were written.

The Anglo-Saxon Chronicles were kept by monks in the monasteries of England starting in the ninth century CE. Each scribe then updated the chronicle locally. The chronicles are sparse yearly annals of the important affairs of the area. They often contradict each other and represent a certain bias in favour of whomever the author approved of or supported.

So why use any of these sources? In some cases, they are the only sources we have. They also contain memories of real characters and events that can be verified elsewhere. They provide accurate descriptions of material culture, landscapes and cultural values, and they are often written with a spontaneity that shows little sign of being reshaped into literary forms.

William Charles Green, *The Story of Egil Skallagrimsson: Being an Icelandic Family History of the Ninth and Tenth Centuries* (London: E. Stock, 1893), Chapter 46.

Chapter 46 Of Thorolf's and Egil's harrying.

Thorolf and Egil stayed that winter with Thorir, and were made much of. But in spring they got ready a large war-ship and gathered men thereto, and in summer they went the eastern way and harried; there won they much wealth and had many battles. They held on even to Courland, and made a peace for half a month with the men of the land and traded with them. But when this was ended, then they took to harrying, and put in at diverse places. One day they put in at the mouth of a large river, where was an extensive forest upon land. They resolved to go up the country, dividing their force into companies of twelve. They went through the wood, and it was not long before they came to peopled parts. There they plundered and slew men, but the people fled, till at last there was no resistance. But as the day wore on, Thorolf had the blast sounded to recall his men down to the shore. Then each turned back from where they were into the wood. But when Thorolf mustered his force, Egil and his company had not come down; and the darkness of night was closing in, so that they could not, as they thought, look for him.

Now Egil and his twelve had gone through a wood and then saw wide plains and tillage. Hard by them stood a house. For this they made, and when they came there they ran into the house, but could see no one there. They took all the loose chattels that they came upon. There were many rooms, so this took them a long time. But when they came out and away from the house, an armed force was there between them and the wood, and this attacked them. High palings ran from the house to the wood; to these Egil bade them keep close, that they might not be come at from all sides. They did so. Egil went first, then the rest, one behind the other, so near that none could come between.

The Courlanders attacked them vigorously, but mostly with spears and javelins, not coming to close quarters. Egil's party going forward along the fence did not find out till too late that another line of palings ran along on the other side, the space between narrowing till there was a bend and all progress barred. The Courlanders pursued after them into this pen, while some set on them from without, thrusting javelins and swords through the palings, while others cast clothes on their weapons. Egil's party were wounded, and after that taken, and all bound, and so brought home to the farmhouse.

The owner of that farm was a powerful and wealthy man; he had a son grown up. Now they debated what they should do with their prisoners. The goodman said that he thought this were best counsel, to kill them one on the heels of another. His son said that the darkness of night was now closing in, and no sport was thus gotten by their torture; he bade them be let bide till the morning. So they were thrust into a room and strongly bound. Egil was bound hand and foot to a post. Then the room was strongly locked, and the Courlanders went into the dining-hall, ate, drank, and were merry.

Egil strained and worked at the post till he loosed it up from the floor. Then the post fell, and Egil slipped himself off it. Next he loosed his hands with his teeth. But when his hands were loose, he loosed therewith the bonds from his feet. And then he freed his comrades; but when they were all loosed they searched round for the likeliest place to get out. The room was made with walls of large wooden beams, but at one end thereof was a smooth planking. At this, they dashed and broke it through. They had now come into another room; this too had walls of wooden beams. Then they heard men's voices below under their feet. Searching about they found a trapdoor in the floor, which they opened. Thereunder was a deep vault; down in it they heard men's voices. Then asked Egil what men were these. He who answered named himself Aki. Would he like to come up, asked Egil. Aki answered, they would like it much.

Then Egil and his comrades lowered into the vault the rope with which they had been bound, and drew up thence three men. Aki said that these were his two sons, and they were Danes, who had been made prisoners of war last summer.

'I was,' he said, 'well treated through the winter, and had the chief care of the goodman's property; but the lads were enslaved and had a hard lot. In spring, we made up our minds to run away, but were retaken. Then we were cast into this vault.'

'You must know all about the plan of this house,' said Egil; 'where have we the best hope to get out?'

Aki said that there was another plank partition: 'Break you up that, you will then come into a corn-store, whereout you may go as you will.'

Egil's men did so; they broke up the planking, came into the granary, and thence out. It was pitch dark.

Then said Egil's comrades that they should hasten to the wood. But Egil said to Aki, 'If you know the house here, you can show us the way to some plunder.'

Aki said there was no lack of chattels. 'Here is a large loft in which the goodman sleeps; therein is no stint of weapons.'

Egil bade them go to that loft. But when they came to the staircase head they saw that the loft was open. A light was inside, and servants, who were making the beds. Egil bade some stay outside and watch that none came out. Egil ran into the loft, seized weapons, of which there was no lack. They slew all the men that were in there, and they armed themselves fully. Aki went to a trapdoor in the floor and opened it, telling them that they should go down by this to the store-room below. They got a light and went thither. It was the goodman's treasury; there were many costly things, and much silver. There the men took them each a load and carried it out. Egil took under his arm a large mead-cask, and bear it so.

But when they came to the wood, then Egil stopped, and he said:

'This our going is all wrong, and not warlike. We have stolen the goodman's property without his knowing thereof. Never ought that shame to be ours. Go we back to the house, and let him know what hath befallen.'

All spoke against that, saying they would make for the ship.

Egil set down the mead-cask, then ran off, and sped him to the house. But when he came there, he saw that serving-lads were coming out of the kitchen with dishes and bearing them to the dining-hall. In the kitchen (he saw) was a large fire and kettles thereon. Thither he went. Great beams had been brought home and lighted, as was the custom there, by setting fire to the beam-end and so burning it lengthwise. Egil seized a beam, carried it to the dining-hall, and thrust the burning end under the eaves, and so into the birch bark of the roof, which soon caught fire. Some fagot-wood lay hard by; this Egil brought and piled before the hall-door. This quickly caught fire. But those who sat drinking within did not find it out till the flame burst in round the roof. Then they rushed to the door; but there was no easy way out, both by reason of the fagot-wood, and because Egil kept the door, and slew most who strove to pass out either in the doorway or outside.

The goodman asked who had the care of the fire.

Egil answered, 'He has now the care of the fire whom you yester-even had thought least likely; nor will you wish to bake you hotter than I shall kindle; you shall have soft bath before soft bed, such as you meant to give to me and my comrades. Here now is that same Egil whom you bound hand and foot to the post in that room you shut so carefully. I will repay you your hospitality as you deserve.'

At this the goodman thought to steal out in the dark, but Egil was near, and dealt him his death-blow, as he did to many others. Brief moment was it ere the hall so burned that it fell in. Most of those who were within perished.

But Egil went back to the wood, where he found his comrades, and they all went together to the ship. Egil said he would have the mead-cask which he carried as his own special prize; it proved to be full of silver. Thorolf and his men were overjoyed when Egil came down. They put out from land as soon as day dawned; Aki and his two sons were with Egil's following. They sailed in the summer, now far spent, to Denmark, where they lay in wait for merchant-ships, and plundered when they got the chance.

James Ingram, trans. *The Anglo-Saxon Chronicle* (London: Everyman Press edition, London, 1912), 49, 51, 55–57, 59, 61, 84, 86.

CE 787. This year King Betric took Edburga the daughter of Offa to wife. And in the days came first three ships of the Northmen from the land of robbers. The reave [officer] then rode thereto and would drive them to the king's town; for he knew not what they were, and there was he slain. These were the first ships of the Danish men that sought the land of the English nation.

CE 793. This year came dreadful fore-warnings over the land of the Northumbrians, terrifying the people most woefully: these were immense sheets of light rushing through the air, and whirlwinds, and fiery, dragons flying across the firmament. These tremendous tokens were soon followed by a great famine: and not long after, on the sixth day before the ides of January in the same year, the harrowing inroads of heathen men made lamentable havoc in the church of God in Holy island, by rapine and slaughter. ...

CE 794. In the meantime, the heathen armies spread devastation among the Northumbrians, and plundered the monastery of King Everth at the mouth of the Wear. There, however, some of their leaders were slain; and some of their ships also were shattered to pieces by the violence of the weather; many of the crew were drowned; and some, who escaped alive to the shore, were soon dispatched at the mouth of the river.

CE 832. This year heathen men overran the Isle of Shepey.

CE 833. This year fought King Egbert with thirty-five pirates at Charmouth, where a great slaughter was made, and the Danes remained masters of the field. Two bishops, Hereferth and Wigen, and two aldermen, Dudda and Osmod, died the same year.

CE 837. This year Alderman Wulfherd fought at Hamton with thirty-three pirates, and after great slaughter obtained the victory, but he died the same year. Alderman Ethelhelm also, with the men of Dorsetshire, fought with the Danish army in Portland-isle, and for a good while put them to flight; but in the end, the Danes became masters of the field, and slew the alderman.

CE 838. This year Alderman Herbert was slain by the heathens, and many men with him, among the Marshlanders. The same year, afterwards, in Lindsey, East-Anglia, and Kent, were many men slain by the army.

CE 851. This year Alderman Ceorl, with the men of Devonshire, fought the heathen army at Wemburg, and after making great slaughter obtained the victory. The same year King Athelstan and Alderman Elchere fought in their ships, and slew a large army at Sandwich in Kent, taking nine ships and dispersing the rest. The heathens now for the first time remained over winter in the Isle of Thanet. The same year came three hundred and fifty ships into the mouth of the Thames; the crew of which went upon land, and stormed Canterbury and London; putting to flight Bertulf, king of the Mercians, with his army; and then marched southward over the Thames into Surrey. Here Ethelwulf and his son Ethelbald, at the head of the West-Saxon army, fought with them at Ockley, and made the greatest slaughter of the heathen army that we have ever heard reported to this present day. There also they obtained the victory.

CE 865. This year sat the heathen army in the isle of Thanet, and made peace with the men of Kent, who promised money therewith; but under the security of peace, and the promise of money, the army in the night stole up the country, and overran all Kent eastward.

CE 870. This year the army rode over Mercia into East-Anglia, and there fixed their winter-quarters at Thetford. And in the winter King Edmund fought with them; but the Danes gained the victory and slew the king; whereupon they overran all that land, and destroyed all the monasteries to which they came. The names of the leaders who slew the king were Hingwar and Hubba. At the same time came they to Medhamsted, burning and breaking, and slaying abbot and monks, and all that they there found. They made such havoc there, that a monastery, which was before full rich, was now reduced to nothing. The same year died Archbishop Ceolnoth; and Ethered, Bishop of Witshire, was chosen Archbishop of Canterbury.

CE 882. This year went the army up along the Maese far into Frankland, and there sat a year; and the same year went King Alfred out to sea with a fleet; and fought with four ship-rovers of the Danes and took two of their ships; wherein all the men were slain; and the other two surrendered; but the men were severely cut and wounded ere they surrendered.

CE 885. This year separated the before-mentioned army in two; one part east, another to Rochester. This city they surrounded and wrought another fortress around themselves. The people, however, defended the city, until King Alfred came out with his army. Then went the enemy to their ships, and forsook their work. There were they provided with horses; and soon after, in the same summer, they went over sea again. The same year sent King Alfred a fleet from Kent into East-Anglia. As soon as they came to Stourmouth, there met them sixteen ships of the pirates. And they fought with them, took all the ships, and slew the men. As they returned homeward with their booty, they met a large fleet of the pirates, and fought with them the same day; but the Danes had the victory.

CE 980. In this year was Ethelgar consecrated bishop, on the sixth day before the nones of May, to the bishopric of Selsey; and in the same year was Southampton plundered by a pirate-army, and most of the population slain or imprisoned. And the same year was the Isle of Thanet overrun, and the county of Chester was plundered by the pirate-army of the North. In this year Alderman Alfere fetched the body of the holy King Edward at Wareham and carried him with great solemnity to Shaftsbury.

CE 991. This year was Ipswich plundered; and very soon afterwards was Alderman Britnoth slain at Maldon. In this same year it was resolved that tribute should be given, for the first time, to the Danes, for the great terror they occasioned by the sea-coast. That was first 10,000 pounds. The first who advised this measure was Archbishop Siric.

Notes

1 Cunliffe, *Europe between the Oceans*, 459.

2 Cunliffe, *Europe between the Oceans*, 459; Price, 'The Scandinavian Landscape', 31–34.

3 Cunliffe, *Europe between the Oceans*, 459–460.

4 Sawyer, 'Scandinavia in the Viking Age', 27–28.

5 Hedeager, 'From Warrior to Trade Economy', 84.

6 Hedeager, 'From Warrior to Trade Economy', 84–85.

7 Cunliffe, *Europe between the Oceans*, 459–462.

8 Brunn, 'The Viking Ship', 1282–1289; Christensen, 'Ships and Navigation', 86–97.

9 Kennedy, *Mongols, Huns and Vikings*, 186–188.

10 Jesch, *Women in the Viking Age*, 176–202.

11 Biddle and Kjølby-Biddle, 'Repton and the Vikings', 36–51.

12 Price, 'Belief and Ritual', 164–195.

13 Noonan, 'Why the Vikings First Came to Russia', 321–348.

14 Clarke, 'The Vikings', 47.

15 Price, 'Ship-Men and Slaughter-Wolves', 63; Price, '"Laid Waste, Plundered, and Burned"', 116–126.

16 Clarke, 'The Vikings', 57–58.

17 Kurrild-Klitgaard and Svendsen, 'Rational Bandits', 255–272.

18 Price, 'Ship-Men and Slaughter-Wolves', 64–65.

19 Bjork, 'Piracy in the Baltic', 39–68.

CHAPTER FOUR

English Sea Dogs and the Pillaging of Empire

Now we enter the period when most Westerners will readily recognize the pirates of their imaginations and their storybooks, such as Francis Drake and Henry Morgan. By the sixteenth century, corsairing (state-sanctioned banditry) and piracy (non-state-sanctioned banditry) had become an endemic part of commerce and warfare in the North Atlantic. Most ports in England and Ireland harboured pirates at one time or another, as did most of the ports of Western Europe. And there was good reason for it. The constant warfare of the fourteenth and fifteenth centuries left coastal areas prone to attack. For cash-poor monarchies, pirates and corsairs provided the most efficient and effective response to seaborne raiders. Consequently, monarchs, such as Henry IV, struggled and failed to control the pirates who carried on their own private war in the English Channel that seriously threatened peace with both France and Flanders.[1]

One of the most famous privateers/pirates/smugglers of the fifteenth century was Henry Pay (died 1419) who sailed out of Poole, England, to raid the shipping and coasts of France and Spain. His exploits included sacking and burning Gijon and Finisterre and demanding a ransom for the prisoners he seized. After being captured by the French in 1404, he managed to escape his bonds, kill his captors and then use their ship to sail up the Seine River to burn and loot several French ships before sailing back to England.[2]

Corsairing became the normal method of forced exchange and warfare all along the western coast of Europe and Africa and into the Mediterranean. The famous Portuguese noble Dom Henrique (1394–1460), erroneously called 'The Navigator', sent his retainers on corsairing missions down the coast of Morocco and far south into the Gulf of Guinea during the first half of the fifteenth century. They seldom bothered to distinguish between Muslim and Christian prey.[3] After the expulsion of the Moors from Portugal in 1250, corsairing against the Muslims in Africa became one of the few remaining ways for aspiring Christian nobles to win their knighthood and enhance their reputations. Land-poor nobles also found corsairing to be an effective method of acquiring the wealth needed to maintain their retainers and to pay their debts. The 'exploration' of the West African coast and the 'discovery' of the Atlantic islands was largely the work of Portuguese and Spanish corsairs. By the end of the fifteenth century, corsairs had come to play a crucial role in the creation of the empire.[4]

Often these armed entrepreneurs acted with the acquiescence of their own monarchies and even held formal commissions from them. These commissions came to be known as 'letters of reprisal' or 'letters of marque'. Letters of reprisal had their origins in the ancient practice of individuals seeking to recover the value of property lost to foreign raiders by acquiring a commission from the crown. The first known letter of reprisal was issued in England in 1295 to Bernard Dongresilli to seek reprisal against the people of Lisbon.[5] The practice of reprisals amounted to 'private warfare between the subjects of foreign states'.[6] These commissions usually listed which enemy nations the holder of the commission could attack and placed limits on the value of property that could be seized. Any surplus property went into the crown coffers.[7]

Letters of marque, first issued in England in 1544 by Henry VIII, developed from the long practice by European monarchs of impressing merchant ships for warfare by giving them commissions. Thus, the letter of marque originated as a tool of the state that sought to both utilize and constrain maritime predation within acceptable limits. Ship captains possessed licence to attack enemy shipping during times of war, but they had to pay to outfit their ships in return for a percentage of the prize. By the sixteenth century, letters of reprisal and letters of marque had become a legitimate means for carrying out attacks for the purpose of profit by private individuals. Raiding was business, pure and simple.[8] So was the selling of commissions by monarchs and governors around the Atlantic world.[9]

Those who carried commissions were called corsairs. The term 'privateer', also often used for them, was first coined in the seventeenth century and should probably not be used for the Elizabethan pirates/corsairs of the sixteenth century.[10] Two kinds of corsairs emerged by the sixteenth century. First were the armed merchantmen whose primary purpose was to carry cargo for trade. They were usually armed for self-defence and carried commissions just in case they should happen upon a prize while carrying out their trade. They needed to carry a commission because if they were attacked and seized the attacking ship without a licence, even in self-defence, they had no legal claim to the prize.[11] The second type was the privately owned men-of-war whose sole purpose was to cruise the oceans looking for prizes. They set out heavily armed and heavily manned with state licences to seize enemy ships and properties. The sailors on the private men-of-war received no regular salaries, but received shares of the profits.[12] The English used both corsairs and privateers as auxiliaries to their small naval forces, but the French used them as their primary naval force. French privateers operating out of Dunkirk and other French ports between 1689 and 1815 became the principal threat to British trade. They often acted on their own initiative, such as the 1711 raid that captured Rio de Janeiro from the Portuguese. Their attacks on Atlantic shipping nearly put an end to the English slave trade to the Americas.[13]

As corsairing became normalized in the sixteenth century, most countries began regulating the practice. In England, the crown created the high court of the admiralty in the seventeenth century. To acquire a licence, the corsair had to get a warrant from the Lord High Admiral; declare the name, tonnage and description of the ship and crew; post bail and undergo an inspection in port by the local customs collector who issued a certificate with a detailed description of the ship and crew. With the letter of marque, the admiralty issued a code of conduct that declared that neutral shipping had to be respected and that the crews of captured vessels were to be well treated. Evidence could not be tampered with. Cargoes could not be embezzled, and all prizes had to be brought to trial in ports friendly to the British for condemnation.[14] To declare a prize, the captain and two of his officers had to submit to examination as to the legality of their prize. Witnesses were questioned, and a declaration was posted for any interested parties to stake a contrary claim to the ship and cargo. If all went well, the prize would be condemned, and the captain would be allowed to sell his prize.[15]

All of these regulations sought to deter abuse and to maximize the military effectiveness of privateers by restricting their activities to enemy shipping. The system worked, more or less, but it could be abused. After all, only the merchants seeking reprisals knew how much property, if any, they had truly lost. Over time, legal proof of loss ceased to matter. Letters of reprisal became nothing more than the purchase of a licence to plunder.[16]

European monarchs could not resist the temptation to allow private, non-state actors to engage in predation that could benefit the state. If things went wrong, they could always blame it on the company or the privateer. Still, monarchs struggled with the paradox that the more they tried to constrain the abuse of private predators, the less effective they became.[17] Privateers often turned pirates and mercantile companies threatened to draw states into wars with other states as they yielded to the temptations for private gain. The temptations for abuse soared after 1500 as the Portuguese and Spanish expanded and consolidated their seaborne empires. By then, the Portuguese had settled the Azores, Cape Verde islands and Madeira, had established fortified trading posts all along the West African coast, and had even reached India in 1498 by sailing around Africa into the Indian Ocean. Pedro Álvares Cabral had landed in what is modern Brazil in 1500 and claimed it for Portugal.

The long-standing rivalry between Spain and Portugal reached a precarious settlement in 1479 with the Treaty of Alcaçovas in which Spain received

sole control over the conquest and colonization of the Canary Islands and
Portugal received exclusive rights to exploit the coasts of Africa. This treaty
was the first to promote the idea that European states could unilaterally
carve out spheres of influence, claim suzerainty over foreign lands and
peoples without their consent or knowledge, and then colonize and exploit
those areas. Columbus's 1492 voyage threw this cosy geopolitical agreement
into a tailspin because it seemed to threaten Portuguese interests in India.
The 1494 Treaty of Tordesillas resolved the dispute by dividing the world in
half. It drew a line in the Atlantic about 2,000 kilometres 'west of the Cape
Verde Islands'. Portugal retained rights to exploit the non-European regions
east of 'the line' and Spain everything west of it.[18]

It should come as no surprise that the emerging sea powers of France,
England and the Netherlands all howled in protest at the arrogance of the
Spanish and Portuguese. The reports of ships laden with gold, silver, sugar
and exotic plants and animals that trickled into northern ports in the early
sixteenth century proved too tempting to resist. Northern European corsairs
from England, Holland and France began haunting the waters in the 'Atlantic
Triangle'. The apex of the triangle was the Azores, Lisbon and the Canaries
forming the other two points. Because the Portuguese and Spanish shipping
that hailed from peninsular ports had to follow predictable sea-lanes and
frequently stopped at the Atlantic islands for resupply, these waters proved
the most lucrative hunting grounds of the Atlantic sea wolves. The other
end of the shipping lanes in the Caribbean proved to be another pinch point
where ships could be easily spotted and chased. The numerous islands and
inlets on both sides of the Atlantic provided safe havens and hideaways for
pirates, such as the rocky, uninhabited island of Berlenga, 12 kilometres off
the Portuguese coast.

The French began their incursions into American waters in 1503 when
a French captain visited Brazil, which was claimed by Portugal, and carried
home a cargo of exotic Brazil wood and birds. Despite Portuguese attempts
to discourage French poaching, the French persisted in raiding and trading
along the Brazilian coast. In the 1550s, they established a colony near
modern Rio de Janeiro called France Antarctique that the Portuguese finally
destroyed in 1567.

Jean de Lery described, in 1555, the subterfuge used by French mariners
to lure ships into an ambush:

> The way it goes is that these mariner gentlemen, striking sail, and meeting
> with the poor merchant ships, usually claim that they have been unable
> to approach any land or port because of tempests and calms, and that
> they are consequently short of supplies, for which they are willing to pay.
> But if, under this pretext, they can set foot on board their neighbor's ship,
> you need hardly ask whether, as an alternative to scuttling the vessel, they
> relieve it of whatever takes their fancy. And if one then protests (as in fact
> we always did) that no order has been given to pillage indiscriminately,

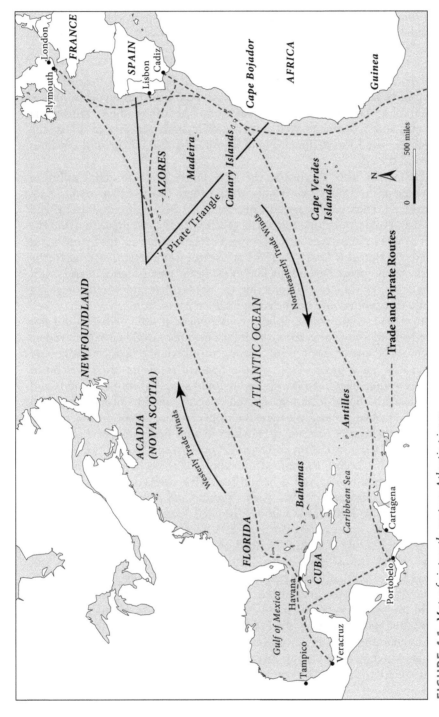

FIGURE 4.1 *Map of sixteenth-century Atlantic piracy.*
Source: Map produced by Barry Levely, Cartographer.

friends as well as enemies, they give you the common cant of our land soldiers, who in such cases offer as sole reason that it's war and custom, and that you have to get used to it.

Armed with such convenient excuses, the French expanded their attacks. In the early seventeenth century, the French established Equinoctial France in Maranhão near the Amazon River from which they raided Portuguese shipping and settlements well into the eighteenth century. In 1710, the French captured Rio de Janeiro and negotiated a 600,000 cruzado ransom to return the city.[19]

The French also conducted the first pirate raids in the Caribbean beginning in the 1520s. They raided the northern coast of Panama in 1536. Successive French pirates seized Cartagena in 1544, Havana in 1555, and looted and raided all along the coasts of Cuba and Hispaniola. To avoid the onset of war in Europe caused by conflict in the Caribbean, the Spanish and the French signed a treaty in 1559 at Cateau-Cambrésis that created the practice of 'no peace beyond the line' 'west of the prime meridian and south of the Tropic of Cancer'.[20] In practice, this meant that piracy and corsairing beyond that point could not be considered an act of war.

After 1555, a growing number of interlopers in the Caribbean did not come to raid. They came to trade. John Hawkins (1532–1595) arrived as a contraband merchant in 1562 hoping to outwit the Spanish monopoly system and get a piece of the action. Spanish residents often welcomed European smugglers like Hawkins who could supply them with goods and slaves that the Spanish monopoly trade system failed to provide. Spanish officials, however, often gave these interlopers a cool reception and refused to give them licences to trade.[21] Hawkins lost his first cargo when he tried, unwisely, to sell it in Lisbon and Seville. On his second expedition in 1564, he was given a licence to trade at unfavourable terms in Venezuela and so landed his men to demand a better deal. This coerced trade became the rule when he returned in 1567 with slaves he had picked up in Africa. He used his men to force trade with the isolated Spanish towns until a storm blew his ships into the Spanish port at Vera Cruz where he was trapped and attacked. Only two ships escaped, one under the command of Francis Drake. Hawkins lost most of his 400-man crew and two of his ships and always suspected that Drake had turned tail and abandoned him.[22]

Hawkins's disaster guaranteed that English pirates in the Caribbean would no longer bother to trade. They came openly to plunder and loot. They found willing allies in the French corsairs operating in the Caribbean, the communities of runaway slaves, known as *cimarrones,* and indigenous peoples who had no reason to love the Spanish who raided them for slaves. Francis Drake (1540–1596) returned to the Caribbean a year later with a letter of reprisal from Queen Elizabeth to seek compensation for the Spanish seizure of Hawkins's ships at Vera Cruz. By this time, the Spanish had developed the famous *carrera de las Índias* by which Spanish ships sailed in convoys guarded by powerful galleons.[23]

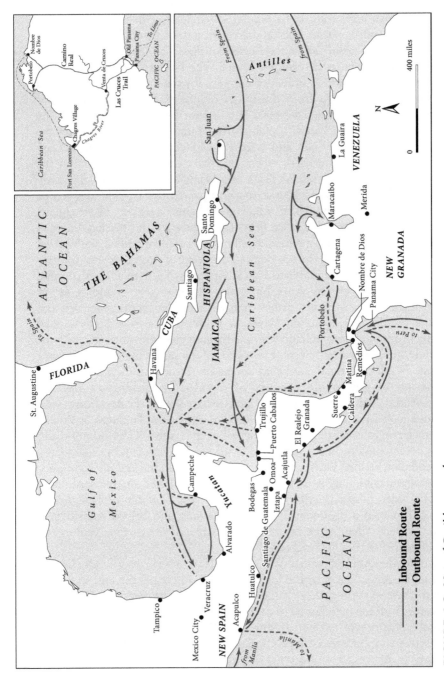

FIGURE 4.2 *Map of Caribbean sea-lanes.*
Source: Map produced by Barry Levely, Cartographer.

The Spanish fleets followed a regular schedule governed by the weather. They sailed from Spain in May and August, passed through the Canaries, and entered the Caribbean at the Lesser Antilles. The main fleet sailed for Vera Cruz and then to Havana by March. The Isthmus fleet anchored off Nombre de Dios, where it unloaded supplies for the Peru trade and loaded the silver coming north from the mines of Potosí, before harbouring at Cartagena, where it loaded supplies. It sailed for Havana in January.[24] The silver shipments from Potosí travelled from Lima to Panama City on the southern Panamanian coast and were then loaded on mules and packed overland to Nombre de Dios, where the silver awaited shipment on the isthmus fleet.[25] The combined fleets left Havana for Spain in the early summer to avoid the hurricane season and passed through the dangerous Florida channel. Pirates lurked amid the Bahamas picking off stragglers, but seldom endangered the large fleet. The regularity and predictability of these routes, amid a fragmented coastline with galleons filled with silver, was guaranteed to draw the sea dogs to the scent of prey. At every transfer point, the silver was vulnerable to attack. The *carrera* system worked, despite widespread fraud, for 150 years, but it also imposed costly shipping delays on the inhabitants of Spanish America, restricted their access to foreign and manufactured goods, including slaves, and carried expensive duties – all of which encouraged their collaboration with smugglers and corsairs.

Trade and plunder had become two sides of the same coin in the sixteenth century. Nobles, criminals and commoners of all social classes were drawn to the sea to pursue the business of plunder. In Elizabethan England (1558–1603), sea-plunder came to be associated with 'Protestantism and patriotism'.[26] To attack the shipping of Catholic Spain, Portugal or France became a religious act of service on behalf of the nation. That did not mean that governments turned a blind eye to all piracy or that pirates suddenly changed their stripes. Pirates were useful only if they attacked the right prey, and governments sought to repress those who insisted on indiscriminate piracy. Under Elizabeth, the gentry of the West Country of Devon and Cornwall played a prominent role in sea raiding and helped transform it from the 'petty Channel roving of earlier years into the oceanic ventures of the [fifteen] seventies and eighties'.[27]

During the Anglo-Spanish War (1585–1603), Elizabeth found herself without an official navy or the financial means to create one and so had to turn to these experienced sea raiders. She relied on private individuals, the sea-gentry and the merchants, to carry on war with Spain. Some sailed with commissions; others did not. In any case, Elizabeth expected them to pay themselves with the prizes they took. Consequently, English privateers joined the fray in droves, 'far outnumbering the queen's ships'. Irregular forces engaging in plunder for plunder's sake became the rule.[28] Approximately 100 ships per year sailed during the war, with numbers rising occasionally to 200. Two hundred thirty-six privateers served in Elizabeth's irregular navy between 1589 and 1591.[29] They captured 299 prizes with a value of

£279,713.[30] English corsairs raided up and down the Brazilian coast in the late sixteenth century, sacking towns, burning sugar plantations and seizing ships. In 1595, James Lancaster occupied Recife for an entire month and carried off a valuable cargo of Brazilwood.[31]

Employing privateers, however, came at a cost. The men may have proclaimed their patriotic fervour, but when the choice between doing their duty and acquiring a prize faced them, they usually chose to take the prize. For example, in 1588 as the English desperately engaged the overwhelming power of the Spanish Armada, Francis Drake served as commander of one of the Queen's squadrons. After a sharp engagement with the Spanish Armada in the Channel, Drake was ordered to post his stern lanterns on his ship, the *Revenge,* so that the rest of the fleet could follow him as he shadowed the Spanish Armada. But Drake found the damaged Spanish ship, the *Rosario,* too tempting a prize. He failed to light his lanterns and pursued the *Rosario* into the night. He captured the vessel the next day with a rich prize, half of which disappeared before the ship reached London for condemnation. As a result of Drake's dereliction of duty, the rest of the English fleet lagged behind the Spanish fleet and lost its ability to attack the Spanish ships.[32] The Armada failed, not because of the prowess and discipline of England's irregular forces, but because of poor weather, poor planning and the failure of Spanish leadership.

After 1580 and the death of the king of Portugal, Dom Sebastião, Portugal became part of the Spanish Empire when Phillip of Spain assumed the throne. Until 1640, when Portugal rebelled against Spanish rule, Portuguese shipping and colonies became legitimate targets for English and Dutch privateers and pirates. Spain, Portugal and their empires were the chief targets of English privateers. The big fleets with their warships protecting the shipments of gold, silver and sugar were imposing prey and were rarely taken, but the smaller vessels that carried on the private trade could provide rich pickings. The Portuguese-Brazil fleet that carried the sugar and Brazilwood back to Portugal suffered terribly from English privateering. Of the fifty ships required to transport the sugar to Portugal, the English captured thirty-four between 1589 and 1591. Despite the legends of hordes of hidden pirate gold, the most common prize the privateers seized was food, such as fish, 'wine, oil, olives, oranges, raisins, figs, walnuts, almonds', grains and manufactured goods, such as textiles, ironware, salt, lumber and hides. Sugar from Brazil and Madeira was the most common prize.[33]

That did not stop men like Francis Drake who specifically targeted the weak points in the system of Spanish silver shipments. English, French and Dutch privateers swarmed into the West Indies, hoping for even a small catch of silver or gold. The isthmus of Panama became a focal point of English depredations because the silver coming from South America was trans-shipped by mule across the isthmus from Panama City to Nombre de Dios. Drake crossed the isthmus in 1572 with *cimarrón* allies, but failed to capture the silver-laden mule train. In July of 1572, he captured Nombre de Dios but had to withdraw without the treasure. He attacked a mule train near Nombre de Dios in April of 1573 and succeeded in making off with some silver. John Oxenham crossed the isthmus again in 1575, built a ship and sailed into the Pacific, where he captured a ship laden with gold and silver. On his raids along the Pacific coast, Oxenham burned and looted settlements, desecrated churches and even paraded a Franciscan priest around with a chamber pot on his head. He paid for these abuses by being captured and executed as a Protestant heretic by the Inquisition in Lima in 1580.[34] Drake followed Oxenham into the Pacific in 1577 by sailing through the Straits of Magellan and raiding his way up the Pacific coast of South America. He captured the treasure ship *Nuestra Señora de la Concepción* and eventually circumnavigated the world. His capture of a Spanish silver ship on the Pacific route forced Spain to establish a fleet system in the Pacific in 1581.

The new fleet system provided better protection, but it did not prevent pirate raids in the Pacific anymore than it did the Caribbean. Thomas Cavendish, who repeated Drake's circumnavigation of the globe, seized the galleon *Santa Ana* along the way. Cavendish returned to England around the time of the Spanish Armada's defeat in 1588 and became a wealthy

FIGURE 4.3 *French filibusters pillage a Spanish town, sixteenth century.*
Source: Theodorus de Bry, *Grands Voyages: America*. Photo by Culture Club/Getty Images.

celebrity. But he died in 1591 trying to repeat his exploits.[35] Between 1588 and 1603, 151 known English ships raided and pillaged in the Caribbean.[36] Drake returned in 1595 with John Hawkins to attack the Spanish Main, but everything went wrong during the expedition. Hawkins took sick and died on the Atlantic crossing. The Spanish had word of Drake's arrival and had fortified San Juan. Drake failed to take it, losing more than fifty men in the fighting. Drake raided a few coastal towns before setting up base at Nombre de Dios, which had been abandoned since his raids. Drake sent men over the isthmus to wait for the Spanish silver shipment. They missed the shipment and retreated to Honduras, where Drake took fever and died. The fleet returned to England in defeat. Drake's failure did not signify an immediate decline in English piracy in the Caribbean, however. Another seventy-three ships raided there between 1575 and 1603 when the Anglo-Spanish War ended.

While Elizabeth encouraged corsairs like Drake, she also established the East India Company (EIC) in 1600, armed it with the power to use violence, and sent it off to trade with East India. For most of its history, the EIC engaged in plundering the shipping and coastlines of the states in India, Bengal, Southeast Asia and China while carrying on a running war with the Dutch East India Company. The EIC brought great wealth into England and delivered a huge empire in India to the British government in the nineteenth century. By then, the crown's opinion had turned against violent commercial companies.[37] Corsairing, armed mercantilism and piracy of the sixteenth century provided much-needed liquid assets to the English, offered lower prices to English consumers and greater access to goods in the Caribbean, failed to stifle interregional trade and pulled resources away from development in Spanish America towards self-defence. The year 1603 saw the end of the Anglo-Spanish War and the reduction in formal legal pillaging of the Spanish Empire. For good or ill, the era of the Elizabethan sea dogs was over and a new era of both state-sanctioned privateering and buccaneering was about to begin.[38]

As you read the sources that follow, consider these questions:

1   How does the account of Drake differ from or confirm that of the Spanish accounts? Whose account do you trust more and why?

2   What do the accounts of the raid at Nombre de Dios reveal about the nature of Elizabethan piracy in the Caribbean?

3   Why might the Spanish accounts disagree with each other about the details of the raid?

4   What tactics did the Spanish use to counter the raid, and how did they respond once it occurred? Why were they unable to prevent the raid?

5   What do the pirates' tactics reveal about their motives?

6 What can the contradictions in the different accounts tell us about the nature of the historical record?

7 Using the Spanish and English documents construct a narrative of what happened during the attack on the mule train.

8 What effect was the parasitic piracy of the English sea dogs having on the hosts upon which they preyed?

Francis Drake (c. 1540–1596) was from Devon, England, and became a protégé of the Hawkins family. He first sailed to the Caribbean at age 23. He was with Hawkins when the fleet was attacked at Vera Cruz in 1568. He escaped and Hawkins accused him of abandoning them in their hour of need. Drake returned to seek vengeance for the losses at Vera Cruz. He apparently sailed three separate times in 1569, 1570 and 1571 to exact retribution, to reconnoitre the area and to seek intelligence before his grand expedition of 1572–1573. He captured Nombre de Dios in 1572, but retreated because of injury. He tried crossing the isthmus to take the mule train near Panama City but failed, only to succeed near Nombre de Dios in the spring of 1573. He circumnavigated the world in 1577–1580, and, in 1585, he rampaged through the Caribbean before returning to Plymouth England via Walter Raleigh's colony at Roanoke. Drake tried to repeat his 1585–1586 raid ten years later, but he died of dysentery in January of 1596 off the coast of Porto Bello.

I. A. Wright, ed., *Documents Concerning English Voyages to the Spanish Main, 1569–1580* (London: Printed for the Hakluyt Society, 1932), 68–70, 81–92. Reprinted with permission.

The Royal Officials of Panama to the Crown, May 9, 1573.
Catholic Royal Majesty

An assault by corsairs has been made in this kingdom, which has resulted in the losses and damages we will here briefly relate.

On the 29th of last April, as the pack-trains engaged in the overland traffic of this realm were proceeding under guard, and with the defense of soldiers and troops considered necessary, from this city to that of Nombre de Dios, the gold and silver belonging to·your majesty and to private persons, to be laden on board ships of the fleet. When they had arrived about a league and a half from that city, there came forth to take the gold and silver carried by these pack-trains a certain number of English, French, and cimarrones, who are negroes who have run away from their masters and advertise that they have allied and confederated themselves with the English and French to destroy this realm, a thing not until this year ever seen or imagined.

The soldiers and other people who were there to protect them being unable to prevent it, they took from the pack-train more than 100,000 pesos, all in gold, including 18,363 pesos, 5 tomines, and 2 grains consigned to your Majesty.

With this prize, they made off, rapidly and in military order, this realm being powerless to prevent or hinder, although proper efforts to do so were made ....

According to the confession of one of the French, taken at the time of this latest attack, it is shown that they have entered into close amity and confederation with the negroes and have promised them that, once this fleet shall have gone from the harbor of the city of Nombre de Dios, they will sack that place and deliver to them what Spanish inhabitants, men and women, it may have, to be their slaves ....

Panama, May 9, 1573. Catholic Royal Majesty
Your majesty's humble servitors and vassals kiss your Catholic royal majesty's feet.
Tristan de Silva Campofrio.
Gonzalo de Carvajal. (Rubrics)
Received August 26, same year, and seen next day.

Diego Calderon, his services; depositions made at Panama, April 22, 1574.]
Very Powerful Sir
I, Diego Calderon, your former alcalde mayor and captain general in the city of Nombre de Dios, state that ... having arrived in the province of Tierra Firme, in this city of Panama, seat of the royal Audiencia, and English and French corsairs having on the north coast of Tierra Firme seized many ships and frigates and barks, and in them killed many of your subjects, and from them stolen large quantities of pesos in gold; having dared to enter and take and sack the city of Nombre de Dios, where they killed many residents and transients in the said city; in view of the necessity of acting in the matter, your president and judges provided and ordered me to go to reside there.

In defense of the said city I served your highness as alcalde mayor and captain-general without pay, all at my cost and expense; for although a salary of 600 pesos in assayed silver was assigned me, there were no proceeds from fines from which to collect the same. And I took with me to the defense of the said city and port of Nombre de Dios, Captain Hernando de Berrio with approximately 100 men, and other residents and good soldiers of this kingdom.

These being in the said city as garrison, there appeared off the port eight sails and three or four launches of English corsairs, and they were off the port and coast more than fifteen days. During that time, I fortified the said city and all the sea coast of the said port with trenches and earthworks, as was suitable, and I advised your royal Audiencia, in consequence of which Licentiate Diego de Vera, your president and governor, came down with 200 men. Seeing the good condition into which I had put the said city, he left the forces he brought as reinforcement for it, and returned to the royal Audiencia. During all this time, I stood guard in person, and made all the sentry rounds, every night, at all hours, along all the works, in these matters laboring, as was my duty and obligation, in your royal service, like a good and loyal servant.

Further, seeing that the said corsairs had not landed, and on the sea were doing much damage by seizing coasting craft, I sent against them an armada of two frigates and shallops, under the command of Captain Francisco Ramirez de Guzman and Admiral Cristóbal García Salon. With more than a hundred men they patrolled all the coast and brought in three frigates which the corsairs had looted and damaged. Similarly, I ordered Captain Hernando de Berrio out to the river called the Sardinilla, for it was understood that the said corsairs might endeavor to land there; and I took all other measures needful for the defense of the said city and coast, as I was under obligation to do in your royal service.

Further, the fleet under General Diego Flores de Valdés, knight of the order of Santiago, being in the city, in the year 1573, in the month of April, there reached the city news that the English and French corsairs and cimarrones had attacked and sacked a mule train numbering more than a hundred animals carrying gold and silver belonging to your highness and to private individuals, to a value of more than 200,000 pesos. As soon as I heard this, in person I sallied forth on the road on foot, and with me went the said Captain Hernando de Berrio and other residents and soldiers. I proceeded to the place where the robbery occurred, which was two leagues from the city. We went into the bush and killed the captain of the French, named Captain Tutila, and others of the corsairs and two of the cimarrones, and captured another of the French corsairs, who said his name was Jacques Laurens. He was executed. And we took from the corsairs a great part of the booty they had stolen, i.e. a great quantity of gold bricks and gold and silver bars, among these being eleven large gold bricks belonging to your highness, duly delivered to your highness' treasurer, Miguel Ordoño, which were worth more than 6,300 pesos. With the said force I pursued the corsairs until night came on, with storm and rain, and we broke them up and scattered them in such manner that they could not keep together; and so it became impossible to follow them further.

As soon as I returned to the city, this same night, I ordered fifty men out, in command of Captain Antonio Suarez de Medina, to occupy the pass to the sea; and I took all other measures possible, according to the lie of the land and the weather, all of which was done with brevity and dispatch; and I delivered the gold and silver over to its owners ...

I ask and request your highness to receive the testimony I intend to present and that the witnesses I may bring forward may be examined accordingly, I furnish this interrogatory ...

In the city of Panama, on the twenty-seventh day of the month of April in the year one thousand five hundred and seventy-four, Diego Calderon ... presented as Witness Juan de Morales Rendon, resident in this city ...

In reply to the eleventh question witness deposed ... that, the fleet and armada which General Diego Flores de Valdés commanded being in the harbor of Nombre de Dios, and Diego Calderon being alcalde mayor and captain general of the said city, one day in April in 1573 news arrived to the effect that at a place two leagues from the city of Nombre de Dios, at the river called Campos, French and English corsairs together with a lot of cimarrones had attacked two pack trains of more than seventy mules which were coming in laden with gold and silver. Immediately, on foot, Diego Calderon appeared in the market-place of the said city and there ordered a summons to be cried, calling upon all the residents, transients and other inhabitants to proceed together to the relief of the bullion, on penalty of death to him who refused to go. Many persons assembled, from whom Diego Calderon selected Captain Hernando de Berrio with some twenty or thirty men, deponent being one of them. With this party Diego Calderon set out down the road on foot, calling upon the many people, who followed him, and they went with all speed to the place where the robbery had occurred. There they found the pack trains in disorder and many boxes broken open, and a Frenchman (his head cut off) and a cimarrón dead. The said alcalde mayor remained here with certain men and by his order, Captain Berrio with about fifteen men pursued the English until night came on, very stormy, with rain and bad weather. Witness knows this, because he saw it, being himself present, and it is public and notorious.

In reply to the twelfth question witness deposes that he knows that in this sally and enterprise Diego Calderon rendered his majesty signal service, because the said English captain was killed, and another Englishman, and also because the corsairs were dispersed and nearly all the loot they had stolen was recovered. Witness believes about 100,000 pesos were recovered, which belonged to private individuals and principally to his majesty. This was accomplished because Diego Calderon came forth so promptly, for the moment the news arrived he set out with the rest of the people ....

In the city of Panama, on the twenty-eighth day of the month of April of the aforesaid year. Diego Calderon presented as witness Alonso de Ribera, notary of the city of Nombre de Dios ...

In reply to the eleventh question witness deposed that while General Diego Flores de Valdés was in the city of Nombre de Dios and his armada and fleet in its harbor, one day in the month of April in the year 1573 ....about mid-day news came that French and English corsairs and cimarrones from the highlands had held up two mule-trains laden with gold and silver at a point two leagues from the city of Nombre de Dios; and witness saw that as soon as the news came, immediately, General Diego Calderon set out ... Because deponent was ill he remained (in the city) ... Night fell; deponent observed that therefore, and because it rained heavily, some persons returned and in the market-place of Nombre de

Dios deponent saw a head exposed which they said was that of Captain Tutila, and so also he saw the head of a negro which they said was that of a cimarron ....

In reply to the fourteenth question deponent said that forthwith, the night that they returned from the bush where the robbery occurred, he knows that next day early Antonio Suarez de Medina went out with a body of soldiers, well-armed and equipped, to cut off the corsairs' retreat where it was deduced that they would come down to the shore to embark. The said Antonio de Medina and Juan Rodriguez, surgeon, who went out on this undertaking, told deponent that they marched three or four days with all diligence and care, and when they arrived at the place where they supposed the corsairs would re-embark, they had already done so ...

This same day, month and year, the said Diego Calderon presented as witness Martin de Hureta, resident in this city ....

In reply to the eleventh question he stated that ... as soon as the news arrived Diego Calderon set out on foot ... with many soldiers and residents of the city of Nombre de Dios, deponent among them .... They arrived where the robbery had occurred and found the mules of the pack trains unpacked and scattered, and many boxes and cases of plate broken open. They killed the captain of the corsairs and another of the band and two cimarrones, and went in pursuit of them until nightfall. The night was very dark and rainy and tempestuous ....

In the city of Panama on the sixth day of the month of May in the said year, Diego Calderon ....as witness presented Luis de Çarate, resident in this city ....

In reply to the eleventh question deponent said that .... the instant the news arrived Captain Diego Calderon with great diligence and speed appeared in the city market place, summoning the people to follow him, for they were going to the place where the corsairs had committed the robbery. By crier he bade all to follow him and so set out; and with him went Captain Hernando de Berrio and deponent and many other persons. With much difficulty, because it was a very muddy bad road, they all proceeded to the place where the robbery had occurred, and Diego Calderon arrived before deponent, for he mounted a mule he met on the way, that he might go more quickly to the relief. Diego Calderon went into the bush with the men who accompanied him, and when deponent reached the place of the robbery he found an Englishman, or a Frenchman, dead and decapitated, and a cimarron, dead. While searching for gold and silver, of the lot they had stolen, deponent came upon the mules of the pack train, in disorder, and at this juncture he saw Diego Calderon emerge from the bush, tired and exhausted ...,

Deponent knew and certainly understood that the dead Englishman or Frenchman was a very valiant captain whom Diego Calderon and the men with him encountered .... Further, witness learned that when Diego

Calderon went into the bush he killed a Frenchman, who they said was the captain of the corsairs ....

In the city of Panama on the seventh day of the month of May in the said year, Diego Calderon ....as witness presented Pero Lopez, carpenter, resident of this city ....

In reply to the eleventh question, he said that at the time mentioned in the question .... news reached the city about noon that two leagues out English and French corsairs and cimarrones had attacked and robbed many mules of a pack train ... Immediately Diego Calderon set out ... and this witness also went with him to the place where the robbery occurred. All went on foot, which was hard work, because of the bad road. When, at top speed, they arrived there they found the mules unpacked and in disorder and many cases and boxes broken open and much silver and gold scattered about. When deponent came up a Frenchman and a cimarron were dead. Hernando de Berrio with twenty-five men went into the bush after the corsairs, whom they had broken up and scattered when they arrived. Deponent knew and understood that in the bush the said soldiers killed the captain of the French who was called Tutila. And so Diego Calderon ordered the people with him to gather up and search for the gold and silver which had been recovered from the corsairs ....

In the city of Panama on the eleventh day of the month of May in the said year, ... Diego Calderon ... as witness presented Pero García de Nuño Álvarez, resident in this city.

In reply to the eleventh question he said that ... he observed that news reached the city that certain squadrons and a company of English and French corsairs and cimarrones from the mountains had held up two trains of 100 mules ... Forthwith Diego Calderon set out by the highway on foot, calling upon the people and soldiers to follow him, deponent among them. They went with all possible haste to the place where the robbery had occurred, and deponent with other soldiers under Captain Berrio went ahead of General Diego Calderon who was getting the people together.

They went two leagues into the wilderness in pursuit of the French and found that the corsairs were fleeing and dropping the gold and silver they had stolen and abandoning their arms. And as they were advancing, they came upon the captain called Tutila, who was the leader of the corsairs, and they killed him.

So they gathered up the money and followed after the enemies until night fell. It was a stormy rainy night. Because this prevented them from carrying the necessary subsistence and munitions, they returned to the city of Nombre de Dios.

When deponent and the other people arrived at the scene of the robbery, they found the pack mules scattered and many cases and boxes broken open, which had contained bullion to a great amount.

They also found a negro and a Frenchman dead; and the alcalde mayor ordered all the gold and silver to be collected which had been recovered from the corsairs … This sally in relief … prevented the corsairs and cimarrones from carrying off all the bullion, and dispersed them. ….

Francis Drake, *Sir Francis Drake Revived: Calling upon This Dull or Effeminate Age, to Follow His Noble Steps for Gold and Silver* (London: Nicholas Bourne, 1653), 75–87. [This account was written with the assistance of Drake in 1592, twenty years after the events it describes.]

Having thus agreed with Captain Testu [to take twenty of his men to sail into the Rio Francisco], we sent for the Cimaroons as before was decreed. Two of them were brought aboard our ships, to give the French assurance of this agreement. And as soon as we could furnish ourselves and refresh the French company, which was within five or six days … taking twenty of the French and fifteen of ours with our Cimaroons, leaving both our ships in safe road, we manned our frigate and two pinnaces … and went towards Rio Francisco, which because it had not water enough for our frigate, caused us to leave her at the Cabezas, manned with English and French, in the charge of Robert Doble, to stay there without attempting any chase until the return of our pinnaces. And then bare to Rio Francisco (March 31) where both Captains landed with such force as aforesaid, and charged them that had the charge of the pinnaces to be there the fourth day next following without any fail. And thus knowing that the carriages went now daily from Panama to Nombre de Dios, we proceeded in covert through the woods, towards the highway that leadeth between them.

It is five leagues accounted by sea between Rio Francisco and Nombre de Dios, but the way which we marched by land we found it above seven leagues. We marched as in our former journey to Panama, both for order and silence, to the great wonder of the French Captain and company, who protested they knew not by any means how to recover the pinnaces, if the Cimaroons (to whom what our Captain commanded was a law, though they little regarded the French, as having no trust in them) should leave us. Our Captain assured him there was no cause of doubt of them, of whom he had had such former trial.

When we were come within an English mile of the way we stayed all night, refreshing ourselves, in stillness, in a most convenient place, where we heard the carpenters, being many in number, working upon their ships, as they usually do by reason of the great heat of the day in Nombre de Dios; and might hear the mules coming from Panama, by reason of the advantage of the ground.

The next morning (April 1), upon hearing of that great number of bells, the Cimaroons rejoiced exceedingly, as though there could not have befallen them a more joyful accident, chiefly having been disappointed before. Now they all assured us we should have more gold and silver than all of us could bear away, as in truth it fell out.

For there came three recoes, one of fifty mules, the other two of seventy each, every one of which carried three hundred pound weight of silver, which in all amounted to near thirty ton.

We, putting ourselves in readiness, went down near the way to hear the bells, where we stayed not long, but we saw what metal they were made, and took such hold on the heads of the foremost and hindmost mules, that all the rest stayed and lay down, as their manner is. These three recoes were guarded with forty-five soldiers or thereabouts, fifteen to each reco, which caused some exchange of bullets and arrows for a time, in which conflict the French Captain was sore wounded with hail-shot in the belly and one Cimaroon slain. But in the end, these soldiers thought it the best way to leave their mules with us, and to seek for more help abroad; in which meantime we took some pain to ease some of the mules which were heaviest loaden of their carriages. And being weary, we were contented with a few bars and quoits of gold, as we could well carry, burying about fifteen ton of silver, partly in the burrows which the great land-crabs had made in the earth, and partly under old trees which are fallen thereabout, and partly in the sand and gravel of a river, not very deep of water.

Thus, when about this business we had spent some two hours and had disposed of all our matters, and were ready to march back the very self-same way that we came, we heard both horse and foot coming, as it seemed, to the mules; for they never followed us after we were once entered the woods, when the French Captain, by reason of his wound not able to travel farther, stayed in hope that some rest would recover him better strength. But after we had marched some two leagues, upon the French soldiers' complaint that they missed one of their men also, examination being made whether he were slain or no, it was found that he had drunk much wine, and overloading himself with pillage and hasting to go before us, had lost himself in the woods. And as we afterwards knew he was taken by the Spaniards that evening, and upon torture discovered unto them where we had hidden our treasure.

We continued our march all that and the next day (April 2, 3) towards Rio Francisco, in hope to meet our pinnaces; but when we came thither, looking out to sea we saw seven Spanish pinnaces, which had been searching all the coast thereabouts; whereupon we mightily suspected that they had taken or spoiled our pinnaces, for that our Captain had given so strait charge that they should repair to this place this afternoon from the Cabezas, where they rode, whence to our sight these Spaniards' pinnaces did come.

But the night before there had fallen very much rain, with westerly wind, which as it enforced the Spaniards to return home the sooner by reason of the storm, so it kept our pinnaces that they could not keep the appointments because the wind was contrary, and blew so strong that with their oars they could all that day get but half the way. Notwithstanding, if they had followed our Captain's direction in setting forth over night, while the wind served, they had arrived at the place appointed with far less labor but with far more danger; because that very day at noon the Spanish shallops, manned out of purpose from Nombre de Dios, were come to this place to take our pinnaces, imagining where we were, after they had heard of our intercepting of the treasure.

Our Captain, seeing the shallops, feared lest having taken our pinnaces, they had compelled our men by torture to confess where his frigate and ships were. Therefore, in this distress and perplexity, the company misdoubting that all means of return to their country were cut off and that their treasure then served them to small purpose, our Captain comforted and encouraged us all, saying we should venture no farther than he did. It was no time now to fear, but rather to haste to prevent that which was feared: 'If the enemy have prevailed against our pinnaces, which God forbid, yet they must have time to search them, time to examine the mariners, time to execute their resolution after it is determined. Before all these times be taken, we may get to our ships if ye will, though not possibly by land, because of the hills, thickets and rivers, yet by water. Let us therefore make a raft with the trees that are here in readiness, as offering themselves, being brought down the river, happily this last storm, and put ourselves to sea! I will be one. Who will be the other?'

John Smith offered himself, and two Frenchmen that could swim very well desired they might accompany our Captain, as did the Cimaroons likewise (who had been very earnest with our Captain to have marched by land, though it were sixteen days' journey, and in case the ships had been surprised to have abode always with them), especially Pedro, who yet was fain to be left behind, because he could not row.

The raft was fitted and fast bound; a sail of a biscuit sack prepared; an oar was shaped out of a young tree to serve instead of a rudder, to direct their course before the wind. At his departure he comforted the company by promising that, if it pleased God he should put his foot in safety aboard his frigate he would, God willing, by one means or other get them all aboard, in despite of all the Spaniards in the Indies.

In this manner putting off to the sea, he sailed some three leagues, sitting up to the waist continually in water, and at every surge of the wave to the arm pits, for the space of six hours, upon this raft. What with the parching of the sun and what with the beating of the salt water, they had all of them their skins much fretted away.

At length God gave them the sight of two pinnaces turning towards them with much wind, but with far greater joy to him that could easily conjecture, and did cheerfully declare to those three with him, that they were our pinnaces and that all was safe, so that there was no cause of fear.

But see, the pinnaces not seeing this raft, nor suspecting any such matter, by reason of the wind and night growing on, were forced to run into a cover behind the point, to take succor for that night; which our Captain seeing, and gathering (because they came not forth again) that they would anchor there, put his raft ashore and ran by land about the point, where he found them; who upon sight of him made as much haste as they could to take him and his company aboard. For our Captain, of purpose to try what haste they could and would make in extremity, himself ran in great haste, and so willed the other three with him, as if they had been chased by the enemy; which they rather suspected because they saw so few with him.

And after his coming aboard, when they demanding how all his company did, he answered coldly, 'Well!' they all doubted that all went scarce well. But he, willing to rid all doubts and fill them with joy, took out of his bosom a quoit of gold, thanking God that our voyage was made. And to the Frenchmen he declared how their Captain indeed was left behind sore wounded, and two of his company with him, but it should be no hindrance to them.

That night (April 4) our Captain, with great pain of his company, rowed to Rio Francisco, where he took the rest in, and the treasure which we had brought with us; making such expedition that by dawning of the day we set sail back again to our frigate, and from thence directly to our ships; where, as soon as we arrived, our Captain divided by weight the gold and silver into two even portions, between the French and the English.

About a fortnight after, when we had set all things in order and, taking out of our ship all such necessaries as we needed for our frigate, had left and given her to the Spaniards, whom we had all this time detained, we put out of that harbor, together with the French ship, riding some few days among the Cabezas.

In the meantime, our Captain made a secret composition with the Cimaroons, that twelve of our men and sixteen of theirs should make another voyage, to get intelligence in what case the country stood and, if it might be, recover Monsieur Testu, the French Captain; at leastwise to bring away that which was hidden in our former surprise and could not then be conveniently carried.

John Oxenham and Thomas Sherwell were put in trust for this service, to the great content of the whole company, who conceived greatest hope of them next our Captain; whom by no means they would condescend to suffer to adventure again this time; yet he himself rowed to set them ashore at Rio Francisco, finding his labor well employed both otherwise and also in saving one of those two Frenchmen that had remained willingly to accompany their wounded Captain.

For this gentleman, having escaped the rage of the Spaniards, was now coming towards our pinnace, where he fell down on his knees, blessing

God for the time that ever our Captain was born, who now beyond all his hopes, was become his deliverer.

He, being demanded what was become of his Captain and other fellow, shewed that within half an hour after our departure the Spaniards had overgotten them, and took his Captain and other fellow. He only escaped by flight, having cast away all his carriage, and among the rest one box of jewels, that he might fly the swifter from the pursuers. But his fellow took it up and burdened himself so sore that he could make no speed, as easily as he might otherwise, if he would have cast down his pillage and laid aside his covetous mind. As for the silver, which we had hidden thereabout in the earth and the sands, he thought that it was all gone, for that he thought there had been near two thousand Spaniards and negroes there to dig and search for it.

This report notwithstanding, our purpose held and our men were sent to the said place, where they found that the earth every way a mile distant had been digged and turned up, in every place of any likelihood to have anything hidden in it. And yet nevertheless, for all that narrow search, all our men's labor was not quite lost, but so considered that the third day after their departure they all returned safe and cheerful, with as much silver as they and all the Cimaroons could find (viz., thirteen bars of silver, and some few quoits of gold), with which they were presently embarked without impeachment, repairing with no less speed than joy to our frigate.

Now was it high time to think of homewards, having sped ourselves as we desired, and therefore our Captain concluded to visit Rio Grande [Magdalena] once again, to see if he could meet with any sufficient ship or bark, to carry victual enough to serve our turn homewards, in which we might in safety and security embark ourselves.

Notes

1   Pistono, 'Henry IV and the English Privateers', 322–330.
2   Little, *Pirate Hunting*, 100–101.
3   Russell, *Prince Henry 'the Navigator'*, 73–74; Disney, *A History of Portugal*, 28, 30–31.
4   Hanna, *Pirate Nests*, 21–57.
5   Elleman, 'Introduction', 3.
6   Hanna, *Pirate Nests*, 34.
7   Starkey, 'The Origins and Regulation of Eighteenth-Century British Privateering', 70–73.
8   Hanna, *Pirate Nests*, 36.
9   Burgess, *The Pirates' Pact*, 117.

10 Rodger, 'The Law and Language', 12.

11 Starkey, 'The Origins and Regulation of Eighteenth-Century British Privateering', 71–72.

12 Starkey, 'The Origins and Regulation of Eighteenth-Century British Privateering', 72–73.

13 Thomson, *Mercenaries*, 24–25.

14 Starkey, 'The Origins and Regulation of Eighteenth-Century British Privateering', 73–75.

15 Starkey, 'The Origins and Regulation of Eighteenth-Century British Privateering', 75–76.

16 Andrews, *Elizabethan Privateering*, 4.

17 Thomson, *Mercenaries*, 43.

18 Lane, *Pillaging the Empire*, 11.

19 Vainfas, *Dicionário do Brasil Colonial*, 487–488; Guerreiro, *O Grande Livro da Pirataria*.

20 Hanna, *Pirate Nests*, 38.

21 Hanna, *Pirate Nests*, 39; Lane, *Pillaging the Empire*, 29–32.

22 Lane, *Pillaging the Empire*, 29–32.

23 Lane, *Pillaging the Empire*, 32–35.

24 Parry, *The Spanish Seaborne Empire*, 134–135.

25 Hanna, *Pirate Nests*, 37–38.

26 Hanna, *Pirate Nests*, 39, 63–64, 159–160.

27 Andrews, *Elizabethan Privateering*, 15–16. See also Hanna, *Pirate Nests*, 21–57; Matthew, 'The Cornish and Welsh Pirates', 337–348.

28 Andrews, *Elizabethan Privateering*, 20–21.

29 Andrews, *Elizabethan Privateering*, 32.

30 Andrews, *Elizabethan Privateering*, 125.

31 Vainfas, *Dicionário do Brasil Colonial*, 488–489.

32 Konstom, *Piracy*, 67.

33 Andrews, *Elizabethan Privateering*, 129–134.

34 Lane, *Pillaging the Empire*, 42–43.

35 Kamen, *Empire*, 230.

36 Andrews, *Elizabethan Privateering*, 175.

37 Thomson, *Mercenaries*, 59–67.

38 Konstom, *Piracy*, 70–72.

CHAPTER FIVE

Dwarf Pirates: Pillaging the Korean and Chinese Coasts

Though largely unknown to most Westerners, Japanese and Chinese piracy thrived in the context of competing states, fragmented geography, vibrant trade and rampant poverty, much like it did in the Western world. It took place in what might be called the Inner Sea – a region that extends from Kamchatka in the northeast to the Malacca Straits in the southeast, bordered by the mainland to the north and west and by the arc of islands from Kamchatka through Japan to Luzon and the northern coast of Borneo.[1] This fragmented coastline, cut by navigable rivers, large bays and dotted with large, inhabited islands, provides the perfect geography for piracy. Rich fisheries, abundant resources, intense geopolitical rivalries, and lucrative and vibrant trade fostered a long tradition of sea raiding. Sometimes these bandits acted independently, sometimes as mercenaries, sometimes in the service of the state and sometimes piratical communities became states themselves. These communities, who often emerged to escape state control of commerce, could become rivals to the very states they had escaped. Pirate communities alternatively competed and cooperated with, ravaged and protected, coerced and extracted from the land-based states.[2] Smuggling and pillaging also created a shadow economy that acted alongside and often in conjunction with the 'legitimate' state-sanctioned economy. This illicit economy proved crucial in the commercial development of the region and in local state formation.[3]

What made this region unique in the history of piracy was China. The colossal dominance of China has defined this region for more than 2,000 years. The reason the Straits of Malacca continues to be the busiest shipping lane in the world is China. But the real anomaly of China has been its maritime policy. No other powerful and wealthy nation with a long coastline erected such imposing barriers to seaborne trade. The Ming dynasty (1368–1644)

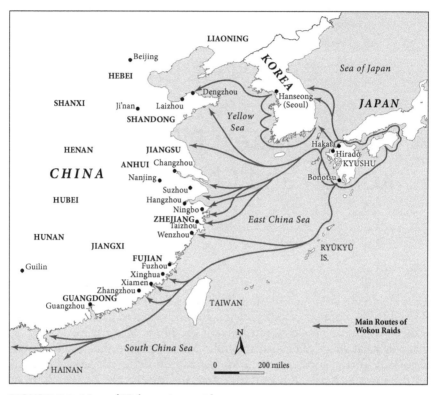

FIGURE 5.1 *Map of* Wokou *pirate raids.*
Source: Map produced by Barry Levely, Cartographer.

attempted to prohibit all seaborne traffic except that associated with official imperial tribute missions.[4] The Qing dynasty (1644–1911) implemented an even stricter policy. Korea and Japan followed suit and imposed bans on seaborne trade. The Korean Chosŏn rulers (1392–1910) and the Japanese Tokugawa shogunate (1603–1868) both placed tight restrictions on trade and prohibited their subjects from sailing abroad. These prohibitions were often ineffectual and difficult to enforce, but they did foster a vibrant illegal trade carried on by smugglers and pirates of all ethnicities.[5]

Piracy in this region, however, began long before the prohibitions were created. In the tenth century, the Japanese rebel Fujiwara no Sumitomo organized a pirate fleet to attack the imperial Heian fleet. He lost the battle and, subsequently, his head. As the Heian Dynasty (794–1185) collapsed in civil war and the samurai seized political power to rule as shoguns during the Kamakura period (1185–1333), Japanese piracy on the Korean coast intensified. In this period, Japanese pirates, some of whom were probably leaderless and landless samurai cut adrift with the fall of the Taira clan to the Minamoto family in 1185, began to appear in Korean waters. In

1223, they burned and pillaged their way along the Korean coast prompting complaints from the Korean government to the Japanese governor of the southern island of Kyushu from which the pirates originated. In response, the governor of Kyushu 'executed ninety pirates in front of the Korean envoys and sent a letter of apology to the Korean governor'.[6] Undeterred, the raiders continued to pillage temples, loot storehouses and destroy communities. The primary objects of the raids were food supplies and captives to be used as forced labourers or to be ransomed.[7] Korean captives and pirate loot were sold at markets in ports such as Naha on Okinawa.[8] In this sense, the Japanese pirates acted as agents of a forced exchange that existed beside the formal and informal trading economy. The raids continued until the eve of the Mongol invasions of Japan in 1274 and 1281. Following the invasions, piracy spread along the Chinese coast and then back to the Korean coast. By 1350, the raids had become so intense that the Korean state faced economic collapse because of the near-total cessation of maritime traffic.[9]

The Korean government desperately petitioned the Japanese shogunate to put a stop to the pirates, but neither the Japanese government nor the other states in the region could do much to stop it.[10] Not until the overthrow of the Mongol Yuan dynasty in China, the creation of the Ming dynasty there in 1368 and the establishment of the Chosŏn dynasty in Korea in 1392 did an active policy of pirate suppression with the collaboration of the three states emerge.[11] The new Ming emperor Hongwu sent missions to Korea and Japan, asking them to control piracy. Tensions remained high as the first Chinese envoy to Japan disappeared and the five members of the second mission were executed. But the Chinese responded, in 1370, by returning fifteen Japanese pirates to Japan and, in 1372, by demanding that the Japanese government do something about the problem. In 1392, the Chosŏn or Yi dynasty emerged in Korea and began sending official missions to Japan seeking an end to piracy. The Korean government finally succeeded in decreasing the pirate threat by 'granting settlement and trade to pirates, thus turning them into traders'.[12] The Japanese government also began to repatriate Korean captives, kidnapped by the pirates. Between 1363 and 1437, some 2,000 Korean captives were sent back to Korea.[13]

The sixteenth century witnessed another surge in piracy in the Inner Sea associated with the Chinese transition to a silver-based economy. Japan possessed massive silver deposits, and smugglers seeking to fill the demand for silver in China could not count on any assistance from the government. They found it necessary to arm themselves for protection against rival bands and soon included piracy in their mix of economic activities. Japan provided safe havens where competing warlords, temples and villages actively sought the foreign commodities and revenue the pirates and smugglers generated.[14]

The Koreans called these pirates *waegu* or rioters. The Chinese referred to them as *wokou* or Japanese pirates. The Chinese term combines characters for dwarf, a pejorative term for the Japanese, and one for bandit.[15] *Wokou* became a catchall term used by the educated land-based elite to 'define the maritime world as a nonagricultural, uncivilized and peripheral region excluded from China proper'.[16]

The use of the term 'pirate' for the seafarers of the sixteenth- and seventeenth-century Inner Sea can be misleading, however.[17] These men were entrepreneurs who created networks for long-distance exchange, distribution and production, and other services to land-based patrons. They often controlled maritime chokepoints and created protection rackets.[18] The Seto Inland Sea between Honshu, Kyushu and Skikoku was one such place. Sea lords established themselves in this peripheral region and acted as go-betweens. They set up protection rackets in the narrow channels and offered their services to land-based patrons as sea raiders and trans-shippers of merchandise. Commerce and violence were not seen as contradictory but as integral parts of seafaring identities.[19] Japanese pirates thus succeeded in making themselves indispensable to local lords, called *daimyo,* who legitimized their activities and provided them with social mobility as retainers in the *daimyo*'s household.[20]

The *Wokou,* however, were not all Japanese. They were, in fact, a hybrid of all the peoples plying the waters of the Inner Sea. Most were Chinese, but the pirate gangs benefitted from cross-cultural pollination including Portuguese and Dutch navigators and weapons, as recent scholars have shown. The pirate ships used a Chinese hull design, employed Western cannon and rigging, carried Japanese warriors and European gunners, navigated by charts produced by the Chinese and the Portuguese, and were manned by mixed crews of Ryukyuans, Japanese, Chinese, Siamese, Spaniards, Portuguese and Dutchmen.[21]

The new surge of piracy decreased after 1567 because the Asian states began relaxing their anti-trade policies. A new Ming policy in 1567 established licensed trade with Southeast Asia, though it still prohibited trade with Japan. A year later, Oda Nobunaga (1534–1582) put an end to Japan's Warring States period (1467–1568) and initiated the red-seal system in 1590 that licensed trade and decreased the autonomy of the warlords. Consequently, the need for smuggling declined and pirates lost access to the Japanese safe havens and patrons who had supported them. The more or less peaceful trade of the 1570s to the 1620s collapsed into another cycle of piratical conflict after the new Tokugawa shogunate of Japan ended the red-seal system, restricted all foreign trade to one port, Nagasaki, and limited foreign trade to Chinese and Dutch merchants.[22] This shift occurred at the same time that the Ming began to withdraw its military presence from the sea and turned its attention to the new threat of a unified Jin state in Manchuria to the north. Merchants turned smugglers and smugglers turned pirates. The maritime weakness of the Ming eventually led them to co-opt the pirates they had pursued into their naval system of defences.[23]

The most prominent of these Chinese pirates was Zheng Zhilong (d. 1661), who rose from a poor background in Quanzhou region of Fujian to

FIGURE 5.2 *Japanese pirate leader with Western revolver.*
Source: Photo by Asian Art & Archaeology, Inc./CORBIS/Corbis via Getty Images.
Note: The presence of the European revolver in this image illustrates the international character of the *Wokou* pirates.

command a powerful pirate fleet. After receiving an official rank from the Ming government in 1628 and assigned to control piracy and smuggling, Zheng set about constructing the most powerful maritime/commercial organization of his era. He created links between Fujian seafarers, Portuguese merchants in Macao, 'the Spanish in the Philippines, the Dutch in Taiwan, and the Japanese of Hirado'. Eventually, Zheng controlled 'ninety percent of all Chinese shipping in maritime East Asia'.[24]

The empire he constructed lasted until 1683, but it struggled with internal dissent, resistance from other pirate/smuggling clans, competition with the Dutch and involvement in the Ming resistance to the Qing dynasty after 1644. The Qing engaged in a long, bitter struggle with the Zheng clan between 1661 and 1683 for control of the Fujian province.[25] During this period, the Qing implemented a series of scorched earth policies collectively known as the Exclusion Policy of 1661–1683.[26] Under this draconian programme, the Qing attempted to deal with Zheng power by depopulating the coast for a 1,000 kilometres from Zhejiang to Guangdong and for 10 kilometres inland. The residents were simply ordered to evacuate. Those who remained were forcibly removed and the towns and villages put to the torch. In the end, at least 100,000 people perished.

Ultimately, the policy probably helped the Zheng clan more than it hurt them, and it was not until the Qing determined to attack the Zheng base in Taiwan that they succeeded in breaking the family's power. In a classic case of pirate turned pirate hunter, the Qing commissioned an old Zhen ally Shi Lang (1621–1696) who had quarrelled with Koxinga, Zheng's successor, and sent him against his old friends. Shi Lang destroyed the Zheng fleet in 1683. A year later, the Kangxi emperor (b. 1645, reigned 1662–1722) removed the ban on foreign trade and, thus, undermined the motivation for smuggling and piracy.[27] Chinese merchants flooded the market cities in Japan and the Philippines, forcing the Dutch East Asian trade into decline. Throughout the eighteenth century, Chinese maritime trade flourished, though the Chinese, the Japanese and the Korean governments continued to regard overseas trade with indifference.[28]

On the southern end of the Inner Sea, the Gulf of Tonkin took part in the long history of piracy. As a frontier region between China and Vietnam, it suffered near-continuous warfare, low-level conflict and trade bans which stimulated smuggling and piracy. Its fragmented coastline cut by rivers, lagoons, islands, isolated coves and mangrove swamps made it a notoriously difficult region to control. During the Chinese bans on trade and the coastal depopulation policy of the Qing, Vietnam provided safe havens for refugees who often turned to smuggling and piracy.[29] Local communities of fishermen, such as the Dan boat people, often combined piracy with fishing, pearl diving and labour as one activity in an overall survival strategy. The bands of smugglers and rebels fleeing state control were often better armed and organized than local pirates. Some settled in the area, but others were *wokou* from Japan operating in the gulf. They were joined by Dutch pirates in the seventeenth century who first came as traders. But when they became embroiled in local wars, they began pillaging Vietnamese towns and shipping.[30]

Other pirates came as political rebels fighting against the Manchu conquest of the Ming. They found refuge among competing polities who gave them safe harbours, official titles and outfitted ships in return for a share of the loot and military aid. Local Vietnamese rulers, such as the Nguyên lords, used pirate-refugees to secure their control of the Mekong delta.[31]

The Inner Sea played a significant role in the political, economic and social construction of the lands washed by its waters. It provided a pathway for trade, diplomacy, warfare and piracy. Contrary to common Western misconceptions, the peoples of this region were not backward and traditional, resistant to change and incapable of competing with Western powers – quite the contrary. These people rapidly overcame any real disadvantages and scored significant victories over Western powers. The seas had always been a place of hybridization, and Asian seafarers readily adopted what worked. They also employed local legal and diplomatic tools to constrain the excesses of Western interlopers. For example, in 1657, the Zheng family sued the Dutch in Japan for capturing a Chinese vessel off the coast of Southern Vietnam. The Japanese court ordered the Dutch to compensate the Zheng, which they had to do or face losing access to the Japanese trade.[32]

We should recognize that calling the people we have examined in this chapter pirates is problematic. It represents an acceptance of the establishment narrative and Western (mis)translations of Asian terms that do not necessarily mean pirate in the modern legal sense of that word. These people were labelled bandits by the Chinese establishment, but they were often far more complicated. The *wokou* were a conglomerate of peoples, often merchants, working outside strict sea bans. The Zheng family represented 'pro-commerce resistance against the Manchu conquest of China'.[33] By the middle of the nineteenth century, Japanese sea bandits had been so thoroughly absorbed into the formal power structures and had shifted to smuggling as their primary source of revenue.[34] It was, and is, a complicated region where Western terms and concepts often confuse more than they reveal. In the Inner Sea, seaborne banditry was at once parasitic, episodic and intrinsic.

As you read the sources that follow, consider these questions:

1   What do these documents reveal about the attitude of government officials towards piracy and pirates?

2   What do they reveal about the motives of the pirates?

3   How might their motives be tied to government policies?

4   What steps did Asian governments take to combat piracy?

5 What evidence suggests that these pirates were an international group from a variety of ethnicities?

6 What do the *Wokou* pirates reveal about how piracy can shift from parasitic to episodic and how might the geography of the region facilitate or foster the different types of piracy?

Zuikei Shuho and Charlotte von Verschuer, 'Japan's Foreign Relations 1200 to 1392 CE: A Translation from "Zenrin Kokuhōki"', *Monumenta Nipponica*, vol. 57, no. 4 (Winter, 2002): 438, 442. Used with permission.

Letter from Korea to the shogun of Japan, 1367.

Too many pirates from your country [Japan] come [to Korea] and plunder the port Happo and other places in this region. They set fire to administrative buildings and trouble the inhabitants, at the worst even killing people. This has gone on for more than ten years. Merchant ships are unable to travel freely and the people in the vicinity cannot live in peace.

Letter from Ashikaga Yoshimitsu to T'aijo Chosŏn of Korea, 1392.

He transmitted a letter from Your Excellencies, to the government of our great shogun [Ashikaga Yoshimitsu] saying that piracy on the seas still has not ceased and that this is hurting [the relations between] our two countries. The situation is indeed as it has been said [many times] before. It would be truly shameful for the rulers of our country to abandon the effort to instruct the coastal people in proper behavior. [The shogun] once more ordered his vassal, the governor of Kyushu [Imagawa Sadayo], to ban and seize [Japanese] pirates' ships and to free and return their [Korean] prisoners to your country. I am sure that eventually good neighborly relations between our two countries will be resumed, providing continuous happiness to you, our benefactor. This is indeed our wish.

Kwan-wai So, *Japanese Piracy in Ming China during the 16th Century* (East Lansing: Michigan State University press, 1975), 15–16, 23, 31, 57–58. Used with permission.

Report by Japanese Pirate: Memoirs of Sato Shinen no shuki, 1570s.

During the Eisho and Taiei eras (1504–1527) several warriors ... from islands ... off the coast of Iyo banded together and crossed the ocean to foreign lands, where they operated as pirates and became wealthy. Murakami Zusho, the lord of Noshima, was selected as their leader. The pirates pillaged coastal towns and seized all kinds of things, making themselves rich. They operated along the coast of China ..., and among the islands of southeast as far as the Philippines, Borneo, and Bali. For several years they continued these forays .... In time ronins, fishermen, scoundrels, and others from the Kyushu-Shikoku area joined the pirate bands, and gradually their size increased from eight to nine hundred to over a thousand men. Consequently, all the islands of the southwestern seas were harassed by pirates. Even Ming China feared them, and as a result sent out her huge armies (to drive them away). China also strengthened her coastal defenses. It was at this time that the pirates came to be known as Wako ....

Iida Koichiro of Oshima in the province of Iyo and Kitaura Kanjuro of Momojima in the province of Bingo were the first (pirate leaders) to sail to foreign lands, pillage the coastal villages, steal property and enrich their families. It is said that at first the two leaders had only fifty or sixty men under them, but with each raid their profits mounted considerably and, as a result, the bands became larger and more powerful.

In foreign countries soldiers were drawn up to guard the coast against our raids. Consequently, we increased our military strength. If we could not destroy the armies, guarding the coast, we could gain no profit. Therefore, before setting sail we made complete preparations for engaging such armies in battle. In regard to these preparations, Wu and Sung had a large number of guns and it became necessary to take proper countermeasures. Toward the end of the Tembun era (1554) we adopted the use of guns, which increased our military strength and enlarged the size of the pirate bands. In 1555, the number of men in the seven groups reached a total of more than 1,000. Each ship was loaded with 700 koku of rice. There were eight or nine main vessels, the best of which were called Hagaibune .... In 1563 our seven bands totaling 1,300 men, attacked Ping-hai in Ming China .... We had one hundred and thirty-seven vessels of various sizes .... The total number of pirates of all classes reached the figure of 1,352 men, plus 60 fishermen and the like who made up the crew. Of the above two or three hundred Chinese pirates had joined our ranks ....

Wang Yü, Memorials by His Excellency Wang Ssu-chih, the Censor in Chief, 1552–1554.

Who have caused this? Generally speaking, the pirates on the high seas are of many different groups. Those who have raided this year do not belong to one group alone. There are notorious pirates of Fukien and Kwangtung who have allied with the Wo (Japanese) and come from Japan: such as T'ien Lao, who attacked Sung-men and Ning-hai; Wang Lao, who attacked Ch'ang-kuo and Hsiang-shan: Li La-ta and Lin Chih, who attacked Hsin-ho and Ai-wan; Ts'en Lao, who attacked Cha-p'u and Cheng Lao, who attacked Shanghai and Tai-ts'ang-are all of one group.

There are treacherous people from Wen [-chou] and Ning [-po] [of Chekiang] who have fled to Japan (and they) number in the thousands. [Their] living abodes have formed lanes or villages, with streets named Ta-t'ang (the Great T'ang), They have induced the famished Japanese people to come as pirates. Such as Mao Lao and P'u Lao, who attacked

Lin-shan and those who occupied Chou-shan, the garrison posts of Ts'en-kang and Kuo-ch'u, form another group.

There are wealthy merchants and traders who own huge men-of-war and crack troops and dominate the seas. Having invited the barbarians to join them. They act recklessly and oppressively. Among these are Wang Chih, Hsü Wei, hsüeh, Mao Hsun, Hsü Ming-shan, Li San, and others. They have occupied Lieh-kang and have recently returned from their trading trip eastward. These form another group ....

Ming historian and magistrate Hsüeh Ying-ch'I, "The Rectification of Names," 1535.

Now the pirates have penetrated deep into our land. The cruelty of their killing, plundering, burning and destroying has never been matched since olden times. Certainly, they want to call themselves by the name Wo. But if we also call them Wo, we would have fallen into their tricks, for we have failed to say that they are really not Wo. It is because, in truth, the rebels of our Middle Kingdom have served as their ringleaders and guides and have invited the Wo barbarians to be their helpers. By the name Wo then they can hide themselves and get under cover, and their families and relatives would be protected from danger. [They would] say that the pirates of today are the Wo and they have taken no part [in the piracy]. Consequently, they could come back with loads of gold, silk, and commodities.

Confession of Chinese smugglers, 1546.

On the 2nd day of the 5th month [June 7] I myself [Ch'en] went ashore on an island and was caught by the patrol. On that day there were on board only twenty Japanese barbarians and there were Japanese swords, Japanese bows, two jars of explosives, four small-size Portuguese cannon, four or five bird-peaked guns, all of which had been obtained by the barbarians in a fight back in Japan the previous year. Among the people aboard were fifty Chinese. Of these six or seven were Cantonese, three or four natives of Chang-chow, more than ten natives of Hui-chow, more than ten natives of Ningpo, and four natives of Shaohsing.

Albert Hastings Markham, ed., 'The Second Voyage of John Davis with Sir Edward Michelborne ... ', in *The Voyages of Works of John Davis, the Navigator* (London: Hakluyt Society, 1880), 178–182.

Here as I stood for Patane about the twenty-seventh of December [1604], I met with a junk of the Japanese which had been pirating along the coast of China and Cambodia. Their pilot being dead, with ignorance and foul weather they had cast away their ship on the shoals of the great island of Borneo; and to enter into the country of Borneo, they durst not. For the Japanese are not suffered to land in any port of India with weapons;

being accounted a people so desperate and daring that they are feared in all places where they come.

These people, their ship being splitted, with their shallops entered the junk wherein I met them, which was of Patane, and killed all the people save one old pilot. This junk was laden with rice, which, when they had possessed and furnished with such furniture, necessaries, and arms as they saved out of their sunken ship, they shaped their course for Japan; but the badness of their junk, contrary winds, and unreasonableness of the year forced them to leeward; which was the cause of my unlucky meeting them.

After I had hailed them, and made them come to leeward, sending my boat aboard them, I found them by their men and furniture very unproportionable for such a ship as they were in; which was a junk not above seventy tons in burden, and they were ninety men and most of them in too gallant a habit for sailors, and such an equality of behavior among them there was that they called captain, but gave him little respect. I caused them to come to an anchor, and upon further examination I found their lading to be only rice; and for the most part spoilt with wet, for their ship was leaking both under and above water. Upon questioning with them, I understood them to be men of war that had pillaged on the coast to China and Cambodia and as I said before, had cast away their ship on the shoals of Borneo.

Here we rode at anchor under a small island near the isle of Bintang, two days entertaining them with good usage, not taking anything from them; thinking to have gathered by their knowledge the place and passage of certain ships on the coast of China to have made my voyage. But these rogues being desperate in winds and fortunes, being hopeless in that paltry junk ever to return to their country, resolved with themselves either to gain my ship or to lose their lives.

And upon mutual courtesies, with gifts and feastings between us, sometimes five and twenty or six and twenty of their chiefest came aboard; whereof I would not suffer above six to have weapons. There was never the like number of our men aboard their junk.

I willed Captain John Davis in the morning to possess himself of their weapons, and to put the company before mast, and to leave some guard on their weapons while they searched in the rice, doubting that by searching and finding that which would dislike them they might suddenly set upon my men and put them to the sword; as the sequel proved.

Captain Davis, being beguiled with their humble semblance, would not possess himself of their weapons, though I sent twice of purpose from my ship to will him to do it. They passed all the day, my men searching in the rice and they looking on. At the sun setting, after long search and nothing found, save a little storax and benzoin, they seeing opportunity, and taking the rest of their company which were in my ship being near to their junk, they resolved at a watchword between them, to set upon us resolutely in both ships. This being concluded they suddenly killed and drave overboard all my men that were in their ship; and those which were aboard my ship sallied out of my cabin, where they were put, with such weapons as they had, finding certain targets in my cabin, and other things that they used as weapons. My self being aloft on the deck, knowing what was likely to follow, leapt into the waste, where, with the boatswain, carpenter and some few more we kept them under the half deck.

At their first coming forth of the cabin, they met Captain Davis coming out of the gunroom, whom they pulled into the cabin, and giving him six or seven mortal wounds they thrust him out of the cabin before them. His wounds were so mortal that he died as soon as he came into the waste. They pressed so fiercely to come to us, as we receiving them on our pikes, they would gather on our pikes with their hands to reach us with their swords. It was near half an hour before we could stone them back into the cabin. In which time we had killed three or four of their leaders.

After they were driven into the cabin, they fought with us at least four hours before we could suppress them, often firing the cabin, burning the bedding, and much other stuff that was there. And had we not with two demy-culverins,[35] from under the half deck, beaten down the bulk head and the pump of the ship we could not have suppressed them from burning the ship. This ordinance being charged with crossbars, bullets, and case shot and bent close to the bulk head, so violently marred therewith boards and splinters that left but one of them standing of two and twenty. Their legs, arms and bodies were so torn as it was strange to see how the shot had massacred them.

In all this conflict, they never would desire their lives, though they were hopeless to escape; such was the desperateness of these Japanese. Only one leapt over board, which afterward swam to our ship again and asked for grace. We took him in and asked him what was their purpose.

He told us that they meant to take our ship and to cut all our throats. He would say no more, but desired that he might be cut in pieces.

The next day, to wit, the eight and twentieth of December, we went to a little island to the leeward of us. And when we were about five miles from land, the general commanded his people to hand him to the Japanese. But he brake the rope and fell into the sea. I cannot tell whether he swam to land or not.

Notes

1   Robinson, 'Centering the King of Chosŏn', 110.
2   MacKay, 'Pirate Nations', 552, 567–568.
3   Chin, 'Merchants, Smugglers, and Pirates', 43–57.
4   Ravina, 'Japan in the Chinese Tribute System', 353–363.

5   Andrade and Hang, 'Introduction', 3–6.

6   Shuho and Verschuer, 'Japan's Foreign Relations', 417.

7   Robinson, 'Centering the King of Chosŏn', 112.

8   Robinson, 'Centering the King of Chosŏn', 112.

9   Shuho and Verschuer, 'Japan's Foreign Relations', 418.

10 Shapinsky, 'Envoys and Escorts', 38–64.

11 Shuho and Verschuer, 'Japan's Foreign Relations', 418.

12 Shuho and Verschuer, 'Japan's Foreign Relations', 440, fn. 72 and 442, fn. 74.

13 Robinson, 'Centering the King of Chosŏn', 113.

14 So, *Japanese Piracy*, 16–36; Andrade and Hang, 'Introduction', 6–8.

15 Antony, 'Introduction', 7.

16 Shapinsky, 'Envoys and Escorts', 41.

17 Reid, 'Violence at Sea', 18.

18 Shapinsky, 'Predators, and Purveyors', 274, 304.

19 Shapinsky, 'From Sea Bandits to Sea Lords', 28–30.

20 Petrucci, 'Pirates, Gunpowder, and Christianity', 59–71.

21 Batchelor, 'Maps, Calendars, and Diagrams', 86–113; Andrade and Hang, 'Introduction', 8.

22 Andrade and Hang, 'Introduction', 8–11; Clulow, 'Like Lambs in Japan', 335–358.

23 Andrade and Hang, 'Introduction', 11.

24 Andrade and Hang, 'Introduction', 11–12.

25 Chin, 'A Hokkien Maritime Empire', 93–112.

26 Ho, 'The Burning Shore', 260–289.

27 Andrade and Hang, 'Introduction', 17–18.

28 Andrade and Hang, 'Introduction', 20–21.

29 Antony, 'Trade, Piracy, and Resistance', 312–316.

30 Antony, 'Trade, Piracy, and Resistance', 320–326.

31 Antony, 'Trade, Piracy, and Resistance', 327–330.

32 Clulow, 'Determining the Law of the Sea', 181–198.

33 Reid, 'Violence at Sea', 18.

34 Hellyer, 'Poor but not Pirates', 113–126.

35 A medium-sized cannon about eleven feet long with a four-inch bore.

CHAPTER SIX

Dutch Sea Beggars and the Business of Piracy

The employees of the Dutch East and West India companies represented the best-funded seaborne bandits the world had ever seen. They enjoyed the support of the state and organized themselves into joint stock companies. For the Dutch, maritime predation began as warfare by other means and became business by other means. Their employees spread over the oceans of the world, attacking shipping and settlements from the North Sea to the Caribbean and from Brazil to the Yellow Sea. They formed alliances with pirates in Taiwan and raided for themselves off the coast of Vietnam. In the end, the Dutch seaborne bandits ran the spectrum from company employees to privateers to pirates.

The Dutch Sea Beggars began as rebels against their Spanish overlords after 1568. They were a 'ragtag assemblage of Dutch aristocrats, ultra-Calvinists, and riffraff who could be quite indiscriminate as to whom they victimized'.[1] Eventually, commercial interests, military exigency and personal profit coalesced to stimulate the rise of mercantile companies who made maritime predation their primary business. Such companies as the English East India Company and the Dutch companies proliferated in sixteenth- and seventeenth-century Europe. They were chartered by states, granted many of the powers of a sovereign state, such as the right to use violence, and were supposed to develop long-distance trade and establish colonies. They often became armed merchant corporations with stockholders who shared the risks and the profits. They also possessed fleets of ships, often larger than state navies, with the will, the ability and the legal sanction to use force for private profit. The problem with mercantile companies, however, was they were difficult to control. They fought among themselves, preyed upon other European states and sometimes attacked the very states which created them.[2]

The Low Countries from which these companies sprang suffered from several challenges that forced them to look beyond their borders for raw materials and economic opportunity. They occupy the delta of the Rhine, the Meuse and the Scheldt rivers in the Netherlands and Belgium. Much of the land in the delta is below sea level, which requires heavy investment in dykes, canals, sluices, windmills and millraces to protect them from the encroachments of the sea. The area is so poor in local resources that it was not effectively settled until the twelfth century. Consequently, the Dutch developed a predisposition towards maritime trade as a means of survival. They imported raw materials from abroad and manufactured finished products, such as cloth, draperies and ships. They also transshipped goods between the Baltic and the Mediterranean. From the Baltic they acquired luxury items, such as fur, but also grains and naval supplies, such as tar, lumber, iron, hemp and flax. By the middle of the sixteenth century, they had become the primary transshippers of salt fish in the North Atlantic with deep ties to the salt producers of Setúbal, Portugal. In return, the cash-poor Portuguese marketed the pepper they brought back from Asia in Antwerp.[3] Despite their challenges, the Low Countries held a fortuitous geographical position that gave them quick access to markets in Denmark, England, France and Germany. The secret to their success was to build ships that required smaller crews, to pay those crews low wages and to feed them minimal rations. This meant that they could offer lower shipping rates than their competitors.[4] But it also meant their crews were more disgruntled and often less effective in battle.

Political tensions also encouraged the development of considerable military capability in the Low Countries. When Phillip II of Spain assumed the Spanish throne and the Hapsburg holdings, which included the Netherlands, from his father, Charles V, in 1556, he decided to root out the growing Calvinist support in the northern provinces of the Low Countries and to impose harsh taxes on Low-Country merchants. The ensuing tensions exploded into a full rebellion in 1568 that would continue off and on until the final peace of Münster in 1648. Meanwhile, Phillip II had assumed the Portuguese throne in 1580 after the death of the Portuguese king, Dom Sebastião. In 1585, Phillip decided to slap embargoes on Dutch and English ships in all of his ports. This meant that the Dutch and the English found themselves excluded from vital supplies of salt, sugar, spices and bullion. Over the next sixty-three years, the Dutch used their war with Spain and Spanish Catholicism to justify ransacking the Spanish and Portuguese Empires from the Caribbean to Japan. The States-General, the Admiralties, the Prince of Orange and the Dutch East and West India Companies all possessed the power to issue commissions to Dutch privateers.[5] Dutch law did not require a state of war to exist before commissions could be issued against another country – only a hostile state. Sometimes the commissions even allowed seizing neutral ships that visited the harbours of hostile nations.

As in England, Dutch privateers were regulated by the Admiralty. Each privateer was required to carry a commission, to undergo an investigation into his background and conduct and to post a bond that could be seized if the captain misbehaved. The captain also had to keep a detailed log or journal of his voyage, and he and the crew had to submit to detailed rules of conduct outlined in the letters of instruction given to each privateer.[6] These instructions included the obligation to say prayers twice daily and to not take the Lord's name in vain. The crew was prohibited from complaining about their wages and their rations. The instructions also imposed brutal punishments administered to those who broke the rules in an attempt to instil fear and discipline in the crew.

> Those striking another seaman with a stick or rope or their fists were to be thrown three times from the yardarm. (This was a severe disciplinary measure in which the perpetrator, his arms fastened behind his back, was taken to one of the upper booms on the ship. There a long rope was tied to his wrists and secured to the boom. He was then pushed off. The resulting drop of 40 or 50 feet inevitably dislocated his shoulders and sometimes crushed the bones in his arms and wrists ....) Those caught smuggling aboard a knife were themselves to suffer its blade, which would be used to skewer the violator's hand to the mast. Any sailor who injured another was to be keelhauled three times ... [A sailor] forfeited all his earnings if he expressed dissatisfaction with his wagers, did not fulfill the duties of his position, opened a prize's cargo containers or disturbed its official papers, or took more than his fair portion of the plunder. If ... one seaman killed another, the culprit was to be bound to the corpse, back to back, and thrown overboard.[7]

All of this was imposed on the crew without offering them any opportunity to air any real grievances or even to tell their side of the story. Their primary responsibility, after all, was to maximize profits.[8] When a prize had been verified and cleared by the Admiralty court, the ship and cargo were sold at public auction, often for half their true market value. The shares were then divided, with the government taking its portion.[9]

At the same time that the Dutch cultivated and regulated their privateers, they developed laws that condemned pirates. Illicit seaborne banditry not only challenged the new state's claims to sovereignty of the seas, but also deprived the state of revenue, and complicated its international relations. The laws were particularly harsh for those who attacked their own countrymen or acquired commissions from other countries.[10] Between the many wars, Dutch seaman, including fishermen, found fewer opportunities for employment and often turned to outright piracy or joined the English as privateers. The Dutch established harsh laws to deal with pirates and renegade privateers, but they did not always apply the laws evenly. Outright pirates often found ready acceptance in Dutch society so long as they had not been too aggressive against Dutch shipping, they had not committed too many violent crimes, such as rape, torture and murder, and they had not worked as privateers for an enemy nation. In other words, they needed to portray themselves as honourable patriots in the service of the fledgling nation.[11]

By the seventeenth century, the Dutch had replaced the English as the primary contraband traders in the Caribbean. They were lured there in the 1580s by the salt deposits of the Punta de Araya in Venezuela after they had been deprived of access to the saltpans of Setúbal, Portugal. They also sought tobacco from Venezuela and Guinea, pearls from Cumaná and hides from Hispaniola. The draconian Spanish response to Dutch encroachments proved as destructive to the colonists as it was to the Dutch. In 1605, Spanish authorities executed Dutch smugglers they had captured without giving them a trial. They prohibited tobacco cultivation in Venezuela, and they forcibly depopulated the north coast of Hispaniola by shifting the population closer to Santo Domingo where they could be watched more closely. Many colonists fled or turned to piracy. Their livestock ran wild and the absence of colonists created a vacuum that buccaneers and the French were happy to fill.

By the seventeenth century, so many companies existed that the Dutch decided to consolidate a variety of competing companies into The United Netherlands Chartered East India Company or the VOC (*Vereenigde Oost-Indishce Compagnie*). In 1602, the States-General chartered the VOC as a joint-stock corporation. The VOC received a twenty-one-year monopoly on trade in Asia from the Cape of Good Hope to the Straits of Magellan with the authority to 'conclude treaties of peace and alliance and to wage defensive war, and to build "fortresses and strongholds"'.[12] After the end of the twelve-year truce with Spain in 1621, the Dutch prepared for a new assault on Spain and Portugal. The Estates General created the West India Company or WIC (*West-Indische Compagnie*) in 1621 with a monopoly on Dutch trade from the Caribbean to the coasts of Africa and with the authority to make offensive war. Backed by the capital of 7 million stockholders, the WIC proved a formidable opponent.[13]

These two companies carried on the assault against Spanish and Portuguese trade, shipping and territories in a truly global campaign. Though the Dutch remained active in the Caribbean and the Pacific coast of South America and even managed to capture the Spanish silver fleet in 1628, Portuguese territories received the brunt of their attacks. The WIC focused on the sugar trade from northern Brazil and securing the West African slave ports of São Jorge de Mina and São Paulo de Luanda. They captured Salvador, Bahia, in 1624, but lost it the next year only to return to seize Pernambuco in 1630. The WIC set up a court in Recife, Brazil, to adjudicate its prizes and commissioned, non-company ships trading with the Americas to capture non-company ships they found in the WIC's jurisdiction.[14] Over the next twenty-four years, the Dutch continued their

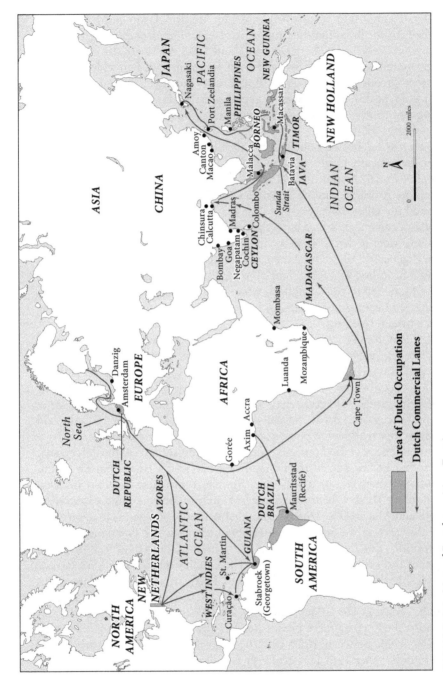

FIGURE 6.1 *Map of Dutch maritime Empire.*
Source: Map produced by Barry Levely, Cartographer.

territorial expansion northward into the Amazon basin until they were expelled from Brazilian territories in 1654. The Dutch also occupied Luanda, in West Africa, between 1641 and 1648, but were driven out by a mostly Brazilian force led by Salvador Correa de Sá e Benevides.[15] Dutch privateers 'trolled the waters of Brazil' and Portugal, seizing every ship they could find.[16] They gained a reputation for ferocity that caused the Portuguese to arm their ships and travel in convoys, which only increased the violence.

The most celebrated Dutch Admiral of this period was the WIC general Pieter Pieterszoon Heyn, known as Piet Heyn. He led the Dutch assault on Bahia in 1624, and, in 1628, he famously trapped the Spanish silver fleet under Admiral Juan de Benavides in Matanzas Bay, Cuba. The Dutch captured the entire fleet, yielding over 4.8 million silver pesos ($25 million in today's currency), which gave their stockholders a 75 per cent return on their investments that year. Benavides was executed in 1634 by the Spanish for negligence.[17] Other Dutchmen, such as Rock Braziliano, became famous for their brutality. Braziliano had lived in Dutch Brazil before it was retaken in 1654. He fled to the Caribbean where he preyed upon Spanish shipping. He enjoyed brutalizing his victims by impaling them on stakes and roasting them between two fires.[18]

The Dutch also ventured into the Pacific to explore trading and settlement opportunities along the Chilean coast. Joris van Speilbergen led an expedition in 1614 that was jointly sponsored by the Estates General and the VOC. Speilbergen spent nearly a year raiding and pillaging up the Pacific coast. He burned villages, seized ships and defeated a Spanish squadron sent to destroy him. Before he sailed for Manilla in December 1615, he had managed to wreak havoc on much of Spain's Pacific defenses.[19]

The Dutch arrived in Southeast Asia in 1596, expecting that the Portuguese, whom they believed to be the unhappy subjects of the same Spanish tyrant, would give them a warm welcome. But the Portuguese were in no such mood. In 1601, they brutally executed Dutch sailors they had captured in Tidore and Macao. The Dutch responded with a prolonged war of attrition over the next thirty years that attempted to drive the Portuguese out of the region. They muscled in on the Portuguese trade, attacked Portuguese shipping and seized Portuguese forts. The Dutch captured the Spice Islands in 1605, besieged Malacca in 1606 and 1607, attacked Mozambique in 1608, seized Malacca in 1641, Colombo in 1658, Sri Lanka in 1659 and the Malabar coast in 1663. The Dutch blockaded Goa in 1638–1644 and again in 1656–1663. Portuguese possessions shrank from fifty fortified areas to nine by 1666. Between 1629 and 1635, the Portuguese lost nearly 5,000 men in India, over 155 ships and over 6 million cruzados.[20]

Once the Dutch arrived in Asia, they quickly set their sights on larger quarry. They began to carve out a trading empire from the long-standing networks that crisscrossed Southeast Asia. Piracy and privateering became their primary tools in acquiring trade agreements and seizing strategic ports.

The grand prize in the imperial game was free trade with China. As we have already seen, the Chinese trade bans stimulated widespread smuggling and piratical merchant communities. Beginning in 1567, the Ming changed their policies to allow Chinese to travel abroad with licences, but still restricted trade with Japan, which was the most lucrative market. The Portuguese and later the Dutch managed to fill an important niche by which Chinese merchants used them as intermediaries to carry out the Japan trade. Initially, the Portuguese had turned to smuggling like everyone else, but, by 1557, they had established themselves at Macao and, by 1571, Nagasaki. The Portuguese were expelled from Nagasaki in 1639 by the Japanese, and the Dutch remained the only European power permitted to trade with Japan until the nineteenth century. The Dutch arrived in the Taiwan Straits in 1600 and set about wresting the China trade from the Portuguese.[21] They began attacking Chinese merchants who traded with Manila, Chinese coastal shipping and intercepting neutral ships at sea for inspection. After a failed attack on Macao in 1622, the Dutch withdrew to the port of Tayouan in Taiwan and rethought their strategy. The Chinese, quite understandably, considered the Dutch to be mere 'piratical sea-robbers'.[22]

The Dutch found the coves and estuaries of Taiwan already filled with Chinese pirates. At first, the Dutch considered the pirates a danger to their attempts to establish free trade with China and actively pursued the pirates in the hope that the Ming would grant them free trade in return. Frustrated by their lack of access to Chinese markets, the Dutch soon joined Zheng

FIGURE 6.2 *Fort Zeelandia, Taiwan.*
Source: Photo by Universal History Archive/UIG via Getty Images.
Note: Fort Zeelandia was built between 1624 and 1634 by the Dutch East India Company on the island of Taiwan.

Zhilong, the founder of the Zheng family pirate dynasty, in seizing ships and raiding towns along the Fujian coast. They used Zhilong as a privateer to attack Spanish, Portuguese and Chinese shipping. They also encouraged defeated pirates to resettle near their Dutch settlement so they could be used as privateers. In 1625, they helped finance Zhilong's expedition to attack the Chinese trade to Manila. In return, Zhilong gave the Dutch nine ships and their cargoes to the value of 28,000 taels of silver (about 2,469 pounds).[23] As Zhilong became more powerful, Ming officials turned to the Dutch for help. In 1627, they promised the Dutch free trade if they would assist them in destroying Zheng Zhilong. Though the Dutch did seize a few of Zhilong's ships, the Chinese lost patience and shifted tactics. They offered Zhilong rank and a title if he would turn pirate hunter. Zhilong accepted the offer and used it to crush his competitors.[24]

The Dutch grew increasingly frustrated that Chinese pirates were being rewarded with titles and rank while the Chinese kept the Dutch at arm's length. In 1629, Hans Putmans, the new Dutch governor of Taiwan, determined that the only way to impress the Chinese and wrest a free trade deal from them was to adopt pirate methods. Consequently, in 1633, the Dutch began capturing junks, demanding protection payments and trying to court pirate groups to join them.[25] The Dutch, however, failed to take into account that Zhilong, their one-time ally, had no intention of stepping aside and allowing the Dutch to become the new chief of the pirates. He attacked the Dutch fleet with 150 ships and forced the Dutch into peace negotiations. Zhilong agreed to grant licences to three Chinese ships to trade with the Dutch in Taiwan so long as the Dutch stayed away from the Chinese coast.[26] Zhilong had become a powerful force, but his political aspirations proved his downfall. After 1644, Zhilong decided to support the Ming in their war with the Manchu invaders but then switched sides in 1646 and let himself get lured into a trap. His son, Zheng Chenggong, assumed leadership and continued the doomed war against the Manchus. After suffering serious defeats, Chenggong returned to Taiwan in 1661 and drove the Dutch from the island.[27]

The Dutch support of, and collaboration with, Zheng Zhilong contributed to the decline of trade and security off the Fujian coast and the weakening of the Ming as it struggled against Manchu incursions in the final decades of the empire. The great irony of this history is that the Dutch presence provided an opening for the creation and expansion of one of the most powerful pirate states in history. And it was this pirate state, not the Ming or the Qing, that finally forced the Dutch from Taiwan.[28] Dutch attempts at piracy, or economic warfare, in China succeeded so long as they limited their actions to non-state-sponsored pirates. When they fought China, they failed. When they fought even small marginal states, such as the Zheng family pirate state, they also lost. Though state-sponsored piracy proved to be a useful tool in European maritime expansion, European states and their agents were always fragile and at a disadvantage in East Asian waters.[29]

One of the greatest weaknesses of the Dutch pirate companies was the way they treated their sailors. The sailors who manned the ships of the VOC and WIC were employees. They received low wages and, unlike privateering crews, no share in the loot they risked their lives to acquire.[30] While their officers dined on fineries, such as pork, olives and wine, the sailors were left to hardtack, dried peas and beans, and salted herring.[31] After Piet Heyn's capture of the Spanish silver fleet, his men rioted in Amsterdam, demanding a fair share of the profits. Dutch sailors also deserted in large numbers to swell the population of Europeans living in Asia, the Caribbean and the North African coast. Indeed, resentful Dutch deserters often joined the famous buccaneers of the latter half of the seventeenth century or moved to the Mediterranean to join the Barbary corsairs.[32]

The glory days of Dutch commercial expansion did not last. The Dutch West India Company went bankrupt in 1674, and the Dutch East India Company was nationalized in 1796 before it came to an end all together in 1799. As with the English East India Company, the Dutch companies succumbed to the transition from non-state forms of predation to state monopolies on extraterritorial violence.[33] Piracy and privateering had been fundamental components of state formation in the Low Countries and to Dutch claims to sovereignty. Piracy became an intrinsic part of the Dutch maritime expansion in which the niceties of legal and illegal predation were frequently ignored.

As you read the documents that follow, consider the following questions:

1   Why were the English employees of the East India Company concerned about the arrival of the Dutch in Asia?

2   What do the injuries suffered by the sailors on the *São João Baptista* in 1622 tell us about the nature of naval warfare?

3   How did the *São João Baptista* attempt to defend itself from attack and remain afloat after being damaged?

4   Notice the areas of the ship where the Dutch concentrated their attacks. What strategy might underlie their choices?

5   What tactics did the Dutch use to seize the *Barkely*, and how did Edward Brant manage to escape?

6   What can the Dutch case tell us about the connection between piracy and state formation in Europe?

7   How did piracy become an intrinsic part of the Dutch state and society?

William Foster, ed. *East India Company from Its Servants in the East: Transcribed from the Original Correspondence Series of the India Office Records*, July to December 1617, vol. 6 (London: Sampson Low, Marston & Co. 1902), 6–7, 14–15.

Richard Wickham to Sir Thomas Smythe, Bantam, early in June 1617.

The Hollanders [Dutch] this year have covered all the seas over, from the Red Sea unto the coast of China, spoiling and robbing all nations whatsoever in the name and under the colors of the English, not so much as excepting the junks of [the] Javas and Malays belonging to Bantam and other places where they hold factories. They are generally feared [in] this part of the world and will, if they be suffered to go on as they begin, overthrow all our trade in these parts and beat us out of these countries. For they have begun already with us in the Islands of Banda, where the *Swan*, a very warlike ship, was shamefully taken by one of their ships and the *Defence* delivered up unto them by a company of treacherous villains who have deserved hanging better than wages. It is reported that the Swan shot not above [?] pieces before she was taken, having five men slain and some hurt, amongst whom was your servant Signor Sophony Cozuck, slain with a great shot, whose death daunted the heartless company. They have sent three tall ships and a drumler[34] and two galliots[35] for the straits of Malacca, two ships and a pinnace for to make spoil about Cape Comorin, Ceylon and the Coast, eleven tall ships under the command of Admiral John Peterson Lam for to rob all the Chinas fleet that cometh to Manila this year and give it out they only go to take Manila, which (as I take it) will be too hot for them for many reasons that I can show; for that since the overthrow of Admiral Witteres by Don John de Silva, the city of Manila is much fortified and a castle built in Cavite in the bay of Manila is much fortified within half a mile of the town, which is always well manned and fortified with fifty-four pieces of brass ordnance, there being no place where to land soldiers nearer than twelve miles of the city but only within command of this castle, which commandeth the whole bay.

George Ball, Agent of Bantam, to Richard Cocks at Firando Bantam, June 9, 1617

For news, here is none but of the Hollanders, whose actions set all men in admiration; and at present more than ever in public robbing of all nations. They lie all seas over with their ships that a boat can hardly escape them. We have lost the *Swan* and *Defence* this year in Banda; the first being of force taken of the Flemings, and the other carried unto them by a company of mutinous villains, that coming again in our hands will hardly escape hanging. They killed us some four or five men, Sophony Cozuck being one of the number, and dismembered and hurt as many more. They let not to say they have the King's letter of [marque] to take us if we presume to go to the eastwards of the Cellebes; but herein I am assured they lie, presuming that a King so loving, gracious and merciful, will not license a mechanic people thus to spoil of his own subjects; and yet I am persuaded that by the favor of some great ones they are emboldened to deal injuriously with us.

Francisco Vaz d'Almada, 'Treatise of the Misfortune That Befell the Great Ship São João Baptista, 1622', in *Tragic History of the Sea,* edited and translated by C. R. Boxer (Minneapolis: University of Minnesota Press, 2001), 191–195, 191 fn 2. Used with permission.

The Mauritius and the Wapen van Rottterdam, two Indiamen bound for Batavia, had left the Cape on 13 June.... [On] (20 June) these two Dutch Indiamen sighted five other Portuguese ships .... These five sails were the outward bound armada under the viceroy Dom Francisco da Gama, Conde da Vidigueira, which was subsequently intercepted and destroyed (save for one galleon) by the Anglo-Dutch 'Fleet of Defence' in the Mozambique Channel on 23–5 July.

On Sunday the 19 July, in the morning, in latitude rather over 35° 30′ S we saw two great Dutch ships ahead and immediately made ready by clearing our ship for action, which we did with great difficulty, as she was much overburdened. Even so, we managed to give them two broadsides that afternoon, and we continued fighting with these two ships for the space of nineteen days until we reached latitude 42° S. We made bulwarks of the liberty-goods, which proved a great help, since thereafter they killed very few of our people, whereas they killed twenty men in the first two days before we adopted this device. During nine of these days, they fought with us from sunrise to sunset, and they finally reduced us to the most miserable condition that can be imagined; for they shot away our bowsprit close to the gammoning and the mainmast a yard and a half above the partners. And the foresail, and the rudder which was an old one, having belonged to a great ship that had been broken up at Goa and been left lying on the beach for two years, and so was rotten, for this is the usual way in which they fit out ships in this country. I say this because the want of a rudder caused our destruction, for it was in such a state that two shots sufficed to shatter it to pieces. Nor was this the only deficiency with which this ship left Goa, for she did not carry sufficient gunpowder and armament for fighting, mounting only eighteen guns of very small caliber; but withal we fought on until we had only two barrels of powder and twenty-eight cartridges left.

Seeing that the ship was completely dismasted, and that the spare spars were so riddled with shot that the least damaged had nine holes in it, and that the ship was foundering through shot which had struck us a fathom under water, while the rudder in breaking wrenched away two of the gudgeons, leaving open their bolt-holes, so that we were slowly sinking without being able to overcome the leak or apply any remedy, although every soul on board worked night and day at the pumps and scoops. The Religious tried to arrange some parley to distract the enemy, so that in the meanwhile we might try to get the better of the water and plug some of the leaks. And for that reason they asked me if I would be willing to be one of the emissaries who would treat with the Dutch for an honorable agreement. I had some sharp words with them over this, telling them that those who wanted such an agreement should go thither themselves, and that they were not friends of mine who gave me such advice; and I went to the station which the captain had assigned to me, so that I neither saw any boat alongside, nor any Dutchmen, thus incurring the hatred of many people in the ship. They afterwards asked Luis da Fonseca[36] and Manuel Peres to go and negotiate this agreement, who went accordingly, but such severe and continual storms supervened that we saw no more of the ship to which these two men went [*Mauritius*].

The other ship [*Wapen van Rotterdam*] followed us without attempting to board us and sent a boat to learn whether we had seen her consort. For they had lost sight of her, and to ask us what we were going to do, in view of the fact that we were leaking so heavily and continuously while being totally dismasted and bereft of all resources. All our people being very miserable and discouraged, we told them that we knew nothing of their ship, and with this answer the boat returned whence it came. We were more wretched every moment. For we were suffering from the most notable storms and cold that ever men endured. It snowed very often, so that many slaves died of the cold, and we felt their loss greatly in working the pump and throwing things overboard, in which tasks we were all employed unceasingly and painfully, because the storms and the rolling of the ship prevented us from lighting the fires, thus making our hardships much worse.

Being in this state, we made a jury-mast of the mizzen-mast and placed it in the prow, with the outrigger for a bowsprit, and so went wherever the wind carried us. In this way, the wind was often favorable for steering landwards but the ship drifted out to sea, for as we had no rudder nor means of steering, we could not point up into the wind but drove helplessly before it. All this occurred in latitude 42° S, with the last Dutch ship following us constantly. One night, as we were going seawards with her in stormy weather and dense darkness, we struck our jury-mast, praying to Our Lady of the Conception that she would allow our ship to go landward, and thus give the slip to the one that was pursuing us. And so it fell out, for at daybreak we were drifting landward, in which direction we continued for many days. The Dutch ship, as we now know, went seaward in quest of us as far as latitude 46° S. They eventually reached Jakarta in the condition which is notorious ....

There were no men of note killed on board ship during the fight, excepting João de Andrade Caminha and João de Lucena. Lopo de Sousa – may he be with God in heaven – and Captain Vidanha were stationed in the waist, where they fought bravely; and Lopo de Sousa lost three toes of his left foot, the foot being completely crushed, receiving at the same time a splinter in the hip, another in the belly, another in the face, and two in the head. Captain Vidanha received two splinter wounds, one in the head and another in the belly. Thome Coelho d'Almeida was stationed on the forecastle, and Rodrigo Affonso de Mello aft on the poop. I was in charge of the stern-chases, which the enemy attacked most frequently, for every time that they gave us a broadside after shooting away the bowsprit. They hit near the stern-chases under the gallery when firing at the rudder. I do not dwell here upon the manner in which we bore ourselves during this long fight, nor upon the hurt which the Dutch received, for I hope that they themselves will be the ones to spread it abroad.

[*Charles Boxer reported that the Mauritius suffered 242 dead and 75 sick while the Wapen van Rotterdam lost 277 dead with 94 survivors. These casualties may help explain the weak Dutch attempts to board the São João Baptista after it was clearly disabled.*]

John Franklin Jameson, ed., *Privateering and Piracy in the Colonial Period: Illustrative Documents* (New York: The Macmillan Company, 1923), 62–63.

35. Declaration of Edward Bant and Others. May 8, 1673.

A Declaration of some events that happened to us in our late voyage from London in the Ship *Barkely* of the said port, Nicholas Prynne Commander, intended for Virginia, Anno 1672/3.

On April 12, 1673, being in said ship about the latitude of the capes of Virginia about 80 leagues distant, we saw a sail towards evening, and being in want of provisions, seeing her to be a fly boat, made towards her and came up with her about eight o'clock and hailed them asking them of whence their ship. They answered of Falmouth. We asked them from whence they came. They answered from Virginia, and called me by my name and asked me how I did.

We asked them what places they loaded at. They answered, in Petuxin River. We told them we wanted some provisions. They answered us if we would hoist out our boat and come on board, they would spare us water and other provisions what they could. In order thereunto we did so, and I being desired by the master and merchant to go on board with the boat to endeavor to get what provisions I could, our Marchant, who was the owner, also desired me to stay, and he and the doctor would go with me as soon as they had sealed their letters.

Our master not having ended his writing, the merchant desired him to go on board with us also and to finish his letter there, and accordingly with three more seamen we went on board said ship, and when we came there founded several Dutchmen on board who had the command of her. They having lately taken her from the English. The Ship was called the *Providence*, belonging to Falmouth. Thomas Radden having been lately master of her. The said Dutchman surprised six of us and kept us prisoners and sent one of our company with three Dutchmen on board our ship, who lay by us until the next morning. Then the Dutch Commander commanded our ships' boat to come on board his ship again, which accordingly they did, he promising our merchant to take out our goods and to give us our ship again, in order whereunto he provided one hogshead of bread to have given us as he said and took our merchant with him and went on board our ship, and about half an hour after our ship made sail and steered to the westward: and then the Dutchmen put us who formerly belonged to her down into the hole and made sail after the said ship for about two hours, and seeing they could not come up with her stood on their course again to the eastward, and by receiving advice from those Englishmen that were at liberty were combined together for them to make way for our coming up and so to rush out upon the Dutchmen at once and to subdue them, for the rescuing of ourselves and ship, which with god's blessing we effected, without loss of life or bloodshed to any, and then agreed among ourselves to come away with said ship to New England, which accordingly we did and after eleven days passage by reason of contrary wind and foggy weather arrived in Piscataquay River on the 23th April 1673.

Edward Bant, Mate
John Ressell
Jonas Lewis

Notes

1 Lunsford, *Piracy and Privateering*, 4.

2 Thomson, *Mercenaries*, 32–42, 59–68.

3 Paine, *The Sea and Civilization*, 425–427.

4 Boxer, *The Dutch Seaborne Empire*, 6.

5 Lunsford, *Piracy and Privateering*, 10.

6 Lunsford, *Piracy and Privateering*, 10–13.

7 Lunsford, *Piracy and Privateering*, 13–14.

8 Lunsford, *Piracy and Privateering*, 12, 14.

9 Lunsford, *Piracy and Privateering*, 16.

10 Lunsford, *Piracy and Privateering*, 36–37.

11 Lunsford, *Piracy and Privateering*, 39–50.

12 Boxer, *The Dutch Seaborne Empire*, 26.

13 Parry, *The Spanish Seaborne Empire*, 260.

14 Lunsford, *Piracy and Privateering*, 19–20.

15 Disney, *A History of Portugal*, 73–74.

16 Lunsford, *Piracy and Privateering*, 32–33.

17 Lunsford, *Piracy and Privateering*, 198–202; Lane, *Pillaging the Empire*, 61–65.

18 Lunsford, *Piracy and Privateering*, 62–63.

19 Lane, *Pillaging the Empire*, 66–83.

20 Pearson, *The Portuguese in India*, 134–141.

21 The following account of the Dutch activities in Taiwan is taken largely from Andrade, 'The Company's Chinese Pirates', 415–444.

22 Willis, *China and Macau*, 63, 95.

23 Chin, 'A Hokkien Maritime Empire', 99.

24 Chin, 'A Hokkien Maritime Empire', 105; Andrade, 'The Company's Chinese Pirates', 430.

25 Andrade, 'The Company's Chinese Pirates', 437.

26 Andrade, 'The Company's Chinese Pirates', 438–439.

27 Andrade, 'The Company's Chinese Pirates', 442.

28 Chin, 'A Hokkien Maritime Empire', 109.

29 Andrade, 'The Company's Chinese Pirates', 443–444.

30 Lunsford, *Piracy and Privateering*, 28–29.

31 Boxer, *The Dutch Seaborne Empire*, 83–85, 774; Lane, *Pillaging the Empire*, 80–81.

32 Lane, *Pillaging the Empire*, 64.

33 Thomson, *Mercenaries*, 97–99.

34 Small, fast transport ship favoured by Dutch pirates.

35 Single-masted Dutch cargo boat was favoured by pirates because it was small and fast.

36 Luís da Fonseca de Sampaio was a rich and important merchant in Goa. He was taken to Batavia, where he spent five years in prison before returning to Goa to serve on the municipal council.

CHAPTER SEVEN

Brethren of the Coast:
Caribbean Buccaneers

As the English sea dogs of the sixteenth century gave way to the Caribbean buccaneers of the seventeenth, we enter the world that most Westerners will recognize from their popular culture. This was the era and the region that birthed the so-called 'golden age' of piracy with swashbuckling rogues who rebelled against the political and social mores of their times and created multi-racial floating democracies filled with Robin Hood–like characters. As entertaining as these perceptions are, they are usually gross exaggerations or downright falsehoods.

The seventeenth-century rise of the buccaneers occurred in the context of the Spanish Empire gasping from the combined assaults of the English, French and Dutch on its shipping, and on its towns and villages throughout the Caribbean. These European interlopers no longer contented themselves with simple raids. They sought bases and territorial acquisitions from which to launch their raids, sell their loot, spend their earnings, recuperate and plan for the next raid. In the 1620s, the English seized St. Kitts, San Cristóbal and Barbados. French refugees from St. Kitts settled Tortuga in 1627. The Dutch captured Curaçao in 1634 and occupied Pernambuco between 1630 and 1654. The French and the English took Martinique and Guadeloupe in the Lesser Antilles in 1635. The English seized Roatán Island in the bay of Honduras in 1642 and Jamaica in 1655. From these bases, they continued their assaults on the open veins of the Spanish Empire – sometimes as private, though illegal, entrepreneurs and sometimes with the authority of letters of marque issued by the colonial governors ensconced in the wet toeholds Europeans now maintained in the Caribbean.

Our English term 'buccaneer' is a perversion of the French term *boucaniers*, which is a perversion of the native Taino word *boucan*, which referred to a

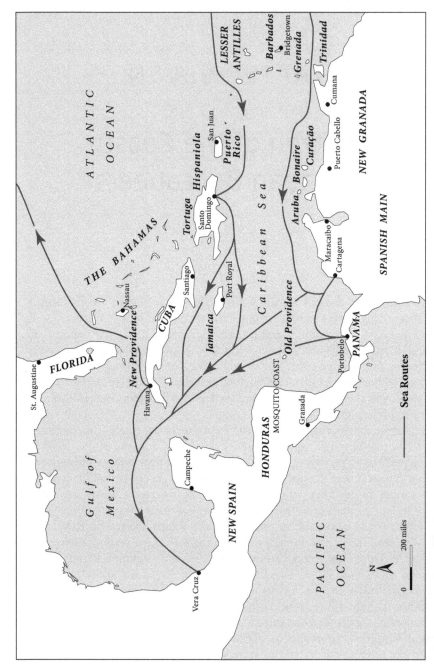

FIGURE 7.1 *Map of the seventeenth-century Caribbean buccaneers.*
Source: Map produced by Barry Levely, Cartographer.

wooden grate upon which meat was roasted or smoked. The French used the term to refer to the motley group of men who lived on the north coast of Hispaniola and the surrounding islands. These men were often French, English, Spanish, Irish, Scotch or Dutch renegades who had deserted their ships, escaped indentured servitude or avoided Spanish depopulation orders.

FIGURE 7.2 *Buccaneer of seventeenth century.*
Source: Photo by Culture Club/Getty Images.
Note: The buccaneer is shown holding the long-barrelled musket typical of buccaneers in the Caribbean. The inset pictures show the *boucan* from which the buccaneers took their name, a duel and a wild boar hunt.

They could also be marooned sailors, escaped African slaves and remnants of the native population.[1] After the 1605 depopulation order, most of the Spanish inhabitants had been cleared from the north coast of Hispaniola. Their livestock went wild and flourished without any predators to thin the herds. Marginal men moved into this vacuum and began hunting the wild livestock and selling the jerked meat and hides to European interlopers and Spanish colonists. In the early years, the buccaneers lived in pairs in a practice called *matelotage*, which was a kind of same-sex marriage. They spent half the year hunting and drying their meat. They then gathered at Tortuga, where they sold the fruits of their labour and spent the next few months preying on passing shipping.[2]

The buccaneers used dugout canoes to sneak up on ships, usually at night, shoot the watchman with their long-barrelled muskets before he could give the warning, throw the crew overboard and seize the ship. Canoes gave the buccaneers a distinct advantage in close, inshore raids because they had a shallow draft, they were very manoeuvrable, and they could be paddled in almost complete silence.[3] Like all pirates everywhere, the buccaneers sought to expend as little energy as possible in pursuit of prey. They haunted the active sea-lanes, hid behind islands and headlands or sailed as if they were part of the legitimate shipping.[4] After their raids, they transported their prizes to Tortuga, where the loot was divided up equally among the participants.

Buccaneer crews also drew up articles of agreement, similar to those used on privateering and merchant vessels. The articles formed a set of checks and balances to restrain the captain's power and to set the rules for discipline, the division of booty into shares and a common welfare fund to provide for men injured in the fighting.[5] The division of shares used on pirate and privateering vessels closely followed the codes used by Reconquista town militias of the Iberian Peninsula, which followed precise rules. After each militia action or pirate raid, the loot was tallied and split into shares. In Spain and Portugal, they followed a specific order: (1) the injured or relatives of the dead, (2) those who had lost a horse, (3) those who had lost equipment in the field, (4) officials of the city council were paid, (5) acts of heroism were compensated, (6) the royal fifth was set aside for the crown and (7) remaining shares were distributed to those who had participated. This spoil increased the town's ability to fight, put military ordinance for combat in the hands of townsmen; supplied, replaced or upgraded weapons; provided insurance for death, injury or loss of weapon; and it brought citizens together in mutual endeavour and concern.[6] The ship's articles served a similar purpose on board pirate and privateer vessels. On privateer vessels the articles were usually drawn up by the ship owners and merchants. Sometimes the government stipulated the wages and shares of corsairing vessels. Among buccaneering groups, however, the men themselves, or their representatives, voted on the articles in a democratic system unusual for the times.[7]

The articles also provided a method of settling disputes on board ship. Pirates, who had witnessed or experienced the harsh discipline of merchantmen and royal navy ships, were not inclined to submit to similar methods when they had a say in the matter. The use of the whip, for example, seldom found its way on board pirate ships. Disputes were to be settled by duels on land with pistol and swords. The one to draw first blood was the winner. Men could be made the 'governor of an island' which was essentially a death sentence by marooning. Or, in extreme cases, they could simply be executed.[8] The system of settling disputes off ship had a practical side. Not only would conflicts disrupt shipboard routine, but in the close confines of a ship, squabbles could lead to larger conflicts that could damage vital rigging and equipment.

Often the articles prohibited women on board ships and outlined punishments for any man who abused a woman on board, but we should take such articles with a grain of salt. Pirates and sailors, after months of living in close quarters with nothing but men to look at, were known to frequent the brothels whenever they were in port. Women captured at sea seldom faired any better. For example, in 1623, pirates working under John Nutt captured a ship near Dungarvan Harbor on the south coast of Ireland that carried a dozen women. The pirates raped all of the women over a period of at least a week.[9]

As buccaneer crews proliferated and spread, the Spanish took action. They repeatedly tried to dislodge the English and then the French from Tortuga without success. After every defeat at the hands of the Spanish, the English and French returned because the Spanish could not afford the resources to hold Tortuga and because the island held no real strategic or economic value. The French finally secured control of the island after 1660, and it remained an important buccaneer haven on the doorstep of Hispaniola. This Spanish weakness only emboldened English interlopers.

After England defeated the Dutch in 1652, Oliver Cromwell wanted to assert England's new identity as a sea power and sought to wrest mastery of the seas from the Spanish. He sent an invasion force of over 5,000 men to seize Hispaniola in 1654. The Spanish defeated the attack on Santo Domingo, and the English retreated to Jamaica in 1655, which they seized and held despite local guerrilla resistance. The ensuing Anglo-Dutch War of 1654–1659 spelt the end of Spain as a major power in Europe. But the empire continued because those who were collecting the golden eggs from this large and unwieldy goose had no intention of killing the goose. For example, the Dutch needed Spain as a counterweight to England and France. Dutch merchants carried Spanish exports, financed the slave trade and escorted Spanish ships to protect them. It was a symbiotic relationship that benefitted both parties.[10] Still, peace might be declared in Europe, but it did not come to the Caribbean. Jamaica soon joined Tortuga as a base for buccaneers who raided up and down the Spanish Main and Central America. This time they held commissions issued by the governors of Jamaica, Tortuga, St. Kitts and others in return for a share of the loot.

One of the most famous buccaneers of this era was Henry Morgan who raided Spanish towns with impunity and brutality. He abused, tortured, murdered, enslaved and robbed Spanish subjects and destroyed Spanish towns in Cuba, Venezuela and Panama. He starved his prisoners and raped his female captives.[11] Some raids yielded high returns, which most buccaneers squandered in riotous living in the brothels and taverns of Port Royal in Jamaica. Most raids were not profitable, however. Morgan's grand raid on Panama City after crossing the isthmus, for example, gave its participants a mere 200 silver pesos each.[12]

The English tried to walk on both sides of the street in the second half of the seventeenth century. They claimed to be in the business of suppressing pirates, while still encouraging privateers and turning a blind eye to the piratical activities of the buccaneers. They even rewarded Morgan for his raid on Panama with a knighthood and a position as the deputy governor of Jamaica in 1674. Their hypocrisy when it came to piracy cannot be chalked up to a mere double standard. Local English governments and communities all around the Atlantic and the Caribbean benefitted from the culture of maritime raiding and so protected maritime predators of all types. They resisted government attempts to redefine commerce raiding as illegitimate and illicit.[13] Pirates brought in much-sought-after supplies, wealth and currency. Buccaneer raids employed sailors who otherwise would have been idle and potentially dangerous. Armed bands of experienced fighters also provided inexpensive defence against attack.

By the last quarter of the seventeenth century, however, the English government was beginning to have more success at shifting local attitudes. In 1677, it became illegal for an English subject to sail under a foreign commission. This was a problem because English buccaneers had long received commissions from the French in Tortuga. In 1677, a pirate captain was executed in Jamaica for carrying a cargo of stolen slaves under non-English commissions.[14] In 1683, the Jamaican legislature outlawed piracy, and Henry Morgan found himself in the ironic position of actively suppressing the very men that had helped him make his fortune.[15] The message was clear enough, but English buccaneers refused to accept it. They continued to sail under French commissions and with French pirates. When European nations went to war, pirates also joined up and used the new façade of legitimacy to pursue their own ends. Nevertheless, by the 1680s, the tide had finally turned against the Caribbean buccaneers as the English began enacting anti-piracy laws and outfitting naval expeditions against them.

Despite the use of commissions to restrain pirate excesses and direct their energies towards enemies, commerce raiders proved difficult to control. They were, after all, accustomed to working outside, or just within, the bounds of the law. The English and the French also had to contend with Spanish, Portuguese and Dutch privateers and pirates. The English and the French also found that, as they collected colonial holdings and needed to protect shipping lanes, the bite of the sea dogs seemed much less alluring when the dogs snapped at their own heels. English and French landowners began investing in slave labour and sugar production. They discovered that sugar was a more profitable and less risky way to get rich than raiding. As their interests shifted away from buccaneering, the laws followed their lead.[16] In 1683, the Jamaican Assembly declared that piracy trials would be held in common-law courts and that those who aided and abetted pirates or privateers could also be prosecuted.[17]

The Caribbean buccaneers, seeing the writing on the wall, scattered to the winds. Some, like Bartholomew Sharp, sailed to the Pacific to raid along the coasts of South America, where he captured the *Santo Rosario* before sailing around Cape Horn to return to the Caribbean, where he met a cold reception. Others fled to the Indian Ocean and Southeast Asia. The Caribbean buccaneers received a small reprieve when King William's War broke out in 1689, and the government issued a new round of commissions. By the end of the century, however, the age of Caribbean buccaneers had passed. Two centuries of continuous assaults had so despoiled the region that buccaneers could find little left to seize. The heady days of Spanish bullion ships filled with the gold and silver were settling down to the more mundane traffic of regular commerce serving the growing plantation societies. This, then, is the real reason pirates and privateers began to abandon the Atlantic and the Caribbean in the late seventeenth and early eighteenth centuries for the Indian Ocean. It had more to do with broad commercial shifts, than campaigns of pirate suppression.

It is tempting to conclude that these multiracial crews of men who selected their own leaders, divided up the ill-gotten gains fairly, and rebelled against government authority and social constraints represent the first blossoming of modern democratic institutions. It is tempting, but we should not succumb. This is not to say that pirate ships of the early eighteenth century did not employ democratic and egalitarian practices that were highly unusual in the societies of their day. They did.[18] Buccaneering could be said to represent a type of resistance to the state's claim on the monopoly of violence and its use of state institutions to protect property and control labour.[19] Pirates moving back and forth across the lines of state-sanctioned predation could chafe under state attempts to control plundering in peripheral areas. Pirate crews in the Caribbean drew their sailors from the same ethnically complex working class of the Atlantic world as did the privateers and merchantmen that sailed the same waters.[20] Like the whaling ships of another generation, these crews represented floating microcosms of the port societies from whence they came. Though we can find examples of more or less racially egalitarian pirate crews, it is unlikely that these were all that common.

We should also avoid confusing the existence of ethnically mixed crews with ethnic equality. Scholars have noted that pirate crews did not restrict African members from carrying weapons and that African pirates could and did occasionally command white crews.[21] This surprises us only because we often choose to see the past in terms of absolutes. Real social systems are far more complex. For example, slave owners in Brazil and the Caribbean regularly armed their slaves for protection and men of African descent could attain high social status through a process of selective reclassification based on achieved merit.[22] But there was always a ceiling. Africans captured by pirates faced an unpredictable fate. As often as not, they were simply sold into slavery. Slaves had long been an important part of the smuggling culture in the Atlantic, and they represented a significant source of profit for pirates. They could also be killed, released or forced to join pirate crews. When given the choice to join pirate crews, many Africans did. When the other options were enslavement or death, joining pirates would certainly appear as the lesser of two evils. Sometimes Africans could account for more than half of pirate crews, and, once they were members of the crew, they were treated as other crew members.[23] Though if they were captured, colonial authorities treated them as slaves.

Likewise, the sometimes-exaggerated reports of black crews should not all be taken at their word. Often these accounts represented the growing concern of emerging slave societies that the human goods they trafficked would themselves turn pirates and attack the order white colonists were trying to establish.[24] Still, African slaves, such as Calico Jack, could escape slavery by joining privateering or pirate crews. Nicholas Cartagena, a slave of Frederick Philipse who went privateering in the Indian Ocean, managed to secure his freedom in 1698 by delivering nine newly enslaved Malagasy to his previous master.[25]

In the same light, buccaneer communities may have been more democratic than the absolutist societies from which they came, but their democracy and egalitarianism had only one purpose – personal gain. There is no evidence that pirates sought to elevate anyone but themselves. They respected no one's freedom save their own. The only poor they hoped to help were themselves.[26] They sought no social or political reform. They shared no class-consciousness with the world's marginalized and deprived. They readily preyed upon and murdered fellow sailors, fishermen, labourers, etc.[27] Their depredations harmed the rich and the poor alike. In short, 'one may describe a thief as a rebel, [a social bandit, or a liberated democratic freethinker] … but if his only purpose is to steal for private purposes, he remains a thief'.[28] That said, we should not forget that piracy flourished because important people did benefit from it. But nowhere do we find the Robin Hood effect. Wealthy land lubbers and government officials who trafficked in pirate loot did so for the same reason the pirates ravaged the seas – personal profit.

As you read the documents that follow, consider the following questions:

1   What strategy did Pierre le Grand and his men use to capture the Spanish ship?

2   What did Pierre le Grand do with the crew of the captured vessel?

3 Why did the pirates of Tortuga increase in number after Pierre's exploits?

4 Why might the pirate articles be considered a type of insurance policy?

5 In what way are the pirate articles both egalitarian and hierarchical?

6 What loot did the pirates seize in their attack on Portobello?

7 Compare Sharp's account of the taking of the *Rosario* with Calderon's. How do the accounts differ, and how might you explain those differences?

8 What were the two techniques the British Crown used to suppress piracy in the early eighteenth century?

9 What reason does the crown's declaration give for repressing piracy?

10 Why might the Caribbean buccaneers be considered episodic pirates responding to political instability?

11 How do the British attempts to suppress pirates fit with their own narrative of state formation and their legal justifications for privateering?

John Esquemeling, *The Buccaneers of America or the Pirates of Panama: A True Account of the Famous Adventures and Daring Deeds of Sir Henry Morgan and Other Notorious Freebooters of the Spanish Main*, edited by George Alfred Williams (New York: Frederick A Stokes Company Publishers, 1914), 35–38, 39–42.

Pierre le Grand was a seventeenth-century French buccaneer who cruised off the coast of Hispaniola with a group of twenty-eight men seeking a prize. After weeks of failure, they discovered and captured a straggler of the Spanish silver fleet.

'The boat,' says he, wherein Pierre le Grand was with his companions, had been at sea a long time without finding any prize worth his taking; and their provisions beginning to fail, they were in danger of starving. Being almost reduced to despair, they spied a great ship of the Spanish *flota*, separated from the rest; this vessel they resolved to take, or die in the attempt. Hereupon, they sailed towards her, to view her strength. And though they judged the vessel to be superior to theirs, yet their covetousness, and the extremity they were reduced to, made them venture. Being come so near that they could not possibly escape, they made an oath to their captain, Pierre le Grand, to stand by him to the last. 'Tis true, the pirates did believe they should find the ship unprovided to fight, and thereby the sooner master her. It was in the dusk of the evening they began to attack; but before they engaged, they ordered the surgeon of the boat to bore a hole in the sides of it, that their own vessel sinking under them, they might be compelled to attack more vigorously, and endeavor more hastily to board the ship. This was done accordingly, and without any other arms than a pistol in one hand and a sword in the other, they immediately climbed up the sides of the ship, and ran altogether into the great cabin, where they found the captain, with several of his companions, playing at cards. Here they set a pistol to his breast, commanding him to deliver up the ship. The Spaniards, surprised to see the pirates on board their ship, cried 'Jesus bless us! are these devils, or what are they?' Meanwhile some of them took possession of the gunroom, and seized the arms, killing as many as made any opposition; whereupon the Spaniards presently surrendered. That very day the captain of the ship had been told by some of the seamen that the boat which was in view, cruising, was a boat of pirates; whom the captain slightly answered, 'What then, must I be afraid of such a pitiful thing as that is? No, though she were a ship as big and as strong as mine is.' As soon as Pierre le Grand had taken this rich prize, he detained in his service as many of the common seamen as he had need of, setting the rest ashore, and then set sail for France, where he continued, without ever returning to America again.

The planters and hunters of Tortuga had no sooner heard of the rich prize those pirates had taken, but they resolved to follow their example. Hereupon, many of them left their employments, and endeavored to get some small boats, wherein to exercise piracy; but not being able to purchase, or build them at Tortuga, they resolved to set forth in their canoes, and seek them elsewhere. With these, they cruised at first upon Cape de Alvarez, where the Spaniards used to trade from one city to another in small vessels, in which they carry hides, tobacco, and other commodities, to the Havana, and to which the Spaniards from Europe do frequently resort.

Here it was that those pirates at first took a great many boats laden with the aforesaid commodities; these they used to carry to Tortuga and sell the whole purchase to the ships that waited for their return, or accidentally happened to be there. With the gains of these prizes they provided themselves with necessaries, wherewith to undertake other voyages, some of which were made to Campeche, and others toward New Spain; in which the Spaniards then drove a great trade. Upon those coasts they found great numbers of trading vessels, and often ships of great burden. Two of the biggest of these vessels, and two great ships which the Spaniards had laden with plate in the port of Campeche, to go to the Caracas, they took in less than a month's time, and carried to Tortuga; where the people of the whole island, encouraged by their success, especially seeing in two years the riches of the country so much increased, they augmented the number of pirates so fast, that in a little time there were, in that small island and port, above twenty ships of this sort of people. Hereupon the Spaniards, not able to bear their robberies any longer, equipped two large men-of-war, both for the defense of their own coasts, and to cruise upon the enemies.

How the pirates arm their vessels, and regulate their voyages:

Before the pirates go to sea, they give notice to all concerned, of the day on which they are to embark; obliging each man to bring so many pounds of powder and ball as they think necessary. Being all come aboard, they consider where to get provisions, especially flesh, seeing they scarce eat anything else; and of this the most common sort is pork; the next food is tortoises, which they salt a little. Sometimes they rob such or such hog yards, where the Spaniards often have a thousand head of swine together. They come to these places in the night, and having beset the keeper's lodge, they force him to rise, and give them as many heads as they desire, threatening to kill him if he refuses, or makes any noise; and these menaces are oftentimes executed on the miserable swine keepers, or any other person that endeavors to hinder their robberies.

Having got flesh sufficient for their voyage, they return to their ship: here they allow, twice a day, every one as much as he can eat, without weight or measure; nor does the steward of the vessel give any more flesh, or anything else, to the captain, than to the meanest mariner. The ship being well victualled, they deliberate whither they shall go to seek their desperate fortunes, and likewise agree upon certain articles, which are put in writing, which everyone is bound to observe; and all of them, or the chiefest part, do set their hands to it. Here they set down distinctly what sums of money each particular person ought to have for that voyage, the fund of all the payments being what is gotten by the whole expedition; for otherwise it is the same law among these people as with other pirates. No prey, no pay. First, therefore, they mention how much the captain is to have for his ship; next, the salary of the carpenter, or shipwright, who careened, mended, and rigged the vessel: this commonly amounts to one hundred or one hundred and fifty pieces of eight, according to the agreement. Afterwards, for provisions and victualling, they draw out of the same common stock about two hundred pieces of eight; also a salary for the surgeon, and his chest of medicaments, which usually is rated at two hundred or two hundred and fifty pieces of eight. Lastly, they agree what rate each one ought to have that is either wounded or maimed in his body, suffering the loss of any limb; as, for the loss of a right arm, six hundred pieces of eight, or six slaves; for the left arm, five hundred pieces of eight, or five slaves; for a right leg, five hundred pieces of eight, or five slaves; for the left leg, four hundred pieces of eight, or four slaves; for an eye, one hundred pieces of eight, or one slave; for a finger, the same as for an eye. All which sums are taken out of the common stock of what is gotten by their piracy, and a very exact and equal dividend is made of the remainder. They have also regard to qualities and places: thus the captain, or chief, is allotted five or six portions, to what the ordinary seamen have: the master's mate only two, and other officers proportionately to their employ: after which, they draw equal parts from the highest to the lowest mariner, the boys not being omitted, who draw half a share; because when they take a better vessel than their own, it is in the boys' duty to fire their former vessel, and then retire to the prize.

They observe among themselves very good orders; for in the prizes which they take, it is severely prohibited, to everyone, to take anything to themselves: hence all they take is equally divided, as hath been said before: yea, they take a solemn oath to each other, not to conceal the least thing they find among the prizes; and if anyone is found false to the said oath, he is immediately turned out of the society. They are very civil and charitable to each other; so that if anyone wants what another has, with great willingness they give it one to another. As soon as these pirates have taken a prize, they immediately set ashore the prisoners, detaining only some few, for their own help and service: whom, also, they release, after two or three years. They refresh themselves at one island or another, but especially at those on the south of Cuba; here they careen their vessels, while some hunt, and others cruise in canoes for prizes.

John Franklin Jameson, ed., *Privateering and Piracy in the Colonial Period: Illustrative Documents* (New York: The Macmillan Company, 1923), 84–92, 124, 136–137.

The Sacking of Portobello, January 1680.
This is the second time the English sacked Portobello. Henry Morgan had sacked it in 1668 and had crossed the isthmus to attack Panama City in 1671. Bartholomew Sharp and the others used a commission from the governor of Jamaica to cut logwood on the isthmus as their cover for the raid. Portobello, like Nombre de Dios, was an important port for the shipment of silver to Spain. This is why the isthmus continued to attract pirates and privateers.

So we went with our parties on with courage, and landed them about twenty leagues short of Portobello in an old ruined port called Puerta Pee. The way was very rocky and bad to march. They went near the seaside to escape the lookout which they saw plainly on a high hill, but as God would have it, the lookout did not see them .... The Saturday following, about ten o'clock, they came into an Indian village. Our people [were], many of them, weak, being three days without any food, and their feet cut with the rocks for want of shoes. An Indian man, crying out. 'Ladrones,' ran and made what speed he could to Portobello. So Coxon, our general, cried out, 'Good boys. You that are able to run get into town before we are descried.' We had then about three miles to Portobello. The Indian being too nimble for us, we being tired afore, he got into Portobello about half an hour before us, and cried out, 'ladrones!' Immediately we heard the alarm gun fire. We then certainly knew that we were descried. We made what haste we could into the town, the [advance group] being led by Captain Robert Alliston, the rest of our party following up so fast as they could.

... In the afternoon we had taken the town, the people of the place taking to their strong castle called the Glory, to secure themselves. The next day the Spaniards, being about two hundred, made an attempt to come out of the Glory. We faced them and made them to retreat back to their castle to some of their sorrow, which fell to the ground. We kept the town two days, plundered what we could of it and put the best of our plunder in canoes, which we took there. Some men marched back by land, guarding the prisoners down to a key about three leagues and a half from Portobello .... Captain Alliston informed us that they had taken Portobello and plundered the most part of the town without the loss of many men. Only five or six men wounded, and that a canoe of the best plunder, [such] as cloth of silver [and] cloth of tissue, [which the men], being so covetous to load [the canoe] deep, sank in the river coming down. The small forts fired [on them], wounding two or three men in the canoes.

[We carried] our plunder down to [Puerto de] Bastimentos and our people which marched by land being come, carrying plunder and prisoners to a key lying about half a mile from the mainland. There came down about three days after from Portobello as near as we could judge seven hundred soldiers, that came from Panama and arrived at Portobello on Tuesday. We came away the Monday before. The Spaniards came down abreast of the key we were upon and fired several small arms, shooting clear over this key. So we took our prisoners with [the] plunder and what we had gotten at Portobello and carried [them] to another key hard by out of the [Spaniards'] reach. So our ships came down where the party lay in dispute what to do having some thoughts the Spaniards would send to relieve the prisoners. Keeping strict watch, we saw the next day a barque longo standing to Portobello, which Captain Bartholomew Sharp went out and took. Her loading was salt and corn come from Cartagena. Keeping very good watch at the top mast head, three days after we saw a good big ship coming from Cartagena. Our ships sloops weighed [anchor] and went out to meet her as she was standing in to Portobello. Captain Allisson came up with her first in his sloop [and] engaged her [with] Coxon seconding him. [Coxon] clapped her aboard and took her without loss of any men. Some Spaniards fell for they fought about one hour. She had eight guns and [was] a new ship of about ninety tons the chiefest of her loading being timber, salt, and corn and about thirty Negros and about four chest of silk besides packets of great concern from the King of Spain ....

The Indians, being very familiar, came upon a key to our ships, men, women, and children [and] informed us that whilst we were at Portobello, the Spaniards had been down with about eighty soldiers and had fallen upon the Indians for their having familiarity with us. The Spaniards did kill of the Indians by their relation about twenty. The rest of the Indians took to the mountains for their security until we came. ... They offered themselves to go with us to take revenge of the Spaniards, which they call by the name of walkers. We, making in all in money, plate, and plunder about 100 pieces of eight a man at Portobello, people were eager for more voyages. And [we] were now fully resolved to go to the Golden Island and haul our ships into a small cove or creek out of sight of any Spaniard.

The Capture of the Ship Rosario
The Rosario *was the last substantial prize Sharp and his men captured on this voyage. Journal of 1680–82.*

Bartholomew Sharp: The Buccaneers on the Isthmus and in the South Sea

We cruise for more purchase and about twelve leagues from the cape, in a drizzly misty morning, a man going to the topmast head saw a sail under our lee, which we made sail to and come up with her, we fired several small arms before they called for quarter. But calling, was presently granted and not a gun fired. Her captain was shot down in taking of her. We found she was a ship bound for Panama come down from the Lima laden with wine and brandies, but very little plate, 700 pigs of pewter, which we thought was silver, found to the contrary. We now resolving to go about this year if pleased God, we took out of her 700 jars of wine, about 100 jars of brandy, to serve us homewards, and had it not been for this wine and brandy was impossible to have subsisted. We cut this ship's main mast by the board and sent her afore the wind to Panama. We kept about 18 Negros and Indians to wash and pump our ship. This last prize gave us full information of the Armada, which was to sail from Lima, about 17 said of ships. The 15 day of September 81, we turned along shore as high as Cape Blanco. ... We all conclude to make the best of our way out of these seas; we having gotten two hundred pieces of eight a man in money and plate upon equal shares.

Deposition of Simon Calderon 1682: Relation of the South Sea Men

Simon Calderon, native of Santiago de Chile, mariner, going from Callao to Panama in the ship called the *Rosario* laden with wine, brandy, pigs of tin, and artichokes, with 24 passengers and all, they met off Cabo Pasado, about halfway in their voyage, a ship, the *Trinidad*, and supposed it to be Spanish, but when they perceived that it was a ship of pirates, they tried to obtain the weather-gauge, but the pirates obtained it, and then they began to fire musket-shots, and with the first three shots they killed the captain of the *Rosario*, who was called Juan Lopez, and fired other shots and captured the ship, and took out with the hooks [?] all that they deemed necessary of the wine and brandy, and all the silver and other things that had value, and tortured two Spaniards in order to learn whether there was more silver, and cut down the sails and rigging, except the mainsail, and turned the ship adrift with the men, excepting five or six whom they took with them, and among others the deponent.

Thence they went to the Isla de La Plata, where they remained three days and a half refreshing themselves, and suspecting that the prisoners were planning to rise and take the ship they killed one and flogged another; and thence they went to Payta, where they sent two canoes ashore with 32 armed men, with design to capture Payta, but meeting with resistance they returned to the ship.

Clarence S. Brigham, ed. *British Royal Proclamations Relating to America, 1603–1783* (Worcester, MA: American Antiquarian Society, 1911), 176–177.

1717, September 5. [For Suppressing Pirates in the West Indies.]

By the King. A Proclamation for Suppressing of Pirates, George R.

Whereas We have received Information, That several Persons, Subjects of Great Britain, have, since the Twenty fourth Day of June, in the Year of our Lord One thousand seven hundred and fifteen, committed divers Piracies and Robberies upon the High Seas in the West-Indies, or adjoining to Our Plantations, which hath, and may Occasion great Damage to the Merchants of Great Britain, and others, Trading into those Parts; And though We have appointed such a Force as We Judge sufficient for Suppressing the said Piracies: Yet the more effectually to put an End to the same, We have thought fit, by and with the Advice of our Privy-Council, to Issue this Our Royal Proclamation; And We do hereby Promise and Declare, That in case any of the said Pirates shall, on or before the Fifth Day of September, in the Year of our Lord One thousand seven hundred and eighteen, Surrender him or themselves to One of Our Principal Secretaries of State in Great Britain or Ireland, or to any Governor or Deputy-Governor of any of Our Plantations or Dominions beyond the Seas, every such Pirate and Pirates, so Surrendering him or themselves, as aforesaid, shall have Our Gracious Pardon of and for such his or their Piracy or Piracies, by him or them

Committed before the Fifth Day of January next ensuing. And We do hereby strictly Charge and Command all Our Admirals, Captains, and other Officers at Sea, and all Our Governors and Commanders of any Forts, Castles, or other Places in Our Plantations, and all other Our Officers Civil and Military, to Seize and Take such of the Pirates who shall refuse or neglect to Surrender themselves accordingly. And We do hereby further Declare, That in case any Person or Persons, on or after the Sixth Day of September, One thousand seven hundred and eighteen, shall Discover or Seize, or cause or procure to be Discovered or Seized, any One or more of the said Pirates, so neglecting or refusing to Surrender themselves, as aforesaid, so as they may be brought to Justice, and Convicted of the said Offence, such Person or Persons, so making such Discovery or Seizure, or causing or procuring such Discovery or

Seizure to be made, shall have and receive as a Reward for the same, viz. For every Commander of any Pirate-Ship or Vessel the Sum of One hundred Pounds; For every Lieutenant, Master, Boatswain, Carpenter, and Gunner, the Sum of Forty Pounds; For every Inferior Officer the Sum of Thirty Pounds; And for every Private Man the Sum of Twenty Pounds. And if any Person or Persons, belonging to, and being Part of the Crew of any such Pirate-Ship or Vessel, shall, on or after the said Sixth Day of September, One thousand seven hundred and eighteen, Seize and Deliver, or cause to be Seized or Delivered, any Commander or Commanders of such Pirate-Ship or Vessel, so as that he or they be brought to Justice, and convicted of the said Offence, such Person or Persons, as a Reward for the same, shall receive for every such Commander the Sum of Two hundred Pounds; which said Sums the Lord Treasurer, or the Commissioners of Our Treasury for the time being, are hereby required and directed to Pay accordingly.

Given at Our Court at Hampton-Court, the Fifth Day of September, 1717. In the Fourth Year of Our Reign.

GOD SAVE THE KING.

Notes

1 Lane, *Pillaging the Empire*, 90.
2 Lane, *Pillaging the Empire*, 90–91.
3 Little, *The Sea Rover's Practice*, 49–50.
4 Senior, *A Nation of Pirates*, 59.
5 Leeson, 'An-*arrgh*-chy', 1065–1076.
6 Powers, *A Society Organized for War*, 213–214.
7 Little, *The Sea Rover's Practice*, 34–37.
8 Rediker, *Between the Devil*, 264–266.
9 Senior, *A Nation of Pirates*, 38.
10 Kamen, *Empire*, 410–413.
11 Hanna, *Pirate Nests*, 163–165.
12 Lane, *Pillaging the Empire*, 112.
13 Chet, *The Ocean Is a Wilderness*, 34–43; Hanna, *Pirate Nests*.
14 Lane, *Pillaging the Empire*, 116–117.
15 Antony, *Pirates in the Age of Sail*, 13–14.
16 Hanna, *Pirate Nests*, 132–133.
17 Hanna, *Pirate Nests*, 136.
18 Rediker, 'Hydrarchy and Libertalia', 29–46.
19 Thomson, *Mercenaries*, 46.

20 Pérez-Mallaína, *Spain's Men of the Sea*, 23–62.

21 Kinkor, 'Black Men under the Black Flag', 200–201.

22 Andrews, *Afro-Latin America, 1800–2000*, 47–49; Johnson and Lipsett-Rivera, 'Introduction', 9–10; Skidmore, *Black into White*, 38–40; Wadsworth, *Agents of Orthodoxy*, 221, 227 n. 45.

23 Kinkor, 'Black Men under the Black Flag', 198, 201.

24 Hanna, *Pirates Nests*, 382–384.

25 McDonald, *Pirates, Merchants, Settlers, and Slaves*, 99–100, 105–106, 109–114.

26 Zheng Zhilong, the founder the powerful Zheng pirate family, did provide food and jobs to poor but always for the purpose of strengthening his own position and reputation. See Calanca, 'Piracy and Coastal Security', 88.

27 Dian Murray shows that the same is true for the Chinese pirates of the late eighteenth and early nineteenth centuries. See Murray, 'Living and Working Conditions', 63–64 and Murray, *Pirates of the South China Coast*, 154–155.

28 Little, *Pirate Hunting*, 162.

CHAPTER EIGHT

Fishers of Men: Piracy and State Formation in Southeast Asia

If ever a region was created to be the perfect habitat for pirates, this region is Southeast Asia. Stretching in a wide triangle from the Malaysian Peninsula to the Philippines down to Papua New Guinea and back across to Java and Sumatra is a water world speckled with islands that create multiple choke points for trade and shipping. Mountainous tropical islands cut by deep mangrove forests and protected by coral reefs have made state building a real challenge. The generally low agricultural potential of the islands has meant that state power would be based on control of trade and people rather than land. Weak centralized statecraft meant that states remained 'unstable and prone to fragmentation', which was exacerbated by the tendency of lesser regional authorities to consolidate their local power at the expense of the state.[1]

The close proximity of rich and powerful cultures such as China and India still loom large in Southeast Asia economic and political identity. Indeed, access to Chinese markets was often the driving force in Southeast Asian economic and political development. As early as 100 BCE, goods travelled through Southeast Asian ports between China and Rome. The Romans sent coral and glass east in return for silk yarn and porcelain. Buddhists and Hindus created a vast trade network throughout the region.[2] They traded cotton with Egypt and acquired gold in Malaysia, Indonesia and Africa. Malay sailors began a long-distance spice trade from the Moluccas to Madagascar carrying cinnamon, pepper, cloves, nutmeg and mace.[3] Muslim traders entered these networks in the eighth and ninth centuries CE and began creating Sultanates throughout Southeast Asia as they consolidated their control over trade. Islam established itself on the Philippine island of Mindanao in 1380, and the Sulu Sultanate, created in 1405, ruled the islands of the Sulu Archipelago and parts of Mindanao,

Palawan and Borneo. Chinese imperial policy under the Song (960–1279) and the Yuan (1279–1368) encouraged trade, causing Chinese merchant communities to spring up throughout the region.[4] The Philippine Islands became a crossroads where trade and piracy developed side by side and connected markets and communities along sea lanes between Japan, China, Vietnam, Malaysia, Java, Borneo and the Moluccas.[5]

In Southeast Asia, trade, raids and state formation have always gone hand-in-hand. Human slaves and spices such as pepper, nutmeg and cloves from the Moluccas, or the Spice Islands as the Europeans called them, were some of the most sought after commodities. Forest products, such as rattan wood, edible bird's nests, aromatic woods, resins and gums, salt, iron and bee's wax, were also traded widely. Outsiders from India and China brought porcelain, brassware and textiles. Chinese sources indicated that raiders plied the waters of Southeast Asia as early as the fifth century CE.[6] The famous monk Shih Fa-Hsien reported in 413 CE that the sea around the Straits of Malacca was infested with murderous pirates.[7] Raiders from the Visayan region of the central Philippines attacked the Chinese coast of Fujian in the twelfth century CE by travelling northward on the Kuroshio Current. They attacked villages, but seemed primarily interested in acquiring iron for their weapons and tools.[8] During the early years of the Ming dynasty (1368–1644), trade and diplomatic missions travelling between China and India were so important that the famous Chinese admiral Zheng He was ordered to clear the seas of 'pirates'. He attacked and defeated Chen Zuyi, whose ships plundered passing vessels from his base in Palembang, Sumatra, as they navigated the Straits of Malacca. Zheng He captured Zuyi and carried him to Nanjing, where he was executed in 1407.[9] Though the Chinese called him a pirate, Zuyi was probably simply engaging in the long-standing practice of effective state craft in Southeast Asia. Plundering vessels that passed one's coastline and forcing them into port to pay duties was a common practice among all Southeast Asian states. Indeed, it was crucial to the success and economic survival of most states.

By the time the Europeans arrived in the region in the sixteenth century, sea raiding had become an endemic part of trade and state formation. The Portuguese, the Dutch and the English who were the first Europeans to enter the region came as pirates. They sacked towns, raided shipping and made military alliances in return for trade concessions. In short, they 'followed the same pattern as indigenous power-struggles' and became just one of many competing power brokers in the region.[10] Of course, they never called what they were doing piracy, but when other Southeast Asian states treated them in the same manner, the Europeans decried them as pirates of the worst kind.

The British 'entry into the Chinese market [in the early eighteenth century], the sudden rise of the Sulu Sultanate as an entrepôt for the Canton trade, and the widespread advent of the Iranun slavers' fostered increased commerce raiding in the region.[11] The Europeans, who had an insatiable desire for Chinese tea, found that trade with Tausug peoples of the Sulu

Archipelago in commodities, such as bird's nests, bee's wax, tortoise shells and mother of pearl, could offset their trade imbalance with China.[12] They actively cultivated relationships with the Tausug of Sulu for access to those goods which allowed the Tausug to insert themselves into the dynamics of China/European trade in a way that stimulated their need for workers to produce or acquire the commodities they needed for the trade. Consequently, they established far-reaching trade and slave raiding networks from Bengal to Canton between 1768 and 1848.[13] The Sulu Sultans wanted textiles, guns, gunpowder and opium to help reinforce their own power and assist them in their ongoing conflicts with their main competitors, the Sultanates of Brunei on Borneo and Cotabato on Mindanao. The combination of trading

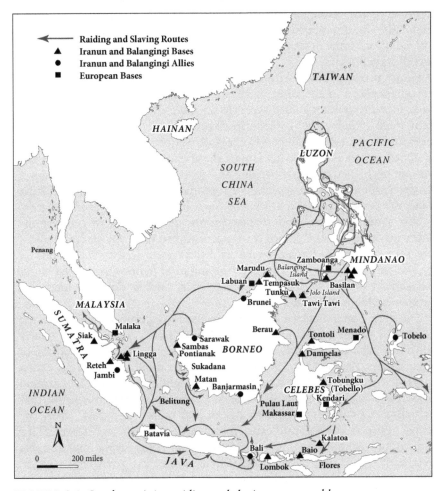

FIGURE 8.1 *Southeast Asian raiding and slaving routes and bases.*
Source: Map produced by Barry Levely, Cartographer.

and raiding they pursued allowed the Tausug to dominate the region. To maintain their competitive edge, they needed vast quantities of labour to procure marine and forest trade products. The only way to ramp up production quickly was to enslave the work force.

Because states often possessed limited direct control over the production of the goods upon which their power rested, they attempted to impose monopoly control over trade, which meant that rivals resorted to raiding to break those monopolies and to weaken their competitors. Because trade monopolies also threatened the autonomy of tribal groups, these groups might participate in trade directly, engage in piracy or migrate in large numbers in search of better trading relationships.[14] The maintenance of monopolies usually required the forced seizure of cargoes, often with state support. Many states in the region developed out of pirate communities or provided the resources and markets that maintained them. Pirate raids might also be stimulated by small-scale conflicts between neighbouring communities, competition between rival states and they could be an integral part of state policies.

Pirates provided states with manpower in the form of inexpensive pirate mercenaries and in the form of the slaves they brought back from their raids. In return, pirates gained access to trade goods that helped them escape local trade monopolies. To acquire slaves and to challenge competitors, three kinds of raids developed in the Sulu Sultanate – those paid for and equipped by the Sultan or his family, those encouraged by the Sultan but without his formal financial backing and those independent of the Sultan.[15] As states, such as the Sulu Sultanate, became more involved in the China trade, the demand for slaves to harvest maritime and forest products grew. It also stimulated the need to incorporate more clients to support the state's maritime needs.[16] James Warren has argued that 'slaving [formed] an integral part of the sultanate's remarkable economic activity with China ... the Iranun and Balanginggi, clients of the sultan of Sulu, who roamed about the island world in their swift raiding boats, finding slaves to meet this burgeoning labor demand'.[17]

The Sulu Sultanate based in Jolo encouraged pirate activities for the purpose of acquiring this much-needed labour force. Pirate fleets regularly sailed throughout the Southeast Asian triangle sometimes in dugout canoes or in galleys manned by 190 oarsmen with cannon and fighting decks. Larger fleets cruised for months, ranging throughout the Philippines around Borneo and into the Straits of Malacca. The raids became so endemic that virtually every community participated in such raids on a regular basis. The primary purpose of these raids was, of course, the acquisition of slaves. Ships and cargoes were taken, but despite European rhetoric, the main targets were native ships and native peoples living in coastal towns and villages. The victims and their cargoes would be taken to one of many markets that specialized in selling pirate loot.[18] These pirate markets also stimulated 'legitimate' trade as merchants from China and elsewhere frequented markets in the Anambas Islands, the Lingga Islands, Sarangani Island or Jolo to trade for pirate loot.

In this commercial environment, slaves became a kind of human currency throughout the region and could be exchanged directly in payment for commodities and services. For the Tausug of Sulu, slaves became the primary source of wealth. Slaves could be ransomed, sold, used as labourers or offered as sacrificial victims at aristocratic funerals or house raising ceremonies. These sacrificial slaves were bound and speared to death in a ritual killing meant to sacralize the proceedings. The ready supply of victims in the eighteenth and nineteenth centuries made the ceremonies more common as lower-ranking members of society could now afford to participate in what had long been an elite privilege.[19]

The economics of slave production meant that in raids, the pirates often slaughtered the men, unless they were fishermen who had seafaring skills the pirates could use, because men were difficult to control. Women and children were thought to be easily controlled and assimilated and so were more highly prized. Pirates also selected certain ethnic groups that were highly prized for their skills. Women from Visaya were esteemed as weavers. Tagalogs were thought to be good at business. Women from Aru Islands and Papua were thought to be especially beautiful. As with ethnicity, education, health and social status could all be considered in the price of a slave. Slaves could be purchased for rice, opium, iron, cloth, brassware, etc.[20] Slavery among the Sulu was not uniform. Slaves could own property. Male slaves could work as labourers, clearing forests, fishing, raiding, building boats, making salt and serving on the crews of raiding ships. Women often worked in rice fields, gathering coastal resources or serving as mistresses or sex slaves. Slaves could purchase their freedom and even experience social mobility.[21] However, slaveholders possessed the power of life and death and could be cruel. Slaves could be purchased or sold, and, as transferable assets, they functioned as a kind of mobile currency in the economy.[22]

Pirate lairs that were scattered throughout the region were never focused solely on piracy. They often had workers who harvested rice, fished and collected sea and forest products for trade. The Pirate leader Datu Camerang lived on Panambangan, an island in the Karimata group west of Borneo, with about 1,000 pirates, blacksmiths and fisherman, who sometimes went on raids as occasional pirates. The Sea Peoples of northern Borneo traded seaweed, sea cucumbers and red coral to the Chinese for salt, tobacco and cotton. They also married into local ruling families and offered their maritime skills for warfare and piracy to local rulers in exchange for special privileges. Sometimes they received land, and sometimes the rulers supplied them with food and support in return for a portion of their booty.[23]

Three groups dominated the pirate networks of Southeast Asia from the late eighteenth century to the middle of the nineteenth century, and all of them were associated with states. The two strongest were the Iranun (also Illanun or Lanun) and the Balangingi Samal. The famous sea nomads of the region, contrary to popular opinion, did not possess the resources or the land bases necessary to carry out extensive pirate raids.[24] In fact, their stories indicated that they took to the sea to escape pirates.[25] The Iranun and the Balangingi emigrated from Mindanao into the Sulu Archipelago around 1750. The Iranun served trading states, such as the Cule, Cotabato, Siak and Sambas, while the Balangingi primarily served the dominant Tausug group in the Sulu Sultanate as specialized raiders. The Iranun, a Maranao-speaking group, settled along the southern Mindanao coast and eventually established communities in Borneo, Celebes and Sumatra. The Samal-speaking Balangingi settled the tiny island of Balangingi and grew to be around 10,000 strong by incorporating people from the regions they raided.[26]

Each group established bases throughout the region near choke points and major sea-lanes.[27] They haunted the narrow straits and targeted their victims during calm weather when the risks were lower for themselves. The Iranun, Balangingi and Tausug were drawn to the Straits of Malacca by the increasing European trade with China and India. Pirate groups established bases in the region for the sole purpose of exploiting this trade. Some expeditions could spend years away from home, and they developed a vast knowledge of local customs and languages. Some were even literate. The Balangingi and the Iranun manned

> well-organized fleets of large swift *prahus*, they navigated along the west coast of Borneo and crossed the South China Sea to the Straits of Malacca and the Bay of Bengal. In the south, their raiding vessels thrust through the Makassar Strait and fanned out over the Indonesian world. They crossed the Banda Sea of New Guinea, made raids along the coasts of Java, and circumnavigated Borneo. In pursuit of captives, Iranun and Balangingi terrorized the Philippine Archipelago. They preyed on the poorly defended lowland coastal villages and towns of southern Luzon and the Visayan Islands. They even sailed and rowed their warships into Manila Bay, their annual cruises reaching the northern extremity of Luzon and beyond. They earned a reputation as daring, fierce marauders who jeopardized the maritime trade routes of Southeast Asia and dominated the capture and transport of slaves to the Sulu Sultanate.[28]

The Iranun also raided the coasts of Vietnam and Thailand and plundered villages and ships in the Straits of Malacca. They tended to raid friend and foe alike, which made them very difficult to anticipate or control. The Iranun and the Balangingi brought back tens of thousands of slaves to work in extracting forest and ocean commodities, such as bird's nests, sea cucumbers and camphor. The Sulu Archipelago located between the Philippines and Borneo on the east and west and China and the Spice Islands on the north and south was perfectly suited to be the gateway for trade between all of these regions.[29]

The Iban or Dayaks of Borneo were a much smaller group that raided in search of human heads and other valuables necessary for social promotion and status. The Iranun and the Balangingi liked to employ the Iban on their pirate ships because the Iban sought mostly human heads and iron, while their fellow pirates wanted the luxury goods and the food supplies. For the Iban, success in headhunting remained necessary for social prestige. Heads also played a role in mourning and fertility rituals. Preferably, the heads used in such rituals should be new, though old heads could be used in an emergency.[30]

FIGURE 8.2 *Dayak Warriors of Borneo, 1876.*
Source: Photo by Universal History Archive/UIG via Getty Images.

All of these pirates captured slaves by attacking small boats, junks, schooners and coastal villages. They carried sails used by local peoples so that they could conceal their attacks. Most often their sailing canoes carried twenty men. These canoes were towed behind the larger *prahus* or boats. When embarking on a raid, the larger boats were hidden, and the canoes were used to approach villages and the mouths of rivers. Most of the men would lie in the bottom of the canoe to conceal their numbers. Sometimes they disguised themselves as Chinese or Filipino merchants to seize fishermen at the mouths of rivers, workers along the coast and even to raid towns. Slave raiders tended to focus on small settlements less capable of defence. The seasonality of their raids was determined by the monsoon trade-winds. The 'pirate wind' blew from April to October, taking the Balangingi and Iranun to the Philippine islands, the Celebes, Brunei on Borneo and beyond.[31]

Because the Sultans of Sulu depended on 'trade, harbor and market fees', tribute and slaves for their income, Sulu officials actively supported pirates. They not only equipped Balangingi vessels, they also extended credit and advances in munitions and supplies to the Iranun. They expected their investment to be repaid in slaves.[32] Sulu expeditions enjoyed considerable organization. The Sultan's officials might supply the expedition and appoint the commanders of the *prahus*. These commanders recruited their own crew. Each expedition had an overall commander who determined the course the expedition would take. Each member of the crew had a specialized task, such as pilot or lookout, and each expedition had at least one imam to oversee religious devotion and to act as judge in the case of disputes. Slaves also formed an integral part of the crews, serving as rowers, cooks and general labour.[33] These expeditions could range from a few boats to as many as fifty or sixty vessels. The Iranun and Balangingi developed three types of vessels specialized for raiding. The Iranun preferred the heavily armed *lanong*, while the Balangingi chose the lighter *garay* as their principal vessel. These ships used both oars and sails much like the galleys of the Mediterranean. Both groups used a canoe-like craft with outriggers called a *salisipan* for coastal raiding.[34]

Throughout the eighteenth and much of the nineteenth centuries, the Sulu and their clients, the Iranun and Balangingi, carried on a near-constant low-level war with the English, the Dutch and the Spanish – though sometimes allied with one or the other as it suited their interests. Spanish authorities pursued a bloody and savage conflict with the pirates from the sixteenth to the nineteenth century.[35] None of these European powers could do much to stop them, until the advent of steamships. The Balangingi, in particular, occupied a supremely defensible island with a dangerous coral reef, shifting sandbars, dangerous currents, mangrove swamps and high tides. They improved the natural fortifications with large wooden stockades reinforced with packed earth. Despite multiple Spanish attempts to drive the Balangingi from the island, they did not succeed until 1848, when they sent a small fleet of steamships to attack the island's defences. After a fierce battle, the Spanish penetrated the stockade and discovered desperate Balangingi men killing the women and children so they would not fall into the hands of the Spanish. It is an ironic twist of fate that the Balangingi were terrified that their women and children would suffer the same fate they had spent the last sixty years inflicting on tens of thousands of victims.[36] The Balangingi scattered and tried to rebuild their strength only to be finally defeated in 1858.[37]

The cause of the Balangingi and Iranun decline was not solely imposed from outside through military force. As the Balangingi and the Iranun became more powerful, some began to pursue their own interest, switched allegiances and resisted the Sultan's demands to pay harbour fees.[38] They weakened themselves by straining their ties to their patrons and relying too much on the defensibleness of their island bases. The Sulu Sultanate also found its economic interests threatened by predatory European commercial interests and the flagging political and economic power of China. The defeat of the Balangingi and the Spanish assault on the Sulu Sultanate spelt the end of their long-distance raiding system. The Iranun continued to raid, but, by the 1870s, the Tausug, their main buyers, had largely disintegrated.

Piracy and slave raiding had been integral to state formation and long-distance trade in Southeast Asia. They intersected with and stimulated legitimate trade even as they preyed upon it. Sultans used the slaves they acquired from their pirate clients to produce trade goods and expand their control over trade monopolies, while piracy allowed the Balangingi and the Iranun to acquire a degree of independence from the power of the Sultan, while resisting Spanish conquest. The entrance of steam power in the mid-nineteenth century changed the dynamics of power in the region. It allowed European states to restrain sea bandits of all types. After 1890, most pirate communities had settled down to fishing, agriculture, collecting sea products and trading, even though the memory of slave raiding remained strong and would resurface in the twentieth century.[39] The piracy that had been intrinsic to state and economic institutions in Southeast Asia shifted back to a parasitic activity that would boil over in episodic spasms of violence into the twenty-first century.

As you read the documents that follow, consider the following questions:

1   How do the prisoner statements reflect the complex nature of piracy in Southeast Asia?

2   What explanations do the captured pirates give for engaging in piracy?

3   How were slaves acquired and utilized in Southeast Asia?

4   Compare the accounts of the two men captured and forced to work for the pirates with the accounts of William Edwards and Henry Keppel. How would you explain the different treatment given to slaves of different genders and ethnic groups?

5   What does the Keppel account reveal about pirate tactics in
    Southeast Asia?

6   Why was piracy in Southeast Asia an intrinsic part of commerce and
    crucial to state formation in the region?

7   Why might Southeast Asian rulers dismiss European complaints
    about native pirates attacking European vessels?

James Francis Warren, *The Sulu Zone, 1768–1898: The Dynamics of
External Trade, Slavery, and Ethnicity in the Transformation of a Southeast
Asian Maritime State* (Singapore: Singapore University Press, 1981), 240,
297–298. Used with permission.

Statements of Balangingi Prisoners, 1836

Statement of Silammkoom

   I am a native of one of the Sulu Isles called Balanguingui and I usually
reside there. I sometimes trade in a small way such as selling Padi at Basilon
and Mindanao. The Sultan lives at Sulu proper. The principal Chief at
Balanguingui is Panglima Alip. It is well inhabited and there are large
fleets of boats which are employed in collecting sea weed, tortoiseshell,
[and] sea cucumbers, ... on account of the Sultan who gives the people in
return, cloth or any other article he may think proper. Our fleet consisting
of six *prahus* came from Balanguingui and left that place about three
months since. The fleet was commanded and under the sole direction of
Orang Kaja Kullul, who is a relation of Panglima Alip. Orang Kaja Kullul
informed us that the Sultan had desired him to plunder and capture all
nations save Europeans. I have never seen the Sultan of Sulu, this is my
first voyage to the east coast of the Malayan Peninsula, but for many years
I have cruised in the vicinity of Manilla, Macassar and other places on
which occasion Orang Kaja Kullul took any boats he happened to meet.

Statement – Prisoner Mah roon alias Mah sandar

   I am a native of Ujang Pandan (? Pandars) Makassar. I was captured
about two years since by a formidable Iranun fleet consisting of twenty-
three *prahus*. When I was taken, I was proceeding to Mandas in company
with two of my countrymen named Sindrah and Pannsil. After cruising
about for some time the piratical fleet went to Balanguingui where I was
treated as a slave and compelled to perform all kinds of work. Panglima
Alip is the chief of Balanguingui, and Orang Kaja Kullul is considered
the second person in authority. The Sultan lives at Sulu proper. We left
Balanguingui about three months since. The fleet consisted of six *prahus* –
the whole under the command of Orang Kaja Kullul. I did not voluntarily
join the pirates. I was compelled to go. Two other of my countrymen
(Sookut and Pula Nea) are in a similar position as myself. Balanguingui
is well peopled and I think there are about 200 *prahus* of the same size as
the one destroyed by the steamer.

Statement made by Daniel

By birth, I am an Iranun and for years have resided at Balanguingui. For six years, I have been pirating near Macassar, Myungka, Yan Le Lah, Seah-Seah, Tambulan, and other places. Panglima Alip is the chief of Balanguingui, he is under the Sultan of Sulu. I cannot pretend to say whether the Sultan and Panglima Alip give any directions touching the fitting out of piratical fleets, but the fact is save pirating we have scarcely any other means of getting a livelihood. Six boats left Balanguingui under the command of Orang Kaja Kullul ... Talagoa was panglima of our boat ... we had a crew of twenty-nine men, six of whom were killed and several wounded.

Statement of Tala Goa

I live at Balanguingui with my family. I occasionally pirate [and] at other times [I am] making salt, planting paddy, [or] collecting tortoise shell. I am a follower of Orang Kaja Kullul and I am compelled to do and act as he may direct. Panglima Alip is the chief of Balanguingui, he of course, was aware of the subject of the cruise and Orang Kaja Kullul received instructions not to molest trading boats to and from the ports of Singapore and Tringanoo. I can say nothing positively relative to the Sultan of Sulu. I am not a panglima. I was placed in charge of one of the boats by Orang Kaja Kullul who had exclusive control of the six *prahus* .... Balanguingui was destroyed by a force from Manilla when I was quite a youth.

Statement by Filipino captive, 1845

I was fishing for sea cucumbers with nine others in a small canoe near Masbate Island when we were pursued by four Balangingi dug out canoes .... One of my companions was killed when he resisted seizure ... I was taken along with 150 other captives to Pitas island and allotted. I fell to Candayo, one of the ship's masters. After two months, Candayo sold me at Jolo to the Muslim Siangu with whom I remained for eight years. Last year [1844] I accompanied my master to Palawan on a trading expedition, and while I was fishing, two Balangingi large raiding craft passed and seized me. I was taken immediately to Pitas and sold.

David Cordingly, ed. *Pirates: Terror on the High Seas – from the Caribbean to the South China Sea* (Atlanta: Turner Publishing, Inc., 1996), 204.

The *Jane Ann* and the Pirate

TO A GENEROUS PUBLIC

I am a poor young man who had the misfortune of having my Tongue cut out of my mouth on my passage home from the coast of China to Liverpool, in 1845, by the Malay Pirates, on the Coast of Malacca. There were Fourteen of our Crew taken prisoners and kept on shore for months; some of whom had their eyes put out, some their ears cut off, for myself I had my Tongue cut out.

We were taken about 120 miles to sea; we were then given a raft and let go, and then were three days and three nights on the raft, and ten out of fourteen were lost. We were picked up by the ship *James*, bound to Boston, in America, and after our arrival we were sent home to Liverpool, in the ship *Sarah James*.

Two of my companions had trades before they went to sea, but unfortunately for me having no Father or Mother living, I went to sea quite young. I am now obliged to appeal to a Generous Public for support, and any small donation you please to give will be Thankfully received by Your obedient servant, William Edwards.

P.S.–I sailed from Liverpool on the 28th day of May, 1844, on board the *Jane Ann*, belonging to Mr. Spade, Williams Jones, Captain. Signed by Mr. Rushton, Magistrate, Liverpool, Mr. Smith, and Mr. Williams, after I landed in Liverpool on the 10th December, 1845.

Henry Keppel, *The Expedition to Borneo of H.M.S. Dido for the Suppression of Piracy: With Extracts from the Journal of James Brooke, of Sarāwak* (New York: Harper & Brothers, Publisher, 1846), 124, 141, 225–227, 303, 306–307.

Henry Keppel became captain of the H.M.S. Dido *in December of 1837. He took part in the First Opium War against China and counter-piracy operations around Borneo.*

The Datus, or chiefs, are incorrigible; for they are pirates by descent, robbers from pride as well as taste, and they look upon the occupation as the most honorable hereditary pursuit. They are indifferent to blood, fond of plunder, but fondest of slaves: they despise trade, though its profits be greater; and, as I have said, they look upon this as their 'calling,' and the noblest occupation of chiefs and free men. Their swords they show with boasts, as having belonged to their ancestors who were pirates, renowned and terrible in their day; and they always speak of their ancestral heirloom as decayed from its pristine vigor, but still deem the wielding of it as the highest of earthly existences. That it is in reality the most accursed, there can be no doubt, for its chief support is slaves they capture on the different coasts. If they attack an island, the women and children, and as many of the young men as they require, are carried off. Every boat they take furnishes its quota of slaves; and when they have a *full cargo*, they quit that coast or country and visit another, in order to dispose of their human spoil to the best advantage. Thus a cargo of slaves, captured on the east coast of Borneo, is sold on the west; and the slaves of the south find ready purchasers to the northward, and *vice versâ*. As the woolly-haired

Papuas are generally prized by the natives, constant visits are made to New Guinea and the easternmost islands, where they are procured, and afterward sold at high prices among any Malay community. The great nests of piracy are [Mindanao], [Sulu], and the northern part of Borneo; and the devastation and misery they inflict on the rest of the Archipelago are well known; yet are no measures adopted for their suppression, as every European community, be it English, Dutch, or Spanish, seems quite satisfied to clear the vicinity of its own ports, and never considers the damage to the native trade which takes place at a distance. To be attacked with success, they must be attacked on their own coasts with two or three steamers. A little money would gain every intelligence as to where they were preparing; and while the steamers were so worthily engaged in suppressing piracy, they might at the same time be acquiring information respecting countries little known, and adding to our stock of geography and science. A few severe examples and constant harassing would soon cure this hereditary and personal mania for a rover's life; and while we conferred the greatest blessings on the rest of the Archipelago, [Mindanao] itself would be improved by the change.

Beside the [Iranuns], there are two other descriptions of pirates infesting these seas: one, the Dyaks of Sakarran and Sarebus, two predatory tribes already mentioned; the other called [Balangingi], a wild people represented to come from the northward of [Sulu]. I have not seen them; but their boats are said to be very long and swift, with sometimes outriggers; and one particular in their mode of attack is too curious to omit. In closing on their victims they use long poles, having a hook made fast at the extremity, with which, being expert, they hook their opponents at a distance and drag them overboard, while others are fighting with *saligis* and spears.

At about three o'clock the following morning, the moon being just about to rise, Lieut. Hunt happening to be awake, observed a savage brandishing a kris, and performing his war-dance on the bit of deck, in an ecstasy of delight, thinking, in all probability, of the ease with which he had got possession of a fine trading-boat, and calculating the cargo of slaves he had to sell, but little dreaming of the hornets nest into which he had fallen. Lieut. Hunt's round face meeting the light of the rising moon, without a turban surmounting it, was the first notice the pirate had of his mistake. He immediately plunged overboard; and before Lieut. Hunt had sufficiently recovered his astonishment to know whether he was dreaming or not, or to rouse his crew up, a discharge from three or four cannon within a few yards, and the cutting through the rigging by the various missiles with which the guns were loaded, soon convinced him there was no mistake.

It was as well the men were still lying down when this discharge took place, as not one of them was hurt; but on jumping to their legs, they found themselves closely pressed by two large war-prahus, one on each bow. To return the fire, cut the cable, man the oars, and back astern to gain room, was the work of a minute; but now came the tug of war; it was a case of life and death. Our men fought as British sailors ought to do; quarter was not expected on either side; and the quick and deadly aim of the marines prevented the pirates from reloading their guns. The [Iranun] prahus are built with strong bulwarks or barricades, grape-shot proof, across the fore part of the boat, through which ports are formed for working the guns; these bulwarks had to be cut away by round shot from the *Jolly Bachelor* before the musketry could bear effectually.

This done, the grape and canister told with fearful execution. In the meantime, the prahus had been pressing forward to board, while the *Jolly Bachelor* backed astern; but, as soon as this service was achieved, our men dropped their oars, and, seizing their muskets, dashed on: the work was sharp, but short, and the slaughter great. While one pirate boat was sinking, and an effort made to secure her, the other effected her escape by rounding the point of rocks, where a third and larger prahu, hitherto unseen, came to her assistance, and putting fresh hands on board, and taking her in tow, succeeded in getting off, although chased by the *Jolly Bachelor*, after setting fire to the crippled prize, which blew up and sunk before the conquerors got back to the scene of action.

While there, a man swam off to them from the shore, who proved to be one of the captured slaves, and had made his escape by leaping overboard during the fight. The three prahus were the same [Iranun] pirates we had so suddenly come upon off Cape Datu in the *Dido*, and they belonged to the same fleet that Lieut. Horton had chased off the Island of Marundum. The slave prisoner had been seized, with a companion, in a small fishing canoe, off Borneo Proper; his companion suffered in the general slaughter. The sight that presented itself on our people boarding the captured boat must indeed have been a frightful one. None of the pirates waited on board for even the chance of receiving either quarter or mercy, but all those capable of moving had thrown themselves into the water. In addition to the killed, some lying across the thwarts, with their oars in their hands, at the bottom of the prahu, in which there was about three feet of blood and water, were seen protruding the mangled remains of eighteen or twenty bodies.

During my last expedition I fell in with a slave belonging to a Malay chief, one of our allies, who informed us that he likewise had been a prisoner, and pulled an oar in one of the two prahus that attacked the *Jolly Bachelor*; that none of the crew of the captured prahu reached the shore alive, with the exception of the lad that swam off to our people; and that there were so few who survived in the second prahu, that, having separated from their consort during the night, the slaves, fifteen in number, rose and put to death the remaining pirates, and then ran the vessel into the first river they reached, which proved to be the Kaleka, where they were seized, and became the property of the governing Datu;

and my informant was again sold to my companion, while on a visit to his friend the Datu. Each of the attacking prahus had between fifty and sixty men, including slaves, and the larger one between ninety and a hundred. The result might have been very different to our gallant but dosy *Jolly Bachelors*.

I have already mentioned the slaughter committed by the fire of the pinnace, under Lieutenant Horton, into the largest Malay prahu; and the account given of the scene which presented itself on the deck of the defeated pirate, when taken possession of, affords a striking proof of the character of these fierce rovers; resembling greatly what we read of the Norsemen and Scandinavians of early ages.

Among the mortally wounded lay the young commander of the prahu, one of the most noble forms of the human race; his countenance handsome as the hero of Oriental romance, and his whole bearing wonderfully impressive and touching. He was shot in front and through the lungs, and his last moments were rapidly approaching. He endeavored to speak, but the blood gushed from his mouth with the voice he vainly essayed to utter in words. Again and again he tried, but again and again the vital fluid drowned the dying effort. He looked as if he had something of importance which he desired to communicate, and a shade of disappointment and regret passed over his brow when he felt that every essay was unavailing, and that his manly strength and daring spirit were dissolving into the dark night of death. The pitying conquerors raised him gently up, and he was seated in comparative ease, for the welling out of the blood was less distressing; but the end speedily came: he folded his arms heroically across his wounded breast, fixed his eyes upon the British seamen around, and, casting one last glance at the ocean – the theater of his daring exploits, on which he had so often fought and triumphed – expired without a sigh.

The pirates on the coast of Borneo may be classed into those who make long voyages in large heavy-armed prahus, such as the [Iranuns, Balangingi], &c., and the lighter [Dayak] fleets, which make short but destructive excursions in swift prahus, and seek to surprise rather than openly to attack their prey. A third, and probably the worst class, are usually half-bred Arab seriffs, who, possessing themselves of the territory of some Malay state, form a nucleus for piracy, a rendezvous and market for all the roving fleets; and although occasionally sending out their own followers, they more frequently seek profit by making advances, in food, arms, and gunpowder, to all who will agree to repay them at an exorbitant rate in slaves.

The [Balangingi] cruise in large prahus, and to each prahu a fleet sampan is attached, which, on occasion, can carry from ten to fifteen men. They seldom carry large guns, like the [Iranuns], but in addition to their other arms, big *lelas* (brass pieces, carrying from a one to a three pound ball), spears, swords, &c., they use long poles with barbed iron points, with which, during an engagement or flight, they hook their prey.

By means of the fleet sampans already mentioned, they are able to capture all small boats; and it is a favorite device with them to disguise one or two men, while the rest lie concealed in the bottom of the boat, and thus to surprise prahus at sea, and fishermen or others at the mouths of rivers.

By being disguised as Chinese they have carried off numbers of that nation from the Sambas and Pontiana rivers. The cruising-grounds of these pirates are very extensive; they frequently make the circuit of Borneo, proceed as far as the south of Celebes, and in the other direction have been met off Tringanu, Calantan, and Patani. Gillolo and the Moluccas lie within easy range, and it is probable that Papua is occasionally visited by them.

It will readily be conceived how harassing to trade must be the continued depredations of the [Balangingi] pirates, and more especially to the trade of Brunei, which seems, from the unwarlike habits of the natives, the chosen field of their operations. The number of Borneons yearly taken into slavery is very considerable, as a fleet of six or eight boats usually hangs about the island of Labuan, to cut off the trade, and to catch the inhabitants of the city. The Borneons, from being so harassed by these pirates, call the easterly wind 'the pirate wind.' The [Balangingi] commence cruising on the northwest coast about the middle of March, and return, or remove to the eastern side of the island, about the end of November.

Notes

1 Healey, 'Tribes and States in "Pre-Colonial" Borneo', 4.
2 Sen, 'The Formation of Chinese Maritime Networks', 421–422.
3 Shaffer, 'Southernization', 1–21.
4 Sen, 'The Formation of Chinese Maritime Networks', 422–435.
5 Kenji, 'At the Crossroads', 73–84.
6 Healey, 'Tribes and States in "Pre-Colonial" Borneo', 6.
7 Wheatley, *The Golden Khersonese*, 37–38.
8 Isorena, 'The Visayan Raiders of the China Coast', 73–95.
9 Levathes, *When China Ruled the Seas*, 102–103.
10 Healey, 'Tribes and States in "Pre-Colonial" Borneo', 7.
11 Warren, *Pirates, Prostitutes and Pullers*, 128.
12 Warren, 'Trade for Bullion', 154–155.
13 Warren, *Pirates, Prostitutes and Pullers*, 61.
14 Healey, 'Tribes and States in "Pre-Colonial" Borneo', 4–5.
15 Warren, 'Who Were the Balangingi Samal?' 486.
16 Warren, *Pirates, Prostitutes and Pullers*, 50.

17 Warren, *Iranun and Balangingi*, 22.

18 Healey, 'Tribes and States in "Pre-Colonial" Borneo', 18.

19 Warren, 'Slave Markets and Exchange', 165–166.

20 Warren, 'Slave Markets and Exchange', 168, 170–173.

21 Warren, *Pirates, Prostitutes and Pullers*, 77–87.

22 For a full discussion of slavery in the Sulu Sultanate, see Warren, *The Sulu Zone*, 215–251.

23 Atsushi, 'Pirates or Entrepreneurs?' 86–87, 90, 92.

24 Sopher, *The Sea Nomads*, 259.

25 Sopher, *The Sea Nomads*, 42–43, 64.

26 Healey, 'Tribes and States in "Pre-Colonial" Borneo', 19.

27 Warren, *Pirates, Prostitutes and Pullers*, 125.

28 Warren, 'Who Were the Balangingi Samal?' 481.

29 Warren, 'The Balangingi Samal', 45–46.

30 Healey, 'Tribes and States in "Pre-Colonial" Borneo', 28.

31 Warren, 'The Balangingi Samal', 50.

32 Warren, 'Who Were the Balangingi Samal?' 486.

33 Warren, 'Who Were the Balangingi Samal?' 487–488.

34 Warren, *Pirates, Prostitutes and Pullers*, 63.

35 Mallari and Malari, 'Camarines Towns', 41–66.

36 Warren, 'The Balangingi Samal', 53–56.

37 Warren, *Iranun and Balangingi*, 343–378.

38 Warren, 'Who Were the Balangingi Samal?' 489.

39 Loyré, 'Living and Working Conditions', 84–85.

CHAPTER NINE

'Our Sea': Corsairs of the Mediterranean

Sea banditry in the Mediterranean remained an integral part of state expansion and of interstate conflict and commerce. The conditions that spawned piracy had not changed since the days of the Greeks and Romans, but the actors and their justifications shifted. New players emerged to ply the waters of the wine dark sea and sea rovers acted sometimes as privateers, pirates, pirate hunters, merchants or members of state navies. Nor had the methods changed. Oared galleys still pursued and plundered merchant ships and raided coastal towns, though cannon and firearms became more common in the fifteenth and sixteenth centuries.[1] The term 'corsair' reflects the nature of Mediterranean piracy. It comes from the Latin word *cursu*, which means to run, track, pursue or course. Hence the name corsair for those who pursued or 'coursed' at sea.

The rise and fall of land-based powers that attempted to project power by sea contributed to the ongoing practice of corsairing. In the sixth century, Justinian constructed a Byzantine navy to counteract the power of the Vandals, Ostrogoths and Visigoths and to reclaim the coastline of the eastern Mediterranean and North Africa. He succeeded, but Byzantium soon faced a new power, Arab Muslims, who carried on their practice of desert raiding in a new context and with new vehicles by boarding ships to attack the coasts and islands of the Mediterranean.[2] Christian kingdoms and city-states responded to the Muslim onslaught with nine Crusades between 1095 and 1272 that used the rhetoric of the defence of Christianity to justify their attempts at economic and territorial expansion into Palestine. The Knights of Saint John, or the Hospitallers, settled on the islands of Cyprus (1291–1310), Rhodes (1310–1523) and Malta (1530–1798) as self-appointed pirate hunters and as religiously and legally sanctioned Christian pirates and privateers.[3] The Muslim kingdoms of the Iberian Peninsula also used

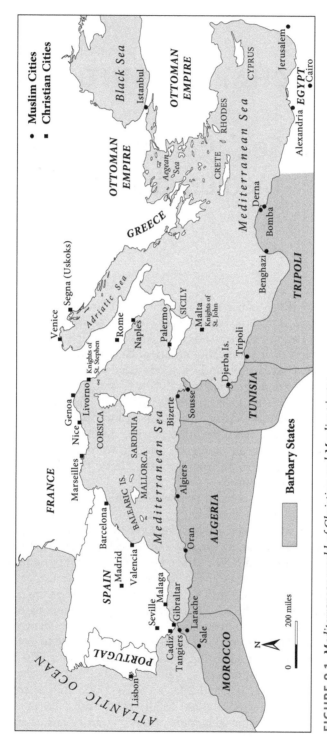

FIGURE 9.1 *Mediterranean world of Christian and Muslim pirates.*
Source: Map produced by Barry Levely, Cartographer.

piracy as 'a coherent form of Statecraft, one that defined, legitimized and financed their state'.[4] The art of piracy had long been a part-time occupation of the inhabitants of the coastal areas of the Mediterranean. In Béjaïa, on the Algerian coast, labourers, artisans, retailers, fishermen and merchants all become involved in raids along the Spanish coast in search of plunder and slaves.[5]

First phase of Barbary corsairs, 1480–1580

Corsairing in the Mediterranean shifted in the late fifteenth century to create a corsairing culture that was distinct from what had gone before. Like the surge of piracy in the Caribbean at the same time, piracy in the Mediterranean was part of a worldwide explosion of violence at sea following the European discovery of the Americas and the European expansion into the Indian Ocean. The new European maritime powers of England, Holland and France all challenged Spanish and Portuguese control of the seas.[6] In the Mediterranean, however, two events set the context for the new upsurge in seaborne banditry.[7] First, as the Byzantine Empire in the east collapsed inward, the Ottoman Turks emerged as the dominant Islamic force. After the Ottomans bombarded Constantinople, the Byzantine capital, into submission in 1453, they turned their sights on expanding into the eastern Mediterranean. Second, in 1492, Isabella, Queen of Castile, and her husband Fernando, King of Aragon, conquered Granada, the last Muslim kingdom to survive on the Iberian Peninsula. Muslim forces had invaded the peninsula in 711 CE from North Africa and established powerful, wealthy and sophisticated states. Their power entered a prolonged period of decline after about 1000 CE, and Christians began to assert greater control over the peninsula. A sizeable Muslim population remained in both Spain and Portugal, but they were now subjects of Christian monarchs.

The Spanish and Portuguese were not satisfied with their victories over Islam. Their crusading zeal caused them to imagine a new sphere of Christian power that would encompass all of North Africa. Consequently, both Spain and Portugal carried out large, amphibious invasions of the North African coast and began attacking Muslim shipping. With an expanding militant Islamic power in the east and an expanding militant Christian power in the west, a clash was perhaps inevitable. Yet, it was the war with Granada that brought the two powers into direct conflict.

The beleaguered Muslim rulers of Granada naturally sought other Muslim allies to assist them. The Mamelukes of Egypt refused because they secretly feared the Ottomans and were hoping for Fernando's support. The Ottoman navy was still small and their forces were preoccupied expanding their own frontiers. In a token of support, however, the Ottoman Sultan Bayezid II authorized Turkish corsairs to establish bases in North Africa to harass the Christians.[8] Kemal Reis, the most famous of these early corsairs, arrived in 1487 and spent five years attacking Christian shipping and coastlines from North African ports, such as Béjaïa and Annaba. His attacks ranged along the Spanish coast, the Balearic Islands, Corsica and Italy. In the end, the Granada war was won by land battles and sieges, so the corsairs could not do much to help. By 1492, Kemal could only assist Muslim refugees fleeing Granada reach the safety of North African ports. Though this early Ottoman intervention had accomplished little, it set a precedent for Turkish corsairing out of North Africa for the next three centuries.[9]

The Ottoman corsairs' use of North African bases also helped the Catholic monarchs justify expanding their war into North Africa and so conceal their true economic and geopolitical motives for seizing control of North African ports. The Portuguese had been sending traders and explorers down the Atlantic coasts of Africa for almost a century and were in the process of creating a maritime Christian Empire that would eventually extend from Portugal to India. Isabella and Fernando attempted a conciliatory stance with the conquered Muslim population in Granada after 1492. But whatever goodwill may have existed was destroyed by the archbishop of Toledo, Cardinal Francisco Jiménez de Cisneros, and other bigoted Christians who refused to accept the Muslim population. The Muslims revolted in Granada in 1499, but were defeated in 1501. The crown then ordered all Muslims in Castile to become Christians or leave. Those who converted and remained were called Moriscos. The rest became refugees in North Africa who carried a grudge against Spain, had little economic opportunity and enjoyed intimate knowledge of the Spanish language, culture and coastline.[10] Cisneros insisted on carrying the war to North Africa, which he did in 1505 and 1509 with attacks on Mers el Kebir near Oran and then on Oran itself. On May 17, 1509, two town officials helped the Spanish enter Oran and a blood bath followed. The Spanish slaughtered 4,000 Muslims and sold the rest into slavery. In 1510, the Spanish captured the ports of Bourgie and Tripoli and then attacked the island of Djerba, west of Tripoli, but were repulsed with the loss of several thousand men.[11]

The famous Barbarossa brothers Aruj and Khizr, who became the principal founders of the Barbary corsairs, first fought the Spanish at Djerba. Aruj had been captured by the Knights of Rhodes in the 1490s and spent three years as a galley slave. He emerged from the experience with a pathological hatred of the Knights and of Christians. In 1500, he received permission from the Sultan of Tunis to use his port as a base for corsairing activity in exchange for part of his profits. Aruj and Khizr raided the Italian and Spanish coasts and even captured two papal ships. Aruj also began seizing control of the North African coast so that, by 1517, he controlled most of the coast of what is now Algeria. He died in a skirmish in 1518, but his brother Khizr, assumed his mantel of leadership and consolidated his control over Algiers, creating a state that lasted for 300 years. His success against the Christians earned him an appointment by the Ottoman Sultan as leader of the entire Ottoman fleet. He died in 1546 after making the Ottoman navy a real force in the

Mediterranean.[12] Under Khizr, Algiers became the most powerful corsair base on the North African coast with a population of between 100,000 and 150,000. Like the other North African states, it relied on the corsairing trade, primarily the sale and ransom of prisoners, for its revenue. Algiers, Tunis and Tripoli all established corsairing as a formal state-run enterprise and became dependent on corsairing for their financial stability. Corsairs organized mercantile companies called *taïfa al-raïs* as joint-stock companies with investors, from every level of society.[13]

Meanwhile, the Christian kings of Spain, Sicily, Tuscany and others issued corsairing commissions of their own. The crusading orders of St John of Jerusalem, based out of Malta, after 1530 and St Stephan, based out of Livorno, were really corsairing religious orders that preyed on Muslim and Christian shipping and settlements alike. They enjoyed fortified ports and political and religious sanction. The Muslim and the Christian corsairs operated under very similar principles. Both were state sponsored for a share of the booty. Both were 'regarded as legal and honorable professions vital to the economies of both sides of the Mediterranean'. Both were 'deeply entrenched in politics and society' with captains being part of the ruling class. Both 'shared their prizes with their respective religious clerics: Barbary corsairs with *marabouts* who prayed for their success' and Christians to the monasteries and convents who prayed for them. Both valued slaves and ships as the primary form of booty.[14]

Livorno serves as a good example of how Christian city-states could benefit from corsairing activity. Livorno had been a secondary port, but under the Medicis it developed into a major Mediterranean port. It benefitted from the decline of Venice and Florence and inserted itself into the corsairing economy in a way that attracted both Christian and Muslim merchants. In 1561, Livorno acquired its own corsairing order, the Knights of Saint Stephen. Like the Knights of St John based on Malta, the Knights of Saint Stephen raided the eastern Mediterranean and North Africa relentlessly. They acquired a reputation of avid and violent corsairs. They seized Jews and Muslims as slaves and carried their loot back to Livorno. More interestingly, however, merchants from Livorno sailed to the Barbary ports of Tunis, Algiers and Tripoli to purchase goods seized by the Muslim corsairs from Christian ships and sold them in Livorno for a handsome profit.[15] The Knights of Saint Stephen provided the ruling Medici clan with 'naval power on the cheap', and the opportunity to profit from corsairing while not appearing to challenge Spanish power. Livorno managed to profit from both Christian and Muslim corsairing at the same time that they touted their ideological hostility towards Muslim peoples. This type of duplicity characterized corsairing in the Mediterranean.[16]

Malta practised a combination of private and public corsairing. The Order of the Knights of Saint John owned corsairing fleets led by knights who went on expeditions that they called caravans. The profits from the caravans were given to the order rather than to the knights, who received glory and honour in the service of God as their reward.[17] Alongside this formal, public system of religious corsairing a 'parallel private corso' emerged. In this case, the ships were privately owned and financed. Knights often backed these private expeditions whose primary purpose was profit. Only a portion of the loot had to be turned over to the order's treasury. Private corsairing on Malta became so popular that, by 1605, a special court was established to regulate corsairing. The knights were driven by an unrelenting hatred for Muslims and Jews, which expressed itself in extreme brutality and a desire to enslave and exploit them. Indeed, the Maltese population contained a higher percentage of slaves than any other European city of the time.[18]

The tide of the Ottoman advance into the Mediterranean turned in 1571 at the Battle of Lepanto. Although the Christians won the battle, they suffered the loss of 12 galleys and 10,000 men. The Ottomans Turks lost some 200 galleys and 30,000 men.[19] Spain and the Ottomans signed a truce in 1580. Together with the defeat of the Spanish Armada in 1588, Lepanto signalled major changes in the balance of power in the Mediterranean and in Europe. The weakness of the Ottomans stimulated a flood of European pirates into the Mediterranean at the same time that the Barbary corsairing states suddenly found themselves free of Ottoman control and able to target European shipping at will.

The golden age of Barbary corsairs, 1580–1660

Following Lepanto and the decline of both Spanish and Ottoman power, corsairing in the Mediterranean changed. Between the Ottoman capture of Tunis in 1574 and the Ottoman invasion of Crete in 1645, the Mediterranean did not experience a major naval war. It became an era characterized by private, low-intensity warfare. The number of Barbary corsairs and their activities expanded. Fleets became stronger and better organized. They spread their raids into the Atlantic. Christian renegades added new blood and new technologies to the corsairing community.[20]

As northern European states like Holland and England became major sea powers, they became increasingly concerned with trade and attempted to hold pirates and privateers at arm's length. When James assumed the English throne in 1603, he expelled pirates from his coast and signed a truce with Spain. The Dutch also declared a twelve-year truce with Spain between 1609 and 1621, which put scores of seamen out of work. Many of them wandered to the Mediterranean seeking employment, where many of them converted to Islam or 'turned Turk' and added a potent force to the Barbary corsairs.[21] These men, called renegades, brought much-needed manpower and new military and naval technology. Between 1550 and 1570, some 300,000 Christians joined the Barbary corsairs.[22] European pirates and privateers discovered that the Barbary states offered safe harbours to refit their ships and to sell their stolen loot. They offered them respectability and bases from which to operate. After 1603, European states referred to the North African states as 'renegade states' to suggest that they could not legitimately sponsor legal privateers, only illegal pirates. English renegades challenged the European fantasy that privateers were somehow different from pirates and that privateers could be used to control pirates.[23] The most important European technological contribution to the Barbary states were the 'round ships' with square-rigging. These ships allowed the Barbary corsairs to expand their activities into the Atlantic because the Mediterranean galleys could not cope with large Atlantic swells. The new sailing ships also decreased their need for large numbers of Christian slaves to serve as rowers. Christian renegades also brought with them knowledge of the North Atlantic coastline, and many of them had already worked as privateers or pirates.[24]

Consequently, the Barbary corsairs, often joined by Spanish Moriscos, surged into the Atlantic attacking ships and coastal settlements from Portugal to Iceland. After 1609, Spain expelled the last of the Morisco population and some 30,000 refugees fled to the Barbary coast. In general, the Moriscos did not take up piracy themselves, though they supported it. But the Moriscos of Hornachos who had used the threat of resistance to leave Spain on their

FIGURE 9.2 *Barbary pirates engage Spanish galleons, seventeenth century.*
Source: Andries van Eertvelt (1590–1652) National Maritime Museum, Greenwich. Photo by Fine Art Images/Heritage Images/Getty Images.

own terms with their weapons and wealth, settled in Salé on the Moroccan coast and turned it into a major corsairing base. Because they could speak Spanish and they wore Spanish clothes, they could fool Spanish patrols. By 1630, North African corsairs had attacked the Atlantic coasts of Portugal, Spain, France, England and Ireland, as well as the Azores, the Newfoundland fisheries off North America and Iceland in 1627.[25] Despite the importance of the new round ships, galleys never disappeared from the Mediterranean and they stimulated a constant demand for slaves to work the oars. The slave trade and the practice of slave ransoms were very sophisticated and were essential to the economy of the Barbary states and Christian states alike. Coastal raids often yielded more captives that could be ransomed or enslaved. For example, in 1566, Turkish corsairs penetrated 100 kilometres into Francavilla on the Eastern Italian coast to capture the local population and then immediately ransom them back to their families.[26]

Between 1500 and 1800, Barbary corsairs seized approximately 1 million Christians, while Christians seized approximately 250,000 Muslims.[27] Buyers could place advanced orders for slaves of certain genders, skills and ages. And slaves were sold at markets in every major Mediterranean port.[28] Barbary states received a portion of the slaves taken in corsairing raids. These slaves were housed in prisons, often suffered great abuse and hard labour in the galleys and on construction projects. Privately owned slaves often lived with their masters and engaged in more household work or skilled labour, such as carpentry. Boys and girls could be shipped east to the Ottoman Empire where the girls entered harems as sex slaves and the boys were trained as Ottoman officials.[29] Slaves also brought in significant financial rewards in ransom payments that may have perpetuated corsairing in the Mediterranean into the nineteenth century. Wealthy captives could rely on their friends and families to provide the ransoms. Merchant networks often handled the details of ransoming negotiations. Those without means had no hope of being ransomed unless one of the Christian orders took pity on them.

The Order of the Holy Trinity (established in 1198) and the Order of Our Lady of Mercy (established in 1218) collected money from alms and family contributions to free Christian captives. They sent regular missions for that purpose that freed some 15,000 captives. Protestants had no such orders but had to rely on their governments to organize ransom payments that might be collected from family, friends and church donations. The Dutch encouraged the formation of liberation societies whose sole purpose was to collect ransom money.[30] From the Christian perspective, the purpose of the ransom was to protect Christians from being forced to convert to Islam. Consequently, Catholic government officials, 'Catholic clergy, women and children' received priority from the Catholic missions. 'Protestants, Christian Renegades and military deserters' were not ransomed by the Catholic orders.[31] Those slaves who could not hope to be ransomed had few options. They could try to escape or accept that they would spend the rest of their lives as slaves. Under those circumstances many chose to convert to Islam and create new lives in North Africa.

Confronting the new sea powers, 1660–1720

The success of the corsairs drew animosity. They had flourished because their ships faced little opposition or distraction. Christian Europe was fighting itself and the Ottomans were not involved in any major war in the Mediterranean. After 1650, however, the three rising sea powers of France, England and the Netherlands began to challenge the corsairs. The corsairs had become so effective that these powers could no longer afford to ignore them. Rather than combining their forces in a coordinated assault, however, they began individually attacking corsair bases. However, the corsairs proved too powerful and forced the European powers to abandon the military solution in favour of separately negotiated treaties. The Europeans accepted the treaties, while still encouraging the corsairs to continue attacking the shipping of their rivals. The treaties allowed the corsairs to absorb the loss of revenue from slave ransoms by replacing it with tribute payments in cash, ships, naval supplies and weapons from European powers. For example, in the 1679 treaty between the Dutch and Algiers, the Dutch paid an annual tribute in cannon, firearms, gunpowder, naval stores such as masts, cordage and shipbuilding timber. What the Dutch had done was provide the resources and equipment Algerian corsairs needed to attack the ships of other nations. In return, they acquired the guarantee that Algerians would not attack Dutch ships. The Dutch agreed to this because it was cheaper to send regular tribute than to cover the cost of naval expeditions against the corsairs. This treaty survived for 100 years.[32]

Decline, 1720–1830

The success of the Barbary corsairs in wringing treaties from European states proved their undoing. By the middle of the eighteenth century, they had so many treaties of immunity that they had very few targets left for corsairing attacks. They also discovered that regular tribute payments provided a much more reliable form of revenue than the hit and miss lottery of corsairing raids. The Ottomans no longer needed corsairs and local rulers began to see trade as more lucrative than raiding.[33] Even though they stepped up raids on smaller and weaker states who could not afford tribute payments, corsairing raids actually decreased. After 1730, even these weaker states began acquiring treaties of immunity – Swedes with Tunis in 1736 and Tripoli in 1741, the Danes with Algiers in 1746, Spain with Algiers in 1786 and Portugal with Algiers in the 1790s. By the end of the eighteenth century, there were very few ships Barbary corsairs could attack.[34] Christian corsairs also experienced a collapse in the number of potential targets as Christian European nations began trading with the Ottoman Empire. Eventually the only ships they could legitimately attack were those of the Barbary states, whose ships seldom held valuable cargoes. Likewise, the Barbary corsairs no longer served as auxiliaries for the Ottoman Sultans, and so neither the Knights of Malta and Saint Stephen nor the Barbary corsairs could justify their roles as 'holy warriors'.[35]

The instability brought about by the wars of the French Revolution (1789–1815) encouraged the Barbary regencies to return to their old corsairing activities.[36] The British blockade of French ports shut the Barbary states out of the French markets, and several European states quit paying their tributes as they came under French control, leaving the Barbary states little option if they were to survive financially. The Christian corsairs of Malta faired worse. On his way to Egypt, Napoleon seized the island of Malta, bringing an end the Knights of Malta as a corsairing order. Faced with the growing loss of revenue and the removal of their major competitor, the Barbary corsairs returned temporarily to full-scale raids on shipping and coastal settlements.[37] After 1806, corsairing declined again because the British blockade and the French continental system allowed neutral ships, either legally or illegally, to import goods into Europe. The new economic opportunities did not last. With the final defeat of Napoleon in 1814, Barbary merchants once again found themselves excluded from European ports and turned back to corsairing.[38]

Meanwhile, the fledgling United States became one of those states that paid tribute after 1776. In 1777, Mohemmed, the ruler of Morocco, recognized the United States and opened his ports to US shipping. He expected the United States to open up diplomatic and commercial relations in return. When they did not, he sent his corsairs against them. In 1794, the United States paid a $642,500 ransom to Algiers for 100 prisoners and promised an annual tribute of '$21,600 in naval stores'.[39] In 1801, Jefferson decided to stand up to the corsairs. At the same time the ruler of Tripoli declared war on the United States because he felt he should receive the same tribute as Algiers and Tunis. Jefferson sent warships to the Mediterranean to force peace on his own terms between 1801 and 1815. The US naval presence forced Tripoli to the peace table. The United States agreed to pay $60,000 for the release of all American prisoners, but refused to pay Tripoli any further tribute.[40] Only after the Napoleonic wars, did the European powers finally decide to work together to attack North African corsairing bases. In 1816, an Anglo-Dutch fleet bombarded Algiers. In 1830, the French finally occupied Algiers with 37,000 soldiers, bringing an end to the Barbary corsairs.[41]

Mediterranean corsairing was a form of both warfare and commerce by other means – often at the same time. It was legally sanctioned and influenced by ongoing political and economic instability. Regular commerce in the form of 'legal' coastal trade intermingled with alternative systems of trade, such as smuggling and corsairing. Barbary states often turned to alternative systems of trade because they had been prevented by the Christian powers from carrying on 'normal' trade. Corsairing remained a clear 'response to the progressive economic marginalization of the North African States'.[42] In Europe, the societies most prone to corsairing were those that found themselves excluded by powerful commercial competitor. These smaller trading centres, such as Livorno and Malta, embraced corsairing, while the major trading centres, like Valencia, Barcelona, Genoa and Venice, suffered from corsairing raids. Indeed, the sixteenth-century decline of Venice had a lot to do with the ravages of the Christian corsairs.[43] Corsairing in the Mediterranean in the early modern period began as an episodic response to political turmoil and state building became an intrinsic part of everyday commerce and warfare before devolving back to episodic predation it had once been.

As you read the documents that follow, consider the following questions:

1 What do the narratives of Joshua Gee and William Okeley reveal about the life of a captive on the Barbary coast?

2 What can these accounts tell us about the military and social operation of piracy in seventeenth-century Barbary?

3 What insight do they provide into the more general business of corsairing?

4 How restricted were the Christian slaves in the exercise of their religion?

5 How often were the slaves physically abused?

6 How much freedom did Christian slaves enjoy, and how might you explain it?

7 What do these accounts tell us about ransom and escape along the Barbary coast?

8 Why might it be appropriate to see corsairing in the Mediterranean as a complex interplay of parasitic, episodic and intrinsic piracy?

9 What role did geography, imperial ambitions and political instability play in the creation and perpetuation of corsairing in the Mediterranean?

Joshua Gee, *Narrative of Joshua Gee of Boston, Mass., while He Was Captive in Algeria of the Barbary Pirates* (Hartford, CT: Wadsworth Atheneum, 1943), 7–30. Used with permission. [Spelling and punctuation have been corrected and updated.]

Joshua Gee's short narrative of his seven years (29 July 1680–14 July 1687) captivity as a slave of the Barbary corsairs represents the first American account of such captivity. In many ways, his narratives represents the long-standing tradition of captivity narratives intended to demonize the enemy and portray the captive as the pious recipient of divine assistance. But Gee's narrative differs in that he did not vilify his captors. He suffered very little physical abuse, was not forced to convert to Islam and enjoyed considerable religious freedom. He was freed because his parents arranged, with the help of Judge Samuel Sewall of Boston, to have a ransom paid to his owner in July of 1687.

In our voyage for England we were short of bread. And in a dream on a day before we were taken I saw a ship that did supply our want of bread but at a dear rate. At sight of an Algerian ship I apprehended it was the same to appearance I had seen in my dream and found it so. We had bread enough at a dear price. I went aboard in the first boat and being asked our loading I answered tobacco. They said in English, "you have brought it to a bad market."

[A] remarkably [?] good slave that waited on the boatswain did frequently show me kindness though he could not understand me nor I him. He first gave me tobacco and often after gave me part of what he had to eat though he had but little – a kindness I never saw him show to any other. And as our being put in irons in the hold of the ship, having nothing but stones for our pillows, he gave me his bag in which he had some clothing to lay under my head. After I came ashore, I never saw him to repay his kindness. Hence, I was led to contemplate divine goodness and his sovereign dominion that can cause the ravens to feed his people, if need be ….

I was sold ….Coming into my masters house in the room where the slaves [were] kept, on a shelf I saw a bible. And with joy [I] took it in my hand and with a sad heart gave thanks to God. Opening the same, the first place come to hand and sight was John 13. Reading the first verse to my great support and surprise [I] was filled with tears. Considering it was God alone that could give a song in the house of pilgrimage, God turned the heart of my first master to favor me and Thomas Corbin bought my bible of an English slave for sixteen pence and gave it me.

The first voyage I went to sea, we had a fight with two English ships. [We] received much damage and were forced to leave them. The next day, we took a ship from New Spain, a right prize. The second voyage we fought an English ship and received much damage. She escaped, the sea being very high. The third voyage we fought a Genoese ship, which got under a castle on Mallorca and escaped.

After that, war was made with France. We took many ships and did recruit ourselves with clothing when we had leave to go on board the prizes, which was a favor shone us. The last voyage I was in my first master's service, cruising off the coast of Spain within the straits which they call Mar Chico, or the little sea. With a mighty wind at west and

[a] great tempest, we stood three days in great distress – our captain never seen in that time to lay down his head or at all to sleep, fearing to trust any other to [conduct] the ship night or day. At the end of three days, having passed a dangerous shoal, passing near a small island called Lampadusa [we] were surprised at three great hollow seas that set the ship almost on end. The moon just rising showed us that we were steering right on the island and very near the wash of the shore. Th[u]s we saw the wonders of god in the deeps (107 Psalm 23 and on). After cruising about Malta, Sicily, and the Coast of Morea[44] in quest of the French, I had opportunity to see and hear of the Greek's hard living under the Turks.

Beside other hard things, the most promising of their children are taken from them and carried to Constantinople and trained in the Mahomaten religion. We put into Hoverene, a maritime port where the Tunis ships of war are kept within a mole[45] with the chains hove to by a windlass in a house for that purpose where are some brass guns to prevent any coming to burn their ships – as also two castles with large guns of brass two big to be mounted on carriages lying on beds without nuts, only rings to slow the[m] ....

The two French ships of war came and did embargo us there and also the six Malta galleys – our ship within the mole. We were sent to the masemoars, or prisons underground about forty steps deep of which there were two. And while we were there, the French appointed us to secure our warden and at midnight they would come with a guard to secure our passage to their boats. Which they did and came to our prison doors armed and waited for us near two hours. But our plot was discovered. It was that while we had our warden at playing cards belo[w] we should surprise him stopping his mou[t]h and the same time surprise the doorkeepe[r] above and go forth. But in the very mome[nt] he apprehended his danger, called hastily to the porter to shut the door and said though you kill me you cann[ot] get out. We were forced to dissemble the mater and the French lost their labor. After that we were removed to another of those prisons farther from the sea.

In each of the prisons, the papist[s] have an altar and place of worship at o[ne] end with candle and [saints?], after their manner, where they, at coming in, go to worship beside what they do when they worship together. And sometimes their padres, fathers or friars, come to preach to them on their great holy days at evening. And those papists did not at all interrupt us in our religious exercises when any of us were so inclined. And here it was I had the first religious acquaintance with Captain Crow. And here had we afforded songs in this night of distress ....

In this time, one of our company, a Frenchman, ran away. Being taken, [he] was beaten by our captain [who] was a renegade Greek, until he ceased to cry, groan, or stir and was taken away for dead. But [he] recovered.

At our return to Algiers, news came of my first master's death in his voyage to visit his friends in the Black Sea. And then I was put to my second master Covo Mustafa, the same that took me being my half master at first sale in the market.

Some small time after my coming to him, one of our company being absent [and] he coming to the knowledge of it, caused us all to be laid down one by one and himself with a great rope (about a three-inch rope) beat us all very severely, which I took as a hassle. The slave thus absent was an Englishman and the next day [he was] beaten so cruelly that his flesh (especially his buttocks) were forced to be dressed by the doctor. His arm [was] so lame that [he] had not the use of his limbs for some time after.

Some[time] after this, the plague came into the family and the second year I had it very dangerous. Mr. Ashly came to visit and pray with me. Most of the family slaves died. I expected the same, but was restored May 20, 1683 ....

The first doctor that dressed my soar, an Englishman, died of the same distemper. The second doctor, a Frenchman, [was] taken sick. A third, belonging to the dey.[46] Both French were sent off on board Monsieur Getane with the rest of the French slaves. My fourth doctor was a Dutchman and my fellow slave with my first master. God blessed his endeavor for my recovery ....

[On] another voyage we took a Portugal flyboat soon after she came out of Portugal. She was bound for Brazil. I had leave to go on board her. I tarried all night and threw away my old clothes and put one new [clothes] and as many as I could well carry.

[In] the morning our boat came on board, my master and others in her. The boat went away laden. My master tarried. None on board were above deck, only two slaves in the foretop. I went over the side to drive in a port. The rope I had to hold by gave way. I fell in the sea. On hauling the rope [I] supposed it would stop. The end came [so] I cast it out of my hand supposing I could swim and take hold of the rudder. Being disappointed, I called for help. Those in the top called to those below deck. My master and others which could afford me no relief, no boat being aboard and the other ship much to windward out of call – the boat on the windward side of her. My master and others made signs. The boat soon put off. My master looking until he could see me no more said 'my little carpenter is lost.' And by signs they warned the boat astern and when within hail said 'there is one overboard.' And as the boat came near me the sea uncovered me [and] I laid hold on a boat hook they put [out].

After war was made with France, we chased a French ship and came not up with her until within night. We boarded her. The ship blew up. I was in the hold to be ready to stop any leak that might happen under water. The blow so listed our ship that all our guns seemed to lift from the deck [and] it seemed as if the deck would fall considering the age and weakness of our ship. Our master esteemed our deliverance miraculous and said 'surely God hath some particular love for someone in this ship for whose sake we are all saved.' Of the French ship's company only three were saved by our boat, which was then out near the ship that blew up. Sometime after their being sold in Algiers, they were ransomed and after that it was known that it was Master Marchand and [the] boatswain and that they blew up their ship on purpose that we, with them, might perish rather then they would be slaves. The captain of our ship said, had he known it before they were sold he would have hung them at the yardarm and shot them to death ....

When I was entering on building my master's ship, I set myself to seek direction from God as well as advice of my friends. Setting apart a day to seek God pleading my interest in his covenant goodness, his promises on which he had caused me to hope, the longings I had to the public worship, the end I had not for gaining money, but that I might have opportunity to grow more in the knowledge of Christ. I wrote the same in my pocket book, and thus before God and the Lord Jesus Christ and the elect angels. And in the end of the day [I] had great inward peace.

I after found myself inclined to the undertaking and the day I began said work [was] the twenty-fifth of June 1685 ....

Captain Crow and Ashly were my most intimate companions and we had all things common to serve each other's necessity. When I went to sea, I left money with Mr. Cole with order to supply them if they called for any of it. And when we had holy days allowed us, as was usual, Christmas and Easter as also their great feasts twice a year, we then used it. We could conveniently meet in some private garden some miles distant from town, carrying with us some provision. And there reading and praying and praising God for his goodness and for his many fold mercies to us in that strange land ....

In building my master's ship, in his great passion [he] swore he would the next day bore out my eyes with his knife, which he shewed to me with many evil treatments. I went home with my heart overwhelmed and spent that night in prayer .... In the morning, I going to my work, God so changed his heart and his countenance, his words were words of kindness. I saw his face as an angel of God .... I was forced to seek a place where to weep tears of joy that God had heard my cry.

William Okeley, *Ebenezer: Or a Small Monument of Great Mercy, Appearing in the Miraculous Deliverance of William Okeley, John Anthony, William Adams, John Jephs, John Carpenter from the Miserable Slavery of Algiers* ... (London: 1675).

William Okeley was captured by Barbary corsairs in 1639, while en route to found a new Puritan colony in the West Indies. He remained a captive until he escaped by boat in 1644. He was nearly killed by his first master for insulting Islam and Mohammad. He was allowed to set up a small shop where he sold tobacco and alcohol so he could earn the two dollars a month his owner required. He was later sold to a second master who owned a farm and treated him kindly. More so than Gee's narrative, Okeley's account follows the captivity narrative agenda of demonizing his captors, denigrating Islam and asserting the superiority of Western Christian societies.

It was not long before we discovered those other three ships to be Turks men of war, who espying their prey endeavored to come up with us, which about night they effected. Whilst they were coming up, the masters of our ships seemed resolved to fight them, and accordingly made preparation to receive them; but in the night, the master and company of the ship wherein I was altered their counsels, let their resolutions dye, and agreed to run for it; uncertain counsels never produce better success; when we might have gone, then we would stay; and when there was no way to escape, then we must needs attempt it. Had we either at first resolved not to fight them, or resolving to fight, had prosecuted our resolutions like men of courage, we might perhaps, either have avoided the danger, or bravely mastered it. The Turks perceiving us begin to run, sent one of their number to chase us, whilst their other two attended the remaining two of our company till the morning. At break of day they began to fight us, and after a short dispute boarded us, and took us all three. In the *Mary*, six were slain, and many wounded ....

As soon as we were put ashore, for the first night we were locked down in a deep nasty cellar ... The next day we were carried, or led, or rather driven to the Viceroys, or Bashaw's palace, who according to the custom, and his own right is to have the tenth man for his dividend of the slaves. When the next market day came, we were driven like beasts thither and exposed to sale .... Their manner of selling slaves is this. They lead them up and down the fair, or market; and when the chapman bids any money, they presently cry ... Here's so much money bidden, who bids more? ... Their first policy is to look in their mouths; and a good, strong, entire set of grinders will advance the price considerably; and they have a good reason for this practice; for first they are rational creatures and know that they who have not teeth cannot eat, and they that cannot eat, cannot work and they that cannot work are not for their turn; and they that are not for their turn, are not for their money. And secondly, they intend to keep them at hard meat all the year, and it must not be gums, but solid teeth ... that must chew it ....

Their next process is to feel their limbs; as whether there be any fracture or dislocation in the bones ... The age is very considerable; but they that sell them, did not breed them, and therefore they know nothing more or less of that. Two ways they have to find out the age; the one is to stand to the courtesy of the slaves, but they are not bound to make any such discovery, and therefore they go by general conjectures from the beard, face, or hair, but a good set of teeth will make any one ten years younger, and a broken one ten years older than the truth ... They are very curious in examining the hands; for if they be callous and brawny, they will shrewdly guess they have been inured to labor; if delicate, and tender, they will suspect some gentleman or merchant, and then the hopes of good price of redemption makes him saleable.

For about a year [my servitude] lay in trudging in errands, bearing burdens, and discharging other domestic services at command ... When [my master's] ship was now fitted for another adventure, my patron tells me, I must go in her ....I pleaded that I was no seaman, understood nothing of the mariners art. ....Nine weeks we were at sea, within and without the straits, cruising and picarooning[47] up and down. At last, we met with one poor Hungarian French man of war, whom we took and so returned.

My patron having been at great charges in fitting, and manning out this ship, and the reprisals so slenderly answering his great cost, and greater hopes, told me, I must allow him two dollars per month, and live ashore where I would and get it where I could.

The Spaniards every year return a considerable sum of money to Algiers to be employed in the redemption of such of their own country as are there in slavery. ... Now there was a Spanish friar that was a slave, who being passed by in the redemption that year took it very heinously to be neglected ... renounces the Christian religion, declares himself a [Muslim] and accordingly appears in his Turkish habit ....

If a Moor shall dare to strike a Turk, he is punished with great severity. I saw two Moors whilst I was there whose right hands were chopped off of this one crime, and hung about their necks in strings. The one was set upon an ass. The other walked by on foot, the common [crier] proclaiming before them their offence, through the chief streets of the city. I saw another also with his heels tied to a horse's tail. He was wholly naked, only he had on a pair of linen drawers. And thus was he dragged through the streets. It was a most lamentable spectacle to see his body all torn with the rugged way, and stones. The skin torn off his back and elbows, his head broken and all covered with blood and dirt and thus was he dragged through the city out at Babazoon, or the East Gate, where he ended his miserable life.

Two others of their own countrymen I saw executed in a most terrible, and dreadful manner ... The one was thrown off from a high wall, and in his fall he was caught by the way by one of the great sharp hooks which were fastened in the wall. It caught him just under the ribs and there he hung roaring in unspeakable pain till he died. The other was fastened to a ladder, his wrists and ankle being nailed through the iron spokes ....and lest his flesh and sinew should fail and the nails not hold, his wrists and ankles were bound fast with small cords to the ladder. Two days I saw him alive under this torture. How much longer he lived under it I cannot tell ...

There was a Dutch youth, a slave to a Turk, who upon some provocation, drew his knife at his patron. For this offer, he was sentenced to be dragged out at one of the gates and there to have his arms and legs broken in pieces with the great sledge hammer, which sentence was accordingly executed, for though I could not see his face for the crowd, yet I heard the blows, and the miserable cries of the poor dying young man ....

[*Okeley's master grew poor and sold him to an old gentleman who was kind and let Okeley continue selling goods from his shop. But Okeley decided to attempt escape.*]

When I had once resolved upon this adventure, and saw it go on hopefully, I gave my patron my wonted visits, kept fair correspondence, paid him his demands duly, but secretly I made off my goods as fast as I could, and turned all into ready money. I had a trunk, for which John Anthony made me a false bottom into which I put what silver or gold I had ... This trunk I took to our dear minister Mr. Sprat ... This trunk he faithfully secured, and carefully brought over, and has honestly delivered to me when he heard I was come safe to London.

[*Okeley and seven companions contrived to construct a collapsible canvas boat with oars and escaped into the Mediterranean.*]

Four of our company took [the boat] upon their shoulders and carried it down towards the sea, which was about half a mile off. When we came to the seaside, we immediately stripped ourselves naked, and putting our clothes into the boat, carried it and them as far into the sea as we could wade; and this we did lest our tender boat should be torn against the stones and rocks. And then all seven of us got into her. But here we soon found how our skill in calculating the lading of our vessel failed us. For we were no sooner embarked, but she was ready to sink under us, the water coming in over the sides ... At last one whose heart most failed him, was willing to shut out and rather hazard the uncertain torment of the land than the certainty [of being] drowned at sea. Then we made a second experiment, but still she was so deep laden that we all concluded there was no venturing out to sea. At length another went ashore. Then she held up her head very stoutly, and seemed heavy enough for our voyage ... And taking our solemn farewell of our two companions whom we left behind ... we launched out upon the thirtieth day of June in the year of our Lord one thousand six hundred forty-four.

[*Okeley and the other four men took turns manning the oars and bailing the water that leaked through the canvas. Their bread became soaked with salt water and the water in the skins became rancid. After three days, they began drinking their own urine to stay alive. They also captured a sea turtle, cut off its head, drank its blood, ate its organs and sucked on its flesh. In this way, they managed to reach the island of Mallorca after six days and nights. The inhabitants of the island gave them clothes and money and helped them find passage back to England.*]

Notes

1 Little, *Pirate Hunting*, 112, 114.

2 Little, *Pirate Hunting*, 112–113; Cunliffe, *Europe between the Oceans*, 456–457.

3 Greene, *Catholic Pirates*, 95–98.

4 Bruce, 'Piracy as Statecraft', 248.

5 Kaiser and Calafat, 'Violence, Protection and Commerce', 71.

6 Greene, *Catholic Pirates*, 78.

7 Jamieson, *Lords of the Sea*, 28–29 is the sources for the next several paragraphs.

8 Jamieson, *Lords of the Sea*, 29.

9 Jamieson, *Lords of the Sea*, 29–30.

10 Jamieson, *Lords of the Sea*, 31–32.

11 Jamieson, *Lords of the Sea*, 32–33.

12 Jamieson, *Lords of the Sea*, 34–47.

13 Antony, *Pirates in the Age of Sail*, 25–26.

14 Antony, *Pirates in the Age of Sail*, 26–27.

15 Greene, *Catholic Pirates*, 91.

16 Greene, *Catholic Pirates*, 81–93.

17 Greene, *Catholic Pirates*, 95–96.

18 Greene, *Catholic Pirates*, 98.

19 Jamieson, *Lords of the Sea*, 68–70.

20 Senior, *A Nation of Pirates*, 78–109; Lunsford, *Piracy and Privateering*, 56–58.

21 Antony, *Pirates in the Age of Sail*, 27–28.

22 Jamieson, *Lords of the Sea*, 60.

23 Fuchs, 'Faithless Empires', 50.

24 Jamieson, *Lords of the Sea*, 86.

25 Jamieson, *Lords of the Sea*, 83–85.

26 Kaiser and Calafat, 'Violence, Protection and Commerce', 75.

27 Jamieson, *Lords of the Sea*, 124.

28 Antony, *Pirates in the Age of Sail*, 29.

29 Jamieson, *Lords of the Sea*, 116.

30 Lunsford, *Piracy and Privateering*, 83–84.

31 Jamieson, *Lords of the Sea*, 117–118.

32 Jamieson, *Lords of the Sea*, 146.

33 Jamieson, *Lords of the Sea*, 178.

34 Jamieson, *Lords of the Sea*, 178–184.

35 Jamieson, *Lords of the Sea*, 182–183.

36 Nadal, 'Mediterranean Privateering', 105–119.

37 Jamieson, *Lords of the Sea*, 191–198.

38 Jamieson, *Lords of the Sea*, 198.

39 Antony, *Pirates in the Age of Sail*, 30.

40 Jamieson, *Lords of the Sea*, 188, 199; Turner, 'President Thomas Jefferson and the Barbary Pirates'.

41 Thomson, *Mercenaries*, 110–113.

42 Nadal, 'Corsairing as a Commercial System', 129.

43 Nadal, 'Corsairing as a Commercial System', 129–130.

44 During the Ottoman period, the Coast of Morea referred to the Peloponnese peninsula in southern Greece.

45 A stone or masonry dike or pier built out into the sea to protect ships.

46 This dey could be Ismail Pasha of Algiers (1659–86).

47 To picaroon is to be a rogue or scoundrel.

CHAPTER TEN

Beneath the Jolly Roger: An Age of Chaos, an Age of Gold

The term 'the Golden Age of Piracy' has been used loosely to describe the period from about 1660 to 1720 in the Atlantic and the Caribbean. This era witnessed a surge in European piracy that expanded into the Pacific and Indian Oceans. This was the age of the pirates of our popular memory – the social bandits who defied the laws of all nations and the hypocrisy of European societies. Rather than think of this as a golden age, however, it is more accurate to portray it as an age of chaos. The non-state predators that states had unleashed in their bid for power, wealth and control of violence led to near-complete chaos by the end of the seventeenth century. During this period, Janice Thomson argues that 'privateers generated organized piracy ....Mercantile companies turned their guns on each other and even on their home states'.[1] The world's oceans experienced a brief moment in which piracy and privateering of all kinds dominated maritime commerce and warfare everywhere. It was an era of nation and empire building and of state collapse. This was the age of the Caribbean buccaneers, the Mediterranean corsairs, Pacific pirates and the Zheng pirate dynasty of Taiwan. It witnessed the rise of Sulu piracy in Southeast Asia and the creation of pirate states on the Malabar coast of India. During this period, the modern state system perched on the edge of complete anarchy because they could not control the predators they had encouraged and empowered.[2] The oceans of the world became a battleground for the myriad competing interests.

Pirates and privateers of this era ran the spectrum from petty criminals knowingly acting outside the bounds of law to state-sponsored raiders. Many moved back and forth across these lines. But none of them would have succeeded without the active support of local communities and patronage from the merchant and political elite.[3] Private prize-taking, whether state-sanctioned or not, became the norm on the oceans of the world.[4] As we have seen, under Queen Elizabeth, the English had recruited pirates for their imperial expansion into the Atlantic. British colonists in North America remained desperately short of specie with which to purchase provisions and trade goods. Pirates began arriving in larger numbers in the 1640s, just when the colonists were experiencing a real crisis in currency.[5] Caribbean pirates also began to shift to North American ports in the 1670s and 1680s as Jamaica became less welcoming. This happy union of supply and demand would eventually transform most colonial maritime communities from Canada to South Carolina into pirate nests, where pirates could find safe havens, supplies and crews. As early as 1612, Peter Easton operated out of Newfoundland, from where he attacked British and Spanish shipping. He also seized Newfoundland fishermen and forced them to sail with him to the Azores.[6] British attempts at creating a centralized regulation of colonial economies further pushed colonials into the arms of the pirates. This should not surprise us. The ports of the south coast of Ireland, Wales, Cornwall and elsewhere, all had strong ties to piracy and privateering.[7] Courts with juries proved hesitant to convict local pirates they knew personally and with whom their families interacted and intermarried.[8]

One might think that the English, who had so vigorously challenged Spanish attempts to enforce a monopoly on trade to their colonies, would have learned something about the futility of such a project. And yet, in 1651, parliament began issuing the Navigation Acts which were renewed and expanded throughout the rest of the century.[9] The Navigation Acts intentionally forced their North American colonies to remain economically underdeveloped. The Acts stipulated that everything imported into England had to come on English ships. Certain products, such as sugar, tobacco and dyes produced in the colonies could only be shipped directly to England and no place else. Any European goods being exported to the colonies had to pass through an English port.[10] The British prohibited the creation of a colonial mint, resisted the use of paper currency and regulated the value of foreign specie, thus leaving the colonies permanently cash poor.[11] They also created monopolies on important trade items, gave trade monopolies to chartered companies and discouraged the creation of import substitution manufacturing of items such as linen and iron that might compete with English producers.[12]

As we might expect, North American colonists, desperate for access to foreign goods and trade, actively supported smuggling and readily purchased cheap, illegal goods. This occurred at just the time that the English colonists and officials in the Caribbean were beginning to take a hard line against illicit pirates, who dispersed around the Atlantic and into the Indian Ocean and the Pacific in search of less aggressive prey. Colonial ports, such as Boston, New York, 'New Haven, Charles Town, and New Providence in the Bahamas', all encouraged and welcomed pirates. The thinly populated, treacherous coastlines allowed pirates to come and go as they pleased. Private colonies supported pirates because they needed access to specie, they wanted cheap exotic trade goods, like calico and silk, and they needed protection.[13]

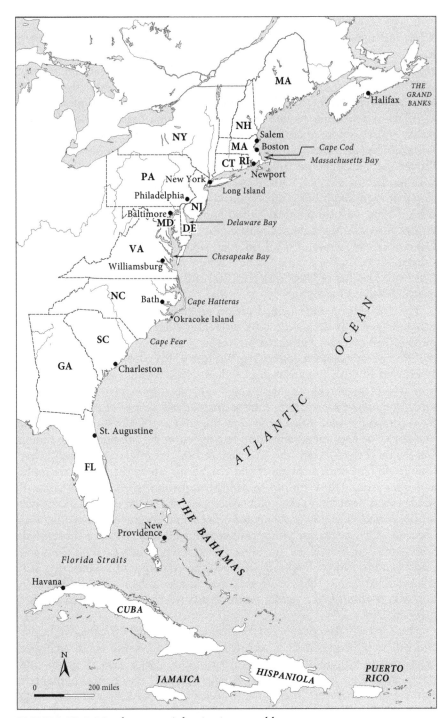

FIGURE 10.1 *Northwestern Atlantic pirate world.*
Source: Map produced by Barry Levely, Cartographer.

North American colonists and their leaders remained cagey about piracy. While many denounced it, others actively supported it and benefitted from it. Even those who denounced it realized that piracy was a temporary activity for most pirates and that it was crucial to the economic and military security of the colonies. The royal colonies, such as New Hampshire, Massachusetts, New York, New Jersey, Virginia, North Carolina, South Carolina and Georgia, tended to be less accepting of pirates, though by no means entirely opposed to them, because their economies depended on legal trade and because they were more susceptible to direct government control. Private colonies, however, tended to supply pirate and privateering vessels with foodstuffs, alcohol, 'sails, rope, pitch, and tar'.[14] They allowed pirates to repair their ships and pirates spent their money in the taverns and inns, offered 'gifts' to local political leaders and married into prominent families. Pirates provided the colonies with exotic goods, slaves, silver and gold.[15] Governors, even those of royal colonies, sold commissions to privateers for substantial sums. For example, Thomas Tew purchased a commission from Governor Fletcher of New York for £300 and one from Governor Cranston of Rhode Island for £200.[16]

The Navigation Acts helped create an economic crisis by the 1690s, which helped this decade become the real golden age of North American pirates. The colonies embraced pirates as a source of desperately needed bullion and consumer goods. King William's War also came to an end in 1697, and English privateers found themselves without employment at a time when the merchant marine could not meet the demand for seafaring jobs. Unemployed privateers and seaman of all stripes came together to form companies that sailed from New England ports, like Boston and New York, with or without commissions to prey upon the shipping of the Indian Ocean, the Persian Gulf, the Red Sea and the west coast of Africa. They found safe harbours throughout the Caribbean where they could resupply, and, once around the Cape of Good Hope, they found shelter on the island of Madagascar or at their principal marketplace, the Island of Saint Marie just off the coast.[17] The lure of piracy for officers and common sailors alike was immense. The profits for pirate captains and officers could be substantial. Some amassed four figure fortunes over their piratical careers. Common pirates could seldom hope for so much, but piracy and privateering still promised better pay than 'legitimate' maritime employment. A sailor could hope to get about £10 a year. A pirate or privateer could get £10 to £60 per prize taken.[18]

These North America–based Englishmen, and the Africans, Malagasy and others who joined them, created informal networks on the margins of the world empires that gave American colonists access to goods and slaves from East India. This Indo-Atlantic pirate network was intimately connected to financiers in colonial American ports and threatened existing trade networks.[19] These men haunted the entrance to the Indian Ocean in search of Muslim pilgrims on their way to the Red Sea port of Jeddah from which they could travel overland to Mecca and Medina. North American merchants and politicians invested in their voyages. Red Sea pirates seldom distinguished between Muslims of the Mediterranean who preyed on Christians and Christian shipping from the Muslim traders and pilgrims of the Indian Ocean, who did not. They lumped them all into the same religious category and justified their predation on religious terms. Once their ships were filled with exotic goods, including African slaves, pirates and privateers returned to North American ports where ready buyers purchased their ill-gotten gains with no questions asked.[20] They sold their goods at low prices, paid colonial leaders and merchants bribes, married into their families and often settled down to become prominent citizens.[21]

Madagascar became an important base for these pirates because it was usually bypassed by European vessels in favour of the Cape of Good Hope as a resupply station and it lay along important shipping lanes and directly south of the Red Sea and the vibrant sea-lanes that crisscrossed the Northern Indian Ocean. The voyage from New York to Madagascar took about eighteen months' round trip.[22] Pirates began to use the island after 1650, and it became the site of large pirate communities from 1690 to about 1720.[23] New York merchants sent provisions to the Madagascar settlements at St Augustine on the southwestern tip of the main island and on St Marie's island. Pirates traded with the local Malagasy people and engaged in the slave trade that sent Malagasy slaves to the North American plantations.[24] Though the pirate presence on St Marie's island depended on good relations with the locals, the pirates squandered it by abusing the natives and even enslaving the children of their own allies. In 1697, the Malagasy living on the Island of St Marie revolted and killed some thirty pirates.[25]

One of the most famous Red Sea pirates, Henry Every, captured two of the Mughal emperor's ships laden with gold and jewels in 1694. One ship, the *Gunj-i-Suwaee,* also carried the emperor's granddaughter, along with other Indian women. The prize netted the pirates about 35 million dollars in modern currency, and the women were raped over a period of three days. The emperor's granddaughter 'married' Every and lived with him on Madagascar. When the Mughal ship reached port at Surat, it caused an international scandal. People rioted against the East India Company, and the Mughal emperor embargoed all English ships and forced the company to sign a bond guaranteeing the safety of his ships. The EIC then petitioned the English parliament to help them restrain piracy in the Indian Ocean.[26] The English Privy Council put a £500 reward on Every's head, but he was never captured. Six of his men were captured and hanged in England in 1696.[27] After 1692, Red Sea pirates, including some of Every's men, began settling down in the North American colonies. In 1695, the British government ordered the governor of Massachusetts to 'suppress the pirates who infested the New England coast'.[28]

Changes like these in imperial policies in the 1690s set the stage for the rejection of the plunder economy in North America. Mark Hanna has argued that 'opening trade in Spanish bullion, African slaves, and East India luxury goods spurred the movement away from illicit markets; but accepting the need for locally regulated privateering was just as important'.[29] Suddenly pirates were no longer needed to provide either slaves or exotic goods. Once colonial politicians accepted that their political liberties would not be infringed by suppressing pirates, they began the transformation from pirate harbors to pirate hunters.

In 1696, after word of the rape of the *Gunj-i-Suwaee* reached England, Richard Coote, the earl of Bellmont and the first lord of the Admiralty Orford, and some friends decided to send a privateer on their own account to the Indian Ocean to hunt for pirates.[30] The problem with pirate hunting was that it was not as lucrative as privateering. Privateers kept their loot as legitimate prizes. Pirate hunters who seized pirate loot could still lose their prize if the original owner sued for its return. This became a problem for William the Kidd in 1696 when he received a commission to hunt down the famous pirates Thomas Tew, John Ireland, Thomas Wake and William Mayes. He signed his crew as 'no prey, no pay', which meant that unless they took a prize, the men could not hope for any income from the voyage.[31] Kidd and his crew found that finding pirates was more difficult than finding merchant vessels, and eventually Kidd and his crew seized several vessels, including the *Quedagh Merchant*. When he returned to New England, Kidd found that he was wanted for piracy, and the earl of Bellmont seized him and sent him to London, where he was hanged for piracy in 1701.[32]

Between 1695 and 1700, at least 1,500 English pirates sailed the waters of the Indian Ocean and visited Madagascar to rest, recuperate, resupply and repair their ships.[33] In 1697, at least forty-five pirates had settled on the Island of St Marie, where they participated in the slave trade and resupplied other pirate ships with the provisions sent to them from merchants in New York.[34] They also continued to attack Muslim shipping and even seized EIC ships. In 1697, the EIC asked the Privy Council to send a fleet to suppress the pirates who used Madagascar as a base. In 1698, the crown dispatched a squadron.[35] Despite these attempts to control pirates sailing from Madagascar, the island continued to be used, but with much less frequency as attitudes towards piracy changed in the North American colonies and the EIC actively defended its monopoly on trade with Asia.[36]

The Wars of the Spanish Succession (1701–1713) drew some of the Red Sea men back home to take up privateering against England's enemies. John Quelch received a commission from Governor Joseph Dudley of Massachusetts to take French and Spanish ships. He unwisely captured nine Portuguese ships off the coast of Brazil and returned triumphant to New England, where he and his crew were tried and executed for piracy in 1704. Quelch had acted beyond the bounds of his commission and had attacked England's ally during a time of war.[37]

Another burst of piracy occurred following the Treaty of Utrecht in 1713, which ended the Wars of the Spanish Succession. The end of the war brought an end to privateering licences and the dramatic drawdown of the English Navy from 49,860 to 13,475. The surplus labour supply contracted wages, increased competition for jobs and intensified the harshness of discipline on board ships, thus stimulating a new round of piracy.[38] By 1713 and the Peace of Utrecht, changes in the British Empire had made piracy less palatable to colonial gentry and more difficult for pirates. Merchants had ready access to markets, planters to slaves, and gentry to exotic goods at cheap prices and paper currency that solved the crisis of bullion of the 1690s. Privateering also became more formalized so that crews could keep their profits and rogue pirates were no longer necessary for defence. Illicit sea robbers had transformed from an economic and military safety net to become a real threat to established colonies.[39]

Some 4,500 to 5,500 Anglo-American pirates plied the waters of the Atlantic in the early eighteenth century. Most of them had worked as privateers or sailors in the merchant marine or the royal navy. A sailor's life was harsh and unpleasant. Marcus Rediker argues that 'disease and accidents were commonplace ... natural disasters threatened incessantly, rations were often meager, and discipline was brutal, even murderous on occasion'. Dr Samuel Johnson expressed this sentiment when he wrote, 'No man will be a sailor who has contrivance enough to get himself into a jail; for being in a ship is being in jail with the chance of being drowned .... A man in jail has more room, better food, and commonly better company.'[40]

By the 1720s, pirates who found themselves unwelcome in colonial ports also found it more difficult to recruit sailors to their crews. They began forcing sailors to join their crews in larger numbers by making sailors sign articles that gave the men a greater interest in the success of the crew, but it also incriminated them. Once a sailor had signed the articles, he could be tried as a pirate, even if he had acted against his will.[41] In some ways, the articles allowed seamen who turned to piracy to correct the worst abuses of the system by creating a rough egalitarianism that shifted much of the authority to the collective will of the crew. As we have already seen, the written articles drawn up by pirate crews 'allocated authority, distributed plunder, and enforced discipline'.[42]

Sailors resented the brutal abuse by naval captains and so restricted their authority and privileges aboard pirate vessels. Pirate captains only had real authority during an action against another ship, and they could be deposed for cowardice, brutality or failure to seize a prize when the opportunity presented itself. The quartermaster was elevated to a position of authority on pirate ships with the power to protect the interests of the crew, settle disputes, and distribute money and food supplies.[43] Pirates also resorted to graphic displays of violence to frighten victims into submission, to extract information about the location of wealth and plunder, for revenge and for simple sadistic pleasure.

Discussions of pirate violence are often taken out of context, however. Societies around the world in the seventeenth and eighteenth centuries used

FIGURE 10.2 *Sweating.*
Source: Photo by Culture Club/Getty Images.
Note: Illustration of the sweating of Portuguese captives on the ship of the British pirate
Francis Spriggs *c*. 1725.

torture as a form of public spectacle in a paternalistic display of power
intended to instruct onlookers in the futility of resistance and the consequences
of disobedience.[44] Europeans regularly used impaling, branding, blinding,
whipping, amputation, beheading, hanging, disemboweling, burning,
crushing, breaking on the rack, etc., as forms of punishment for even trivial
crimes. Children experienced severe physical punishment as a normal part
of home life. Discipline on board merchant and naval ships relied on the
liberal use of the whip.[45] A pirate captured by the authorities could hope
for nothing but death. In a macabre tit-for-tat, pirates returned the brutality
they experienced in kind.

Though walking the plank has become the most popular trope for pirate
brutality, there is no evidence that this practice was common. Pirates were
far more creative. Normal methods of torture on pirate ships included
keelhauling, in which the victim was dragged underneath the ship from side
to side. If they did not drown, their bodies were horribly lacerated from the
barnacles that clung to the bottom of the ships. Sweating and pickling was
another favourite, in which the victim was forced to run naked through a
gauntlet of the crew who stabbed him with sharp objects. His 'sweating'
body was then stuffed in a barrel filled with cockroaches and left to 'pickle'
in the hot tropical sun. Henry Morgan whipped and beat Spanish residents
of captured towns until they revealed the whereabouts of hidden treasure.
Victims could have burning fuses placed between their fingers and toes. They
could be hung by their thumbs, roasted over flames, stretched on a rack,

clubbed, castrated or otherwise mutilated. The practice of woolding used a rope tied around the head that was twisted with a stick to cause unbearable suffering that might even force the eyeballs to bulge from their sockets.[46]

Most pirate violence served the very practical purposes of maintaining discipline and gaining intelligence or access to booty. Sometimes it was religiously motivated in the heated religious climate of the time. Pirates also resorted to violence to seek revenge, and they sometimes justified it on rather shaky moral grounds. They argued that they had been sent to punish the Spanish for their brutality towards the native peoples.[47] Gratuitous, sadistic torture was done for humour. Blackbeard fired his pistol into the knee of his mate while at a game of cards. Edward Low 'sliced the ears from the captain's head and then supplying salt and pepper to improve the flavor, he gave his prisoner the order to eat them'. Rock Braziliano chopped off the 'arms and legs of bystanders' in a drunken fit.[48] The French buccaneer François l'Olonnais, after the capture of Puerto Cavallo, hacked his victims to pieces, 'licking the blood off his sword, eating the heart out of one disemboweled prisoner, and threatening to do the same to others. Daniel Montbars, the Exterminator, another Frenchman, opened the abdomen of a captive, took out a portion of the intestine, nailed it to a post, and then chased the prisoner with a firebrand, the intestines unraveling from his stomach as he ran and danced about frantically trying to avoid the flame'.[49] Pirates of the golden age often saved their most vicious attacks for the captains and shipmasters of the merchantmen who had been the authors of much of their suffering. In acts that might be called a type of social banditry, pirates rebelled against the larger shares officers received, their own low wages, poor food and harsh discipline.[50] The captains of pirated vessels were often tortured or simply executed unless their crew spoke up for them.[51]

Contrary to popular myth, pirates did not usually sail under the famous skull and crossbones. For most of history, pirates sailed under a bewildering array of flags and banners. The iconic Jolly Roger with its black background and skull and crossbones did not appear prior to the 1700s and was only popular for a short time. Pirates and privateers used a variety colours and images. Flags, or colours, as they were called, were flown to identify ships, but only when needed. The colours might also have various symbols sewn into them. Each state had their own colours. The Dutch flew a red, white and blue flag. The French flew a white flag. The Spanish flew a white flag with a red cross. The English flew a red flag with a red cross on a white background. Obviously, it was an easy matter to fly a false standard to deceive a potential enemy.[52] Privateers and men-of-war often used a plain red flag called the 'bloody flag', which indicated they would offer no quarter to their prey. Most pirates flew the colours of their home state because they were pretending to be legitimate privateers or merchantmen. After the end of the Wars of the Spanish Succession in 1713, however, pirates began to fly the black flag often called the Jolly Roger.[53] The term Roger referred to the devil. Marcus Rediker shows that the images of skulls, hourglasses, bleeding hearts and skeletons served as 'interlocking symbols [of] death, violence, and limited time' in which pirates expressed their sense of being both predator and prey.[54] The Jolly Roger symbolized both death and rebirth. The pirates declared that having abandoned the law they were now dead to the law and sailed under the standard of King Death. But it also symbolized that they had been reborn as freemen loyal only to their brethren under the Jolly Roger.[55]

This sense of existing outside of law and society increased in the early eighteenth century. By 1707, the pirates of this golden age found themselves increasingly rejected by the societies that had once accepted and supported them. Those communities, in turn, found themselves the targets of piratical raids. By the 1720s, Atlantic pirates had become genuine outlaws often bent on retribution. 'Captains Blackbeard, Edwards, Gow, Bonnet, and Phillips all named their vessels the *Revenge*. Low, Spriggs, and Blackbeard swore vengeance against New Englanders for hanging pirates. Captain Rackham vowed, "Destruction to all those who belong to" New Providence.'[56] Edward Low began his career in the Caribbean in the early 1720s, but soon found that the world had changed. Twenty-six of his former crewmen were executed in Rhode Island in 1723. Low then cruised along the New England coast, seizing dozens of vessels and resorting to increasingly violent behaviour even against his own crew.[57] These pirates often tried to work the old system. Blackbeard (Edward Teach) went to the trouble of acquiring signed letters of support from prominent New Yorkers. Jack Rackham kept searching for a royal pardon. Both men were disappointed. Blackbeard died in the assault on his vessel in November of 1718 and Rackham was tried and hanged in 1720.[58]

Sea banditry served a vital role in the expansion of the English Empire and the economic and military viability of the North American colonies. Pirate nests supplied and protected pirates in return for scarce commodities, labour, specie and military protection. The 1690s represented both a high point in North American piracy and a shift away from a reliance on the plunder economy. By the 1720s, pirates found it more difficult to operate. As the pirate nests withdrew their support, pirate ships struggled to recruit men who knew they would not be able to return home to enjoy their ill-gotten gains. Consequently, the old notion of the free-floating, independent pirate democracies who were the enemies of all nations can no longer be accepted. Without the land/sea connection, pirate communities could not survive. This withdrawal of support from port societies proved far more important for the eventual collapse of the golden age of North American piracy than naval patrols or the royal courts.[59]

Even as piracy declined, legitimate sea raiding remained popular throughout the colonies. Both the War of Jenkins' Ear (1739–1748) and King George's War (1744–1748) provided ample opportunities for privateering licences. This new generation of privateers 'played *the* leading role in America's war effort and made a major contribution to British sea power by disrupting Spanish and French commerce'.[60] The lessons of the

1690s, however, were forgotten after the Seven Years War (1754–1763). The crown re-imposed customs restrictions, impressed sailors, created monopolies and challenged charters.[61] Riots and rebellion ensued along with the rise of a new brand of patriotic privateer. George Washington and the Continental Congress understood that their tiny navy could do nothing against the British in 1775, so they invited private citizens to attack British shipping. Over 2,500 privateers received commission from the Continental Congress who went on to seize 2,300 British ships.[62] Motivated by greed and patriotism, these privateers swarmed colonial waters to ravage British ships in close hand-to-hand combat. Privateering once again stimulated the economy by supporting maritime industries like shipbuilding, employing sailors and allowing investment in privateering vessels.[63] The patriotic privateers of the Wars of Independence may not have won the war, but they were a continual annoyance to the British, and they showed, once again, that seaborne banditry would play an important role in the creation of nation states. The war of 1812 brought a new batch of privateering commissions for American and Canadian seamen. Between 1812 and 1815, 41 Canadian seamen from Nova Scotia, New Brunswick, and 500 Americans petitioned to receive commissions to attack one another's shipping.[64]

Despite this outbreak of privateering, the seeds for dissolution of widespread privateering had already been sown. By the late eighteenth century, seamen serving on privateering vessels began to receive wages rather than a share of the prizes. The business of privateering could no longer offer the quick financial rewards it had once done.[65] Poorly enforced and observed laws, insurance companies' protection of merchants from the costs of piracy, local resistance to government crackdowns on what they saw as illegitimate commerce and the benefits accrued to local merchants and politicians all allowed piracy to flourish in the Atlantic and the Indian Oceans during the golden age of piracy and beyond. Guy Chet has argued:

> The result of this widespread embrace and support for commerce raiding and of the expansive market for pirated goods was a consistent increase in the scope of commerce raiding in the Atlantic from the mid-eighteenth century to the early decades of the nineteenth century. As wartime economies created profitable conditions for freebooting, so freebooting stimulated local economies on both sides of the Atlantic.[66]

This process created a repetitive system in which the state authorized legal piracy during a war. After the war, unemployed seamen who had worked on the privateering vessels simply carried on what they had done during the war. The state declared them outlaws and half-heartedly tried to suppress them. They simply went somewhere else until another outbreak of war and the state called them back to work as privateers. In the Atlantic world, 'privateering reflected state ruler's efforts to build state power; piracy reflected some people's efforts to resist that project'.[67] The north Atlantic piracy of this age of chaos managed to be simultaneously parasitic, episodic and intrinsic. Its practitioners, however, were seldom the romantic social bandits of our imaginations.

As you read the documents that follow, consider the following questions:

1　How does the Portuguese commission to Charles Bill justify giving him a licence to raid?

2　What does Robert's treatment of his captives reveal about his motives?

3　What does the English treatment of the African captain reveal about race relations in the eighteenth-century Atlantic and about privateer attitudes towards race?

4　Why does Peter Vezian criticize the Captain Benjamin Brown of the *Revenge*?

5　What does Peter Vezian's journal reveal about the dangers and challenges of privateering?

6　What do Peter's journal and Snelgrave's account reveal about pirate/ privateering boarding tactics?

7　Why did the pirates initially seek to kill Captain Snelgrave, and why did his men defend him?

8　What did Captain Davis give as his excuse for going pirating?

9　How does the reality of piracy during the 'Golden Age' challenge modern romantic conceptions of pirates as social bandits?

10　How did the chaos of this period reveal the hypocrisy of European use of, and support for, seaborne bandits?

11　How did the support of local communities foster piracy in the British North American colonies?

12　Why were pirates so central to the formation of state institutions and the assertions of governmental authority in the British world?

John Franklin Jameson, ed., *Privateering and Piracy in the Colonial Period: Illustrative Documents* (New York: The Macmillan Company, 1923), 27–28, 313–316, 401–403.

Portuguese Commission (Letter of Marque) to Charles de Bils. For the Blue Dove. 10 February 1658.

Alfonso, by the grace of God King of Portugal and of the Algarves [on both sides] of the seas in Africa, Lord of Guiney and of the Conquest, navigation, and Commerce of Ethiopia, Arabia, Persia, and of India, Know all to whom this my letter patent shall appear that it behooving me to provide ships to oppose sea rovers that frequent the coasts of these my kingdoms, for the convenience of trading to them. And considering the merits and Parts that do concur in the person of Charles de Bils, confiding in him that in all that I shall impose to his trust he will serve me to my content, it is my will and pleasure to nominate and by these presents do name for Captain of a ship of war, by virtue of which power he may provide at his own charge a ship of one hundred tons with what boats necessary, and provide her with guns, people, ammunition and the provisions as he shall think convenient, to wage war with the subjects of the King of Spain, Turks, pirates, sea rovers, take their ships and their merchandise and all that belongs unto them and carry them to any port of this kingdom to give an account of them in my office, where they shall be taken account of in a book kept for said purpose, where they shall be judged if lawful prizes. He may visit or search what ships he thinks go laden with our enemies' goods, go to their ports, favoring in all things any allied to this Crown, paying the customs of said prizes, according to the rates of the custom houses of this kingdom ....

Sealed with the arms of Portugal

THE KING

Bartholomew Roberts, a Welshman, ravaged the Atlantic from Newfoundland to Cuba and over to the Canaries between 1718 and 1722. He is supposed to have captured over 400 ships in four years. His crew was tried at Cape Corso Castle in Africa on April 1722. Fifty-two of them were executed.

Extract from the Boston News Letter, August 22, 1720; Bartholomew Roberts

Boston, on Monday last, the 15th current, arrived here the ship *Samuel*, about eleven weeks from London, and ten from land's end, Captain Samuel Carry commander, who in his voyage hither, on the 13th of July past, in the Latitude of 44, about 30 or 40 leagues to the eastward of the banks of Newfoundland, was accosted and taken by two pirates, viz. A ship of 26 guns and a sloop of ten both commanded by Captain Bartholomew Roberts, having on board about a hundred men, all English; The dismal account whereof follows:

The first thing the pirates did, was to strip both passengers and seamen of all their money and clothes which they had on board, with a loaded pistol held to everyone's breast ready to sho[o]t him down, who did not immediately give an account of both and resign them up. The next thing they did was, with madness and rage to tear up the hatches, enter the hold like a parcel of furies, where with axes, cutlasses, etc., they cut, tore and broke open trunks, boxes, cases and bales, and when any of the goods came upon deck which they did not like to carry with them aboard their ship, instead of tossing them into the hold again they threw them over-board into the sea. The usual method they had to open chests was by shooting a brace of bullets with a pistol into the key-hole to force them open. The pirates carried away from Captain Carry's ship aboard their own 40 barrels of powder, two great guns, his cables, etc. and to the value of about nine or ten thousand pounds sterling worth of the choicest goods he had on board.

There was nothing heard among the pirates all the while, but cursing, swearing, damning and blaspheming to the greatest degree imaginable, and often saying they would not go to Hope point in the River of Thames to be hung up in gibbets a sun drying as Kidd and Bradish's company did, for if it would change that they should be attacked by any superior power or force, which they could not master, they would immediately put fire with one of their pistols to their powder, and go all merrily to Hell together! They often ridiculed and made a mock of King George's Acts of Grace with an oath that they had not got money enough, but when they had, if he then did grant them one, after they sent him word, they would thank him for it. They forced and took away with them Captain Carry's mate, and his seamen, … holding a pistol with a brace of bullets to each of their breasts to go with them, or be presently shot down, telling them that at present they wanted none of their service; but when they came to any action, they should have liberty to fight and defend the ship as they did, or else immediately be shot, that they should not tell tales. They had on board the pirate near 20 tons of brandy. However, the pirates made themselves very merry aboard of Captain Carry's ship with some hampers of fine wines that were either presents, or sent to some gentlemen in Boston it seems they would not wait to untie them and pull out the corks with screws, but each man took his bottle and with his cutlass cut of the neck and put it to their mouths and drank it out. Whilst the pirates were disputing whether to sink or burn Captain Carry's ship they spied a sail that same evening, and so let him go free.

Captain Benjamin Norton received a commission as a privateer against Spanish shipping for twelve months, on 2 June 1741, at Providence, Rhode Island, from Richard Ward, governor and commander in chief of the colony. Norton had joined forces with the merchant John Freebody to equip the ship Revenge. *For Norton and Freebody, this was simply a business adventure. We know about the voyage because Peter Vezian, the captain's quartermaster, kept a journal.*

'Journal of the Sloop *Revenge*,' written by Peter Vezian Captain's quartermaster June 5–Oct. 5, 1741.

Wednesday 29th About 4 pm saw a sloop. Gave chase but the weather being calm was forced to get out our oars. Fired our bow chase to bring her too, but we tacking about and the people in confusion, night coming on, it being very foggy, could not speak to her. By her course, she was bound to Northward. Lost sight of our prize. The two Englishman that were taken prisoners by the Spanish privateer signed our articles, their names John Evergin and Samuel Elderidge.

Thursday 30th Nothing remarkable these 24 hours. At 5 AM saw a sloop standing to the northward and another astern of us. Bore down the latter and made our signal agreed on. Found her to our prize. Opened a BB of beef and one tierce of bread. The two men that had signed the day before had arms given them.

Saturday August 1st The prize still alongside of us. Ordered the master to send us 2 hogs for the sloop's use. Also the negro prisoner, having been informed that he was Captain of the Company of Indians, Mulatoes, and Negroes that was at the retaking of the fort at St. Augustine formerly taken under the command of that worthless G – O – pe who by his treachery suffered so many brave fellows to be mangled by those barbarians. The Negro went under the name of Signor Capitano Francisco. Sent one of the mulatoes in his room on board the prize. Gave the people a pale of punch.

Sunday 2d At 1 PM we examined the Negro who frankly owned that he was captain of the company as aforesaid and that his commission was on board the privateer, that he went privateering in hopes of getting to Havana and that there he might get passage for to go to old Spain to get the reward of his brave actions. We then asked him if it was his company that had used the English so barbarously when taken at the Fort. He denied that it was his company but laid that cruel action to the Florida Indians and nothing more could we get out of him. We then tied him to a gun and made the doctor come with instruments seemingly to castrate him as they had served the English, thinking by that means to get some confession out of him, but he still denied it. We then tied a mulato one that [he] was taking with him to know if he knew anything about the matter. We gave him a dozen stripes and he declared that he knew nothing more than his being captain of a company at the time but that the other fellow on board the sloop knew all about it. We sent to him and he declared the whole truth that it was the Florida Indians that had committed the fact under his command but knew not if he was consenting to it. However, to make sure and to make him remember that he bore such a commission we gave him 200 lashes and then pickled him and left him to the doctor to take care of his sore ass. Opened a tierce of bread and killed the two hogs.

Thursday 6th Still in Chase of the 5 vessels. Our spritsail, topsail and square sail with a fine breeze of wind. About 11 AM one of Ships brought too and fired a gun to wait for a sloop that was in company with her, and to wait for us. We took in all our small sails and bore down to her and hoisted our pennant. When alongside of her, she fired 6 shot at us but did us no damage, we still hedging upon her and gave her our broadside and then stood off. The sloop tacked immediately and bore down upon us in hopes to get us between the ships, as we suppose, to pepper us at the sight of which we gave them three cheers. Our people all agreed in general to fight them and told the captain if he'd venture his sloop they'd venture their lives, but the captain seemed unwilling and gave for reason that the prizes of which he was in possession of would be of little profit if taken by us for we could only come in for a share which would be allowed us by the court. And that perhaps would not make good a limb if it was lost, also that we had not hands sufficient to man them, and to bring those vessels to Providence.

No one was able to buy any part of them and to carry them to the northward would be the breaking up of the voyage without profit. Nevertheless, we let the sloop come alongside us and received her shot. We gave her a broadside and a volley of small arms with three huzas, then bore down to the ship, who all this time had been pelting us with her shot but to no purpose, and gave her another broadside which did her some damage, for she bore down to the sloop and never fired one more shoot, but got her on the careen and men over the side to stop her holes, also several hands at her rigging to man it, her sails being full of shot holes, as also those of the sloop. All the damage we got was one shot through our main sail. The ship mounted six guns of a side and the sloop eight. She was a Spanish privateer that had been cruising to the northward and had taken five ships and that sloop which we took some time before. It grieved us to think that that fellow should go off with those prizes which he would not have done had the captain been as willing as we."

Thursday 13th. Landed all our corn and made a clear hole of the prize. At 9 PM it began to thunder and lightning very hard. Our sloop received great damage by a thunder bolt that struck our mast and shivered it very much, tore a large piece off the hounds and as it fell tore up the bits and broke in the hatchway, burst through both our sides, and stared the planks under gunwale, melting several cutlasses pistols and fired off several small arms, the bullets of which stuck in her beam. It was some time before we perceived that she leaked being all thunder struck, the master stepping over the side to examine her put his foot on a plank that was started on the larboard side, and all this time the water was pouring in. We immediately brought all our guns on the starboard side to give her a heel and sent the boat ashore for our doctor, a man being hurt by the lightening, William Jackson. When we got her on a heel we tried the pumps, not being able to do it before, for our careful carpenter had never a pump-box rigged nor fit to work so had it not been for the kind assistance of the man of war's people, who hearing of our misfortune ashore come immediately off and put our guns onboard the prize, we must certainly have sunk."

Saturday 26th. About 5 PM. Thought we saw a vessel at anchor under land. Lay off and on until 5 AM then saw two sails a brigantine and a sloop. Gave them chase, the sloop laying to for us and the brigantine making the best of her way to leeward. We presently came up with the sloop and when in gunshot hoisted our pennant. The compliment was returned with a Spanish ensign at mast head and a gun to confirm it. We then went along side of him and received a broadside, which we cheerfully returned with another. We then tacked, she dropping astern, and bore away before the wind crowding all the sail she could and we doing the like. Came again within gunshot. In the time of chase, we shifted out bow guns to our fore ports and they had done the like with their after guns to their cabin windows, pelting us with their stern chase and we peppering of them with our fore guns. So that after several brisk firing they at last struck. We ordered his canoe on board, which was directly manned. The captain came on board and delivered his commission and sword to our captain and surrendered himself a prisoner of war. He was desperately wounded in the arm and several small shot in his head and body. Three more of his hands was wounded and one negro boy killed. This vessel was fitted out in November last from Havana and had been on our coast early in the spring and had taken several vessels and brought them to Havana and was again fitted out last August and had met with good success on the coast of Virginia … She mounted six guns and twelve swivels and thirty-eight hands, two of which were Englishmen that had been made prisoners and entered in their service … The damage we received was not much. Only one man slightly wounded in the engagement by a splinter, John Taylor, two more by an accident, a piece going off after the fight and shot them both in the arm. We received upwards of twenty shot in our sails, two through our mast and one through our gunnel port and all this day the *Revenge* established her honor having almost lost it by letting the other privateer go off with them four ships as is mentioned before.

William Snelgrave, *A New Account of Some Parts of Guinea and the Slave Trade* (London: James, John, and Paul Knapton, 1734), 193–288.

William Snelgrave was an English slave trader and ivory merchant who was captured in March 1719, by pirates, while at anchor in the mouth of the Sierra Leon River. Just prior to his arrival, three pirate ships had seized ten English ships in the river.

About eight o'clock the officer of the watch upon deck sent me word, 'He heard the rowing of a boat.' Whereupon we all immediately went upon deck; and the night being very dark, I ordered lanterns and candles to be got ready … I ordered also, by way of precaution, the first mate to go into the steerage, to put all things in order, and to send me forthwith twenty men on the quarter-deck with fire arms and cutlasses, which I thought he went about … I ordered the boat to be hailed again; to which the people in it answered, 'they were from America:' And at the same time fired a volley of small shot at the ship, though they were then above pistol shot from us ….

When they first began to fire, I called aloud to the first mate, to fire at the boat out of the steerage port holes, which not being done, and the people I had ordered upon deck with small arms not appearing, I was extremely surprised ... I went thereupon down into the steerage, where I saw a great many of them looking at one another ... I asked them with some roughness, 'Why they had not obeyed my orders?' ... some of them replied, 'They would have taken arms, but the chest they were kept in could not be found' ... By this time the boat was along the ship's side, and there being nobody to oppose them, the pirates immediately boarded us; and coming on the quarter-deck, fired their pieces several times down into the steerage, and shot a sailor in the kidneys, of which wound he died afterwards. They likewise threw several grenade shells, which burst amongst us, so that 'tis a great wonder several of us were not killed by them, or by their shot.

At last some of our people bethought themselves to call for quarter; which the pirates granting, the quartermaster came down into the steerage, enquiring, 'Where the Captain was?' I told him, 'I had been so till now.' Upon that he asked me, 'How I durst order my people to fire at their boat out of the steerage? Saying that they had heard me repeat it several times.' I answered, 'I thought it my duty to defend the ship, if my people would have fought.' Upon that he presented a pistol to my breast, which I had but just time to parry before it went off; so that the bullet passed between my side and arm. The rogue finding he had not shot me, he turned the but-end of the pistol, and gave me such a blow on the head as stunned me; so that I fell upon my knees; but immediately recovering myself, I forthwith jumped out of the steerage upon the quarterdeck, where the pirate boatswain was.

... This cruel monster was asking some of my people, 'Where their captain was,' so at my coming upon deck, one of them, pointing to me, said, 'There he is. ' ... Whereupon lifting up his broad sword, he swore, 'No quarter should be given to any captain that offered to defend his ship,' aiming at the same time a full stroke at my head. To avoid it, I stooped so low, that the quarterdeck rail received the blow; and was cut in at least an inch deep; which happily saved my head from being cleft asunder; And the sword breaking at the same time, with the force of the blow on the rail, it prevented his cutting me to pieces.

By good fortune, his pistols, that hung at his girdle, were all discharged, otherwise he would doubtless have shot me. But he took one of them, and with the but-end endeavored to beat out my brains, which some of my people that were then on the quarterdeck observed, cried out loud, 'For God's sake don't kill our captain, for we never were with a better man.' This turned the rage of him and two other pirates on my people, and saved my life. But they cruelly used my poor men, cutting and beating them unmercifully. One of them had his chin almost cut off, and another received such a wound on his head, that he fell on the deck as dead; but afterwards, by the care of our surgeon he recovered. All of this happened in a few minutes, and the quartermaster then coming up, ordered the pirates to tie our people's hands ....

[*Snelgrave was taken aboard the pirate ship to Captain Cocklyn.*] Their commander saluted me in this manner 'I am sorry you have met with bad usage after quarter given, but 'tis the fortune of war sometimes. I expect you will answer truly to all such questions as I shall ask you; otherwise you shall be cut to pieces; but if you tell the truth, and your men make no complaints against you, you shall be kindly used ... '[Captain Davis came to him and said,] He was ashamed to hear how I had been used by them. That they should remember, their reasons for going a pirating were to revenge themselves on base merchants, and cruel commanders of ships ... That as for my part no one of my people, even those that had entered with them, gave me the least ill character, but by their respect since shown me, it was plain they loved me.

Notes

1   Thomson, *Mercenaries*, 43.
2   Thomson, *Mercenaries*, 43.
3   Hanna, *Pirate Nests*, 2.
4   Starkey and McCarthy, 'A Persistent Phenomenon', 131–151.
5   Hanna, *Pirate Nests*, 91.
6   Senior, *A Nation of Pirates*, 62–63.
7   Senior, *A Nation of Pirates*, 53–57.
8   Burgess, *The Pirates' Pact*, 13–14, 21–22.
9   Hanna, *Pirate Nests*, 96.
10 McCusker and Menard, *The Economy of British America*, 46–49.
11 McCallum, 'Money and Prices', 145; Davisson, 'Essex County Price Trends', 146–148.
12 Newell, *From Dependency to Independence*, 78–80; Newell, 'The Birth of New England', 15–16.
13 Hanna, *Pirate Nests*, 145–158.
14 Hanna, *Pirate Nests*, 167.
15 Hanna, *Pirate Nests*, 174.
16 Burgess, *The Pirates' Pact*, 116–117.
17 Gosse, *The History of Piracy*, 177–178.
18 Senior, *A Nation of Pirates*, 39–41.
19 McDonald, *Pirates, Merchants, Settlers, and Slaves*, 1–6.
20 Hanna, *Pirate Nests*, 185–189.
21 Hanna, *Pirate Nests*, 194–198, 204–209.

22 Bialuschewski, 'Pirates, Slavers, and the Indigenous Population', 404.

23 McDonald, *Pirates, Merchants, Settlers, and Slaves*, 37–60; Hooper, 'Pirates and Kings', 226.

24 Platt, 'The East India Company', 548–577.

25 McDonald, *Pirates, Merchants, Settlers and Slaves*, 82–87.

26 Nutting, 'The Madagascar Connection', 206.

27 Hanna, *Pirate Nests*, 189–192, 242.

28 Gosse, *The History of Piracy*, 181; Burgess, 'Piracy in the Public Sphere', 887–913; Burgess, *The Pirates' Pact*, 129–147.

29 Hanna, *Pirate Nests*, 420.

30 Nutting, 'The Madagascar Connection', 208.

31 Ritchie, *Captain Kid*, 54–55; Hanna, *Pirate Nests*, 231.

32 Ritchie, *Captain Kid*, 206–227.

33 Bialuschewski, 'Pirates, Slavers, and the Indigenous Population of Madagascar', 408.

34 McDonald, *Pirates, Merchants, Settlers, and Slaves*, 37–60; Hooper, 'Pirates and Kings', 223.

35 Nutting, 'The Madagascar Connection', 208–209.

36 McDonald, *Pirates, Merchants, Settlers, and Slaves*, 61–80.

37 Hanna, *Pirate Nests*, 330–364; Beal, *Quelch's Gold*.

38 Rediker, 'The Seaman as Pirate', 153.

39 Hanna, *Pirate Nests*, 366.

40 Rediker, *Between the Devil*, 258.

41 Hanna, *Pirate Nests*, 385.

42 Rediker, *Between the Devil*, 261–262.

43 Rediker, *Between the Devil*, 261–263.

44 Foucault, *Discipline and Punish*, 101–140.

45 Rediker, *Between the Devil*, 215–223; Burg, 'The Buccaneer Community', 227–233.

46 Cordingly, *Under the Black Flag*, 127–140; Burg, 'The Buccaneer Community', 229–231.

47 Hanna, *Pirate Nests*, 159–161.

48 Both quotes are from Burg, 'The Buccaneer Community', 225.

49 Both quotes are from Burg, 'The Buccaneer Community', 228–229.

50 Bromley, 'Outlaws at Sea, 1660–1720', 171–174.

51 Rediker, *Between the Devil*, 269–273.

52 Little, *The Sea Rover's Practice*, 111–115.

53 Little, *The Sea Rover's Practice*, 114.

54 Rediker, 'The Seaman as Pirate', 151–152.

55 Kinkor, 'Black Men under the Black Flag', 197.

56 Hanna, *Pirate Nests*, 408.

57 Hanna, *Pirate Nests*, 365–366, 373–374.

58 Burgess, *The Pirates' Pact*, 1–11; Konstam, *Piracy*, 162–166.

59 Hanna, *Pirate Nests*, 416–421.

60 Swanson, 'American Privateering and Imperial Warfare', 359.

61 Hanna, *Pirate Nests*, 421.

62 Elleman, 'Introduction', 8.

63 Patton, *Patriot Pirates*, xvi–xvii.

64 Kert, 'Cruising Colonial Waters', 145.

65 Starkey, 'A Restless Spirit", 139.

66 Chet, *The Ocean Is a Wilderness*, 44.

67 Thomson, *Mercenaries*, 54.

CHAPTER ELEVEN

Maritime Marginals: Piracy in Late Imperial China

After the successful 1683 Qing assault on the Zheng family pirate stronghold on Taiwan and the removal of the sea bans in 1684, piracy in the waters of the South China Sea settled down to the petty raiding that had characterized the region for centuries. This relatively stable period of small-time sea bandits who raided from Vietnam to Korea endured until the end of the eighteenth century.[1] Chinese pirates enjoyed thousands of miles of fragmented coastline, offshore islands, dense populations, vibrant trade routes near at hand and vast river deltas, such as the 3,500-square-mile Pearl River Delta with its 1,500 miles of channels and 3,000 miles of canals and waterways.[2] By the late seventeenth century, traders from around the world flocked to Chinese ports. Malaysians, Persians, Arabs, Siamese, Filipinos, Indians, Vietnamese, Portuguese, Dutch, British, Swedish, French, Germans and Americans all struggled for a piece of the Chinese trade.[3]

Piracy remained small scale and sporadic until the end of the eighteenth century, carried out primarily by fishermen as a form of seasonal activity, like smuggling, that supplemented their meagre incomes.[4] These pirates/fishermen were opportunists in that they robbed vessels that happened by them while they were fishing. They might also sail north during the summer when fishing stocks dwindled to raid along the coast only to return home in the fall to continue fishing. Fishing was always a risky endeavour, as incomes vacillated with the markets, and injury and death at sea were common. Fishermen needed cash to purchase supplies and gear and so depended on loans and credit to stay afloat – which also meant they were often deeply indebted.[5]

In the last two decades of the eighteenth century, the status quo shifted. The Qing dynasty suffered a period of sustained instability. Four major rebellions rocked China. Vietnam experienced the prolonged Tâyson

Rebellion (1771–1802). Between 1790 and 1810, China was ravaged by twenty-nine famines and many typhoons.[6] The population of the Pearl River Delta between 1723 and 1820 rose from 1.3 million to 5.3 million.[7] The cost of rice soared, and wages fell. The instability and the preoccupation of the government officials with these crises gave space for petty pirate gangs to coalesce into larger, more menacing organizations. Pirates also found ready patrons willing to employ their skills in return for safe harbours, supplies, weapons, ranks and titles.[8]

The city of Jiangping on the border of Vietnam and China became a haven for fishermen who engaged in smuggling and piracy. It was far from the power centres of either country, inaccessible by land, close to vibrant sea-lanes and within striking distance of the south China coast. Jiangping and other Vietnamese coastal cities, such as Doan Mien and Hue and the port city of Hanoi, became pirate nests whose economies depended on pirate commerce.[9] Other pirate nests emerged near major Chinese commercial

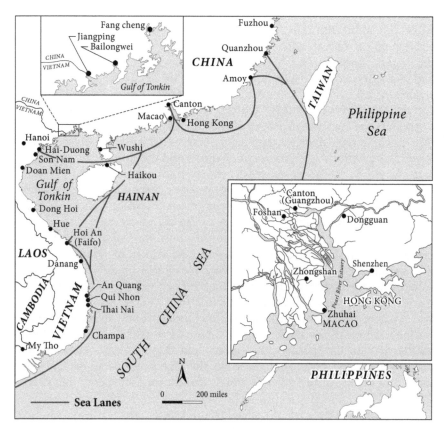

FIGURE 11.1 *Nineteenth-century Chinese piracy.*
Source: Map produced by Barry Levely, Cartographer.

and political centres in Guangdong and Fujian provinces. By the end of the eighteenth century, a shadowy network of pirate lairs and officially sanctioned and unsanctioned ports had developed with the active participation of smugglers, local officials, merchants, soldiers and pirate gangs.[10]

The spark that turned these petty pirate gangs into the most formidable pirate fleets the world has ever seen was the Tâyson Rebellion in Vietnam. The country was ruled by an emperor, but the real power lay in two families – the Trinh in the north and the Nguyen in the south. Three brothers from the Nguyen family who lived in a village called Tâyson rebelled against their lord in 1771.[11] The Tâyson recruited Chinese pirates to fill the ranks of their navy and to raid the Chinese coasts of Guangdong and Fujien for much-needed supplies. Small-time pirates/fishermen and professional pirates alike discovered that the Tâyson would provide them with ships, weapons, military ranks, titles and safe havens in return for their services. The Tâyson legitimized the pirates' activities by granting them seals, permits, certificates and passes that effectively turned them into privateers with licence to raid and plunder.[12] The Tâyson patronage and the support of pirate bosses helped systematize the pirate ranks. Pirate gangs grew in size. They became more disciplined and hierarchical. They gained prestige as 'sailors in a King's navy' rather than simply being seen as sea scum. And they gained valuable fighting and tactical experience that allowed them to openly confront fully equipped Chinese squadrons.[13]

Chinese pirates sailed from their bases in northern Vietnam with the southeast monsoon to raid along the south China coast for foodstuffs, supplies and new pirate recruits. They targeted Western merchantmen and Chinese junks in the hopes of valuable prizes, but more commonly plundered fishing vessels and smaller coastal trading ships. These pirates fought in most of the major naval engagements of the Tâyson war and proved vital in provisioning and supporting the Tâyson rebels. The rebels managed to establish a new regime that was recognized by the Chinese emperor in 1788. It survived for fourteen years largely because of the crucial support of the Chinese pirates. The Tâyson were finally defeated by combined Vietnamese and French forces in 1802.[14]

Several large pirate coalitions emerged from the Tâyson Rebellion as pirates fled to China once they lost their patrons in Vietnam. Pirates struggled with each other for three bloody years until seven pirate leaders signed a pact in 1805 to regulate their activities around the Guangdong province. They continued to raid villages and shipping, both local and foreign, to engage in bribery and extortion, and to sell protection to villages and ships.[15] Unlike legitimate merchants and smugglers, however, pirates dealt in stolen loot, which they usually sold it on the open market. Piracy was business and pirates actively sought to diversify their business activities.[16]

One of the signers of the 1805 pact was Zheng Yi. He was a descendant of the powerful Zheng family of pirates that had been defeated in 1683. His family had taken up residence in Guangdong, and he and his cousin,

Zheng Qi, had joined the Tâyson rebels and become powerful pirate leaders. When Zheng Qi died in 1802, Zheng Yi took command and created a gang of pirates that numbered over 10,000 strong by 1804. Zheng Yi used his Guangdong connections to secure anchorages at the entrance to the Pearl River Delta, including the island of Lantau.[17] By 1807, when he died, Zheng Yi had manoeuvred to become the most powerful leader of the Guangdong pirate confederation.[18]

When Zheng Yi died at the young age of forty-two, his wife Shi Xianguu, otherwise known as Zheng Yi Sao (wife of Zheng Yi), manoeuvred to seize control of the confederation.[19] Within weeks of Zheng Yi's death, Zheng Yi Sao selected her stepson, Zhang Bao, to be her second-in-command and her sexual partner. Zhang Bao was a fisherman who had been captured by Zheng Yi, initiated into the pirate's world through a homosexual relationship with Zheng Yi, and adopted by Zheng Yi as his son and protégé.[20] Zheng Yi Sao and Zhang Bao imposed a code of conduct that regulated the division of booty, prohibited the raping of women, though this was seldom enforced, and provided for the provisioning of ships that were unsuccessful in their raids.[21] These articles demonstrate that the primary motive of the Chinese pirates was personal advancement and financial gain.[22] It also demonstrates that because this shadow economy existed outside the control of the state, pirates had to self-regulate. They relied on codes of conduct and personal relationships, often by marriage or by creating fictive kin ties, such as Zheng Yi did by adopting Zhang Bao.[23] By 1807, the Guangdong confederation had become self-sustaining with 2,000 junks and 50,000–70,000 pirates divided into six fleets with their own coloured banners (Red, Black, Blue, Yellow, White and Green). Zheng Yi Sao and Zhang Bao commanded the Red Banner, which was the largest fleet with more than 20,000 pirates and 300 ships.[24]

The pirates who manned these fleets mostly came from the impoverished and marginalized maritime classes who occupied low-prestige positions in Confucian society.[25] They could be recruited by offers of money, boats, women or leadership positions, or they could be abducted and forced to join. During the horrible famines, desperate parents could sell their sons to the pirates.[26] Pirate ships usually contained a large number of captives who could outnumber the actual pirate crews. Captives played a crucial role in the success of the pirate confederations as sources of recruits, labour and income. Captives could be tortured or sexually abused into joining the pirate crews. But most captives served the pirates as free labour and lookouts. Captives did the unpleasant work on the pirate ships, such as cleaning, cooking and helping unload pirate prizes, which made them accomplices and punishable under Chinese law. Captive men, women and boys were also kept to serve the sexual needs of the crew.[27]

Despite having coalesced into large fleets, pirates usually attacked in small groups or as single vessels. Pirates preferred to attack easy stationary targets, close to shore and at night using small craft with oars. Large trading junks proved to be challenging targets because they were more difficult to board, carried cannon and used 'layers of ox hides and fishing nets to deflect cannon shot'.[28] To the pirates, however, they were the most desirable. The junks carried valuable cargoes of rice, silver, dried fish, wine, betel nuts, oil, porcelain, tea, sugar, birds' nests and other trade items.[29] As with bandits the world over, Chinese pirates preferred to attack from ambush. They would conceal their vessels behind islands and hire fishermen to scout for them. Robert Antony described their tactics this way:

> When attacking another vessel, the pirates would run their boats alongside the victim's ship, fire a volley of cannon or musket shot, then shower the ship with 'a great quantity of stink-pots' to set the sails on fire. Once the victim's ship was disabled, the pirates would jump aboard with their knives and spears to take command.[30]

After the prize was secured and reported to the confederation, ships, cargoes and captives could be held for ransom. The ransoms would be set according the perceived value of the cargo or of the captive's ability to pay. If ransoms were not paid, the victims would simply be executed. Even when ransoms were paid, the pirates might choose to keep their captives and take the men and the ship sent to deliver the ransom.[31]

The pirates of Guangdong also sold safe conduct passes, controlled the salt and opium trades through the use of passports, and imposed tribute payments on villages and markets. Robert Antony argues that 'through systematic use of extortion, bribery, and terror, the pirates gained a firm hold over coastal villages, towns and markets as well as over fishing and shipping enterprise. In fact, they constituted a level of control over south China's maritime society that operated independent of that exercised by officials and local elites'.[32] By diversifying their income in this way, pirates ensured predictable profits year round.

A key tool in the pirates' playbook was dramatic displays of violence. Just as in Europe, Chinese pirates followed the example of the state in the deliberate use of terror and violence to intimidate and to display their power and authority. Sexual violence and rape against men and women was normal, despite the pirate codes against it. Pirates used violence to intimidate crews, to get revenge against those who dared to fight back and to coerce men to join their crews. Their most common form of torture was to string their victims up by their hands, strip them and beat them with canes. They saved their most vicious attacks for the crews of naval ships. These men were dismembered, disemboweled and some even had their feet nailed to the deck and were beaten to death.[33] Chinese pirates also engaged in various forms of cannibalism. They drank their victims' blood and ate their livers and hearts, which they did to display their hatred of their enemies and to acquire their enemy's power and life force. Participating in acts of violence and cannibalism also helped solidify group identity and the bonds of

FIGURE 11.2 *Public execution of Chinese pirates, 1880s.*
Source: *L'Illustration*, year 49, no 2522, 4 July 1891. Via Getty Images.

brotherhood.[34] In doing so, they imitated the violence the state used against them, in much the same way that pirates in the Caribbean and the Atlantic did a century before. Most pirates, especially repeat offenders, could expect to be executed by the state. One of the most graphic and popular forms of execution was death by slicing, in which the victim's body would be slowly carved up into 120, 72, 36 or 24 pieces. Pirates witnessed these barbarous executions and copied the state brutality.[35]

Zheng Yi Sao's unusual rise to power highlights the question of women and sexuality on board pirate ships. In European waters, women at sea were usually considered bad luck, and pirate codes restricted the presence of women on board ships – though, as we have seen, these codes were honoured in the breach as often as not. Both European traditions and Chinese Confucian philosophy assigned women to subservient, domestic non-public roles. Women could obviously break those boundaries by cross-dressing, as Mary Read and Anny Bonny did, or by seizing the mantel of power after the death of a powerful husband, as in the cases of Zhen Yi Sao in China and Grace O'Malley in Ireland.[36] There may have been a few hundred women globally who were formally accepted as part of pirate crews. But the evidence is thin, and only a few are known by name. Still fewer commanded pirate ships or fleets. Even so, because women formed an integral part of maritime communities, their role in the success of pirate adventures is hard to overstate. Women were the wives, daughters and lovers of pirates. They were cooks, prostitutes, seamstresses, informants, suppliers, tavern keepers, and buyers and sellers of pirate loot. In China and Southeast Asia, women lived on board ships and worked alongside the men. Chinese women at sea seldom had their feet bound like many women did on land. They accompanied their husbands, helped sail and pilot the ships, cooked, cleaned, served the sexual desires of the men and fought alongside them. Women on board pirate vessels in China enjoyed greater freedom than women on land, and they were less likely to receive the death penalty if caught.[37]

The near-absence of women on board European pirate vessels, the close proximity of men and limited availability of sexual partners made homosexual liaisons and rape common. When homosexual relations disrupted shipboard discipline, they were punished.[38] But in China, homosexual activity was widely accepted and even a key part of the initiation of new pirate recruits that established patron–client relationship, strengthened male bonding and proved essential for the stability of pirate confederations. Chinese pirate leaders were often bisexual and transitioned easily between men, women and boys.[39] Nonetheless, it is easy to exaggerate the role of women and homosexuality on board pirate vessels. Pirate ships were not homosexual havens or liberated sexual spaces for women, even though sexuality may have been more fluid there than on land.

Between 1807 and 1810, the Guangdong pirate confederation acted like a state unto itself. It levied duties, collected 'taxes', issued passes, authorized executions, engaged in trade and defended its territory. However, by 1809, the patience of the emperor had grown thin. He sent Bai Ling to rein them in.[40] Bai Ling imposed a blockade on the coast to cut the pirates off from their food and supplies. The famine of 1809 exacerbated the situation for the pirates, who became desperate for food and began to raid further inland in search of rice. Zhang Bao and Zheng Yi Sao took their Red Banner fleet into the Pearl River Delta with Guo Podai of the Black Banner fleet. Bai Ling encouraged towns to create their own militias and to erect fortifications to resist the pirates. He sent in the Chinese fleet, together with their Portuguese allies, who fought several pitched battles with the pirates.[41] The combination of the blockade, stepped up naval campaigns, town resistance and famine wore down the pirates' resolve. When several of the important pirate leaders died in 1809, others began to surrender to the authorities. Bai Ling began encouraging pirates to surrender in return for pardons. In 1810, Zheng Yi Sao and Zhang Bao surrendered. Zhang Bao and Guo Podai were given naval commissions and ordered to hunt the remaining pirates.[42]

After 1810, piracy along the south China coast returned to the small-scale petty activities of gangs of bandits or opportunistic fishermen and sailors. During the Opium War (1839–1842), the state armed pirates and encouraged them to attack British ships. In 1844, another large pirate fleet of 150 ships emerged to prey on shipping on the south China coast. The British and the Vietnamese attacked and destroyed two pirate fleets in

1849.[43] The age of the great pirate fleets had come to an end, but piracy would persist along the south China coast into the twenty-first century as a parasitic activity that fed on global commerce.[44]

As you read the documents that follow, consider the following questions:

1   What can we learn about the nature of Chinese piracy from Glasspoole's captivity account?

2   How does Glasspoole's account differ from that of Joshua Gee?

3   Why were Glasspoole and his men not tortured and enslaved as was the common lot for many other pirate victims?

4   What evidence do Glasspoole and Yung-lun provide that might demonstrate the existence of a pirate shadow economy?

5   Why were the pirates raiding so far inland? What motived them to enter a river system where they could be trapped?

6   What tactics did the pirates employ in attacking Chinese towns and villages?

7   What measures did the villagers and townspeople take to resist pirate attacks? How successful were they?

8   Can you find any evidence in Yung-lun's account that might suggest that Glasspoole or his men were fighting with the pirates?

9   Where do Yung-lun and Glasspoole corroborate each other's accounts? Where do they contradict each other? How might you explain this?

10   What role did political instability and vibrant trade play in creating the huge pirate confederacies in China in the early nineteenth century?

11   How would you characterize the piracy of this period (i.e. parasitic, episodic or intrinsic)?

Richard Glasspoole, 'A Brief History of My Captivity', in the Appendix of Yung Lun Yuen, *The History of the Pirates Who Infested the Seas,* translated by Charles Neumann (Canton, 1830), 97–128.

Richard Glasspoole worked for the British East India Company on the ship Marquis of Ely *in the early nineteenth century. He was tasked with taking a cutter and twelve men to deliver the purser and a packet of documents to Macāo and to pick up a Chinese pilot for the ship. On 18 September 1809, Glasspoole set out to return to the* Marquis of Ely, *which had weighed anchor while they were gone. The cutter nearly reached the* Marquis of Ely *when it encountered a hard squall, heavy seas, and a strong tide that pulled it towards the shore. The* Marquis of Ely *disappeared in the haze. Glasspoole and his men narrowly missed being wrecked on the rocks by pulling hard at the oars. They then attempted to reach another company ship, the* Glatton, *but it did not see them and sailed away. Glasspoole decided to make for Macão. He and his crew fought the rough weather and evaded pirates for four days before they were captured on 21 September 1809, by pirates, which Glasspoole called Ladrones, who belonged to the fleet of Zheng Yi Sao. He was not ransomed until 4 December 1809, eleven weeks later.*

Thursday the 21st … a large row-boat pulled after us; she soon came along-side, when about twenty savage-looking villains, who were stowed at the bottom of the boat, leaped on board us. They were armed with a short sword in each hand, one of which they laid on our necks, and the other pointed to our breasts, keeping their eyes fixed on their officer, waiting his signal to cut or desist. Seeing we were incapable of making any resistance, he sheathed his sword, and the others immediately followed his example. They then dragged us into their boat, and carried us on board one of their junks, with the most savage demonstrations of joy, and as we supposed, to torture and put us to a cruel death. When on board the junk, they searched all our pockets, took the handkerchiefs from our necks, and brought heavy chains to chain us to the guns.

…. I was then taken before the chief. He was seated on deck, in a large chair, dressed in purple silk, with a black turban on. He appeared to be about thirty years of age, a stout commanding-looking man. He took me by the coat and drew me close to him; then questioned the interpreter very strictly, asking who we were, and what was our business in that part of the country. I told him to say we were Englishmen in distress, having been four days at sea without provisions. This he would not credit, but said we were bad men, and that he would put us all to death; and then ordered some men to put the interpreter to the torture until he confessed the truth.

Upon this occasion, a Ladrone, who had been once to England and spoke a few words of English, came to the chief, and told him we were really Englishmen, and that we had plenty of money, adding, that the buttons on my coat were gold. The chief then ordered us some coarse brown rice, of which we made a tolerable meal, having eat[en] nothing for nearly four days, except a few green oranges. During our repast, a number of Ladrones crowded round us, examining our clothes and hair, and giving us every possible annoyance. Several of them brought swords, and laid them on our necks, making signs that they would soon take us on shore, and cut us in pieces, which I'm sorry to say was the fate of some hundreds during my captivity.

I was now summoned before the chief, who had been conversing with the interpreter; he said I must write to my captain, and tell him, if he did not send an hundred thousand dollars for our ransom, in ten days he would put us all to death. In vain did I assure him it was useless writing unless he would agree to take a much smaller sum; saying we were all poor men, and the most we could possibly raise would not exceed two thousand dollars. Finding that he was much exasperated at my expostulations, I embraced the offer of writing to inform my commander of our unfortunate situation, though there appeared not the least probability of relieving us. They said the letter should be conveyed to Macao in a fishing-boat, which would bring an answer in the morning. A small boat accordingly came alongside and took the letter.

About six o'clock in the evening they gave us some rice and a little salt fish, which we [ate], and they made signs for us to lay down on the deck to sleep; but such numbers of Ladrones were constantly coming from different vessels to see us, and examine our clothes and hair, they would not allow us a moment's quiet. They were particularly anxious for the buttons of my coat, which were new, and as they supposed gold. I took it off and laid it on the deck to avoid being disturbed by them; it was taken away in the night, and I saw it on the next day stripped of its buttons.

About nine o'clock a boat came and hailed the chief's vessel; he immediately hoisted his mainsail, and the fleet weighed apparently in great confusion. They worked to windward all night and part of the next day, and anchored about one o'clock in a bay under the island of [Lantau], where the head admiral of Ladrones was lying at anchor, with about two hundred vessels and a Portuguese brig they had captured a few days before, and murdered the captain and part of the crew.

Saturday the 23d, early in the morning, a fishing boat came to the fleet to inquire if they had captured a European boat; being answered in the affirmative, they came to the vessel I was in. One of them spoke a few words of English, and told me he had a Ladrone-pass, and was sent by Captain Kay in search of us; I was rather surprised to find he had no letter. He appeared to be well acquainted with the chief, and remained in his cabin smoking opium, and playing cards all the day.

In the evening, I was summoned with the interpreter before the chief. He questioned us in a much milder tone, saying, he now believed we were Englishmen, a people he wished to be friendly with; and that if our captain would lend him seventy thousand dollars 'till he returned from his cruise up the river, he would repay him, and send us all to Macao. I assured him it was useless writing on those terms, and unless our ransom was speedily settled, the English fleet would sail, and render our enlargement altogether ineffectual. He remained determined, and said if it were not sent, he would keep us, and make us fight, or put us to death. I accordingly wrote, and gave my letter to the man belonging to the boat before mentioned. He said he could not return with an answer in less than five days.

The chief now gave me the letter I wrote when first taken. I have never been able to ascertain his reasons for detaining it, but suppose he dare not negotiate for our ransom without orders from the head admiral, who I understood was sorry at our being captured. He said the English ships would join the Mandarins and attack them. He told the chief that captured us, to dispose of us as he pleased.

Monday the 24th, it blew a strong gale, with constant hard rain; we suffered much from the cold and wet, being obliged to remain on deck with no covering but an old mat, which was frequently taken from us in the night, by the Ladrones who were on watch ....

Tuesday the 25th, at daylight in the morning, the fleet, amounting to about five hundred sail of different sizes, weighed, to proceed on their intended cruise up the rivers, to levy contributions on the towns and villages ....the only method of communication is by boats, that have a pass from the Ladrones, and they dare not venture above twenty miles from Macão, being obliged to come and go in the night, to avoid the Mandarins; and if these boats should be detected in having any intercourse with the Ladrones, they are immediately put to death, and all their relations, though they had not joined in the crime, share in the punishment, in order that not a single person of their families should be left to imitate their crimes or revenge their death. This severity renders communication both dangerous and expensive; no boat would venture out for less than a hundred Spanish dollars.

Wednesday the 26th, ...The fleet now divided into two squadrons (the red and the black) and sailed up different branches of the river. At midnight the division we were in anchored close to an immense hill, on the top of which a number of fires were burning, which at daylight I perceived proceeded from a Chinese camp. At the back of the hill was a most beautiful town, surrounded by water, and embellished with groves of orange-trees. The chop-house (custom-house) and a few cottages were immediately plundered, and burnt down; most of the inhabitants, however, escaped to the camp.

The Ladrones now prepared to attack the town with a formidable force, collected in rowboats from the different vessels. They sent a messenger to the town, demanding a tribute of ten thousand dollars annually, saying, if these terms were not complied with, they would land, destroy the town, and murder all the inhabitants; which they would certainly have done, had the town laid in a more advantageous situation for their purpose; but being placed out of the reach of their shot, they allowed them to come to terms. The inhabitants agreed to pay six thousand dollars, which they were to collect by the time of our return down the river. This finesse had the desired effect, for during our absence they mounted a few guns on a hill, which commanded the passage, and gave us in lieu of the dollars a warm salute on our return.

October the 1st, the fleet weighed in the night, dropped by the tide up the river, and anchored very quietly before a town surrounded by a thick wood. Early in the morning, the Ladrones assembled in rowboats, and landed; then gave a shout, and rushed into the town, sword in hand. The inhabitants fled to the adjacent hills, in numbers apparently superior to the Ladrones. We may easily imagine to ourselves the horror with which these miserable people must be seized, on being obliged to leave their homes, and everything dear to them. It was a most melancholy sight to see women in tears, clasping their infants in their arms, and imploring mercy for them from those brutal robbers. The old and the sick, who were unable to fly, or to make resistance, were either made prisoners or most inhumanely butchered. The boats continued passing and repassing from the junks to the shore, in quick succession, laden with booty, and the men besmeared with blood. Two hundred and fifty women, and several children, were made prisoners, and sent on board different vessels. They were unable to escape with the men, owing to that abominable practice of cramping their feet: several of them were not able to move without assistance, in fact, they might all be said to totter, rather than walk. Twenty of these poor women were sent on board the vessel I was in; they were hauled on board by the hair and treated in a most savage manner.

When the chief came on board, he questioned them respecting the circumstances of their friends, and demanded ransoms accordingly, from six thousand to six hundred dollars each. He ordered them a berth on deck, at the after part of the vessel, where they had nothing to shelter them from the weather, which at this time was very variable – the days excessively hot, and the nights cold, with heavy rains. The town being plundered of everything valuable, it was set on fire, and reduced to ashes by the morning. The fleet remained here three days, negotiating for the ransom of the prisoners, and plundering the fish-tanks and gardens ....

October the 5th, the fleet proceeded up another branch of the river, stopping at several small villages to receive tribute, which was generally paid in dollars, sugar and rice, with a few large pigs roasted whole ....Nothing particular occurred 'till the 10th, except frequent skirmishes on shore between small parties of Ladrones and Chinese soldiers. They frequently obliged my men to go on shore and fight with the muskets we had when taken, which did great execution, the Chinese principally using bows and arrows. They have matchlocks, but use them very unskillfully.

On the 10th, we formed a junction with the Black squadron, and proceeded many miles up a wide and beautiful river, passing several ruins of villages that had been destroyed by the Black squadron ....

The fleet now anchored opposite the ruins of the town where the women had been made prisoners. Here we remained five or six days, during which time about an hundred of the women were ransomed; the remainder were offered for sale amongst the Ladrones, for forty dollars each. The woman is considered the lawful wife of the purchaser, who would be put to death if he discarded her. Several of them leaped overboard and drowned themselves, rather than submit to some infamous degradation.

The fleet then weighed and made sail down the river, to receive the ransom from the town before-mentioned. As we passed the hill, they fired several shots at us, but without effect. The Ladrones were much exasperated, and determined to revenge themselves; they dropped out of reach of their shot and anchored. Every junk sent about a hundred men each on shore to cut [rice] paddy and destroy their orange-groves, which was most effectually performed for several miles down the river. During our stay here, they received information of nine boats lying up a creek, laden with paddy; boats were immediately dispatched after them.

Next morning these boats were brought to the fleet; ten or twelve men were taken in them. As these had made no resistance, the chief said he would allow them to become Ladrones, if they agreed to take the usual oaths ....Three or four of them refused to comply, for which they were punished in the following cruel manner: their hands were tied behind their backs, a rope from the masthead rove through their arms, and hoisted three or four feet from the deck, and five or six men flogged them with three rattans twisted together 'till they were apparently dead; then hoisted them up to the masthead, and left them hanging nearly an hour, then lowered them down and repeated the punishment, 'till they died or complied with the oath.

October the 20th, in the night, an express boat came with the information that a large Mandarin fleet was proceeding up the river to attack us. The chief immediately weighed, with fifty of the largest vessels, and sailed down the river to meet them. About one in the morning they commenced a heavy fire till day-light, when an express was sent for the remainder of the fleet to join them: about an hour after a counter order to anchor came, the Mandarin fleet having run. Two or three hours afterwards the chief returned with three captured vessels in tow, having sunk two, and eighty-three sail made their escape. The admiral of the Mandarins blew his vessel up, by throwing a lighted match into the magazine as the Ladrones were boarding her; she ran on shore, and they succeeded in getting twenty of her guns.

In this action very few prisoners were taken: the men belonging to the captured vessel drowned themselves, as they were sure of suffering a lingering and cruel death if taken after making resistance ....

On the 28th of October, I received a letter from Captain Kay, brought by a fisherman, who had told him he would get us all back for three thousand dollars. He advised me to offer three thousand, and if not accepted, extend it to four; but not farther, as it was bad policy to offer much at first: at the same time assuring me we should be liberated, let the ransom be what it would. I offered the chief the three thousand, which he disdainfully refused, saying he was not to be played with: and unless they sent ten thousand dollars, and two large guns, with several casks of gunpowder, he would soon put us all to death. I wrote to Captain Kay, and informed him of the chief's determination, requesting if an opportunity offered, to send us a shift of clothes, for which it may be easily imagined we were much distressed, having been seven weeks without a shift; although constantly exposed to the weather, and of course frequently wet.

On the first of November, the fleet sailed up a narrow river·, and anchored at night within two miles of a town called Little Whampoa. In front of it was a small fort, and several Mandarin vessels lying in the harbor. The chief sent the interpreter to me, saying, I must order my men to make cartridges and clean their muskets, ready to go on shore in the morning. I assured the interpreter I should give the men no such orders, that they must please themselves. Soon after the chief came on board, threatening to put us all to a cruel death if we refused to obey his orders. For my own part, I remained determined, and advised the men not to comply, as I thought by making ourselves useful we should be accounted too valuable.

A few hours afterwards he sent to me again, saying, that if myself and the quartermaster would assist them at the great guns, that if also the rest of the men went on shore and succeeded in taking the place, he would then take the money offered for our ransom, and give them twenty dollars for every Chinaman's head they cut off. To these proposals we cheerfully acceded, in hopes of facilitating our deliverance.

Early in the morning, the forces intended for landing were assembled in rowboats, amounting in the whole to three or four thousand men. The largest vessels weighed, and hauled in shore, to cover the landing of the forces, and attack the fort and Mandarin vessels. About nine o'clock, the action commenced and continued with great spirit for nearly an hour, when the walls of the fort gave way, and the men retreated in the greatest confusion.

The Mandarin vessels still continued firing, having blocked up the entrance of the harbor to prevent the Ladrone boats entering. At this the Ladrones were much exasperated, and about three hundred of them swam on shore, with a short sword lashed close under each arm; they then ran along the banks of the river 'till they came abreast of the vessels, and then swam off again and boarded them. The Chinese thus attacked, leaped overboard, and endeavored to reach the opposite shore: the Ladrones followed, and cut the greater number of them to pieces in the water. They next towed the vessels out of the harbor, and attacked the town with increased fury. The inhabitants fought about a quarter of an hour and then retreated to an adjacent hill, from which they were soon driven with great slaughter.

After this, the Ladrones returned and plundered the town, every boat leaving it when laden. The Chinese on the hills perceiving most of the boats were off, rallied, and retook the town, after killing near two hundred Ladrones. One of my men was unfortunately lost in this dreadful massacre. The Ladrones landed a second time, drove the Chinese out of the town, then reduced it to ashes, and put all their prisoners to death, without regarding either age or sex!

I must not omit to mention a most horrid (though ludicrous) circumstance which happened at this place. The Ladrones were paid by their chief ten dollars for every Chinaman's head they produced. One of my men turning the corner of a street was met by a Ladrone running furiously after a Chinese; he had a drawn sword in his hand, and two Chinaman's heads which he had cut off, tied by their· tails, and slung round his neck. I was witness myself to some of them producing five or six to obtain payment! ...

On the 20th of November, early in the morning, discovered an immense fleet of Mandarin vessels standing for the bay. On nearing us, they formed a line, and stood close in; each vessel as she discharged her guns tacked to join the rear and reload. They kept up a constant fire for about two hours, when one of their largest vessels was blown up by a firebrand thrown from a Ladrone junk; after which they kept at a more respectful distance but continued firing without intermission 'till the 21st at night, when it fell calm.

The Ladrones towed out seven large vessels, with about two hundred rowboats to board them; but a breeze springing up, they made sail and escaped. The Ladrones returned into the bay, and anchored. The Portuguese and Mandarins followed, and continued a heavy cannonading during that night and the next day. The vessel I was in had her foremast shot away, which they supplied very expeditiously by taking a mainmast from a smaller vessel ....

On the 28th, at night, they sent in eight fire-vessels, which if properly constructed must have done great execution, having every advantage they could wish for to effect their purpose; a strong breeze and tide directly into the bay, and the vessels lying so close together that it was impossible to miss them. On their first appearance, the Ladrones gave a general shout, supposing them to be Mandarin vessels on fire but were very soon convinced of their mistake. They came very regularly into the center of the fleet, two and two, burning furiously; one of them came alongside of the vessel I was in, but they succeeded in booming her off. She appeared to be a vessel of about thirty tons; her hold was filled with straw and wood, and there were a few small boxes of combustibles on her deck, which exploded alongside of us without doing any damage. The Ladrones, however, towed them all on shore, extinguished the fire, and broke them up for firewood. The Portuguese claim the credit of constructing these destructive machines, and actually sent a dispatch to the Governor of Macão, saying they had destroyed at least one third of the Ladrones' fleet, and hoped soon to effect their purpose by totally annihilating them.

On the 29th of November, the Ladrones being all ready for sea, they weighed and stood boldly out, bidding defiance to the invincible squadron and imperial fleet, consisting of ninety-three war-junks, six Portuguese ships, a brig, and a schooner. Immediately the Ladrones weighed, they made all sail. The Ladrones chased them two or three hours, keeping up a constant fire; finding they did not come up with them, they hauled their wind and stood to the eastward.

Thus terminated the boasted blockade, which lasted nine days, during which time the Ladrones completed all their repairs. In this action, not a single Ladrone vessel was destroyed, and their loss about thirty or forty men. An American was also killed, one of three that remained out of eight taken in a schooner. I had two very narrow escapes: the first, a twelve-pounder shot fell within three or four feet of me; another took a piece out of a small brass swivel on which I was standing ...

On the 2nd of December I received a letter from Lieutenant Maughn, commander of the Honorable Company's cruiser *Antelope*, saying that he had the ransom on board, and had been three days cruising after us, and wished me to settle with the chief on the securest method of delivering it. The chief agreed to send us in a small gun-boat, 'till we came within sight of the *Antelope*; then the Comprador's boat was to bring the ransom and receive us.

I was so agitated at receiving this joyful news that it was with considerable difficulty I could scrawl about two or three lines to inform Lieutenant Maughn of the arrangements I had made. We were all so deeply affected by the gratifying tidings, that we seldom closed our eyes, but continued watching day and night for the boat. On the 6th she returned with Lieutenant Maughn's answer, saying, he would respect any single boat; but would not allow the fleet to approach him. The chief then, according to his first proposal, ordered a gunboat to take us, and with no small degree of pleasure we left the Ladrone fleet about four o'clock in the morning.

At one P.M. [we] saw the *Antelope* under all sail, standing toward us. The Ladrone boat immediately anchored, and dispatched the Comprador's boat for the ransom, saying, that if she approached nearer, they would return to the fleet; and they were just weighing when she shortened sail, and anchored about two miles from us. The boat did not reach her 'till late in the afternoon, owing to the tide's being strong against her. She received the ransom and left the *Antelope* just before dark. A Mandarin boat that had been lying concealed under the land, and watching their maneuvers, gave chase to her, and was within a few fathoms of taking her, when she saw a light, which the Ladrones answered, and the Mandarin hauled off.

Our situation was now a most critical one; the ransom was in the hands of the Ladrones, and the Comprador dare not return with us for fear of a second attack from the Mandarin boat. The Ladrones would not remain 'till morning, so we were obliged to return with them to the fleet.

In the morning, the chief inspected the ransom, which consisted of the following articles: two bales of superfine scarlet cloth; two chests of opium; two casks of gunpowder; and a telescope; the rest in dollars. He objected to the telescope not being new; and said he should detain one of us 'till another was sent, or a hundred dollars in lieu of it. The Comprador, however, agreed with him for the hundred dollars.

Everything being at length settled, the chief ordered two gun-boats to convey us near the *Antelope*; we saw her just before dusk when the Ladrone boats left us. We had the inexpressible pleasure of arriving on board the *Antelope* at 7 P.M., where we were most cordially received, and heartily congratulated on our safe and happy deliverance from a miserable captivity, which we had endured for eleven weeks and three days.
RICHARD GLASSPOOLE.
CHINA, December 8th, 1809.

Yuan Yung-lun, 'The History of the Chinese Pirates', in *History of the Pirates Who Infested the China Sea, from 1807–1810*, translated by Charles Fried Neumann (London: J. L. Cox, 1831), 30–61.

Yuan Yun-lun served the governor-general as a low-level government employee. He knew Chinese officials who had died at the hands of the pirates during the Chinese government's attempts to suppress them. He collected first-hand accounts from men who had been involved in the battles and sought to narrate an accurate account of the pirates' deprivations so that the memory of those who had perished would endure. His narrative overlaps with Glasspoole's account and provides important details that Glasspoole could not have known. Both accounts provide insights into pirate methods and motivations. They also show that the pirates were hard-pressed and often failed in their attempts to pillage towns along the delta. A comparison of the two accounts reveals both how serious the pirate threat was to the local economy and populace, and how effective the government campaigns against them became.

1809 ' ... If the valiant men let their spirits droop, and the soldiers themselves become frightened at these repeated defeats, the pirates will certainly overpower us at last; we can really not look for any assistance to destroy them. We must try to cut off all provisions and starve them.' In consequence of this, all vessels were ordered to remain, or to return into harbor, that the pirates might not have any opportunity to plunder, and thus be destroyed by famine – the government officers being very vigilant about this regulation. The pirates were not able to get provisions for some months. They became at last tired of it and resolved to go into the river itself.

The pirates came now into the river by three different passages. The wife of Ching yih [Zheng Yi] plundered about Sin hwy, Chang paou [Zheng Pao] about Tung- kwan, and O po tae about Fan yu and Shun tih, and all other smaller places connected with Shun tih they were together explored by the pirates, who guarded the passage from Fan to Shun.

On the first day of the seventh moon, O po tae came with about a hundred vessels and burnt the custom-house of Tsze ne. On the second day he divided his squadron into four divisions, extending to Peih keang,

Wei yung, Lin yo, Shih peih, and other villages. The *Chang lung* division surrounded the whole country from Ta wang yin to Shwy sse ying. The Ta chow, or large-vessel division, blockaded Ke kung shih, which is below the custom-house of Tsze ne. The pirates sent to the village Tsze ne, demanding ten thousand pieces of money as tribute and of San shen, a small village near Tsze ne on the right side, they demanded two thousand ....

As soon as it was resolved to resist the demands of the pirates, weapons were prepared, and all able men, from sixteen years and upwards to sixty, were summoned to appear with their arms near the palisades. They kept quiet the whole of the second day, and proceeded not to fighting but the people were much disturbed, and did not sleep the whole night. On the following day, they armed and posted themselves on the sea-coast. The pirates, seeing that the villagers would not pay the tribute, became enraged, and made a severe attack during the night but they could not pass the ditch before the village.

On the morning of the fourth, O po tae headed his men, forced the ditch, took the provisions, and killed the cattle. The pirates in great numbers went on shore but the villagers made such a vigorous resistance that they began to withdraw. O po tae therefore surrounded the village on both sides, and the pirates took possession of the mountain in the rear. They then threw the frightened villagers into disorder, pursued them, and killed about eighty. After this, the pirates proceeded with their van to the sea-shore, without encountering any resistance from the front. The villagers were, from the beginning, very much alarmed for their wives and daughters. They collected them in the temple and shut it up. But the pirates being victorious, opened the temple, and carried the women by force all away on board ship. One pirate set off with two very fine women; a villager, on seeing this, pursued after and killed him in a hidden place. He then took the women and carried them safe through the water ... A great number of the pirates were killed and wounded, and the villagers lost about two thousand persons. What a cruel misfortune it is hard indeed only to relate it ....

The pirates tried many stratagems and frauds to get into the villages. One came as a country gentleman to take charge of the government guns; another came in a government vessel as if to assist the village; after which they, on a sudden, attacked and plundered all, when people were not aware of them. One pirate went round as a peddler, to see and hear all, and to explore every place. The country people became therefore at last enraged and were in future always on their guard. If they found any foreigner, they took him for a pirate and killed him ....

On the sixteenth day of the seventh moon, the pirates attacked a village near Tung kwan. The villagers knowing what would happen, made fences and palisades, and obstructed the passage with large guns. Armed with lances and targets they hid themselves in a secret place, and selected ten men only to oppose the pirates. The pirates seeing that there were so few people, went on shore to pursue them. As soon as they came near the ambuscade the guns were fired the pirates became alarmed and dared not advance farther. Not being hurt by the fire, they again advanced but three pirates presuming that there was an ambush, thought of retreating, and being very hard pressed by the enemy, they gave a sign to their comrades to come on shore. The ten villagers then retired near the ambush, and when the pirates pursued them, about a hundred were killed by their guns, and the whole force of the banditti was brought into disorder. The villagers pursued them killing many. Those also who had been taken alive were afterwards beheaded. They captured one small and two large vessels ...

The twenty-first [Zheng Pao] came to Lin tow, and the twenty-second to Kan shin. He made an attack but could not overpower the place. He then returned to Pwan peen jow and lay before its fence. The inhabitants of Chow po chin, knowing that the pirates would make an attack, assembled behind the wall to oppose them. The pirates fired their guns and wounded some, when the villagers ran away. The pirates then went on shore, but the villagers crowded together and fired on them; the pirates cast themselves on the ground, and the shots passed over their heads without doing any harm. Before the gunners could again load, the pirates sprang up and put them to death. Out of the three thousand men who were in the battle, five hundred were carried away by the pirates. One of the most daring pirates, bearing the flag, was killed by the musket of a villager; a second pirate then took the flag, and he also was killed. The pirates now pressed against the wall and advanced. There was also a foreign pirate engaged in the battle with a fowling-piece.

The pirates assembled in great numbers to cut the wall with their [halberds], but they were disappointed on seeing they could not attain their object in such a manner. The pirates lost their hold, fell down, and were killed. The engagement now became general, and great numbers were killed and wounded on both sides. The villagers at last were driven from their fortifications, and the pirates pursued them to *Mih ke*, or the rocks about *Mih*, where they were hindered from going farther by foggy weather; they retired and burned about twenty houses, with all they contained.

On the following day, the pirates appeared again on the shore, but the inhabitants made a vigorous resistance, and being driven back, they retired to the citadel *Chih hwa*, where a thousand of them fought so hard that the pirates withdrew. It was reported that ten of them were killed, and that the villagers lost eight men ....

On the twenty-fourth Chang paou and Po tae divided this district between themselves and robbed and burned all. Pao had to plunder the north part to Fo shin; he carried away about ten thousand stones of rice, and burned down about thirty houses ....

On the twenty-ninth they returned to plunder Kan shin. They went into the river with small vessels, and the inhabitants opposing them, wounded two pirates, which all the pirates resented. They next came with large vessels, surrounded the village, and made preparations to mount the narrow passes. The inhabitants remained within the entrenchments, and dared not come forward. The pirates then divided their force according to the various passes, and made an attack. The inhabitants prepared themselves to make a strong resistance near the entrance from the sea on the east side of the fence but the pirates stormed the fence, planted their flag on the shore, and then the whole squadron followed. The inhabitants fought bravely and made a dreadful slaughter when the pirates crossed the entrance at Lin tow. The boxing-master, Wei tang chow, made a vigorous resistance, and killed about ten pirates. The pirates then began to withdraw, but Chang paou himself headed the battle, which lasted very long. The inhabitants were not strong enough. Wei tang was surrounded by the pirates nevertheless that his wife fought valiantly by his side. On seeing that they were surrounded and exhausted, the father of the lady rushed forward and killed some pirates. The pirates then retired in opposite directions, in order to surround their opponents in such a manner that they might not escape and could be killed without being able to make any resistance and thus it happened, the wife of Wei tang being slain with the others.

The pirates now pursued the inhabitants of the place, who cut the bridge and retired to the neighboring hills. The pirates swam through the water and attacked the inhabitants, who were unable to escape. The whole force of the pirates being now on shore, the inhabitants suffered a severe loss, it is supposed about a hundred of them were killed. The loss of the pirates also was considerable.

The pirates went in four divisions to plunder they took here an immense quantity of clothes and other goods and carried away one thousand one hundred and forty captives of both sexes. They set on fire about ten houses the flames could not be extinguished for some days in the whole village you could not hear the cry of a dog or a hen. The other inhabitants retired far from the village or hid themselves in the fields. In the paddy fields about a hundred women were hidden, but the pirates on hearing a child crying, went to the place and carried them away. Mei ying, the wife of Ke choo yang, was very beautiful, and a pirate being about to seize her by the head, she abused him exceedingly. The pirate bound her to the yardarm, but on abusing him yet more, the pirate dragged her down and broke two of her teeth, which filled her mouth and jaws with blood. The pirate sprang up again to bind her. Ying allowed him to approach, but as soon as he came near her, she laid hold of his garments with her bleeding mouth, and threw both him and herself into the river, where they were drowned. The remaining captives of both sexes were after some months liberated, on having paid a ransom of fifteen thousand *leang* or ounces of silver …

On the thirteenth day of the ninth moon our Admiral Tsuen mow sun mustered about eighty vessels to go to Shaou wan and obstruct the passage. The pirates heard of these preparations, and on the night of the fourteenth every vessel of the different flags was ordered to go to Shaou wan. Their order was, that being within ten le from the place, they should stop and prepare themselves to begin the battle when it was dark. From the first night watch, the cannon began to fire, and only ceased with daylight. At the end of the day, the cannon were again roaring without any intermission, and the country people mounted on the green Lo shang, to look at the progress of the fight. They saw the wrecks of vessels floating on the sea, the waves were rolling, the bullets flying, and the cries of dying people mounted to the skies. The valleys reechoed the noise; beasts and birds started alarmed and found no place where they might repose themselves. The vessels were thrown into disorder, and our army was pressed down by the overpowering force of the enemy. Our commander lost four vessels, but the palisade before the village could not be taken, by which means it was protected against pillage. Our admiral said, "Since I cannot conquer these wicked pirates, I will blow myself up." In this manner the admiral and many other officers met their death.

The wife of Ching yih then ordered the pirates to go up the river, she herself remaining with the larger vessels in the sea to blockade the different harbors or entrances from the seaside, but the government officers made preparations to oppose her. There were about this time three foreign vessels returning to Portugal. Yih's wife attacked them, took one vessel, and killed about ten of the foreigners; the two other vessels escaped. The Major Pang noo of Heang shan about this time fitted out a hundred vessels to attack the pirates; he had before hired six foreign vessels, and the two Portuguese ships, which had before run away, united also with him. Yih's wife, seeing that she had not vessels enough, and that she might be surrounded, ordered a greater number to her assistance. She appointed Chang paou to command them and sail up the river but to keep quiet with his squadron [un]till he saw the Chang lung, or government vessels come on. On the third of the tenth moon, the government vessels went higher up the river, and Chang paou following and attacking them, the foreign vessels sustained a great loss, and all the other vessels then ran away. The foreigners showed themselves very courageous; they petitioned the mayor of Heang shan to place himself at the head of the foreign vessels, to go and fight the pirates ....

The Admiral Tsuen mow sun was exceedingly eager to destroy the pirates, but he was confident that he was not strong enough to vanquish them ... In consequence of this determination all commanders and officers of the different vessels were ordered to meet on the seventeenth at Chih leih keo, to blockade the pirates in Ta yu shan, and to cut off all supplies of provisions that might be sent to them. To annoy them yet more, the officers were ordered to prepare the materials for the fire vessels. These fire vessels were filled with gunpowder, nitre, and other combustibles; after being filled, they were set on fire by a match from the stern, and were instantly all in a blaze ...

The pirates knowing our design were well prepared, for it they had bars with very long pincers, by which they took hold of the fire vessels and kept them off so that they could not come near. Our commander, however, would not leave the place and being very eager to fight, he ordered that an attack should be made, and it is presumed that about three hundred pirates were killed.

Notes

1 Murray, *Pirates of the South China Coast*, 1; Paola Calanca has shown that there was a brief period between 1690 and 1726 when two large pirate gangs flourished around Fujian and Guangdong provinces. See Calanca, 'Piracy and Coastal Security', 91.

2 Murray, *Pirates of the South China Coast*, 7.

3 Murray, *Pirates of the South China Coast*, 10–11.

4 Calanca, 'Piracy and Coastal Security', 97–98.

5 Murray, *Pirates of the South China Coast*, 16–17; Antony, *Like Froth Floating on the Sea*, 82–88, 94–97.

6 Antony, *Like Froth Floating on the Sea*, 37–38.

7 Antony, *Like Froth Floating on the Sea*, 72.

8 Antony, *Like Froth Floating on the Sea*, 38–43.

9 Murray, *Pirates of the South China Coast*, 22–23.

10 Antony, 'Piracy and the Shadow Economy', 102–108, 111–112.

11 Murray, *Pirates of the South China Coast*, 32–56; For full study of the rebellion, see Dutton, *The Tay Son Uprising*.

12 Murray, *Pirates of the South China Coast*, 35–41.

13 Antony, 'Maritime Violence and State Formation in Vietnam', 118–123; Murray, *Pirates of the South China Coast*, 48–56.

14 Antony, 'Maritime Violence and State Formation in Vietnam', 114–118.

15 Murray, *Pirates of the South China Coast*, 57–60; Antony, *Like Froth Floating on the Sea*, 44–45.

16 Antony, 'Piracy and the Shadow Economy', 109.

17 Murray, *Pirates of the South China Coast*, 68–69.

18 Antony, *Like Froth Floating on the Sea*, 43–44.

19 Murray, 'Cheng I Sao in Fact and Fiction', 253–282.

20 Antony, *Like Froth Floating on the Sea*, 48; Murray, *Pirates of the South China Coast*, 71–72.

21 Murray, *Pirates of the South China Coast*, 72.

22 Murray, 'Living and Working Conditions', 64.

23 Antony, 'Piracy and the Shadow Economy', 111.

24 Antony, *Like Froth Floating on the Sea*, 49; Murray, *Pirates of the South China Coast*, 71.

25 Calanca, 'Piracy and Coastal Security', 91.

26 Antony, *Like Froth Floating on the Sea*, 74, 90; Calanca 'Piracy and Coastal Security', 88.

27 Antony, *Like Froth Floating on the Sea*, 88, 90–91, 99–102.

28 Antony, *Like Froth Floating on the Sea*, 106–109.

29 Murray, *Pirates of the South China Coast*, 82–83.

30 Antony, *Like Froth Floating on the Sea*, 110.

31 Antony, *Like Froth Floating on the Sea*, 112–114.

32 Antony, *Like Froth Floating on the Sea*, 121, 118.

33 Murray, *Pirates of the South China Coast*, 81–82.

34 Antony, *Like Froth Floating on the Sea*, 115–117, 161–163.

35 Antony, *Like Froth Floating on the Sea*, 116.

36 Murray, *Pirates of the South China Coast*, 152–153; Stanley, *Bold in Her Britches*, 36–38; Chambers, *Ireland's Pirate Queen*; Cook, *Pirate Queen*; Druett, *She Captains*.

37 Murray, 'Cheng I Sao in Fact and Fiction'; Stanley, *Bold in Her Britches*, 38–48; Appleby, 'Women and Piracy in Ireland', 283–298; Rediker, 'Liberty beneath the Jolly Roger', 299–320; Bracewell, 'Women among the Uskoks of Senj', 321–334.

38 Burg, 'The Buccaneer Community', 215–221; Burg, *Sodomy and the Perception of Evil*; Murray, 'The Practice of Homosexuality among the Pirates of China', 244–252; Pérez-Mallaína, *Spain's Men of the Sea*, 170–176.

39 Murray, 'The Practice of Homosexuality among the Pirates of China', 246–247.

40 For a detail analysis of Quin attempts to defeat the pirates, see Murray, *Pirates of the South China Coast*, 99–136.

41 Murray, *Pirates of the South China Coast*, 131–136.

42 Murray, *Pirates of the South China Coast*, 137–150; Antony, *Like Froth Floating on the Sea*, 51–52.

43 Murray, 'Living and Working Conditions in Chinese Pirate Communities', 49.

44 Antony, 'Piracy on the South China Coast', 35–50; Elleman, 'The Taiping Rebellion', 51–63; Koburger, 'Selamat Datang, Kapitan', 64–77.

CHAPTER TWELVE

Community of Thieves: Piracy in the Western Indian Ocean

One of the persistent, self-serving myths of the European expansion into the Indian Ocean is that Europeans disrupted the quiet, peaceful, unarmed trade that had defined the region for millennia.[1] European interlopers claimed that no Indian, African or Asian state had bothered to assert sovereignty over the seas until the Europeans arrived – which, of course, meant that Europeans were free to do so. Consequently, any sign of pre-European maritime violence has been quickly discounted as an aberration.[2] These misconceptions persist because little scholarly work has been done on the pirates of the western Indian Ocean and because these myths served the needs of European powers who sought to justify their imperial expansion into the region.[3] However, the Indian Ocean enjoyed a history of maritime exploration, commerce and political claims to sovereignty over the seas that long pre-dated such efforts in the Atlantic Ocean.[4]

These claims were facilitated and constrained by the unique and complicated human geography of the greater Indian Ocean world. To the west, its waters wash the shores of East Africa with its many states, chiefdoms and diverse linguistic and cultural groups. To the north, the Saudi Arabia peninsula is separated from Africa by the Red Sea and from Persia or Iran by the Persian Gulf. The densely populated Indian subcontinent sits astride long-distance trade routes that connect the Arabian Sea and the Bay of Bengal. To the east, the Malacca Straits connects the Bay of Bengal and, hence, the Indian Ocean to the South China Sea. Ancient sea-lanes have linked the great empires of the east with those of the west for thousands of years.

The long coastlines, scattered islands, deep bays, and the regularity and predictability of the monsoon winds allowed for the easy flow of ideas, people and commodities. From April to August, the trade winds blow northeast,

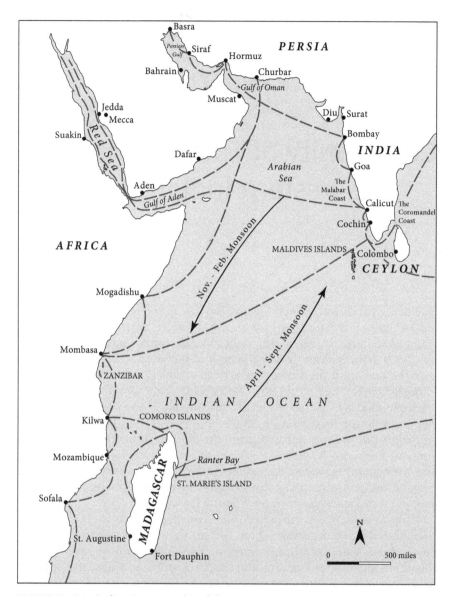

FIGURE 12.1 *Indian Ocean and Malabar coast.*
Source: Map produced by Barry Levely, Cartographer.

and, from December to March, they blow southwest. This geography created four major choke points for trade – the Malacca Straits, the tip of the Indian subcontinent, the entrance to the Persian Gulf and the entrance to the Red Sea – all of which became focal points for piratical activity. Trade routes coming from China and Southeast Asia through the Straits of Malacca

rounded the southern tip of India to cross the Arabian Sea to the Persian
Gulf and to the Gulf of Aden. Spices, such as pepper, ginger, nutmeg and
mace, sugar, as well as porcelain, sandalwood and silk, moved west while
horses, frankincense, myrrh, ivory, cotton cloth and metal goods came east
to India.[5] The Red Sea was the gateway to the Mediterranean, while the
Persian Gulf tapped into the overland trade across the Arabian Peninsula.
The competition for trade stimulated both state claims of sovereignty over
the seas and piracy.

Pirates haunted the waters of the Indian Ocean from the Red Sea and the
Persian Gulf to the Straits of Malacca since at least the seventh century BCE.
Necho II (610–595 BCE) of Egypt constructed a fleet of triremes in the Red
Sea to protect his ships against pirates.[6] Pliny the Elder (23–70 CE) described
this region as 'infested with pirates' and recommended that Roman vessels
travelling there should carry a contingent of archers for defence.[7] Ptolemy
(c. 100–170 CE) referred to pirate dens scattered along the west coast of
India. Pirates sailed the waters between Ceylon and the Indian mainland. In
the Persian Gulf, the island of Kish (Qays) and the shores of Oman became
famous pirate dens. These pirates regularly pillaged the coasts of India and
travelled as far south as Zanzibar in search of slaves. Around 1000 CE, Kish
developed into a pirate state.[8] In the 1200s, Jewish merchants organized a
group of ship owners called the *karim* who travelled in convoys and hired
local maritime toughs to protect themselves from the ravages of pirates in
the Red Sea who attacked merchants and Muslim pilgrimage vessels.[9] Al-
Muqadasi in the tenth century warned anyone travelling in the Arabian Sea
to take soldiers who could throw Greek fire, a combustible mixture used to
disable enemy ships. Marco Polo noted that all the merchants in the Indian
Ocean went about heavily armed to protect themselves from pirates.[10]

Local states also sought to secure control over the valuable sea-lanes. The
Chola dynasty (c. 300 BCE–1279 CE) of southern India asserted control
over the Straits of Malacca and even sent fleets to attack the Andaman
Islands, Sri Lanka and the Maldives in a heated competition over control of
the trade routes from China to Egypt. The ruler of the island of Kish (Qays)
attacked the shipping of the king of Makran in the Gulf of Oman to contest
control of the sea-lanes, which they jealously guarded. In 1130, Kish sent a
fleet against Aden in an attempt to keep the trade they had long encouraged
in the Persian Gulf from being diverted to the Gulf of Aden.[11] Pirate attacks
forced the merchants of the twelfth century who sailed between Cairo and
India to travel in convoys and to hire military escorts. The Muslim rulers of
Aden, under the Rasulid dynasty (1229–1454), sent their galleys to patrol
the sea-lanes and to protect merchants. The grateful merchants paid them
a galley tax in exchange. The Hindu ruler of Barkur on the Malabar coast
sent out his ships to raid passing shipping.[12] Chinese sources claimed that
the Srivijaya state based in Sumatra used to send out ships to attack any
merchant vessel that did not stop at their ports to pay duties.[13] In every
case, states justified their pillaging by assertions of sovereignty over the sea-

lanes in much the same way as European monarchs were only beginning to do.

Perhaps the most famous pirate region in the western Indian Ocean was the Malabar coast of India.[14] This region of the Indian subcontinent developed dynamic cosmopolitan trading cities with merchants from China and the Mediterranean, Persia, Africa and Malaysia. By the eleventh century CE, Hindus belonging to the Mukkuvar caste of fishermen had also developed a highly organized form of communal piracy in which twenty or thirty vessels sailed together. The pirates took their wives and children with them for the entire sailing season in the summer in oared vessels outfitted with triangular rigged sails. When seeking ships, they extended their boats in a line several miles apart, which allowed them to surveil hundreds of miles of sea at a time. Prearranged smoke or fire signals allowed them to communicate the sighting of any ships so the rest could converge to plunder it in strength. They surrounded their prey and attacked them with a hail of arrows and spears before boarding.[15]

These communities operated on their own, but also with the support of local rulers. The port cities of Aden and Calicut benefitted directly from the licit trade, while smaller communities had to find other ways to tap into the immense wealth that sailed past their shores. For example, the ruler of Thana on the Konkan coast, just north of the Malabar region, cut a deal to allow pirates to use his city in return for any horses they might capture in their raids. The Hindu ruler of Barkur, in the sixteenth century, maintained a fleet of warships to attack passing merchants or force them to pay a tribute. The political fragmentation of the region meant that some rulers benefitted more from peaceful trade while others benefitted more by allowing pirates to attack it in return for a share of the loot.[16] These pirate communities were seen as 'integral parts of society and as connected to states'.[17] They specialized in maritime violence as mercenaries hired either by merchants to protect trade or by rulers to steal it.[18] Pirates along the Malabar coast did not, however, operate outside the realm of regular trade and the distinction between pirate and merchant could be blurred. Pirates marketed their wares during the winter after the raiding season ended at below market value in places like Goa or Cochin and often sold them to the very merchants from whom they had stolen the goods.[19]

As Muslim traders expanded into the region in the 700s CE, some local inhabitants adopted Islam and found that they paradoxically enjoyed access to Muslim markets and laws, while being relegated to specific roles in regional commerce. The foreign Muslims called *paradesi* tended to dominate the long-distance trade through the Red Sea. The Marakkar Muslim merchants were natives of the Coromandel area who had converted to Islam and moved to Malabar. They controlled the medium-range Indian trade from the Coromandel coast on the eastern side of the subcontinent with the Malabar coast on the west. Local Mapilla Muslims native to Malabar found themselves relegated to small-time coastal peddling.[20]

When the Portuguese arrived in the region at the end of the fifteenth century, they viewed the peoples of the Indian Ocean with a crusader mentality. In 1498, Vasco da Gama and his three caravels attacked Muslim shipping and executed Muslim sailors. Pedro Álvares Cabral returned in 1500 with specific instructions from the crown to begin corsairing activity. He established a *feitoria* (trading factory) in Calicut, but a mob of angry Muslim merchants destroyed the *feitoria* and massacred the men there. The Portuguese responded by shelling Calicut. Da Gama shelled it again in 1502 on his return voyage.[21] The long-distance *paradesi* Muslims found themselves in conflict with the Portuguese who tried to wrest control of the long-distance spice trade, especially in pepper, from them. The Marakkar and Mapilla Muslims, however, allied with the Portuguese in the hopes of carving out a larger market share for themselves.[22]

The Portuguese activity in Asia remained a mixture of private and public finance. The Portuguese strategy amounted to opportunistic plundering of the rich inter-port trade. This plunder took two main forms: first, the spectacular wealth taken in territorial raids and conquests, and second, the institutionalized corsairing operations against Asian shipping – especially long-distance Muslim shipping. The crown received 20 per cent shares in all of these activities. Thus, even though much of the Portuguese raiding and corsairing in the Indian Ocean was done by private individuals without formal state sanction, the crown had little incentive and little capacity to stop it.[23] The crown eventually shifted from an overt policy of corsairing to promoting and participating in trade and creating a crown monopoly on pepper. The Portuguese also set up an official protection racket through the *cartaz* system. Merchants had to purchase a safe conduct pass from the Portuguese. If they did not, their ship was subject to attack and confiscation by patrolling Portuguese fleets. The real intent of the *cartaz* system was to force passing ships into Portuguese-controlled ports where they would have to pay customs duties.[24] As we have already seen, states throughout India and Asia had long practised this form of raiding as a fundamental part of state craft.

The Portuguese claims to dominance of the sea-lanes and a monopoly of the pepper trade, however, stimulated a violent response from the *paradesi* Muslims who found their livelihoods threatened by Portuguese attacks. Local rulers, Muslim merchants and mixed-race Portuguese settlers, called *casados,* collaborated in building ships and raiding Portuguese shipping.[25] These pirates, in their small-oared ships, called *paráos,* used guerrilla tactics to encircle the more cumbersome Portuguese caravels, get in close where the cannons were useless and then swarm up the sides of the vessels. They could also outrun Portuguese ships and seek shelter in the many protected bays, backwaters and hidden coves along the coast.[26] Though the Muslim conflicts with the Portuguese off the Malabar coast were intense, the Muslim pirates raided Christian, Hindu and Muslim shipping with equal ease because, to them, raiding was simply a traditional communal activity.[27]

By the 1540s, Muslim merchants understood that the only way to counter Portuguese control of the spice trade was to construct a state to counteract them. Ali Raja seized power in Cannanore in 1545 and created a Cannanore–Maldives–Red Sea trade network that was able to keep the Portuguese at arm's length despite ongoing corsairing raids by both sides and the occasional outright sea battle. By the 1580s, Malabar Muslims had constructed a maritime corsairing state that controlled most of the west Indian coast and had formed an alliance with the ruler of Calicut to fight the Portuguese.[28] Malabar pirates also raided south into the Maldives. In 1609, a group of Malabar pirates attacked and killed the sultan of the Maldives before looting his boat and setting it adrift.[29] By 1645, the Portuguese had signed an agreement with the sultan of the Maldives to provide protection against both Malabar and European pirates, but they were incapable of doing so. A band of Malabar pirates descended on the islands, butchered royal officials and carried off 'great riches' without anyone being able to stop them.[30] The ongoing competition with the Portuguese drove Muslims into closer ties with Malabari rulers who received tribute from the pirates that they could then turn around and pay as tribute to the kings of powerful cities, like Calicut. This system integrated the pirates into networks of patronage that allowed them to outfit their fleets, sell their loot and anchor their ships.[31]

The English and the Dutch arrived in the early seventeenth century, and the Muslim corsairs initially partnered with them to resist Portuguese control of the trade. The corsairs then took their stolen goods to be sold in the market at Calicut. As European power increased in the region, Muslim corsairing also increased with the support of local rulers until, 'by the middle of the seventeenth century, corsairing [evolved] into an anti-European maritime campaign, in which all Europeans, including the Portuguese, the Dutch, and the English became a target of frequent attacks'.[32]

By the end of the seventeenth century, the Muslim Mughal state that had governed much of India, and with whom the English had formed an alliance, was falling into decay. In the 1690s, Hindu Maratha rebels hired their own navy under Kanhoji Angre to harass Mughal and European shipping. Kanhoji, also known as 'the pirate king', established a federation of forts and gained his independence from the Maratha state in 1698. He employed grabs, which were '150–300 tons, two-masted, shallow draft, and fast sailing' ships, and 'gallivants, which were 40–70 ton, one-sail' ships manned by twenty to forty rowers.[33] He also employed European gunners. Kanhoji began seizing ports and raiding local fishing boats and Portuguese, Bengali and English vessels. He attacked an East India Company ship and captured the wife of an EIC official, whom he ransomed for 30,000 rupees.[34] Kanhoji himself, his Maratha allies and his Mughal enemies did not share the English legal definition of maritime violence. To them, maritime predation was a normal part of ongoing state conflicts and was necessary for economic survival.

Brigantin donnant chasse a une Felouque, et prest alaborder

FIGURE 12.2 *Giving chase.*
Source: Photo by Culture Club/Getty Images.
Note: Despite the caption, the larger vessel is not really a brigantine. The creator of the image probably called it that because it was larger than a normal *felucca*. A *felucca* is a small sailing vessel powered by oars or one or two lateen sails that was traditionally used in the Red Sea, the Nile and the eastern Mediterranean.

Kanhoji also imitated the Portuguese *cartaz* system by 'issuing [protection] passes to merchants and attacking those ships that carried the passes of either the Sidi or the Portuguese'.[35] What was important to Kanhoji was the 'existence or absence of personal non-aggression agreements'.[36] Though Kanhoji had such agreements with the governor of Bombay, he continued to attack English ships hailing from Madras or Calcutta with whom he had no personal agreements.[37] Kanhoji died in 1729, and his state fell into civil war while his sons struggled for power. By 1749, under the leadership of the victorious son, the Angres resumed their attacks on English, Portuguese and Dutch shipping. The English Royal Navy finally destroyed Angres forts in 1756, and the pirate state ceased to exist.[38]

Omanis from the Saudi Arabian Peninsula also developed a reputation as sea raiders in the seventeenth century. After retaking control of their own coasts from the Portuguese in 1649, they began raiding indiscriminately 'along the coasts of southern Arabia, eastern Africa, and western India'. By 1710, they controlled 'the southern Arabian coast, the Gulf of Oman, and the Persian Gulf'.[39] In 1721, an EIC agent in Mocha described the region: 'All the people along [Omani] coast quite up to Muscatt, live upon plunder, and seize all they can over power, be [their victims] of what nation whatsoever.'[40]

In the latter part of the eighteenth century, the Arab tribesmen called the Qawasim became a nuisance to all shipping entering the Persian

Gulf through the Straits of Hormuz. They lived along the Musandam Peninsula where the modern state of the United Arab Emirates lies. The part of the coastline facing the Gulf was called the Pirate Coast by the British. Qawasim raids began in 1778, when they attacked and captured an English vessel. They soon began raiding along the Omani coast and even down the coast of India almost to Bombay and had a base on Socotra Island at the mouth of the Gulf of Aden adjacent to the Somali coast.[41] They had come under the influence of the expansive jihadist group called the Wahhabis who used them to oppose Omani power on the seas and to generate revenue for the emerging Wahhabi state. The British sent two naval expeditions against them and finally forced the local rulers to the peace table in 1820, after destroying Qawasim bases.[42] A study of piracy in the western Indian Ocean blurs the lines between legal and illegal raiding, between legitimate and illegitimate trade. It demonstrates that pirate communities could operate with considerable autonomy under local leadership. In any case, piracy did not arrive with the Europeans, though European competition for trade could and did stimulate the evolution of pirate communities into full-blown states. Piracy in the western Indian Ocean 'plugged into circuits and networks of labour, information, markets, and social support'.[43] It evolved with economic, military and political change as a key tool in state formation, the creation of empire and local resistance to both. Piracy in the region declined as the EIC (which operated as a pirate organization)[44] consolidated its control of India by the middle of the nineteenth century. As in the Mediterranean, piracy in the western Indian Ocean came to an end only by imperial conquest.[45]

As you read the documents that follow, consider the following questions:

1 What evidence do you find in these accounts that pirates of the Indian Ocean were connected to local states and relied on local communities for their survival?

2 Did pirate tactics described in the accounts change over time? How do you explain what you find?

3 Why might the pirates in the accounts be described as part-time pirates? What does this indicate about the nature of piracy in the Indian Ocean?

4 How was piracy in the Indian Ocean similar to piracy in the Mediterranean and the Atlantic? How would you explain these similarities?

5 What role did piracy in the Indian Ocean play in state formation, imperial expansion and claims of sovereignty over the seas?

6 How did pirate communities evolve into full-blown pirate states? What historical trends contributed to this evolution?

7   When pirate communities become states, do they cease to be parasitic? Why or why not?

8   Why might Middle Eastern, African, Indian and Asian rulers reject European claims to sovereignty of the seas?

9   How did the claims of European historians and chroniclers that piracy came to the 'peaceful' Indian trade only with the arrival of the Europeans serve European imperial interests?

'Narrative of the Voyage of Abd-er-Razzak, Ambassador of Shah Rukh, A.H. 845, A.D. 1442'. Translated from the Persian into French by M. Quatremere. Rendered into English with notes, by R. H. Major, Esq. F.S.A. in *India in the Fifteenth Century: Being a Collection of Narratives of Voyages to India in the Century Preceding the Portuguese Discovery of the Cape of Good Hope from Latin, Persian, Russian, and Italian Sources* (London: Hakluyt Society, 1857), 7, 18.

> Ormuz. The governors sought all kinds of pretexts to detain me; so that the favorable time for departing by sea, that is to say the beginning and middle of the monsoon, was allowed to pass, and we came to the end of the monsoon, which is the season when tempests and attacks from pirates are to be dreaded.
>
> 1443–1444
>   Several individuals, who brought with them a certain number of horses, and all sorts of things besides, had been shipped on board another vessel by order of the king of Ormuz; but being captured on the road by some cruel pirates, they were plundered of all their wealth, and narrowly escaped with their lives. Meeting them at Calicut, we had the honor to see some distinguished friends.

Henry Yule and Henri Cordier, eds. and trans., *The Book of Ser. Marco Polo, the Venetian, Concerning the Kingdoms and Marvels of the East,* 3rd rev. ed. 2 vols. (London: J. Murray, 1903), 2:389.
Marco Polo [1271–1295]

> And you must know that from this kingdom of Malabar, and from another near it called [Gujarat], there go forth every year more than a hundred corsair vessels on cruise. These pirates take with them their wives and children, and stay out the whole summer. Their method is to join in fleets of 20 or 30 of these pirate vessels together, and then they form what they call a sea cordon, that is, they drop off till there is an interval of 5 or 6 miles between ship and ship, so that they cover something like a hundred miles of sea, and no merchant ship can escape them. For when any one corsair sights a vessel a signal is made by fire or smoke, and then the whole of them make for this, and seize the merchants and plunder them.

H. A. R. Gibb and C.F. Beckingham, trans., *The Travels of Ibn Battūta, CE 1325–1354*, 5 vols. (London: Hakluyt Society, 1956–2000), 4: 808. Used with permission.

Ibn Battuta was an Islamic scholar from Morocco who travelled most of the Muslim world between 1325 and 1354. He recorded detailed accounts of his travels.

> [The infidel ruler of Barkur] possesses about thirty warships, commanded by a Muslim called Lūlā, an evildoer who robs at sea and plunders merchants on the sea .... It is a custom of theirs that every ship that passes by a town must anchor at it and give a present to the ruler. This they call the right of the harbor. If anyone omits to do this, they sail out in pursuit of him, bring him to the port by force, double the tax on him, and prevent him from proceeding on his journey for as long as they wish.

Mansel Longworth Dames, ed. and trans., *The Book of Duarte Barbosa: An Account of the Countries Bordering on the Indian Ocean and Their Inhabitants*, 2 vols. (London: Hakluyt Society, 1918–1921) 2: 95–96.

Duarte Barbosa sailed in the third Portuguese armada to India in 1501. He served as interpreter for the viceroy Alfonso de Albuquerque with the local Malabar speakers of the language Malayalam. After writing this account of his time in India in 1516, he sailed with Ferdinand Magellan, his brother-in-law, on his fateful voyage around the world in 1519. After helping Magellan quell a mutiny, Magellan made Barbosa captain of the Victoria. *Barbosa survived the battle of Mactan in the Philippines, where Magellan died, and became co-commander of the expedition. He was killed at a banquet by the rajah Humabon on 1 May, 1521, in the Philippines.*

> Midway between [Quilon] and the Kingdom of Cochim is a small town which they call Porqua under its own Lord, where dwell many Heathen fishers whose livelihood in the winter season is naught but fishery, and in the summer they live by robbery of all they can find, and everything they can take on the sea. They make use of small rowing vessels like the *bargatim*. They are great oarsman and a multitude of them gather together all armed with bows and arrows in plenty, and thus they surround any vessel they find becalmed, with flights of arrows until they take and rob it. Those who are taken therein they put ashore. Thus with these boats of theirs which they call *catures*, they take much spoil, part whereof they give to the lord of the land.

Albert Gray and H. C. P. Bell, eds. and trans., *The Voyage of François Pyrard of Laval to the East Indies, the Maldives, the Moluccas and Brazil*, 2 vols. (London: Hakluyt Society, 1887) 1:47–50.

Pyrard de Laval was a French sailor who sailed to India in 1601. He was shipwrecked in the Maldives Islands in 1602, and he and his shipmates were held captive for five years. They escaped in 1607 during the confusion of a Bengali raid on the islands. Pyrard returned home in 1611 and wrote an account of his experience.

Of these Malabars, too, some are corsairs and pirates, who for the six summer months, when the navigation is good sweep the seas for more than two hundred leagues of coast, so to harry all the ships they find, as well Portuguese as Indian, and even those of their own brethren of Malabars (who carry their merchandise at that season alone); this often happens. While at sea they are no respecters of persons further than this: they choose a chief when they set sail; when they return the chief is so no longer, and has no more power; they usually have as many as eighty to one hundred *galiots* well equipped. Moreover, they make the best soldiers in the world, being exceedingly brave and courageous. They are always at war with the Portuguese, to whom they give great trouble ....The war between them is very cruel and merciless, for the Malabars are so courageous that they never surrender, and prefer death. I have seen them, when in battle with the Portuguese, on perceiving that they were the weaker side, and could not avoid being taken, all come to one side of their *galiot*, and go down with their booty, *galiot* and all, and even sometimes wait till the Portuguese had boarded their vessel, so as they should perish with them.

When they take any of the Portuguese, they usually put them to death or keep them for some time, to see if any will come and redeem them; if not redeemed they are put to death ... To the Indians, of whatever race they may be, the pirates do no harm beyond pillaging them, for they let them go with their vessels and more bulky goods. What is passing strange is that it is their trade and custom to be sea-rovers, and they must seize every opportunity when it presents itself. For all that, they are by land the best folks in the world, the most humane and tractable. They have four harbors of refuge in the realms of Nair kings, where they build their galleys, whence they sally forth, and whither they return with their booty. These harbors are well fortified on the sea side only, for they have a good understanding, being subject to their judicature and paying them tribute. This understanding is highly profitable to these petty Nair kings, who are inaccessible by land. These ports are Moutingué, Badara, Chombaye, and Congelotte, which these kings have given them permission to build. When in the winter time, they return from sea they become good merchants, going hither and thither among the neighboring places to sell their goods, both by land and by sea, using then merchant ships that also belong to them. They often go to Goa and Cochin to sell their merchandise and trade with the Portuguese, obtaining Portuguese passports, though in the previous summer they may have been at war. It is not only the Malabars of these ports who lead this kind of life, but also all others of the whole coast, when they are minded thereto, as indeed they usually are; but inasmuch as they durst not embark at other places, they come overland to these ports and there take ship; they afterwards return home to resume their ordinary life, and then only when they think fit. It is a thing worthy of admiration how these people, whether at sea or in their towns, although they have no masters, nevertheless agree so well together that no dispute, quarrel, or discord arises among them. In these towns, they have indeed some very rich and great Malabar lords, who build and equip these *galiots*, pay the soldiers and pressed hands, and send them to sea without budging from home themselves, except to be chiefs of a large expedition, on which occasion the booty belongs to them ....In the town of Cananor is a fine market every day, called Basar ...

All the Malabars of Cananor and the neighborhood have but two professions those of merchant or corsair; the merchants buy the goods filched by the others to sell at a higher price, even though they have been taken from their own relatives and friends ... The Malabar merchants are recognized by their dress, and not otherwise; for while both the merchants and corsairs usually carry arms, the merchants do not wear their hair long; ... The corsairs wear their hair long like women, and never cut it; they tie it in a bunch like all the other Indians, and cover it with one of these pretty kerchiefs; they go quite naked, except that they are covered with silk cloth as far as the knees, and have another handkerchief round the waist. All the Malabars, as well corsairs as merchants, carry knives with hafts and sheaths of silver – that is, such as can afford it; these are all beautifully fitted with little pendants, such as toothpicks, earpicks, and other instruments. The corsairs wear the beard shaved, but never shave over the mouth nor the moustaches ...

After making a prize, and before coming ashore, they search every man on board and the whole ship. The captain and chief men lay hands on everything, and account conscientiously to the owner of the *galiot*, or *pados*. It is incredible the fatigues these fellows will undergo at sea, and how they endure hunger and thirst. They have plenty of cannon and other arms ... As soon as they have taken a prize they come in to discharge, and return to sea at once, if there seems a likelihood of other booty.

Notes

1   Panikkar, *India and the Indian Ocean*, 35; Abu-Lughod, *Before European Hegemony*, 276; Chaudhuri, *Trade and Civilisation*, 14; Hourani, *Arab Navigation in the Indian Ocean*, 61; McDonald, *Pirates, Merchants, Settlers, and Slaves*, 2–3.

2   Anderson, 'Piracy and World History', 175.

3   Prange, 'The Contested Sea', 10–11.

4   Prange, 'The Contested Sea', 11.

5   Chaudhuri, *Trade and Civilisation*, 39.

6   Paine, *The Sea and Civilization*, 91. The Nabataeans also practised piracy against Ptolemy's Egypt in the late fourth century. See Toussaint, 'La course et la Pirateria', 705.

7   Saletore, *Indian Pirates*, 16.

8   Paine, *The Sea and Civilization*, 267; Saletore, *Indian Pirates*, 1–27.

9   Paine, *The Sea and Civilization*, 361.

10   Prange, 'A Trade of No Dishonor', 1278; Chakravarti, 'Horse Trade and Piracy', 159–182.

11   Prange, 'The Contested Sea', 13–19.

12   Prange, 'The Contested Sea', 20–25.

13   Rugua, *Chau Ju-Kua*, 62.

14   Saletore, *Indian Pirates*, 1–27.

15   Prange, 'A Trade of No Dishonor', 1272–1274.

16   Prange, 'A Trade of No Dishonor', 1275–1277.

17   Prange, 'A Trade of No Dishonor', 1277.

18   Prange, 'A Trade of No Dishonor', 1278–1279.

19   Prange, 'A Trade of No Dishonor', 1279.

20   Malekandathil, 'From Merchant Capitalists to Corsairs', 75–78.

21   Disney, *A History of Portugal*, 127.

22   Malekandathil, 'From Merchant Capitalists to Corsairs', 79–82.

23   Disney, *A History of Portugal*, 153–155.

24   Disney, *A History of Portugal*, 156; Prange, 'A Trade of No Dishonor', 1281.

25   Malekandathil, 'From Merchant Capitalists to Corsairs', 88–89.

26   Prange, 'A Trade of No Dishonor', 1282–1283.

27   Prange, 'A Trade of No Dishonor', 1285.

28   Malekandathil, 'From Merchant Capitalists to Corsairs', 89–93.

29   'Excerpts from an Islamic History of the Maldives', 210.

30   'Memorandum on the Maldive Islands, 1645', 218–219.

31   Prange, 'A Trade of No Dishonor', 1286–1289.

32   Malekandathil, 'From Merchant Capitalists to Corsairs', 94.

33   Thomas, 'Merchants and Maritime Marauders', 91.

34   Risso, 'Cross-Cultural Perceptions of Piracy', 302–305.

35   Subramanian, *The Sovereign and the Pirate*, 10.

36   Risso, 'Cross-Cultural Perceptions of Piracy', 309.

37   Risso, 'Cross-Cultural Perceptions of Piracy', 305.

38   Thomson, *Mercenaries*, 113.

39 Risso, 'Cross-Cultural Perceptions of Piracy', 306.

40 Risso, 'Cross-Cultural Perceptions of Piracy', 307.

41 Davies, *Blood-Red Arab Flag*, 89.

42 Risso, 'Cross-Cultural Perceptions of Piracy', 311–314; See also Davies, *Blood-Red Arab Flag*.

43 Subramanian, *The Sovereign and the Pirate*, 229.

44 Thomson, *Mercenaries*, 39–40.

45 Saletore, *Indian Pirates*, 90.

CHAPTER THIRTEEN

Terror on the Seas: Piracy in Modern Southeast Asia

It is probably not too far of a stretch to say that the modern era of piracy began with the introduction of the steamboat. For the first time, sailors of all kinds did not have to rely on wind- or human-powered oars. Those who acquired the steamboat first enjoyed a distinct advantage in range, speed and manoeuvrability as the British demonstrated during the Opium War (1839–1842) with China. Fleets of Chinese junks could not compete with the heavily armed and more manoeuvrable steamships. The advent of steamships also forced pirates to rethink their tactics and strategies. Pirates along the South China Coast understood that attempting to seize an ironsided steamship using wooden sailing ships was a losing proposition. So they changed tactics from direct assaults to hijackings. Gangs of pirates disguised as passengers would board a steamer and then seize it once it was underway, rob the other passengers and crew, and take a few hostages for ransom.[1]

As Chinese power began to wane in the nineteenth century, European and Malaysian pirates mobbed the Chinese coastline. Americans and Portuguese pirates and smugglers in particular gained a reputation for brutality. The Chinese responded by hiring their own pirates to repel the foreign threat. In 1911, the Qing state finally collapsed into a prolonged period of civil war that persisted until the 1950s. Piracy flourished as professional gangs of hijackers belonging to large, well-organized crime syndicates became much more sophisticated, taking weeks to plan the hijacking of a steamboat.[2] The British worked with the Nationalist Party (Kuomintang) to suppress piracy in the 1930s, but to little effect.[3]

Steam power also assisted the Dutch and the English in their ongoing struggle against Malay, Orang Laut, Iranun and Chinese marauders around Singapore in the early nineteenth century. Local rulers, especially the Malay royal family, recruited sea bandits like the Orang Laut, who were fishermen that plundered as part of a broader economic strategy, to help them resist European incursions.[4] In response, the Dutch and the British signed treaties with local rulers demanding that they stop using pirates. These demands are quite interesting given that their own governments used privateers in much the same fashion that local rulers used the sea bandits of their region. When treaties did not reduce attacks against European shipping, they used their steamships to patrol the islands around Singapore and to attack known pirate lairs. The Dutch and the British were able to force pirates to shift their bases to safer locations, but they proved unable to suppress piracy in the region.[5]

The Second World War forced a fundamental realignment of power in Southeast Asia and China and created the conditions for piracy to flourish. The Japanese conquests toppled colonial regimes and drove out the European navies that had patrolled the waters of Southeast Asia. Following the war, new states emerged who saw little reason to suppress pirates who were cast as patriotic heroes struggling against foreign invaders and global commerce. International disputes over territorial claims often left vast areas of ocean and coastlines unpatrolled and uncontrolled. A huge American surplus of outboard motors, weapons and ammunition left behind in Southeast Asia gave pirates the technological advantage of speed and manoeuvrability that allowed them to chase down their prey on the high seas and to quickly disappear into the intricate maze of islands, swamps, bays and estuaries.[6] A new era in maritime piracy was born.

The old centres of piracy became hotspots once again as Borneo, the Philippines, the Sulu Archipelago and the Straits of Malacca all became centres of piratical activity. Between 1959 and 1962, some 232 reported attacks occurred in Borneo. Pirates now used speedboats and came armed with shotguns, rifles, submachine guns, pistols and homemade bombs. The Tausug of Jolo and the Balangingi in the Sulu region returned to piracy with a vengeance. They considered piracy a traditional activity and saw themselves as Muslims resisting the efforts of Christians to dominate their homeland. Rather than focusing on slaves, as their ancestors had, they stole 'cattle, money, jewelry, weapons, brass work and gongs ... shoes, watches, transistor radios, and sewing machines'.[7] Piracy also returned to the South China Sea in the 1970s and 1980s. Both small-time outfits using small craft to loot, rape and pillage and large gangs that hijacked vessels and sold their cargos proliferated. Often these vessels became 'phantom ships'. They were repainted, renamed and given false registrations so they could be used to smuggle drugs or illegal immigrants.[8]

Perhaps one of the most vicious and most often overlooked episodes of piracy in the twentieth century occurred in the Gulf of Thailand in the 1970s and 1980s. The political instability following the Vietnam War (1955–1975) led to a massive outflow of some 3 million people from Vietnam, Laos and Cambodia. Many of them were ethnic Chinese, but others were Vietnamese

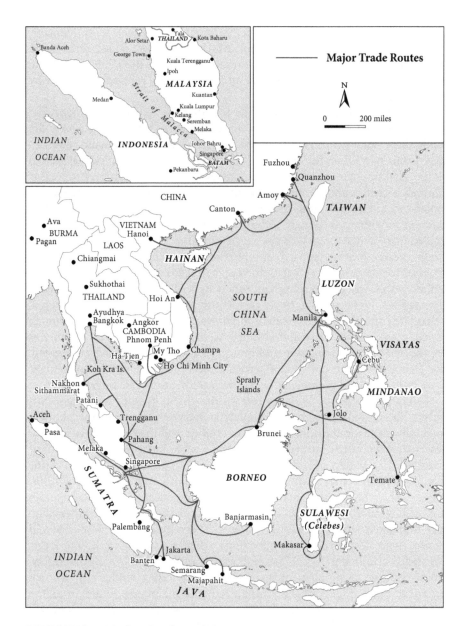

FIGURE 13.1 *Modern Southeast Asia.*
Source: Map produced by Barry Levely, Cartographer.

businessmen who had not supported the new Vietnamese government's economic policies, who rejected communism or who fled government repression.[9] Often, these refugees took to the sea hoping to find sanctuary in Thailand or Malaysia. But they found themselves in political limbo.

The Vietnamese government saw them as traitors and their navy regularly attacked refugee boats. The Thai and Malaysians chose to see them as an invasion force meant to destabilize their countries. By 1979, Indonesia, Malaysia, the Philippines, Singapore and Thailand all refused to accept any more refugees.[10]

The lack of any protection and the fact that the refugees often travelled with all the wealth they could carry in the hopes of establishing a new life made them vulnerable. Thai fisherman discovered that they could make an easy profit by raiding the ships for valuables. These raids quickly escalated as the Thai government encouraged pirates to attack the refugees in a clear campaign to discourage immigration into Thailand. The attacks became more violent, including gratuitous torture and gang rapes. Ships that were attacked three or four times soon had nothing left to take. A clear campaign to rape and kidnap women and girls for service in Thai brothels ensued as pirate gangs became more organized and more effective. Though the attacks came to an end as the flood of refugees dried up and international efforts, led by the United States, worked to stamp out piracy in the Gulf, the human costs were tremendous. Perhaps some thirty to forty thousand people were murdered. Uncounted thousands of women and girls were systematically and brutally raped, many on the uninhabited jungle island of Koh Kra, 130 kilometres southeast of Koh Samui, and sold into prostitution in Thailand. In the end, the Thai government policy of deterrence succeeded. The number of refugee arrivals in Thailand plummeted by 62 per cent between 1981 and 1982.[11]

Today, the Straits of Malacca remain the global hotspot for piracy. Not only is the region's geography uniquely suited for piracy, but the political instability, territorial disputes, religious conflict and the existence of vibrant sea-lanes over which a third of the world's trade passes make it a pirates' paradise. The Malacca Straits create a funnel that all east/west ocean traffic has to use, unless they want to go around Sumatra and add nearly a 1,000 miles to their trip, which increases fuel costs significantly. Most companies are willing to run the risks of the occasional pirate attack rather than pay the added costs in fuel and salaries. These pirates include occasional pirates, who simply seize an opportunity when it presents itself, and large, organized criminal gangs. Most of the opportunistic pirates are fishermen simply seeking to supplement their income. The large, syndicated criminal organizations are hierarchically organized, and maintain spotters in all the major ports who can provide information on ships, cargoes, schedules, crews, etc.[12] Other pirates operate as part of nationalist or religious organizations, such as the Free Aceh Movement, Islamic fundamentalists from Sumatra and the Jamaah Islamiyah in Malaysia and Indonesia.[13]

In the southern Malacca Straits, piracy tends to focus on Singapore and the Phillip Channel where ships have to slow down to navigate the narrow channel. Pirates in this region tend be Indonesian men from the island of Batam. They can see the thriving port of Singapore with its skyscrapers and the world's wealth anchored in its harbour from their own doorsteps.

Because the industries established on Batam prefer to employ women, men are often left with few options for legitimate employment.[14] These pirates use outboard motors and hit-and-run tactics to board ships in search of cash and easily portable, resalable valuables, such as 'binoculars, cameras, audio-visual electronic equipment, clothing, credit cards, medicine and medical equipment, jewelry, [and] watches'. The pirates usually attack at night by approaching the vessel from the stern and use grappling hooks and ropes or bamboo poles to climb onboard while the vessel is still underway. They rarely seize the ship and its cargo, and they rarely kill or kidnap their victims, though they are not averse to using their knives and machetes to intimidate crews.[15] They understand that the sight of a little blood is an effective psychological tool. Piracy in the northern Malacca Straits is much more violent as the pirates are armed with automatic weapons and grenades launchers. These pirates kidnap foreign crews and vessels and hold them for ransom. They also prey on local fishing and trading vessels and extort protection money from them.

After the 2004 tsunami that devastated the coastal areas, piracy declined, probably because of the loss of equipment but also because of the increased military presence as rescue and relief efforts took place. After 2005, piracy in the northern Malacca Straits returned, together with the shootings and kidnappings.[16] Piracy in recent years in the northern Malacca Straits has diminished while that in the Singapore Straits and Indonesia continues unabated. Pirate attacks in the region continue to include robbery of vessels at sea or anchored in harbours, hijacking, kidnap-for-ransom and stolen vessels that become 'phantom ships'.[17]

Recent decades have also witnessed the rise in insurance fraud in Southeast Asia run by large crime syndicates. Ship owners can arrange to have their ships 'pirated'. The pirates can keep the ship and sometimes the cargo, and the ship owner claims the loss on his insurance. Often these ships become phantom ships registered to Honduras or Panama where temporary registration papers are easy to obtain.[18] It is a cost-effective way for a ship owner to dispose of ageing ships.

Another more recent development is the connection between piracy and terrorism. Insurgent groups have discovered that piracy can be an effective way of raising funds and upgrading equipment and weapons. The Moro National Liberation Front (MNLF) in the Philippines began collecting protection money from local fisherman in the 1980s. Some of them began raiding coastal towns in Malaysia in the 1980s in raids reminiscent of the buccaneer raids on Spanish towns in the Caribbean. The Abu Sayyaf Group of Islamists, who operated out of Jolo and Basilan, regularly targets civilians and uses indiscriminate violence. It is tied to international terror networks and is classified as a Terrorist Organization by the US State Department. But after 1998 and the death of its founder, the Abu Sayyaf Group has turned increasingly towards piracy. In 2000, they raided the Sipadan Island Diving Resort, robbed the tourists and took nine hostages that they later ransomed

FIGURE 13.2 *Philippine pirates in South China Sea, c. 1994.*
Source: Photo by Eric-Paul-Pierre Pasquier/Gamma-Rapho. Via Getty Images.

for 5 million dollars. Then, in 2004, they combined terrorism with piracy when they blew up the Manila *SuperFerry 14* killing 100 civilians and then sent a letter to the ferry company demanding 1 million dollars in protection money.[19]

This cross-pollination of piracy with terrorism has led some to argue that piracy and terrorism are simply two sides of the same coin – that they are essentially the same thing.[20] To argue that piracy equals terrorism is to profoundly misunderstand, misconstrue and over-simplify both the history of piracy and the history of terrorism.[21] Similarities can be found, of course. Pirates do use terror to intimidate their victims – all violent criminals do whether on land or sea. Likewise, terrorist groups are seldom purely political. They also come together for criminal purposes. Pirates use terror for profit or personal pleasure. Terrorists use terror as propaganda and seldom see direct profit from sending a suicide bomber into a school or military base. Likewise, pirates are seldom willing to die to achieve their goal. Terrorists often are.[22] As we noted in the introduction, the one key factor that distinguishes pirates from other forms of banditry or criminal organizations is the use of ships. In most other regards, they are very similar. If all pirates can be classified as terrorists and all terrorist as pirates, then all bank robbers, mafia organizations and crime syndicates the world over are both pirates and terrorists and neither word has any real meaning anymore.

Equating pirates with terrorists might appeal to legal experts wrestling to cope with an upsurge in piracy and global terrorism, but it does little to deepen our understanding of piracy. One does not have to run roughshod over the history or piracy to argue that the United States should prosecute terrorists under piracy statutes. This is not to say that those fighting terrorism cannot learn lessons from historical efforts to fight piracy. I believe they can. But perhaps the most salient lesson is the most unpalatable. Piracy has always been with us, so we can probably expect that terrorism will persist as well. Global piracy was not defeated in the eighteenth or the nineteenth century. It was contained and constrained. That was all. That may be all we can expect in our global fight against terrorism and political extremism.

As you read the documents that follow, consider the following questions:

1   What similarities can you see between the 1962 raid on Borneo and the 1980 attacks on the Vietnamese ship?

2   What are the costs associated with pirate attacks, both human and financial? Who bears the costs of pirate attacks?

3   What tactics do pirates in the Malacca Straits employ? What do they hope to acquire in their raids?

4   Why is piracy easier in the Malacca Straits than in other areas of the world?

5   What evidence can you find that indicates that pirates continue to have support from governments and land-based communities and businesses?

6   What role does organized crime play in modern piracy?

7   What complicates attempts to fight piracy in the Malacca Straits?

8   What patterns does the 2017 ICC IMB report reveal about modern piracy?

9   How did pirates adjust to changes in technologies?

10   Why does piracy tend to emerge and re-emerge in the same places over time?

11   What is the challenge of equating piracy with terrorism?

12   Why are modern pirates not cast as romantic social bandits in popular culture?

13   How do pirates use what might be called a vocabulary of violence in their raids and what purpose does it serve?

Stefan Eklöf, *Pirates in Paradise: A Modern History of Southeast Asia's Maritime Marauders* (Copenhagen: NIAS Press, 2009), 20–22, 38–39. Reproduced with Permission.

A pirate raid on a timber camp at Kunak on the east coast of Borneo in 1962.

The raid began about 1740 hours ... when a vessel (technically a *kumpit*, but more like a Chinese launch in appearance and about 24 feet long) approached Kunak from the Semporna Channel. It had a *kajang* covering, badly maintained. At the time, the government launch *Rusakan* was alongside the steps of the wharf, and the British Borneo Timber Company log towing boat, *Darvel Bay* was alongside the longest part of the wharf. As the *kumpit* came alongside the *Rusakan*, the muzzles of four rifles appeared over its side. The occupants of the *kumpit* opened fire and in the first burst killed the Engineer of the *Rusakan*, who was sitting on the forward deck, and wounded two children also on deck. The two sailors, the Engineer's wife and one of the sailor's wives jumped into the sea. The *serang* (skipper) was wounded in the left arm as he also jumped for the sea. The *kumpit* then pulled up to the wharf. Four raiders ran across the wharf to the *Darvel Bay*, which had its engine running, shot four members of the crew and did some damage to the engine. One man returned to the *Rusakan*, smashed the copper pipes of the engine, tore out the radio and transferred it and the *Rusakan's* binoculars to the *kumpit*. While one raider stayed in the *kumpit*, the rest, some seven in number, advanced from the wharf, with two firing up the road, while others entered the shops near the wharf and forced local people to carry goods and money back to the *kumpit*. The telephone-line was cut and an attempt was made to launch the Mostyn Estates launch *Lucinda*. This was unsuccessful, as it was locked up. The raiders then stove in the boat and damaged the engine. ...

After the raiders had loaded their boat, they saw a Chinese launch coming in round the coral. They intercepted it, tied up their own boat to it, told the passengers to jump into the sea and ordered the skipper and engineer, named Kamaludin, to tow the *kumpit* out.

Attack on Vietnamese junk carrying forty-two refugees in March of 1980. After being robbed by a Vietnamese naval vessel, they were attacked by Thai pirates.

At 3 p.m. on Mar. 22, a Thai pirate boat attacked them, searching the refugees, wrecking the motor and then letting them go. The junk drifted on and the next morning the scene was repeated. The third time came that afternoon when 2 pirate boats came upon them at once. Both vessels had cloths spread over their bows to hide their numbers. At the time, 3 Vietnamese youths were standing on the bow of the junk holding out a sail. All of a sudden, the pirates fired into the three. Nguyen Van Y., 29, was struck by a bullet and fell while his brother-in-law, Nguyen Ngoc Ly, 32, a former air force officer, ran to break the fall. The pirates shot him, too. Then the pirates leaped onto the junk and threw the victims into the sea. Ly and Y., only wounded by the gunshots, struggled to get back to the boat, but they were beaten off by the pirates. ...

The remaining 40 refugees were driven onto the pirate vessel. The men were put in the ice hold and the women were raped. After that, they forced everyone back on the junk and left. The refugees continued to drift without an engine to power them. They had run out of food and water.

On Mar. 24, they met another pirate boat. In terror, the women smeared their faces and bodies with viscous oil, hoping in this way to repulse the pirates, but this plan did not deter the attackers who went on with the raping. They pounded holes in the junk, pried up boards as they searched for hidden gold and finally took with them two girls Nguyen Thi A., 16, and Le Thi Y., 18.

[*After being attacked a fifth time, the junk was towed to Koh Kra.*]

[Seven] other pirate vessels were there waiting when they arrived. What ensued could only be described as chaos. The different bands fought over the valuables and women. The 11 women left, with ages ranging from 12–43, were the victims of the most vicious rape right on the beach when everyone was exhausted, hungry, thirsty and sick, and their bodies still slimy with oil.

Ms. Vo Thi No., 40, with her 2 daughters, aged 14 and 12, were all three raped at the same time. The pirates didn't bother to take them off to some hidden place, but went right ahead with their rape there on the beach in front of everyone.

The next days, from Mar. 24 to April 1, hundreds of pirates from numerous boat[s] poured onto the island and barbarous scenes took place each day: the hunting of women and the torture of men. The women spread out, some hiding in the jungle, some climbing the mountain, but by now the pirates were well acquainted with the territory and kept up the search. Sometimes they set fire to the jungle to drive the women out.

Ted Kemp, 'Crime on the High Seas: The World's Most Pirated Waters', *CNBC*, 15 September 2014. Used with Permission.

SINGAPORE – The Ai Maru steamed alone under night skies on June 14 when a speedboat slipped in from the darkness and overtook the tanker about 30 miles off the coast of Malaysia. At 9:15 p.m., seven men with handguns and knives clambered up over the side, smashed through doors, tied up crew members at gunpoint and bashed the Ai Maru's communications equipment.

The attackers stripped the 13 crew members of their personal belongings, locked them in a room and spent the next hours getting to the real work at hand: stealing the cargo. A second tanker, this one piloted by more pirates, pulled alongside. The maritime robbers siphoned a total of 620 metric tons of marine gas oil from Ai Maru to their own ship.

At 5 a.m., when naval and coast guard vessels arrived at the Ai Maru, dead in the water with its lights glowing, the pirates were long gone. Their total haul, at black market fuel prices, came in at about $550,000.

Welcome to the world's most dangerous waters, where a whole new style of piracy is rewriting the playbook of maritime crime. The attack on the Ai Maru, which was documented by *ReCAAP*, a multinational body that combats piracy, and the International Chamber of Commerce's International Maritime Bureau (IMB), is a textbook example of the piracy plaguing the seas of the Singapore Strait and Strait of Malacca – the world's busiest commercial waterway.

Unlike the Somali pirates – who, incidentally, are now almost out of business – the pirates of southern Asia rarely, if ever, seize hostages. They're in the business of stealing cargoes of liquid fuel. And they're often not small-time, ad hoc gangs from coastal villages like the Somali crews. Instead, experts say, they're highly organized criminal enterprises that gather intelligence, coordinate attacks, work in discrete teams, sometimes have their own tankers and then sell what they steal to big, pre-arranged buyers ....

Why here, why now

From a business standpoint, the boom in south Asian piracy makes a lot of sense. A third of the world's shipping moves through the Strait of Malacca and Singapore Strait each year, including most trade between Europe and China, and nearly all the crude oil that moves from the Persian Gulf to the big Asian economies like China, Japan, and South Korea. About 130,000 vessels arrive in Singapore each year alone, according to both Singaporean and international estimates. That breaks down to a ship entering the strait every four minutes. And the global trade that flows through that bottleneck – only 1.7 miles wide at its narrowest point – is growing.

The great majority of those vessels make it to their destination without any problems. The Singapore Strait is in no danger of shutting down. But the number of attacks is on the rise. There were 125 pirate attacks reported in the region in 2013, triple the number from 2009. (Over the same period, attacks off the Horn of Africa shrank from 197 to 13.)

And even those estimates from Asia are conservative. Only a minority of attacks are reported, experts contend, since handing over such information is voluntary, and many shippers don't want their names associated with lost cargoes or a perception of lax security.

But the costs of piracy extend far beyond the actual vessels that are attacked. The U.S. Merchant Marine estimates that global piracy costs shippers $4.9 billion to $8.3 billion a year. Half of the world's attacks now take place in the waters off Indonesia, Singapore, and Malaysia.

Those higher costs come in the form of lost cargo, higher insurance, added shipping times, extra compensation to crews, litigation and legal fees. Even cruising faster in an effort to discourage pirates adds costs. (Pirates prefer their targets "low and slow," in the parlance of the shipping trade.) Jon Helmick, a captain with the United States Merchant Marine

Academy, overseen by the Maritime Administration at the Department of Transportation, said that cruising at 17.9 knots in a supertanker, versus the typical 12.8 knots, adds an extra $88,000 in fuel expense per ship per day.

Those extra costs inevitably get passed on to consumers in the increasingly interconnected global markets, where losses in one part of the world affect costs in another. And while it's impossible to quantify exactly how much more Americans pay for regular consumer goods as a result of piracy and higher shipping costs, it's worth considering that more than 90 percent of the world's trade is carried by sea, according the United Nations International Maritime Organization.

How it works: Pirating in plain sight

As the example of the Ai Maru shows, pirates in the Strait of Malacca and Singapore Strait prefer tactics that are very different from the chasing, seizing and kidnapping that were employed in the past by Somali pirates on the *Maersk Alabama* and hundreds of other targets.

Maritime bandits in south Asia prefer stealth, and they make money by selling what they steal, not by ransoming seafarers. But that doesn't mean that hair-raising confrontations with a high possibility of violence don't occur from time to time.

Capt. David Watkins, a former ship's master who now works as fleet quality assurance manager for Swire Group's China Navigation unit, tells a story of being awakened by a crewmate in the middle of the night who said that nine pirates wielding ropes, grappling hooks and machetes were swarming up over the stern of his crude carrier as it sailed through the strait close enough to see the nighttime lights of Singapore in the distance. His 19-man crew armed itself with crowbars, mustered on deck and got ready for a nasty hand-to-hand fight.

'Nobody went to sleep that night,' he said. 'No one wants to get into the conflict, I have to admit. Sometimes there's this bravado about attacking pirates. But when push comes to shove, all you want to do is constrain them or subdue them.'

Two pirates drowned that night as they tried to escape from the superior numbers of the crew.

Pirates in the Strait of Malacca and Singapore Strait prefer small cargo ships carrying scrap metal, and small tankers transporting liquid fuel or other petroleum products. Those cargoes are difficult to trace on the black market, experts said. At least nine tankers in the straits and east of Singapore in the South China Sea had their liquid cargoes siphoned off between April and August, according to the IMB.

Such heists require precise intelligence – about what a ship is hauling, where it will be at a specific time, the security measures in place and details about the crew. Most pirate operations obtain that information from a variety of sources, from crooked seafarers or their family members to port workers and even government and military sources, according to several sources who spoke with CNBC, including Nicholas Teo, deputy director at the Information Sharing Centre of ReCAAP.

When Western navies first began combating Somali pirates toward the end of the last decade, they often cited the vast watery expanses of that region one of the main reasons it was so hard to stamp out the perpetrators. So naturally, one may wonder how a choke point running from the Strait of Malacca through the Singapore Strait has become a choice operating region for gangs of thieves on tankers.

Rather than making it harder to operate, experts said, the crowded waterways of the region make it easier for pirates to blend in. It's a regular occurrence for two vessels in the area to lash together alongside one another and transfer fuel or other cargoes, for entirely legitimate, commercial reasons. Standing on the shore at East Coast Park in Singapore last month, a *CNBC* reporter could see it happening simultaneously in two different places. 'Ships pass by and see two vessels together transferring cargo, that's not uncommon at sea. And on radar, it just looks like two little blips. Those could be fishing boats,' said the IMB's Pottengal Mukundan.

Crew members standing at the controls on the ship's bridge with a gun to their head are unlikely to sound an alarm, even if a patrol boat passes nearby, experts said. After a cargo transfer or robbery is done, pirates usually destroy victim ships' communications gear and steal crew members' phones. And even if the seafaring thieves are on a big vessel, they can blend in with the hundreds of others in the area before the authorities arrive. If Somali pirates act like muggers, attacking isolated targets out of sight of the authorities, south Asia's pirates act more like pick-pockets, using the crowd itself as cover.

In the waters of the Singapore Strait, there have been at least four attacks this year in broad daylight, said Capt. K.A. Pillai, a former Indian navy officer and bulk carrier master who is now a maritime security consultant and a member of the Singapore Chamber of Maritime Arbitrators. The area is well patrolled by marine police from Singapore, Malaysia, and Indonesia, but it's possible to be in the area of an ongoing attack and not be able to recognize that it's happening.

Organized crime

The pirates' high level of coordination and business model bear the hallmarks of organized crime, experts from across the industry and government agencies agree. One big tell: A growing number of attacks in the area involve commandeering vessels and stealing whole cargoes, especially liquid fuel, as opposed to simple theft of whatever pirates can find laying around. That means finding a buyer for a particular product in advance, often an international buyer with plenty of capital. Next, pirate groups have to gather intelligence that will let them target a ship containing that specific cargo. Then they have to make big capital expenditures, such as acquiring their own tanker that will carry the stolen cargo. Then they need to fence the fuel.

'It's definitely organized crime,' said Michael McNicholas, managing director of Phoenix Group, a maritime security firm. 'And they have to have international links. They're taking it ashore. They need a refinery that will turn their head. And those refineries are cutting them deals.'

Given current market prices for, say, naval fuel, and the quantities that pirates have been able to siphon away in attacks that have been documented, a gang can steal fuel worth upwards of $2 million in one robbery. Certainly, pirates are unlikely to get fair market value, since part of the way they draw buyers is by offering heavily discounted prices. Their huge operating margins make slashing prices easy. But even accounting for discounted pricing, they're engaged in transactions that require them to line up a major buyer ahead of time, said Derek Baldwin, director of Worldwide Operations at IBIS Risk Management Services, which investigates fraud and other crimes for the U.S. government and corporate clients.

'If I know you buy oil, and I have dealt with you before, I call you up and say, "Can you use 10,000 gallons?" I'm getting it for free, so I can quote you a really good price,' Baldwin said.

Small tankers are perfect targets in more ways than one. When they're loaded, their decks are close to the water line and they move slowly, making them easy to board.

Just before midnight on June 17, the Budi Mesra Dua was overcome by a high-speed wooden boat as it steamed slowly with a cargo of diesel oil, according to an account from *ReCAAP*. Six pirates armed with swords tied down the crew of the Budi Mesra Dua and forced its master and chief officer to sail to a new location close to land. There, a barge with 20 more pirates arrived. They boarded and siphoned off 940 metric tons of diesel onto the barge. They fled at 9 a.m. the next day, leaving the crew unharmed, after smashing the diesel tanker's communication and navigation equipment.

Current liquid fuel prices make their cargoes appealing to organized crime. Marine gas oil can go for $900 a metric ton on the open market. Plus, liquid fuels are hard to track, and pirates sometimes make them even more difficult to trace by moving them through multiple middlemen or by mixing refined products with other grades of fuel. In fact, those mixtures are turning up on the market more and more, said Pottengal Mukundan of the IMB.

That can pose its own danger to vessels far away from the scene of pirate attacks. A growing problem of 'contaminated' oils turning up in Southeast Asia means many buyers are unknowingly adding fuel that can damage engines because it doesn't meet the ship's specifications.

A region posing its own problems

Another challenge for governments trying to catch pirates is the sheer number of governments and other groups trying to combat the problem, often with limited collaboration. The region has three major national jurisdictions – Indonesia, Malaysia, and Singapore. The geography of the region makes intercepting and tracking down pirates extra difficult. Malaysia is broken into two main parts, one on a peninsula north of Singapore, and the other on a huge island it shares with Indonesia, south of Singapore. And then Indonesia is a vast archipelago in its own right, with 17,000 islands that provide endless villages, grottoes, inlets and other nooks where pirates can hide out.

Indeed, more governments involved in anti-piracy efforts don't necessarily translate into better enforcement. In the case of the Ai Maru, a distress signal reached the IMB's Piracy Reporting Centre in Kuala Lumpur, Malaysia. Six vessels responded, from the Royal Malaysian Navy, the Malaysian Maritime Enforcement Agency, the Indonesian Navy and the Republic of Singapore Navy. The pirates still got away.

Stefan Eklöf, *Pirates in Paradise: A Modern History of Southeast Asia's Maritime Marauders* (Copenhagen: NIAS Press, 2009), 70–71. Reproduced with Permission.

On 12 September [1995], the Cyprus-registered bulk carrier *Anna Sierra* left Ko Si Chang, southeast of Bangkok, bound for Manila. On board, she carried a crew of 23 and a cargo of 12,000 tons of sugar worth US$ 5 million. Shortly after midnight on 13 September the Anna Sierra was proceeding south in the Gulf of Thailand when she was attacked by 30 pirates armed with submachine guns. After boarding the ship, the pirates handcuffed the crew and locked them in two small cabins. Two days later, off the south Vietnamese coast, the crew was forced off the ship in two life rafts. They were rescued later the same day by Vietnamese fishermen. Around half of the pirate gang left the ship [i]n the motor boat, which they had used for boarding the ship, taking cash and valuables with them. Left on board were 14 of the pirates acting as crew.

The *Anna Sierra* then proceeded north to the Chinese port or Beihai in Guanxi province, where she arrived on 20 September, one week after the hijacking. The ship had now been renamed the *Artic Sea* and provided with false documents from the Honduras Registry of Shipping. Apparently, the pirates intended to unload the cargo of sugar in Beihai; it later transpired that a trader in Beihai had ordered the shipment in early September, that is, already before the *Anna Sierra* was hijacked. For unknown reasons, however, the cargo was not unloaded. The ship was instead detained by Chinese Frontier Defence Authority (Banfong) which put two armed guards on board and seized the ship's documents and the passports of the crew.

At the beginning of October, investigators of the IMB, which had been contacted by the shipowner after the ship had been hijacked, arrived in Beihai and were able positively to identify the ship as the *Anna Sierra*. Eventually, in December, the Chinese authorities recognized that the ship was in fact the *Anna Sierra*, but nevertheless refused to return the ship to the shipowner, claiming that they were still investigating the case. However, none of the detained crew members was formally interviewed by China's Public Security Bureau (PSB) the authority in charge of the investigation.

In February 1996, the PSB offered to release the ship provided the shipowner paid a fee of US$ 400,000 to the Bureau for its costs and other expenses. As the shipowner refused to pay, however, the ship remained in Beihai, where its maintenance was neglected. In July, the crew of pirates was taken off the ship – they were subsequently repatriated to their countries of origin with no legal prosecution – and the ship was left unmanned. In early 1997, the PSB noticed that the ship's engine room and holds were partially flooded with sea water, and the cargo was discharged to a warehouse. As the *Anna Sierra* continued to take in sea water and developed a ten degree list, the port authorities decided to tow her to a nearby beach. In August, the PSB auctioned the cargo without consulting the owners.

Piracy and Armed Robbery against Ships: Report for the Period 1 January–31 December 2016 (London: ICC International Maritime Bureau, 2017), 17–18, 20–22, 24. Used with Permission.

Bangladesh: Robbers usually target ships preparing to anchor. Most attacks reported at Chittagong anchorages and approaches. However, Attacks in Bangladesh have fallen significantly over the past few years due to the efforts by the Bangladesh Authorities.

China: Tianjin/Caofeidian – Incidents mostly at anchorage area.

India: Kandla – Incidents reported at port and anchorage areas.

Indonesia: Tanjung Priok – Jakarta, Dumai, Nipah, Batu Ampar/Batam, Samarinda, Muara Berau and Belawan anchorage and surrounding waters. Pirates/robbers normally armed with guns/knives and/or machetes. Generally, be vigilant in other areas. Many attacks may have gone unreported. Pirates/robbers normally attack vessels during the night. When spotted and alarm sounded, the pirates/robbers usually escape without confronting the crew.

Malacca Straits: The number of reported attacks continue to drop due to the patrols by the littoral states authorities since July 2005. Ships are, however, advised to continue maintaining strict anti-piracy/robbery watches when transiting the Straits. Currently, there are no indications as to how long these patrols will continue or reduce. In some cases, attacks may have gone unreported.

Malaysia: Of Sabah – Militant activities resulting in a number of tugs/barges/fishing boats being attacked and crews kidnapped.

Philippines: Pirates/militants in the southern Philippines attacking vessels in/off Sibutu passage/off Sibutu island/Tawi Tawi/Sulu Sea/Celebes Sea/off eastern Sabah. Initially tug/barges and fishing vessels were targeted to rob and kidnap crews for ransom. Merchant ships and their crews have also recently been targeted.

Singapore Straits: Vessels are advised to remain vigilant and to continue maintaining adequate anti-piracy/robbery watch and measures. Pirates/robbers attack ships while underway or while at anchor especially during the night.

South China Sea: Although attacks have dropped significantly in the vicinity off Tioman/off Pulan Aur/off Anambas/Natuna/Mangkai Islands/Subi Besar/Merundung areas, vessels are advised to continue to remain vigilant. In the past, a number of hijackings of small product tankers have occurred off the coast of Malaysia, Indonesia, Singapore and in the South China Sea Area. This trend started in April 2014 and the hijackings stopped abruptly late 2015. The IMB is monitoring the situation. It has been reported that some criminals have been arrested by local authorities both in Malaysia and in Indonesia.

Vietnam: Vung Tau – Increase in attacks especially at anchorages.

Observations:
Indonesia:
On 07 May 2016, a Cook Islands flagged Product Tanker MT Hai Soon 12 was attacked and hijacked by armed pirates while underway at position latitude 02:04:48 South and Longitude 108:39:27 East, around 21nm south of Pulau Serutu, Indonesia at approximately 2045 LT. The Tanker while en route from Singapore to Sunda Straits was attacked and boarded by armed pirates. They took hostage all crew members and hijacked the tanker. As the Owners failed to receive the updates from the Master, they reported the incident to the IMB PRC who had then reported and liaised with the Indonesian Authorities. The IMB PRC also broadcast to all ships to keep a lookout for the missing tanker. The Indonesian Navy dispatched their patrol boats who had subsequently located and intercepted the hijacked tanker and rescued all crew members on board. Nine pirates were detained. All crew members reported safe.

On 28 June 2016, a Panamanian flagged Product Tanker MT Chamtang was attacked and boarded by armed pirates while steaming at position Latitude 03:00 North and Longitude 105:10 East, around 26nm WSW of Mangkai Island, Indonesia at approximately 1945 UTC. About ten pirates armed with guns and knives attacked and successfully boarded the tanker underway. They entered the bridge as the Second Officer was altering course. They held the Second Officer and the duty AB at gun point and beat them. The pirates wore face masks and were aggressive and violent. They took the Second Officer to the Master's cabin and then took the Master and the other crew hostage. The pirates stole the ship's GPS and Navtex equipment and removed the cabling from the remaining satellite communication equipment. Before escaping, they stole cash and other personal effects from the crew and released the Master.

Malaysia:
On 02 June 2016, a Malaysia flagged Tug TB Ever Prosper and Barge Ever Dignity were attacked and hijacked by armed pirates while underway at position Latitude 03:07:24 North and Longitude 112:35.14 East, around 11nm NNE of Balingian, Sarawak, Malaysia at approximately 2300 LT. Armed persons in two speed boats approached and attacked the tug and barge underway. They boarded the tug, took hostage all 10 crew members and tied them up. They then damaged the communication equipment and hijacked the tug and barge. As the Owners were unable to contact the tug, they reported the incident to MMEA. The hijackers stole the cargo and the crew's valuables. One crew was reported injured during the incident. MMEA patrol boats escorted the tug and barge to a safe port for investigation.

On 19 November 2016, a Malaysian flagged fishing vessel was attacked by armed persons while anchored at position Latitude 04:49.15 North and Longitude 118:46.22 East, around 8.7 nm south of Merabung, Lahad Datu, Sabah, Malaysia at approximately 1930 LT. About five armed persons wearing masks in a small boat attacked and boarded the vessel engaged in fishing activities. Crew personal belongings and an outboard engine were stolen. Before escaping, they kidnapped two crew members. The Malaysian Authorities are investigating the incident.

Notes

1   Antony, 'Piracy on the South China Coast', 45.
2   Antony, 'Piracy on the South China Coast', 42–43, 46.
3   Singleton, 'Defining Piracy', 48–63.
4   Atsushi, 'The Business of Violence', 131–132.
5   Atsushi, 'The Business of Violence', 137–140; Anderson, 'Piracy in the Eastern Seas', 96–97.
6   Koburger, 'Selamat Datang, Kapitan', 65–67.
7   Koburger, 'Selamat Datang, Kapitan', 67–70.
8   Koburger, 'Selamat Datang, Kapitan', 70.
9   Elleman, 'The Looting and Rape of Vietnamese Boat People', 97, 102.
10 Elleman, 'The Looting and Rape of Vietnamese Boat People', 102.
11 Elleman, 'The Looting and Rape of Vietnamese Boat People', 103. See also Eklöf, *Pirates in Paradise*, 17–34.

12 Lis, 'Maritime Piracy in Southeast Asia', 62–63.

13 Koburger, 'Selamat Datang, Kapitan', 72–73.

14 Eklöf, *Pirates in Paradise*, 44–48.

15 Eklöf, *Pirates in Paradise*, 46–47.

16 Eklöf, *Pirates in Paradise*, 53–55.

17 Raymond, 'Piracy and Armed Robbery', 111.

18 Eklöf, *Pirates in Paradise*, 66–69.

19 Eklöf, *Pirates in Paradise*, 110–116.

20 See Burgess, *The World for Ransom*.

21 Young and Valencia, 'Conflation of Piracy', 269–283; Bateman, 'The Threat of Maritime Terrorism', 95–107.

22 Little, *Pirate Hunting*, 273–274; Lehr, *Violence at Sea*, 85.

CHAPTER FOURTEEN

Oil-Soaked Pirates in the Gulf of Guinea

The scramble for Africa has begun again. Only this time, land is not the issue. It is oil. And the Gulf of Guinea and the country of Nigeria are at the centre of the scramble. Nigeria has 37.2 billion barrels of oil reserve, the eleventh largest reserve in the world. It also has over 182 million people, 100 million of whom live in poverty.[1] The Gulf of Guinea has a 5,000-mile-long coastline with numerous harbours, bays, estuaries, rivers and islands. It is rich in oil and fisheries. The massive Niger River spills into the gulf through an intricate network of channels and estuaries that create the perfect geography for pirate hideaways. The region is ethnically diverse with multiple competing state and non-state actors who frequently engage in violent conflicts. It is also a major transit route for international shipping and is becoming increasingly important as a supplier of fossil fuels. Unlike the transit areas of Malaysia and the Gulf of Aden, there are no choke points in the Gulf of Guinea.[2] Instead of congregating around choke points, pirates take advantage of the numerous harbours and the oil rigs that dot the seascape.

Oil exploration in the delta began in the 1930s and commercial quantities were found in 1958. Real interest by Western powers in Nigerian oil came only when the 1967 Six Day War in the Middle East disrupted oil flows to Europe and the United States. The British responded by seeking more oil from Nigeria. To maintain the flow of oil, they interfered in a civil war to prop up the Nigerian government.[3] The United States also began to turn to Nigeria, which would eventually supply over 12 per cent of US oil imports.[4] By 2005, China had also moved in to exploit Nigerian oil.[5] Most of the oil money flowing into Nigeria remains at the top of the social hierarchy where politicians and wealthy families scramble for what, in Nigeria, is called 'cake' – government-controlled

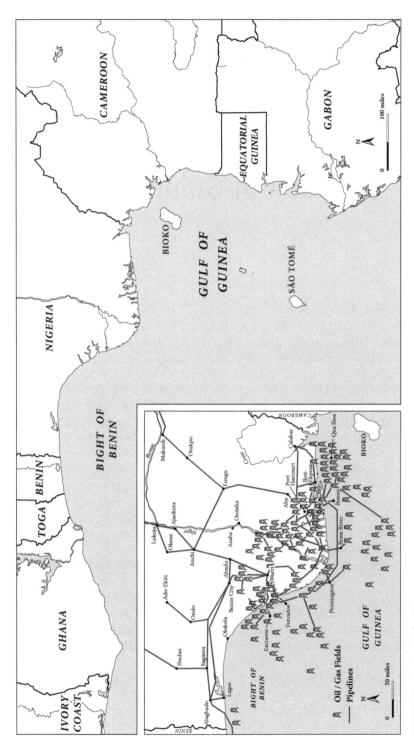

FIGURE 14.1 *Gulf of Guinea.*
Source: Map produced by Barry Levely, Cartographer.

jobs, construction projects, university access, state and national budgets, foreign business deals and oil money that can be funnelled into foreign banks. Meanwhile, 61 per cent of Nigerians live in squalid huts trying to scratch out an existence from depleted soils and polluted waterways.[6] The Gulf of Guinea sits astride a major commercial route where thousands of ships pass every year carrying the world's wealth. Those ships need to anchor when unloading at African ports or to refuel and so become tempting targets for pirate attacks.

In the 1990s, communities in the delta began attacking the 'predatory activities of the Western Oil multinationals: Shell, Chevron Texaco, Exxon Mobil, Total and Agip-ENI'.[7] From 1990 to 2010, oil companies spent 70 billion dollars in Nigeria. They erected massive oilrigs and a network of pipelines, brought in foreign workers and built resort-style residences for them. They also spilled more than 1.5 million tonnes of oil in the mangrove swamps and waterways – 'the equivalent of an *Exxon Valdez* disaster every twelve months'.[8] There were more than 7,000 spills in the delta between 1970 and 2000 alone. The ecological and economic damage done to the delta is incalculable. Thousands of acres of forests, farmlands, rivers and estuaries are now coated in a layer of oil. Drinking water and wells are polluted. Tar balls wash up on shore. Fish and wildlife drown in a sea of oil.[9] Farmers and fisherman are deprived of their livelihoods. For many millions, the situation is desperate, compounded by the arrogance of foreign oil companies, the lack of international attention and the refusal of government authorities to acknowledge the scale of the devastation.

Insurgents, pirates and angry and desperate individuals have attacked the rigs and pipelines or simply siphoned off oil to sell on the black market. This siphoning is called bunkering. Oil bunkering can be a small-time affair with young men seeking to make a few dollars or it can involve organized criminal gangs who siphon thousands of gallons of oil from the pipelines into ships to sell on the black market. Pirates also seize oil tankers and siphon the oil directly from the ships. Some oil smugglers set up rudimentary refineries to produce diesel fuel. Political insurgents and pirates alike have found that kidnapping oil workers and selling them for ransom can also be a lucrative sideline. All of this activity costs the oil companies and the states that support them a lot of money. Shell Nigeria reported in November of 2006 that they were losing $61 million a day.[10] Nigerian oil production is 400,000 barrels below its productive capacity of 2.5 million per day.

Political insurgents, such as the Movement for the Emancipation of the Niger Delta (MEND) and others, have received the most attention in the news, though most pirate attacks are linked to autonomous criminal gangs and community activists. The lines between the groups remain fluid and an attacker might work for any or all of these groups in a given week.[11] Even those who work for militant groups seldom act out of purely ideological, religious or political motives. One such pirate who had participated in a

FIGURE 14.2 *Bunkering in Bolo Creek, Nigeria, 2009.*
Source: Photo by Veronique de Viguerie/Getty Images Reportage.

kidnapping for ransom and walked away with $20,000 explained his motives. 'I do everything (kidnapping) to help myself and to live fine.'[12]

Small pirate gangs inhabit the network of mangrove swamps and come out at night to seek unwary prey. They almost always carry firearms and are more prone to violence than the Somali pirates. They use canoes equipped with outboard motors and other motorboats to approach their targets. They prefer approaching anchored ships under the cover of darkness, but they will also fire on the ships to get them to stop. Nigerian pirates can be bold, even attempting to storm well-armed vessels.[13] Like pirates in Southeast Asia, pirates in the Gulf of Guinea are after portable wealth – 'money, watches, televisions, equipment, food', synthetic mooring ropes which they use to make fishing nets and crew members to kidnap and hold for ransom.[14] In 2013, 1,871 seamen were attacked by pirates and 279 were kidnapped in the Gulf of Guinea. Violent injuries and fatalities are on the rise. Pirates are even beginning to attack Nigerian naval vessels. Oil theft has become increasingly better organized and relies on collusion between workers in the oil industry, security personnel and criminal networks.[15]

West Africa has become the most active pirate region in the world. Attacks are so common that most remain unreported. Shipping companies who understand that no one cares much about piracy in the Gulf of Guinea seldom bother to report attacks. Local law enforcement also worries about retaliation from villagers if they resist pirates too aggressively.[16] In 2016, ninety-five reported attacks occurred along the West African coastline from Senegal to Angola. Two-thirds of them came from Nigeria. Militant attacks on oil infrastructure cost the Nigeria government some $5 billion in 2016 and caused a mid-year recession. Ninety-six seafarers were taken hostage and held for ransom the same year.[17] The attacks are also spreading farther from Nigerian territorial waters. Because most of the incidents remain in the territorial waters of sovereign states, piracy in the Gulf of Guinea has not generated the same kind of international response that has occurred in Somalia. Indeed, according to the United Nations Convention on Law of the Sea, these attacks are not considered piracy. Corruption, unemployment, pollution, greed and political instability continue to foster piracy in the region. Collusion between naval officers and criminal gangs combined with the serious lack of naval resources has meant that effective suppression of piracy has been virtually non-existent.[18] Shipping companies have begun to hire private security agencies to protect their crews and to deter pirate attacks.[19]

The year 2017 witnessed ongoing pirate activity in the Gulf of Guinea. Thirty-three attacks occurred within twelve miles of the coast. Sixty-five crewmen were kidnapped in the Gulf out of the global total of seventy-five in 2017. Nigeria has become one of the most active and dangerous pirate regions in the world, second only to Indonesia.[20] In response to international pressure, in late 2017, the Nigerian government agreed to spend $186 million in its campaign against piracy. The money is supposed to purchase 'three new ready-for-war ships, three aircrafts, 12 vessels and 20 amphibious vehicles' in addition to increased training for the Nigerian navy and improvements in infrastructure.[21] The problem with the government approach is that it avoids the underlying issues that created the upsurge in piracy in the first place.

Ultimately, small-time bandits and militant groups in Nigeria demand more of the 'cake' in return for their oil-soaked waterways, polluted forests, lack of economic opportunity, governmental corruption and predatory foreign companies. So long as the 'cake' is not more equitably shared, political aspirations are not addressed and ecological devastation is not halted and reversed, piracy will persist in the Gulf of Guinea.

As you read the documents that follow, consider the following questions:

1   Describe the Black Devil's tactics. How do they compare to the tactics used in Southeast Asia?

2   Why does the Black Devil say he doesn't like to raid Indian and Filipino vessels?

3   How does the Black Devil justify his pirate activities?

4   What measures did the crews take to thwart pirate attacks, and how effective were they?

5 What does Captain Thomas's account reveal about the nature of pirate groups?

6 What recommendations does the UN make regarding Nigerian piracy? What do these recommendations reveal about the international community's views regarding the responsibility for repressing piracy and the appropriate tactics to be used?

7 What does the 2017 IMB report on the Gulf of Guinea reveal about the nature of piracy and the effectiveness of countermeasures?

8 What role does political instability and economic poverty play in the perpetuation of piracy?

9 How might modern legal definitions of piracy complicate understanding and responding to pirate attacks in the Gulf of Guinea?

10 How might foreign economic empires contribute to the rise of piracy in the Gulf of Guinea?

Transcript of an interview from the film *Pirates: Threatening Global Trade,* produced by Magneto Press and distributed by Java Films in 2016. Reproduced here with permission. All rights reserved by the copyright owner.

Bertrand Monnet interview with the Black Devil, Niger Delta, 2016.

Narrator: Two hours later, we are directed towards the pirate's base. Their leader appears. He's still very aggressive.

Black Devil: Get out. Quick. Get out!
Interviewer: Okay. Okay.
Black Devil: Get out, now! Before I blow your head off.
Pirate: Move. Move. Move. Move. Move.
Black Devil: What is your mission here, my friend? Talk to me before I (he swings a machete at the interviewer's head).
Interviewer: I want to talk to you. Calm down, please.
Black Devil: You want to talk to me, how?
Interviewer: I want to ask questions.
Black Devil: Questions? As in?
Interviewer: Just questions. Okay?
Black Devil: Okay come.
Interviewer: Okay. Okay. Calm down. I just want to talk questions. Don't be scared. Don't be scared about me.
Black Devil: I'm not scared.
Interviewer: I just want to ask you a few questions.
Black Devil: Questions?
Interviewer: Is okay?
Black Devil: Okay, Come inside. Inside quick.

Narrator: The pirates drink a cocktail of alcohol and cocaine which they believe wards off bad spirits. Once they've sprayed some on us, we are allowed behind this so-called protective curtain.

Interviewer: Can I sit?

Black Devil: Sit there. Oh, you want to sit face to face with me?

Interviewer: Yes.

Black Devil: Okay, sit there.

Interviewer: Can you tell me who you are?

Black Devil: This is Black Devil alias [?] Omega 5.

Interviewer: How many guys do you have with you?

Black Devil: I have forty-five men on the ground.

Interviewer: They are not all with you?

Black Devil: No. No. I send some for operation.

Interviewer: Which operation?

Black Devil: Operation for any especial kidnapping at sea.

Interviewer: Okay. How does it work when you do an attack?

Black Devil: I use my [?] speedboat 200. Two speed boats attack and come to our camp.

Interviewer: How many guys do you have in a speed boat when you do attack?

Black Devil: Seven per boat – plus the driver. Seven men.

Interviewer: How do you choose your targets when you do an attack?

Black Devil: My target? It depends on the kind of security over the ship. Before you get there, the security mans, they will open fire on you. Before you come closer, they will open fire.

Interviewer: It happens often that they open fire?

Black Devil: Yes.

Interviewer: So what do you do?

Black Devil: When they open fire, me too, I ask my boys to open fire.

Interviewer: So sometimes you have casualties?

Black Devil: Yes.

Interviewer: How many people belonging to the security did you kill?

Black Devil: The soldiers I killed are countable, maybe if twenty men on the boat, maybe I kill three. I kill five. I take their guns. That is part of my job.

Interviewer: So, once you have opened fire you go on board?

Black Devil: I cease fire and I climb.

Interviewer: You climb?

Black Devil: Yes. Go straight to the engine room and the captain.

Interviewer: The captain?

Black Devil: Ask the captain to come down. How much do you have on board? I have one million. I have three million. Okay, give me. If you don't want to release the money, sorry for you. You go straight to hell. Blow your head off.

Interviewer: Do you target specific nationalities?

Black Devil: Yes. Like those Indians. We don't go for Indians. Because they are very cheap people. Like the Filipinos. No. Very cheap. We target fat people like you. I know if I kidnap you, I get much money for myself.

Interviewer: How much do you think you could get if you would kidnap me?

Black Devil: From you? At least 50 million Naira [about $141,000].

Interviewer: Which are the most bankable hostages you target?

Black Devil: Americans and French.

Interviewer: How is the ransom paid? How do you get the cash?

Black Devil: I will direct you where to drop them. I don't use bank. Just street. Okay. Take the money to this point. My men are there to collect the money. Don't go with army. Don't contact the police. If you do, we are watching you. If you make any move, we kill your man here.

Interviewer: What do you do with this money?

Black Devil: The money? I use to buy ammunitions and speedboats and the rest to take care of our families, because we don't have jobs. That is how we are doing this dirty job. You come to exploit here, and you don't want to employ us That is why. That is main reason why we do this. You don't want to employ us. And you are exploiting from us. Anybody, any expatriate companies that come into our [?] here. If you don't settle with us. You won't operate. I swear to God the Black Devils are always stand by.

World Maritime News Staff, 'Six Pirate Attacks in 24 Hours off Nigeria, Two Crew Kidnapped' (posted on 22 April 2016) http://worldmaritimenews. com/archives/189767/six-pirate-attacks-in-24-hours-off-nigeria-two-crew-kidnapped/. Used with permission.

Two crew members of an offshore supply vessel were kidnapped by pirates while their ship was underway around 97 nautical miles south west of Brass, Nigeria.

According to the information provided by the International Maritime Bureau's (IMB) piracy reporting center, a group of pirates attacked and boarded an unidentified offshore supply vessel while underway on April 19th.

The crew managed to raise the alarm and non-essential crew members retreated into the citadel. Once onboard, pirates robbed and kidnapped two crew members, identified as the vessel's Captain and Chief Engineer.

All remaining crew are reported to be safe and proceeding to a safe port. Two more attacks occurred on the same day in the region. Namely, seven pirates armed with guns approached a Panama-flagged tanker some 58 nautical miles south west of Brass, Nigeria.

However, the crew activated the water hose and the master commenced evasive maneuvers that enabled the ship to fend off the attack.

'*Due to the high free board and hardening measures deployed by the vessel, the pirates aborted the attack and moved away,*' the reporting center said.

All crew of 28 members are reported to be safe. The third target of the day was a multipurpose offshore vessel, which was attacked by pirates causing damage to the bridge. However, the crew managed to escape pirates by retreating to the citadel and has been escorted to Agbami terminal. The pirate activity did not subside the day after, as a Spanish-flagged LNG tanker was attacked on route to Port Harcourt.

The ship's identity has not been disclosed, but it is believed that the ship is Bilbao Knutsen, owned by Knutsen OAS. The attack has been confirmed to World Maritime News by UK-based security agency Clearwater, saying that this incident is the sixth incident that occurred in and around this area within 24 hrs.

The LNG tanker managed to thwart the attack and proceeded to Bonny with all crew members accounted for. Clearwater received reports of two further separate pirate attacks on Wednesday targeting two offshore supply vessels in close proximity. A Nigerian Navy vessel has been tasked and managed to deter the pirates from the scene. All crew members are accounted for and the vessels were escorted by the navy to Onne port.

Rob Almeida, 'Kidnapped off Nigeria – An American Ship Captain Unveils the Truth', *gCaptain* (4 April 2014): http://gcaptain.com/captain-wren-thomas-kidnapped-off-nigeria-c-retriever/. Used with Permission

On 22 October 2013, Captain Thomas' day started with a bit more angst than normal. His boat was carrying radioactive materials which meant a lot more paperwork and his ship would be the last to onload at Onne.

At 0845, 15 minutes before the convoy was scheduled to depart from the port, his sailing orders came in, directing him somewhere else besides his normal Agbami run.

'I don't know where the supply boats for those fields were,' notes Captain Thomas. 'Each field has its own supply vessels. If more are needed, they usually hire a boat for what they call a spot job. Even my Nigerian chief officer and the crew found it strange.'

At 0910, the C-Retriever was slightly delayed in leaving with the convoy and the Beachmaster announced over VHF Channel 16 the ship's departure and destination – a practice generally avoided to conceal ship's movements. Announcing the location and destination could make the ship easy prey for pirates.

Considering the very real security threats faced by him and his colleagues in Nigeria, this violation of operational security was a daily occurrence, and it infuriated him.

'All the people who needed to know that information had the access to gain that information via secure channels,' he commented.

After leaving the convoy at 'Charlie Charlie,' approximately 10 nautical miles past the fairway buoy, the C-Retriever was on its own and heading toward its destination to the east of the Agbami Field.

At 0300 the next morning, his ship came under attack, and Captain Thomas and most of his crew were soon barricaded inside the Bulk Tank Room, awaiting the inevitable.

Using angle grinders, the pirates slowly cut their way into the room.

In a futile attempt to avoid capture, Captain Thomas and the Engineer sprayed water at the grinder, eventually electrocuting the pirate using it.

'That made them mad.'

As soon as the grinder had cut a large enough hole, the pirates began firing 7.62mm rounds from an AK-47 blindly into the room.

Captain Thomas and his engineer looked at each other and soon came to the conclusion that the ricocheting bullets presented a far greater immediate danger than whatever the pirates were intending to do to them.

They shouted at the pirates in an effort to explain their intentions to give up. The pirates understood, and the door was opened shortly after.

After profuse apologizing and making up excuses why he threw water on the angle grinder, Captain Thomas was able to gain the trust of the pirates.

The pirates allowed him to gather his malaria pills and a few items of clothing, before he and his engineer were placed aboard a speedboat with six other pirates bound for God-knows-where.

That was the start of an 18-day saga that continues to haunt him to this day ....

Did you have a citadel?

No, we used the Bulk Tank Room, with the engine room to the front of it and the z-drive room to the back of it. The pirates had 2 ways to get to us – either through the watertight door dividing the engine room or the emergency escape hatch in the z-drive room. It was easier and more convenient for them to cut through the door to the engine room. When the pirates came through, they were armed with AK-47s and an M-60.

Where did they take you?

When the pirates kidnapped me and the other American, we were immediately taken ashore. For the first week, we stayed in the bush farther inland and then I talked them into moving us. I told them I was going to die from a heart attack at this location because of the high traffic-causing noises. Every time they heard anything, they chambered rounds in their weapons. This is how we existed every night and day. So finally, I talked enough sense to them that they moved us to the swamps right off the beach. We were hidden very well in the creeks.

What did they feed you?

Indomie Noodles (ramen noodles) – we got a packet of these every other day. And on the days the negotiators would make them angry, we wouldn't eat.

How did they treat you?

Horribly. Very inhumane. They fought with each other the entire time, they would chamber rounds on each other and they would beat each other. They treated us like animals. It's about as close as a person could get to being a POW. Some of them were particularly cruel to us. The stifling air was filled with smoke from crack and pot the entire time. I found my training as a Marine kicked in and provided me with survival skills. I knew not to [mess] with these people. I did push them as far as I could and then I would back down. I knew not to piss off a Nigerian. Or worse a Nigerian pirate, or even worse a Nigerian pirate on drugs. I was surrounded by the last kind ….

Did any of the pirates try to befriend you while you were kidnapped?

Yes, one of their community boys (slaves) who cooked for us did. I actually got close to him. He was alone it seemed. Most of the other Nigerians hated him, although he was good friends with the leader. He was very scared and often wanted to sleep on the piece of foam with my Engineer and me. He was like a scared kid. He asked if I wanted some tea. I told him yes then when he got around to it about an hour later I told him I didn't want it, since the caffeine probably wouldn't be good for me. Even this kid could snap – he went completely nuts and told me not to ever make him angry again or I would regret it. He had Satan in his eyes. I apologized to him and accepted some tea.

Under what circumstances were you released?

We were taken up the river and exchanged after the money was counted. We were given to a team of three Nigerians that were sent by one of the tribal chiefs acting as a 3rd party for ECO.

United Nations Security Council
Resolution 2039 (2012) Adopted by the Security Council at its 6727th meeting, on 29 February, 2012.

Affirming its full commitment to promoting the maintenance of peace and stability in the Gulf of Guinea region ….

  3. *Stresses* the primary responsibility of the States of the Gulf of Guinea to counter piracy and armed robbery at sea in the Gulf of Guinea and in this context urges them through ECCAS, ECOWAS and the GGC to work towards the convening of the planned joint Summit of Gulf of Guinea States to develop a regional anti-piracy strategy, in cooperation with the African Union;

4. *Requests* the Secretary-General through the United Nations Office of West Africa (UNOWA) and the United Nations Office of Central Africa (UNOCA) to support States and sub-regional organizations in convening the joint Summit, as referenced in resolution 2018 (2011), to the extent feasible;

5. *Urges* States of the region of the Gulf of Guinea to take prompt action, at national and regional levels with the support of the international community where able, and by mutual agreement, to develop and implement national maritime security strategies, including for the establishment of a legal framework for the prevention, and repression of piracy and armed robbery at sea and as well as prosecution of persons engaging in those crimes, and punishment of those convicted of those crimes and encourages regional cooperation in this regard;

6. *Encourages* Benin and Nigeria to extend their joint patrols beyond March 2012, while the countries of the Gulf of Guinea continue to work towards building their capacities to independently secure their coastlines and also encourages international partners to consider providing support, as needed, in that regard and to the extent feasible;

7. *Encourages* the States of the Gulf of Guinea, ... to develop and implement transnational and transregional maritime security coordination centres covering the whole region of the Gulf of Guinea, building on existing initiatives, such as those under the auspices of the International Maritime Organization (IMO);

8. *Encourages* international partners to provide support to regional States and organizations for the enhancement of their capabilities to counter piracy and armed robbery at sea in the Gulf of Guinea, including their capacity to conduct regional patrols, to establish and maintain joint coordination centres and joint information-sharing centres, and for the effective implementation of the regional strategy, once adopted;

9. *Requests* the Secretary-General to support efforts towards mobilizing resources following the creation of the regional strategy to assist in building national and regional capacities in close consultation with States and regional and extra-regional organizations.

Piracy and Armed Robbery against Ships: Report for the Period 1 January–31 December 2016 (London: ICC International Maritime Bureau, 2017), 17–18, 20–22, 24. Used with Permission.

Africa
Benin: Cotonou – Although the number of attacks has dropped significantly, the area remains risky. Past attacks showed that the pirates/ robbers in this area are well-armed and violent and, in some incidents, have fired upon and hijacked ships. The pirates force Masters to sail to unknown locations where ship's properties and sometimes part cargo is stolen (gas oil). Crew members have been injured in the past. Recent

patrols by Benin and Nigerian Authorities have resulted in a drop in the number of attacks. However, vessels are advised to continue to be vigilant and maintain strict anti-piracy/robbery watches and measures.

Nigeria: Lagos – Pirates/robbers are often well-armed, violent and have attacked hijacked and robbed vessels/kidnapped crews along the coast, rivers, anchorages, ports and surrounding waters. In the past, attacks reported up to about 170nm from coast. In many past incidents, pirates hijacked the vessels for several days and ransacked the vessels and stole part cargo – usually gas oil. A number of crew members were also injured and kidnapped in past 4 attacks. Generally, all waters in/off Nigeria remain risky. Vessels are advised to be vigilant, as many attacks may have gone unreported.

Observations:
Benin:
On 27 November 2016, a Panamanian-flagged Refrigerated Cargo Ship was attacked and hijacked by armed persons while anchored at position Latitude 06:14.09 North and Longitude 002:34.54 East, Cotonaou Outer Anchorage, Benin at approximately 2145 LT. Owners of the vessel reported to the IMB PRC that they had lost contact with their anchored ship. The IMB PRC immediately relayed the message to all the authorities in the region including Benin and Nigerian Authorities. The Nigerian Navy dispatched two warships to locate and intercept the missing ship with 20 crews on board. As the warships approached the hijacked ship, it was reported that 15 pirates escaped along with three kidnapped crew members. The remaining crew then managed to sail the ship to a safe port.

Ivory Coast:
On 11 February 2016, a Panamanian-flagged Product Tanker MT Maximus was attacked and hijacked by armed pirates while underway at position Latitude 04:00 North and Longitude 004:00 West, around 77 nm south of Abidjan, Ivory Coast, at approximately 2000 UTC. Fourteen pirates armed with guns attacked and hijacked the tanker. All 18 crew members were taken hostage. The pirates ransacked all cabins and stole crew personal effects. Eight pirates then disembarked the tanker on the high seas with two kidnapped crew members. A Togo Navy patrol boat managed to intercept and took a picture of the tanker. The pirates had repainted the tanker's name and provided false information to the Togo Navy. The picture as sent to the owners for verification. As the tanker sailed into the Nigerian EEZ waters, the Togo Navy handed over the coordination to the Nigerian Navy who had dispatched a warship to shadow the tanker. On 20 February 2016, the Nigerian Navy boarded the tanker. After an exchange of gunfire, the pirates surrendered, and the crews were rescued. One pirate was reportedly killed. The two kidnapped crew members were released on 20 March 2016. Throughout

the incident, the IMB PRC liaised and shared information among the regional authorities, vessel owner, and flag state.

Nigeria:
On 11 February 2016, a Marshall Islands-flagged Product Tanker MT Nave Jupiter was attacked by armed pirates while underway at position Latitude 03:35 North and Longitude 005:42 East, around 54nm SW of Brass, Nigeria at approximately 1510 LT. The tanker was sailing from Bonny to Amsterdam when she spotted two skiffs approaching from the stern. Master quickly raised the alarm, increased speed, commenced evasive maneuvers and contacted the CSO. Owners contacted the IMB PRC who immediately liaised with the Nigerian Authorities, and the IMB PRC were advised that an armed patrol boat had been dispatched to the location. As the skiffs closed in, weapons and ladders were sighted. The pirates opened fire at the tanker's superstructure and threw homemade explosive devices onto the main deck, which luckily did not explode. Three pirates managed to board the tanker using a ladder and fired several rounds. Non-essential crew retreated to the citadel. Master continued with evasive maneuvers. The Pirates cut of the fuel to the main engines and generators. Master then instructed the bridge team to go to the citadel. The pirates later tried to gain access to the citadel but failed. Before escaping, the pirates damaged all communication equipment and stole crew personal effects. The Nigerian Navy arrived and boarded the tanker and rescued the crew members. The tanker thereafter sailed to a safe port.

Notes

1 'Nigerians living in poverty rise to nearly 61%'.
2 Osinowo, 'Combating Piracy', 1.
3 Uche, 'Oil, British Interests and the Nigerian Civil War', 111–135.
4 Watts, 'Imperial Oil', 29.
5 Obi, 'Enter the Dragon?' 417–434.
6 Nodland, 'Guns, Oil, and "Cake"', 194, 204.
7 Obi, 'Enter the Dragon?' 418.
8 Nodland, 'Guns, Oil, and "Cake"', 193.
9 Vidal, 'Nigeria's Agony Dwarfs the Gulf Oil Spill'.
10 Watts, 'Imperial Oil', 30.
11 Nodland, 'Guns, Oil, and "Cake"', 197.
12 As quoted in Nodland, 'Guns, Oil, and "Cake"', 200.
13 Burnett, *Dangerous Waters*, 111–115.
14 Burnett, *Dangerous Waters*, 114.

15 Osinowo, 'Combating Piracy', 3.

16 Burnett, *Dangerous Waters*, 110.

17 Gaffey, 'Pirate Attacks on the Rise in West Africa'.

18 Nodland, 'Guns, Oil, and "Cake"', 200–201.

19 Burnett, *Dangerous Waters*, 101–116.

20 *Piracy and Armed Robbery*, 2018, 5–6.

21 'Ending Piracy in Nigerian Waters'.

CHAPTER FIFTEEN

Saviours of the Sea: Pirates of the Somalia Coast

The Gulf of Aden has long been a choke point in ocean-going traffic and so has drawn pirates to its waters and coastlines. In Chapter 12, we briefly discussed the ongoing efforts of merchants and mercantile city-states, such as Aden, to resist piracy in the region prior to the 1500s.[1] After the sixteenth century, first the Portuguese and later other European pirates sailing out of African bases such as Madagascar, regularly cruised the entrance to the Gulf of Aden seeking prizes. In the early nineteenth century, American merchants operating out of Zanzibar complained of native pirates in the region. For example, in December of 1827 an American ship was chased by pirates twice near Lamu in Kenya. In 1835, an American ship stranded on Masirah Island off the coast of Oman was harassed by pirates who then chased the rescue boat the ship sent out to seek aid.[2] All along the coast of modern Somalia, fishermen and tribal peoples developed a culture of raiding and pillaging shipwrecks and shipwrecked sailors that was linked to local warlords and clans who struggled for control of the loot.[3]

With the opening of the Suez Canal in 1869, the Gulf of Aden became an even busier sea-lane because ships travelling between Europe and Asia no longer had to make the long, costly and dangerous journey around Africa. Roughly 8 per cent of the world's trade now passes through the Gulf of Aden, into the Red Sea, and through the Suez Canal. Pirates operating out of Somali ports continued to prey upon passing shipping throughout the nineteenth century and into the twentieth when pirates, apparently operating out of Bosaso in northern Somalia, attacked British pearl fisheries off the island of Socotra. These Somali pirates were suppressed only with the Italian invasion and occupation of northern Somalia in 1927. They did not resurface in strength until the political turmoil of 1980s.[4]

Consequently, rather than seeing modern Somali piracy as a new phenomenon, as many reporters and academics have done, we need to see it in this long history of predation at sea and against wrecked ships and their crews. Maritime predation has long existed there as a parasitic, part-time activity of local peoples around the Gulf of Aden and the Horn of Africa. In the late nineteenth and early twentieth centuries, it evolved into an episodic outburst of piracy that riveted the world's attention until it devolved back to the parasitic predation that has characterized the region for a very long time. Though the modern upsurge of piratical activity in Somali was unusual in that the pirates ventured far beyond the Gulf of Aden into international waters hundreds of miles from the coast, it was not unprecedented.

This modern explosion of piratical activity occurred in the context of ongoing political instability, military conflict, economic deprivation, natural disaster and foreign predation on Somali maritime resources. The Somali Republic, created in 1960 after decades of colonial domination by the British, Italians and French, survived for only nine years. Muhammad Siad Barre seized power in 1969, created a small navy to protect Somali fisheries, sold fishing licenses to foreign companies and suppressed piracy along the 2,060-mile coastline. As his regime came under increased pressure in the 1980s, politically motivated pirates tied to the Somali National Movement began attacking foreign ships to keep the government from receiving foreign supplies. When the regime collapsed in 1991, this politically motivated piracy ended abruptly.[5] The United Nations sent a peacekeeping force that met with considerable local resistance, which compelled the United Nations to pull out in 1995. Somalia then descended into clan warfare with no government to police the seas or regulate foreign vessels.[6]

Somalia sits on the Horn of Africa along what has long been one of the most productive fishing areas in the world, rich with shrimp, lobster and tuna. For hundreds of years, entire communities made their living from the sea. But with no government to regulate fishing and protect it from foreign encroachments, Somali fisherman soon found themselves competing against large commercial fishing vessels from Russia, Japan, Germany, the European Union and Yemen who employed modern industrial fishing techniques that rapidly depleted the local fisheries. Some 300 foreign ships were fishing off Somalia in 1998. They focused on the high-value shrimp and lobster while simply throwing away all the other fish caught in their trawlers. The trawlers tore up the sea beds and destroyed the ecosystems the marine species relied upon. They also caught up Somali fishing nets and traps, which meant local fishermen and their families went hungry.[7]

Italian, Swiss and other foreign ships also entered Somali territorial waters to dump toxic waste, such as radioactive uranium, 'lead, cadmium, mercury, industrial, hospital, chemical, leather treatment and other toxic waste'. Often barrels of waste were simply dumped on the beaches.[8] The 2004 tsunami that devastated so much of the Indian Ocean coastlines also hit Somalia. Fisherman lost their boats. Villages were swept away. Water supplies were polluted. The tsunami stirred up the hazardous waste on the beaches, exacerbating the already severe health crisis caused by the tsunami.[9] The devastation to fishing and the communities who depended upon it is difficult to overstate, especially in the context of a failed state, indiscriminate violence among the competing political factions and the lack of basic services, such as electricity and clean water.

Somali fishermen initially tried to confront the foreign vessels and were met with high-pressured hoses that swamped their boats. So, they formed armed vigilante groups that boarded foreign vessels fishing in Somali waters to demand compensation for the fish they were taking.[10] In the beginning, the pirates robbed the ships but did not take hostages or vessels. Eventually, however, as the potential for financial gain became obvious, these vigilantes began to call themselves the coastguard and began taking some of the ships back to Somalia to force the companies to compensate Somalis for their lost revenues and resources. Foreign fishing companies began arming their crews and seeking fishing licences from local clan leaders and warlords.[11]

Warlords and clan leaders realized that 'licencing' foreign vessels to fish in Somali waters could be a reliable source of income in the war-torn country and actively tried to control piracy because they did not want to lose their licencing business. But over the next eight or nine years, the ongoing efforts to limit foreign incursions and the growth of illicit business opportunities associated with it led to full-blown pirate organizations seeking ransoms under the cloak of the self-serving narrative that they were protecting Somali resources.[12] Pirate gangs gave themselves names such as '"Kismayo Volunteer Coastguards", the "Somalia Marines for Hobyo and Harardhere", or "National Volunteer Coastguard"'.[13] This coastguard narrative has some basis in reality as we have seen. However, the existence of highly organized criminal operations whose sole purpose is plundering and ransoming kidnapped ships and crews of vessels unassociated with the illegal fishing or dumping and that are seized hundreds of miles from Somali coastal waters puts the lie to their claims. Still the narrative serves a useful purpose of creating a mutual identity, justifying maritime predation, recruiting pirates and garnering community support.[14]

Central Somalia became the epicentre of the best organized and most aggressive pirate ring called the Harardhere. This was a clan-based ring from the Mugdug region that has been traditionally very poor and received very little attention from the provisional governments or the warlords. Fishing had been the region's only means of income. The Harardhere justified their attacks by the need to protect Somali resources and argued they were simply collecting fees from those who exploited their waters without paying.[15] They had become the saviours of the sea. Though some authors have criticized the pirates' claims that their ransoms are merely normal taxation of trade,[16] this idea has deep roots in the ancient practice of statecraft and commerce in the wider Indian Ocean and Southeast Asia. As we have seen, this kind of 'taxation' (i.e. forcing passing ships into port to pay duties) was a fundamental part of the projection of sovereignty over the seas and was intimately tied to state formation.

FIGURE 15.1 *Somali mothership with two ships in tow.*
Source: Photo by Pierre Verdy/AFP/Getty Images.

Somali pirates used their traditional fiberglass boats with styrofoam cores and outboard motors that could outrun most commercial vessels. After 2004, the pirates extended their range over 200 miles off the coast and began using 'mother ships' to tow speedboats out to the target area with two week's worth of supplies. This had been a traditional practice of fishermen that was simply adapted to piracy. In effect, the pirates were simply fishermen who had become fishers of boats and crews. This practice also helped conceal their intentions, as a large vessel could not distinguish between a legitimate fishing operation and a band of pirates.[17]

Pirate raids usually include ten to twelve men who were backed by investors. Investors expected to pay about $5,000 a day to keep the operation going, which could amount to over $150,000 a month. The investors supplied the pirates with 'boats, fuel, arms, ammunition, communications, and salaries'.[18] The larger pirate gangs had regional networks with spotters in major ports feeding them information about ships, their cargoes and their sailing schedules. Pirates watched the shipping lanes for slow-moving, isolated ships with low freeboards. When a target was spotted, two skiffs approached the vessels at high speeds. One skiff fired a rocket-propelled grenade over the ship to get it to stop. If the ship refused, they fired directly at the bridge. As the ship slowed, the pirates used ladders to get one of their members on board, called the jumper, to intimidate the crew while the other

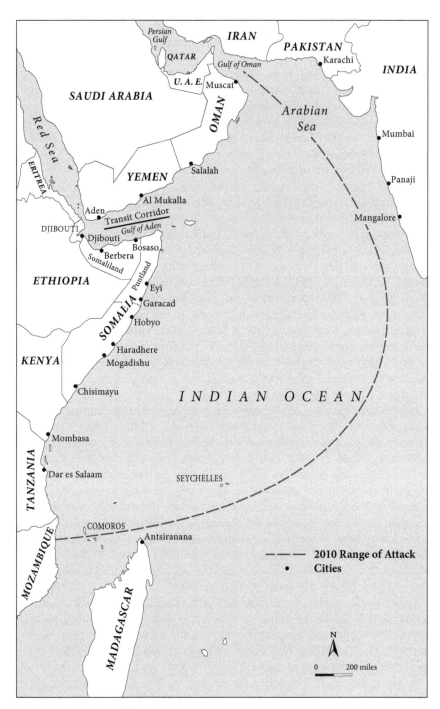

FIGURE 15.2 *Somali piracy.*
Source: Map produced by Barry Levely, Cartographer.

pirates boarded. They then tied their skiffs to the back of the pirated vessel and towed them into port, where their ransom negotiators contacted the ship's owner to demand the ransom.[19]

Once a ransom had been collected, it was divided up among the various participants in a system, reminiscent of the old pirate articles of the seventeenth and the eighteenth centuries. The hijackers received 30 per cent, which was distributed in equal shares. Peter Eichstaedt described the system this way: 'The first pirate to board a ship, the jumper, gets a double share or a bonus, such as cash or a vehicle like a Toyota Land Cruiser. Pirates who fight with other pirates are fined.' Families of pirates who died during the operation were compensated. The security at the port and the local community received 10 per cent, while 'the financier gets 20%' and 'the hijacking sponsor gets 30%'.[20]

Between 2005 and 2012, $339 to $413 million in ransoms were paid to Somali pirates for the 179 ships hijacked during that same period. The average ransom per ship was $2.7 million with the pirates receiving on average between $30,000 and $75,000 per hijacking, which amounts to a mere 0.01 to 0.025 per cent of the total ransom. This is still fifty-four times higher than the average annual income in Somalia, where the average life expectancy is fifty-four years.[21] A Somali could expect to 'earn $30,000 over a lifetime compared to $35,000 to $75,000 for one job'.[22] The ransom money is also vital to the economy as it filters out through the various groups who host and support the pirates, but it also goes to fund ongoing militia and Islamist organizations.[23]

This revenue has allowed the increasingly more sophisticated organizations to adapt to anti-piracy measures. Pirates have moved their bases 'to remote islands in the Gulf of Aden historically used by pirates and smugglers [such as Socotra]. Here they are able to stash weapons and equipment needed for hijacking, such as ladders, night goggles, and satellite phones, and they also use these islands as outposts to watch ships passing in the gulf'.[24] The glamour of being a pirate can be real, but so are the dangers. Not only do they risk capture or injury in their attacks, but most Somali pirates also do not know how to swim. For example, in 2009 after the hijackers of the *Sirius Star* were gleefully returning home with their portion of the 3 million dollar ransom, they wrecked their boat. Five out of the nine pirates on board drowned and the rest lost most of their money.[25]

After several spectacular attacks in 2005, including the failed attack on the cruise ship *Seabourn Spirit,* in which the pirates fired several rocket-propelled grenades and automatic weapons, the attacks finally drew media attention. The Combined Task Force 150, which had been established as an international naval force in the Gulf of Aden after 9/11 to counter terrorism in the area, began to respond to pirate attacks. The pirates changed their tactics again in response to the new threat. They 'began using captured low-value vessels as mother ships for the skiffs', so that they would appear to be part of the normal ocean traffic.[26]

The international response to Somali piracy, which has focused on military suppression and prosecution of pirates, has enjoyed some success, however inadequate and misdirected it has been. In June of 2008, the UN published Resolution 1816, which allowed foreign navies to 'enter the territorial waters of Somalia for the purpose of repressing acts of piracy and armed robbery at sea' and to deploy ships and military aircraft for that purpose. They also 'authorized natives to arrest pirates'.[27] The Combined Maritime Forces that include three different task forces with thirty-six ships from the different countries were assigned to patrol 2.5 million square miles of ocean from the Suez Canal to the Straits of Hormuz. The Gulf of Aden alone comprises 1.1 million square miles.[28] To cope with this vast area, they created an Internationally Recognized Transit Corridor in 2009 in the Gulf of Aden that they would patrol and encouraged ships to use the corridor. Obviously, that meant that ships approaching, leaving or sailing outside the corridor had very little protection. The narrow transit corridor also had the unintended consequence of concentrating 'shipping traffic' and 'taking the guesswork out of piracy'.[29] The pirates simply sat in the corridor waiting for the prey to approach. After the development of more robust countermeasures in 2009 and 2010, pirates shifted away from the transit corridor to the greater Somali basin in search of prey hundreds of miles from shore. By 2011, they had extended their range even further to 800 miles from the coast.[30]

The naval patrols used drones to identify potential pirate ships. Then they boarded and searched them. If weapons were found, the pirates were fingerprinted and taken to shore, while their boats and equipment were sunk. These pirates could not be prosecuted because they were not caught in the act. Still, Puntland opened a special pirate prison in 2014. But the challenge with arresting pirates is to know how to prosecute them effectively. This became clear in 2010 when Russian troops captured ten Somali pirates who had hijacked the ship *Russian University*. Initially, they considered taking them back to Russia for trial, but after realizing that it would be difficult to convict them under international law, they set the pirates adrift in a raft some 350 miles off the Somali coast. The men disappeared and are presumed dead. Kenya and Yemen have agreed to try Somali pirates, but have found themselves overwhelmed by cases.[31]

Ship owners and insurers exacerbated the situation by lobbying for naval protection while refusing to allow naval operations to attack pirates who had boarded their ships for fear of damaging expensive boats and cargoes and injuring the crews. So long as national governments shouldered the costs of pirate suppression, the costs of ransoming ships remained comparatively low, and negotiations could be carried out quickly, ship owners saw little reason to change their approach. The desire to free the ships quickly caused some ship owners to pay increasingly higher ransoms, which, in turn, encouraged the pirates to ask for more, which, in turn, caused long delays in negotiations and higher costs to ship owners. Insurance companies, facing the sudden increase in successful hijackings after 2008, began to encourage ship owners to get serious about hardening their ships against attack by following the Best Management Practice guidelines, which we will discuss in the next chapter. Extended negotiations also hit the pirate financers who had to pay to keep the pirates and their prisoners fed.[32] Combined with the ongoing counter-piracy measures these economic transformations made piracy more costly for both the ship owners and the pirates and pirate attacks fell dramatically after 2011. It can, therefore, be argued that the economics of piracy played a more important role than military suppression or legal action in suppressing Somali piracy.

We should not be overly optimistic, however, that piracy in Somali will disappear. It is true that the international response has made piracy much more difficult, costly and dangerous to the pirates, but it has not, as yet, focused on the real problem. The response has treated the symptom, rather than the cause. Somalia remains a failed state. Over $300 million of seafood is stolen from Somali waters every year. Fishermen have few options. Safe havens remain available. People are still desperate and organized crime is able and willing to exploit them. Nothing has been done to correct the policies and practices that helped create the modern pirate problem. Though it is true that pirate attacks off the coast of Somalia are way down from their 2011 high, the recurrence of attacks in 2016 and 2017 demonstrates that Somali piracy is not yet suppressed, claims to the contrary notwithstanding. (There were at least two attacks in 2016, three in 2017 and at least two in the first half of 2018.) (See Table 15.1.)

TABLE 15.1 Pirate attacks by Somali attackers, 2008–2017

Year	Number of Attacks
2008	111
2009	219
2010	219
2011	237
2012	75
2013	15
2014	11
2015	0
2016	2
2017	9
Total	**898**

Source: ICC International Maritime Bureau, *Annual Reports*.

Somali piracy cost the international community $31.9 billion in naval activities, security, vessel protection measures, counter-piracy organizations, increased fuel costs caused by higher vessel speeds, and prosecuting and imprisoning pirates. We spent $1.5 billion in 2016 alone.[33] If even a portion of that money could have been spent restraining foreign abuses in Somali waters and offering Somali fishermen other alternatives to fishing, the downturn might be made permanent. But as naval patrols have declined and ship owners' vigilance has waned, we may see the recent uptick in Somali piracy expand. It seems clear that, unless real reform occurs inside Somalia, piracy in the Gulf of Aden can be maintained within acceptable limits only so long as international naval coalitions continue to patrol the region.[34]

Modern Somali pirate attacks should not be construed as another Golden Age of Islamic piracy, though it may be tempting to do so. The Islamic piracy of the Somali pirates of Africa and the Sulu pirates of the Philippines do not represent a new tradition of Islamic corsairing like the Barbary corsairs. No Islamic superpower exists today that is comparable to the Ottoman Empire. The Somali pirates are motivated by a desire for profit, not religious zeal and they thrived because of the absence of political authority. The Barbary corsairs operated during a time of nation state expansion and faced the combined power of several European states. The Barbary corsairs also were not defeated until North Africa was conquered and colonized by European imperialists.[35] Though piracy has diminished off the Somali coast through an international military presence, economic changes in the ransoming model and attempts to subject pirates to legal trials, we have not seen the end of Somali piracy. So long as the underlying conditions that spawned the rise of Somali piracy exist, the temptation to pluck wealth from the sea will draw Somalis into piracy.

As you read the following documents, consider the following questions:

1 How does Shamun Indhabur explain the rise in Somali piracy? Can you find any similarities between his arguments and those used by pirates in the seventeenth-century Caribbean or in Southeast Asia?

2 What does he believe will end piracy in Somalia?

3 How does Shamun Indhabur explain their bravery in the face of increased countermeasures by ships' captains and crews? Do you have evidence of drug use among any other pirate groups?

4 How does the presence of legitimate fisherman intent on protecting their catch complicate efforts to identify real pirates off the coast of Somalia?

5 What is the emphasis of the United Nations' efforts to combat piracy? How might this approach be incomplete?

6 What similarities can you find between piracy in Somalia and the Gulf of Guinea?

7 What role do issues of state sovereignty over the seas play in Somali piracy?

8 How would you characterize Somali piracy (i.e. parasitic, episodic, or intrinsic) and why?

Rod Nordland, 'Q&A Somali Pirate Explains How to Steal Ships', *NewsWeek* (17 December, 2008). Used with Permission.

Somali pirates last September captured a Ukrainian cargo ship, the *MV Faina*, loaded to the gunnels with heavy weaponry, including 33 Russian-designed T-72 battle tanks. Since then, American and Russian naval vessels have been shadowing the ship at its anchorage off the fishing village of Hindawao, 300 miles north of Mogadishu. This month there were reports that the ship's owners had agreed on ransom terms, but the *Faina* and its crew are still being held.

NewsWeek's Rod Nordland interviewed Shamun Indhabur, who is thought to be the leader of the pirates who took the *Faina*, and the *Sirius Star*, a Saudi supertanker with $100 million worth of oil aboard. The interview was conducted by satellite telephone to the bridge of the *Faina*, through Somali translator Abukar al-Badri. Excerpts:

Q: What is your background, and how did you capture the *MV Faina*?
A: Shamun Indhabur: I was a fisherman before I turned to piracy, a crewmember of a small fishing boat. We used to capture lobsters and sharks.

When we hijacked *MV Faina* it was early morning 24 September 2008, in Somali waters. We took it after 60 minutes of fighting between the crewmembers and our gunmen and eventually the captain decided to surrender after we fired some rockets to warn them that we were close to destroying the ship if they didn't surrender. The captain tried to escape, but he didn't succeed. He had a pistol, and he refused to surrender until we were close to killing him. When we intercepted the ship and saw the shipment [of arms], then we thought it was going to Somalia and belonged to the Ethiopians [whose army is supporting the transitional government in Somalia], but the captain told us that it was going to South Africa. Then later we saw that it was going to southern Sudan, after we forced the captain to show us the manifests.

Q: What's the situation on board the *Faina* now?
A: The middlemen tried to steal some of the money we agreed on [estimated at more than $3 million]. And now we can't trust them. They're trying to take the money, and we are the criminals. We can't accept that.

Q: How are your ransoms paid?
A: We get the money two ways. A boat takes the money from Djibouti, then a helicopter takes the money from the boat, then it drops the

money in waterproof cartons on assigned [small] boats. Then we collect it, check if it is false or not, then we release the ship. The other way we get the money is a boat from Mombasa.

Q: Isn't it dangerous for middlemen to be carrying so much money into a lawless place like Somalia? I've heard some of them have been killed doing it, is that true?

A: The pirates are different groups. Those in Puntland may have problems with the middlemen and sometimes kill them.

Q: Why has there been such an increase Somali piracy?

A: In Somalia all the young men are desperate. There is wide unemployment in the country; there are no sources of income. One of the only sources we have had is fishing, and the superpowers and Asian countries sidelined us in our own sea. So, at first, we started out just to counter illegal fishing, but international forces started to protect them.

Q: Now the European Union is sending an additional naval force. Are you worried about the increased naval presence?

A: We know the EU and NATO forces are coming, but that is not the solution. The solution is to restore peace in Somalia so that we can have a better life and more job opportunities. I can tell you that sending forces will not stop us going into piracy. They can arrest us if they find us out at sea, they've arrested our friends several times, but that will never deter us from this business. The only thing that can stop piracy is a strong government in Somalia.

The most friendly forces in Somali waters are the U.S. forces. They arrest us and release us, because they know we are not going to hurt them. But the French and the Indians treat us badly, and sometimes they don't know what they're doing. The Indians sunk that Thai boat [a fishing vessel reportedly taken over by pirates this month] and said it was pirates, but I tell you there was not a single pirate on that boat.

Q: Are you worried about another attack ashore, such as the one the French conducted, now that the U.N. has approved such attacks?

A: The French forces made two attacks. They arrested our friends, but French nationals will pay for that. If we get a ship with French nationals, we will punish the crew, and they will pay double ransom. We're not worried about another attack [against pirates on land], because now we are on very high alert, and they will never succeed with another raid.

Q: You justify piracy against all shipping even though your only complaint was against foreign fishing boats operating in your waters. Does that really make sense?

A: I justify it as a dirty business encouraged by the foreign forces that were escorting illegal fishing boats and toxic waste dumpers. And if they are escorting fishing boats, they can't escort all commercial shipping, and if we are forced to avoid fishing our waters, then those [commercial] ships are all our fish.

Q: How do you justify attacking pleasure yachts hundreds of miles offshore, or cruise liners, or even any vessel so far from Somalia?

A: Luxury yachts are what we are looking for, because what we need is money, and if we get a luxury yacht, we make a fortune.

Q: Some ships have started putting armed guards on their vessels. Others have used weapons such as sonic guns, which use beams of loud noise to deter pirates. Does any of that worry you?

A: It will not protect them. We also have rocket-propelled grenades, and we can destroy them. For those with the sonic guns, we hijacked some of them even after they fired the sonic guns. Truly speaking, when we go to sea we are drunk, and we are like hungry wolves running after meat. We don't even know what we are doing until we have boarded.

Q: Some of the leaders of the Islamists now fighting the Somali government have criticized pirates for giving the country a bad name, and for attacking Muslim-owned ships like the *Sirius Star*.

A: The Islamists have a memorandum of understanding with us. What they are saying to the media is not their real position. They just want to send a message to their Arab friends who sometimes fund them.

Q: What if the Islamists come back to power?

A: The Islamists are not homogenous groups, they are heterogeneous. I can guess they'll never come back to power as in 2006, but they can fight one another and create a huge mess. If they did take power, they must restore law and order and create job opportunities for us. If they don't, then piracy will never stop.

Q: How are the Somali pirates organized? Do you all coordinate your actions?

A: The pirates belong to different groups, but we have umbrella groups. There are two main groups, one in Puntland and the other in south and central Somalia, which is my group. I am a member of the seven top committee members in south and central. We are a group of men with norms and terms, and we respect them.

Q: The pirates holding the *Sirius Star* have threatened to dump its oil if their demands are not met. Is that a serious threat, and do they realize how much damage that could do not only to Somalia, but other countries as well?

A: Those holding the *Sirius Star* and the *MV Faina* I'm aboard now, we are the same group. And we know the risk of spilling the oil shipment. But when evil is the only solution, you do evil. That is why we are doing piracy. I know it is evil, but it is a solution.

Piracy and Armed Robbery against Ships: Report for the Period 1 January–31 December 2016 (London: ICC International Maritime Bureau, 2017), 18–19, 25. Used with Permission.

Piracy and Armed Robbery Prone Areas and Warnings

Red Sea/Gulf of Aden/Somalia/Arabian Sea/Indian Ocean: Attacks related to Somali pirates have reduced. However, the risk of being approached or attacked still exists. Vessels are advised and encouraged to remain vigilant and comply with all BMP4 procedures. The threat of those attacks still exist in the waters off southern Red Sea/Bab el Mandeb. Gulf of Aden, including Yemen and the northern Somali Coast, Arabian Sea/ of Oman, Gulf of Oman, and off the eastern and southern Somali cost. In the past, vessels have been attacked off Kenya, Tanzania, Seychelles, Madagascar, and Mozambique, as well as in the Indian Ocean and off the west and south coast of India and west Maldives. Incidents have also been reported close to the east African coastlines.

Somali pirates tend to be well-armed with automatic weapons and RPG and sometimes use skiffs launched from mother vessels, which may be hijacked fishing vessels or dhows, to conduct attacks far from the Somali coast. Masters and shipowners are encouraged to follow the latest BMP procedures and ensure that the vessel is hardened prior to entering the High Risk Area. While transiting through these waters, it is essential to maintain a 24-hour visual and radar watch. Early sightings/detection enable and accurate assessment, keeping in mind the warnings and alerts for the area, allowing the Masters and PCASP to make informed decisions to keep clear of small boats, dhow, and fishing vessels and, if necessary, take evasive actions, increase speed, and request assistance as needed.

Masters are reminded that fishermen in this region may try to protect their nets by attempting to aggressively approach merchant vessels. Some of the fisherman may be armed to protect their catch, and they should not be confused with pirates.

Observations:

Somalia:

On 22 October 2016, a United Kingdom-flagged Product Tanker MT CPO Korea was attacked and fired upon by armed persons while underway at position 04:28.1 North and Longitude 053:22.2 East, about 300 nm east of Somali Coast, Somalia, at approximately 0955 LT. A blue hulled boat with five to six persons attacked the tanker with 21 crews and three security guards on board. At a CPA of two cables, the on board security team fired warning shots. Persons in the boat retuned fire and tried to board the tanker but failed. The boat later aborted the attempt and moved away.

United Nations Security Council Resolution 2382 (2017) Adopted by the Security Council at its 8088th meeting, on 7 November, 2017. S/RES/2383 (2017).

Noting that the joint counter-piracy efforts of States, regions, organizations, the maritime industry, the private sector, think tanks, and civil society have resulted in a steady decline in pirate attacks as well as hijackings since 2011, and expressing concern about the recent piracy incidents that occurred during 2017, and by the ongoing threat that resurgent piracy and armed robbery at sea poses to the prompt, safe, and effective delivery of humanitarian aid to Somalia and the region, to the safety of seafarers and other persons, to international navigation and the safety of commercial maritime routes, and to other ships, including fishing vessels operating in conformity with international law, commending Chinese and Indian naval forces for thwarting an attack on the OS-35, Chinese operations soldiers for capturing three pirates, and Chinese and European Union Naval Forces (EU NAVFOR) for preventing an attack on *MV Al Heera*, and further commending countries that have deployed naval forces in the Gulf of Aden and the Somali Basin to dissuade piracy networks from carrying out acts of piracy, ...

Recognizing the need to investigate and prosecute not only suspects captured at sea, but also anyone who incites or intentionally facilitates piracy operations, including key figures of criminal networks involved in piracy who plan, organize, facilitate, or illicitly finance or profit from such attacks, and reiterating its concern over persons suspected of piracy having been released without facing justice, reaffirming that the failure to prosecute persons responsible for acts of piracy and armed robbery at sea off the coast of Somalia undermines anti-piracy efforts, ... noting with concern that the continuing limited capacity and domestic legislation to facilitate the custody and prosecution of suspected pirates after their capture has hindered more robust international action against pirates off the coast of Somalia, which has led to pirates in many cases being released without facing justice, regardless of whether there is sufficient evidence to support prosecution. ...

Determining that the incidents of piracy and armed robbery at sea off the coast of Somalia, as well as the activity of pirate groups in Somalia, are an important factor exacerbating the situation in Somalia, which continues to constitute a threat to international peace and security in the region, ...

12. Renews its call upon States and regional organizations that are able to do so to take part in the fight against piracy and armed robbery at sea off the coast of Somalia, in particular, consistent with this resolution and international law, by deploying naval vessels, arms, and military aircraft, by providing basing and logistical support for counter-piracy forces, and by seizing and disposing of boats, vessels, arms, and other related equipment used in the commission of piracy and armed robbery at sea off the coast of Somalia, or for which there are reasonable grounds for suspecting such use;

13. Highlights the importance of coordination among States and international organizations in order to deter acts of piracy and armed robbery at sea off the coast of Somalia ...

14. Encourages Member States to continue to cooperate with Somali authorities in the fight against piracy and armed robbery at sea, notes the primary role of Somali authorities in the fight against piracy and armed robbery at sea off the coast of Somalia, and decides that, for a further period of 12 months from the date of this resolution to renew the authorizations as set out in paragraph 14 of resolution 2316 (2016) granted to States and regional organizations cooperating with Somali authorities in the fight against piracy and armed robbery at sea off the coast of Somalia, for which advance notification has been provided by Somali authorities to the Secretary-General.

Notes

1 Prange, 'The Contested Sea', 20–25.

2 Brooks and Bennet, *New England Merchants in Africa*, 102–104, 160–161.

3 Ingiriis, 'The History of Somali Piracy', 242–246, 257.

4 Ingiriis, 'The History of Somali Piracy', 260–261; Samatar, Lindberg, and Mahayni, 'The Dialects of Piracy in Somalia', 1384.

5 Samatar, Lindberg, and Mahayni, 'The Dialects of Piracy in Somalia', 1384.

6 Weir, 'Fish, Family and Profit', 1–27.

7 Daniels, *Somali Piracy and Terrorism*, 33–34.

8 Eichstaedt, *Pirate State*, 28–30; quote from page 38.

9 Eichstaedt, *Pirate State*, 33, 38; Daniels, *Somali Piracy and Terrorism*, 34–35.

10 Samatar, Lindberg, and Mahayni, 'The Dialects of Piracy in Somalia', 1385–1386, 1387–1389.

11 Weir, 'Fish, Family and Profit', 210–211.

12 Bueger, 'Practice, Pirates and Coast Guards', 1817–1820.

13 Bueger, 'Practice, Pirates and Coast Guards', 1817.

14 Bueger, 'Practice, Pirates and Coast Guards', 1820–1824.

15 Weir, 'Fish, Family and Profit', 211–212.

16 Bueger, 'Practice, Pirates and Coast Guards', 1818.

17 Weir, 'Fish, Family and Profit', 212.

18 Eichstaedt, *Pirate State*, 57, 62.

19 Eichstaedt, *Pirate State*, 61.

20 Eichstaedt, *Pirate State*, 57.

21 Yikona, *Pirate Trails*, 40–42, 45.

22 Daniels, *Somali Piracy and Terrorism*, 40.

23 Yikona, *Pirate Trails*, 46–49.

24 Eichstaedt, *Pirate State*, 60.

25 Eichstaedt, *Pirate State*, 35.

26 Weir, 'Fish, Family and Profit', 213.

27 Eichstaedt, *Pirate State*, 53–54.

28 Daniels, *Somali Piracy and Terrorism*, 80–81.

29 Shortland, 'Can We Stop Talking about Somali Piracy Now?' 422.

30 Daniels, *Somali Piracy and Terrorism*, 36.

31 Daniels, *Somali Piracy and Terrorism*, 73, 82.

32 Shortland, 'Can We Stop Talking about Somali Piracy Now?' 426–428.

33 *Oceans beyond Piracy* 2016 Report. http://oceansbeyondpiracy.org/reports/sop/east-africa.

34 Hansen, 'Piracy, Security and State-Formation', 177–178.

35 Jamieson, *Lords of the Sea*, 217–221.

CHAPTER SIXTEEN

Modern Pirate Hunting – What Is to Be Done?

Pirate hunting is as old as piracy itself because, with few exceptions, piracy has proven very durable and very difficult to control. In truth, little has changed since the days of the Greeks. Benerson Little describes the situation well: 'Pirates remain for the most part small gangs of lightly armed men in swift, light vessels in pursuit of large, slow-moving, poorly armed merchant vessels. The tactics of lying in wait, ruse, and swift pursuit have not changed, nor has the value placed on people as plunder.'[1] The conditions that foster piracy also remain unchanged. Piracy still flourishes around fragmented coastlines that are difficult to patrol and that provide havens and hideaways for pirates. It thrives amid widespread poverty, political fragmentation or the absence of strong unified rule, the corruption or acquiescence of government officials, the presence of vibrant trade along predictable sea-lanes, the support of local communities and the existence of markets willing to buy and sell pirate loot. When these conditions coincide, piracy persists.

The real challenge in suppressing piracy is that the practice of piracy is almost always profitable, while pirate hunting rarely is. This is one reason why privateers have so readily turned to piracy when given the chance. Modern pirate hunting is even less profitable. Somali pirates capture vessels and crews to be held for ransom. A pirate hunter who captures these pirates will not be rewarded with the hijacked ship and its cargo as in the past. Those will be returned to their owners. Pirate hunters in Malaysia may be able to intervene in the robbery of a vessel's payroll and its crew members, but they will not be allowed to keep the payroll. Discoverers of phantom ships will not be allowed to sell the ships for a profit. Today, pirate hunters are employees of the state who cannot hope for any more profit than their promised salaries, and taxpayers are left to carry the burden of pirate suppression.

We also confront the problem of a complete misunderstanding of how and why piracy declined when and where it did. The story we have told ourselves for a very long time is that pirate suppression came about as more civilized nation states tamed the wild frontiers of the oceans.[2] This story always focuses on violent suppression by state authorities, which includes military action and effective use of legal systems.[3] In this narrative, military and legal action are thought to make piracy too costly and, thus, deter pirates from taking to the sea in the first place. However, as we have seen, this story is largely fiction. If it were true that violent military action and robust legal systems could defeat criminal activity by themselves, then prisons in the West would be largely empty. Police forces and prosecuting attorneys would have very little to do. This story is a nationalistic and imperialistic narrative that makes us feel good, but it is not true.

The much-vaunted pirate wars of the first two decades of the eighteenth century that supposedly brought piracy in the Atlantic to an end and inaugurated the era of controlled privateering are exaggerated.[4] Beyond the fact, as discussed in Chapter 1, that the distinction between piracy and privateering remains largely academic, piracy never came to an end in the Atlantic and Caribbean in the 1730s. This is clearly demonstrated by the ongoing complaints about piracy, pirate trials, new piracy laws and campaigns dedicated to pirate suppression that persisted well into the nineteenth century throughout the Atlantic world. Pirates habitually acquired privateering commissions to provide legal cover for practices already considered legitimate on board ships.[5] Indeed, piracy and privateering in the Atlantic and the Caribbean actually increased in the 1820s with the Latin American wars of independence.[6] The American Civil War brought a new upsurge in privateering and piracy in the mid-nineteenth century[7] as did the British struggle against the Riff pirates off the coast of Morocco into the 1850s.[8]

The simple truth is that laws have very little capacity to 'change the ethical and legal beliefs of local communities'.[9] This is especially true of marginal or peripheral communities who see little benefit from centralized government, distrust law enforcement efforts, see maritime commerce as beyond the jurisdiction of nation states and doubt the central governments' ability to enforce the laws they create.[10] Likewise, no European state has ever ended piracy through military means. The costs were too high, and they required the continual occupation of all available pirate lairs, harbours and markets. So if the accepted narrative is not correct, why did piracy recede from some areas of the world – even if only temporarily? The truth is that the reduction or elimination of piracy had more to do with transformations in the economic realities of the Atlantic world than in legal changes and military action.

Piracy in the Atlantic and Caribbean slowly diminished because of the new 'economic and commercial conditions' that prevailed in the eighteenth and nineteenth centuries. The value of cargoes declined as the trade shifted from bullion to consumer goods. Pirates abandoned the Atlantic for the Pacific and the Indian Oceans because of the promise of more profitable loot. Peaceful trade also became more profitable as tariffs were reduced, insurance costs declined, convoy protection improved and markets opened up.[11] Smugglers and pirates found that they could no longer compete as suppliers of cheap goods. As commerce raiding became less important to the survival of maritime communities, those communities closed their doors to pirates. The free-floating pirate communities of the 'Golden Age' could not last without the land-based communities that supported them.[12]

By the mid-nineteenth century, European powers had determined that private property and commerce on the high seas were essential to national economies and national security and began reining in the non-state predators they had unleashed. They went after the monopoly mercantile companies, who enjoyed coercive power and who had been the source of much of the maritime predation in international waters. These companies either went bankrupt, were co-opted by the state or became purely commercial enterprises. The Dutch West Indies Company went bankrupt in 1674 after the 1661 treaty with Portugal opened up trade in the Americas to the Dutch. The English East India Company faced growing opposition until it was abolished in 1833.[13] Local communities who had supported pirates and privateers began to see these activities as disruptive to legal trade and damaging to profits and social stability. With the mounting protests of 'friendly nations, neutrals and insurance companies' against the depredations of privateers, in the latter half of the eighteenth century, states began to turn against them.[14] This led most European states to sign the 1856 Paris Declaration Respecting Maritime Law, which prohibited privateering. Though the agreement was intended to bring an end to private warfare at sea, it really gave an advantage to nations with powerful navies who did not need to rely on privateers. The United States, Mexico and Spain all refused to sign the agreement for that reason. Consequently, privateering remained legal in the United States and was used by the Confederacy in the American Civil War.[15]

The decline in piracy in the Mediterranean experienced a similar trend. Peaceful commerce became more profitable, and the religious justifications for corsairing disappeared. Though the combined military efforts of the Western nations in attacking Barbary corsairing bases did make corsairing more costly and difficult to pursue, it did not bring it to an end by itself. Napoleon's conquest of Malta in 1798 and the French imperial conquest of North Africa beginning in 1830 combined with the changed commercial environment to bring about the end of corsairing in the Mediterranean.[16] Pirates lost their bases and private trade became more profitable. In the Philippines, Spain's use of steamships gave them a temporary advantage that allowed them to suppress Balangingi piracy against European shipping in 1848, though slave raiding continued until 1898.[17] The Chinese managed to maintain piracy within acceptable limits in the later part of the nineteenth century with a combination of violent suppression, pardons, the conquest and occupation of pirate lairs, and the assistance of the English. The one constant in all of these stories is that military and legal repression were never sufficient to end piracy by themselves. All they did was keep it within tolerable limits, which is what European naval power in Southeast Asia did until the Second World War.

The rise in global piracy in the last half of the twentieth century, followed by the dramatic increase off the coast of Somali at the beginning of the twenty-first century, riveted the world's attention for a brief moment on the problem of suppressing piracy. All the major players fell back on only a few of the methods practised in Europe during the long 200-year 'war on piracy' from 1650 to 1850. Those techniques were complex and varied. They included 'changing public attitudes, hiring private pirate hunters, rooting out corruption, improving the administration of justice, offering pardons to pirates who voluntarily surrendered, increasing the number of naval ships dedicated to anti-piracy duty, cooperating with other nations, convoying merchant ships, blockading and bombarding pirate ports, chasing pirates both at sea and on land, and finally occupying and dismantling pirate lairs'.[18] Despite the evidence to the contrary, the lesson most commonly drawn by modern observers was that only a vigorous military and legal response could rein in the pirates.[19] The military responses contemplated almost never included occupying the territory of failed states or even sovereign states that pirates use as bases. As I argued in the previous chapter, the apparent success of these efforts in Somalia by 2015 has created a false sense of accomplishment. The conditions that created the pirate menace remain unaltered. The same is true in the Gulf of Guinea, in Southeast Asia and in the Straits of Malacca.

The trend continues elsewhere in the world. Following the eruption of the Arab Spring in 2011 and the collapse of the Libyan government, piracy began to appear in Libyan waters, though still in small numbers. There was one reported attack in 2013. In 2014, Libyan rebels seized the oil tanker, MV *Morning Glory* and its 234,000 barrels of crude oil. In 2015, pirates seized 'a Sicilian fishing boat and its seven crew members' 'sixty kilometers off the Libyan coast'.[20] There were seven attacks off Egyptian shores in 2013 and another one in 2015.[21] The recent rise in piracy off the coasts of Venezuela suggests that the age-old pattern is reasserting itself yet again. As Venezuela struggles with political and economic instability and its people have become increasingly desperate, piracy has increased. In 2013, there were no attacks and in 2014 and 2015 there was only one attack each year. But, in 2016 as the political and economic crisis began to intensify, five attacks occurred followed by twelve in 2017.[22]

The lesson that should be drawn from a global study of piracy, but is consistently overlooked, is that enduring peace and shared prosperity remain the two most important tools in combating piracy. Wherever piracy is practised today, poverty, instability, the lack of economic opportunity, corruption, organized crime and community support are the real culprits. Vast riches flowing past communities wallowing in wretched poverty can only exacerbate a sense of betrayal and deprivation. Certainly being a victim does not justify victimizing others, but blaming the victim for his victimization is equally useless. Aggressive assaults on pirates are probably necessary, but these tactics tend to treat the symptoms while ignoring the real causes of piracy.

Attempts to confront modern piracy are also hampered by a multitude of challenges. Piracy remains a low priority for governments in Southeast Asia and Africa who have much bigger political, economic and social fish to fry. Western nations remain preoccupied with the threat of terrorism and the rise of isolationist nationalism. Piracy tends to thrive along the coasts of poor countries or failed states that cannot police their territories effectively. The international community cannot agree on who should bear the burden of covering the costs of pirate suppression. Shipping companies prefer to bet on the odds that their ships will not be pirated and then pay the costs of occasional raids rather than face the expense of improving shipboard security. Corruption and collusion of state officials with pirates in Puntland, China, Nigeria and the Philippines feeds piracy. Poor reporting makes it difficult to adequately assess the real pirate threat. Law enforcement is expensive and requires international organizations and agreements to be effective. Economic crises and political instability continue to punish the communities least able to deal with them.[23]

Despite ongoing pirate attacks around the world, the only region to stimulate a sustained and forceful international response against piracy was Somalia after 2005 when pirate attacks rose dramatically. Given the considerable human and economic costs of piracy, we should ask why? Almost $2.5 billion were spent in 2016 on anti-piracy measures, 5,276 seafarers were attacked, 172 hostages were taken, 9 people were killed and 37 injured. Poor countries of Africa, such as Kenya, end up paying higher prices for food as the increased insurance costs for shipping are passed on to consumers.[24] Since 2012, when the Somali threat seemed to have been contained, the international response has declined. NATO ended its operation Ocean Shield in the Gulf of Aden in 2016. Spending on anti-piracy measures is down from about $12 billion in 2010 to $2.5 billion in 2016 (see Table 16.1). These costs should not be minimized. However, examined from a global perspective, the economic costs of piracy are not very substantial. The average loss is $5,000 for a robbery and $1–2 million for a hijacking. Insurance companies continue to insulate ship owners from these losses, and ships have about 0.01–0.02 per cent chance of being attacked.[25] On the whole, piracy is still maintained within tolerable limits and, until, or unless, that changes, it is unlikely there will be a significant and sustained international response.[26]

If the international community did decide to get serious about ending piracy, the effort would have to be multi-national and sustained.

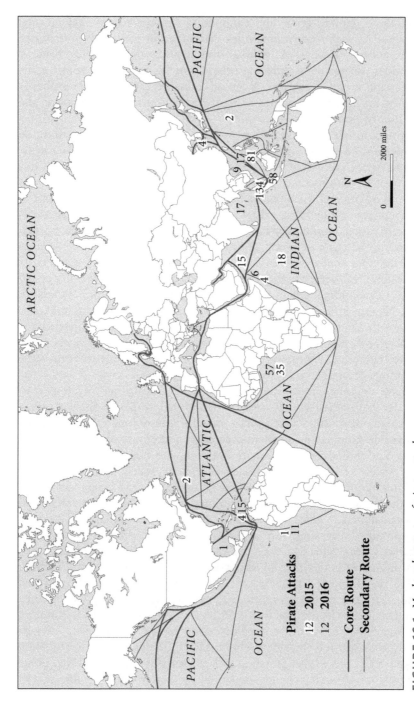

FIGURE 16.1 *Modern hotspots of pirate attacks.*
Source: Map produced by Barry Levely, Cartographer.

TABLE 16.1 Human and economic costs of piracy in 2016

Region	Number of Attacks	Total Cost	Cost of Contracted Maritime Security Services	Cost of International Naval Activities	Cost of Stolen Goods	Seafarers Subjected to Attack	Seafarers Taken Hostage	Seafarers Killed	Seafarers Injured
East Africa	27	$1.7 Billion	$726.1 Million	$228.3 Million	$202.578 Million	545	8	1	15
West Africa	95	$793.7 Million	$345.9 Million	$41,000	$931.248 Million	1,921	96	0	7
Asia	129				$4.5 Million	2,283	67	6	8
Latin America	27				$302,000	527	1	2	7
Total	**278**	**$2.494 Billion**	**$1.072 Billion**	**$228.341 Million**	**$1.139 Billion**	**5,276**	**172**	**9**	**37**

Source: Oceans beyond Piracy. http://oceansbeyondpiracy.org/reports/sop.

International cooperation would be necessary to eliminate pirate bases and the conditions that support piracy. This would require an international alliance to establish bases in Somaliland, and build up the Somaliland coast guard and judiciary system. Where regional governments exist, they need to be encouraged to take piracy seriously and to share intelligence information. They need to be given the resources to create formal anti-piracy military units and judiciary systems.[27] The connections between pirate leaders and corrupt officials must be severed, which means governmental corruption must be tackled. The international banking community should be forced to 'end easy money laundering and transfers by pirate financiers in Europe and elsewhere'.[28] Naval patrols, aerial surveillance and security need to be intensified to make it more dangerous to be a pirate. International piracy law needs to be clarified and punishments need to be more effective. World governments need to cooperate in depriving pirates of bases and going after the shadowy world of organized crime that often finances and benefits from pirate activity.

More importantly, however, something must be done to revitalize sagging economies and promote stable, functioning states. The fishing industries in Somalia and Nigeria could be revived by retracting foreign fishing permits and giving them to Somalis, cleaning up oil spills along the Nigerian coast and rebuilding fishing infrastructure like port facilities and processing plants. Attacking the problem of poverty alone, however, will not solve the problems either because as long as piracy remains easy and profitable, it will continue. These methods will help only in conjunction with measures that make piracy so risky that alternative employment becomes appealing.[29]

Foreign companies and governments who dump hazardous waste in Somali waters or spill oil in the Gulf of Guinea must be punished and forced to pay to clean up the mess. Governments around the world need to create and enforce fair and moral immigration policies and more equitable distribution of wealth. Insurance companies must crack down on companies who contract pirates to take ships so they can collect insurance money. Southeast Asian countries need to create clear maritime boundaries and allow naval patrols to move across those boundaries in pursuit of pirates.[30] Governments need to crack down on kidnapping, human trafficking and sex trafficking. A multi-national convoy system to protect international shipping through global choke points would also be necessary.

This international response must coincide with effective deterrents by shipping companies. They can use enhanced surveillance techniques by illuminating their decks and the area around their ships at night. They can sweep surrounding seas with searchlights and monitor radar up to at least one nautical mile away from the ship. A wide variety of inexpensive deterrents to boarding are available. Ships can travel at increased speeds to create dangerous wakes around their ships. For now, at least, pirates cannot board a vessel travelling faster than eighteen knots.[31] Heavy wheel movements can make it difficult to board. They can install barbed wire or electric fencing all around the ship. They can expand the width of gunnels to prevent grappling hooks from gaining a purchase. They can use slippery paint on areas where boarding is likely. They can spray slippery foam on decks and gunwales. They can trail mooring lines or cargo nets astern to entangle the propellers of boats approaching from the rear. They can spread broken glass on deck, use fire hoses to spray intruders, fire flares at pirates, use sonic lasers and post dummy dogs or guards. If all that fails, they need to create safe rooms to prevent pirates from taking hostages, and they should be prepared to use lethal force either by training and arming their crews or by hiring security professionals.[32] The problem with all of these efforts is that they cost money – lots of it. Countries facing terrorist attacks, insurgencies, economic crises and political strife are unlikely to muster the interest or resources to tackle piracy, despite UN resolutions that encourage it. The effort also requires trust and cooperation at an international level. Given the worldwide rise in populist nationalism that makes it nearly impossible to tackle clear global challenges, such as climate change, we can be forgiven for being sceptical that such cooperation is likely to emerge anytime soon.

Modern calls for creating a formal system for issuing letters of marque to private companies to solve the pirate problem are also likely to fall flat.[33] Not only do they drastically overstate the value of privateers in fighting pirates, but the recent use of private contractors in the war in Iraq has proven that private forces are very difficult to control, less effective, very costly and given to excess.[34] Privateers, like pirates, only work for a profit. In the past, privateers were paid from the loot they stole from the pirates. That practice is no longer viable and taxpayers will be left holding the bill.

Conclusion

Like the Romans before them, the European states of the nineteenth century agreed to define piracy as a common evil they should cooperate in eradicating. They created the category of the privateer, or the legally sanctioned legitimate raider of the civilized state, as the opposite of the pirate – the illegal, illegitimate raider of barbarous or backward peoples, so they could justify both the private wars European entrepreneurs carried out around the globe and their own imperial expansion. The hypocrisy of empire allowed them to define away the illegitimacy of their own raiding, looting and pillaging, while castigating those who sought to resist European domination and maintain their own traditional rights over their own sea-lanes.[35] As European powers created and maintained their own navies of steam-powered ships, privateers became unnecessary. Economies adjusted to peaceful exchange. Merchants accepted governmental control over maritime commerce, and taxpayers picked up the tab for protecting the shipping of private companies.

The cosy agreement that pirates are a common evil to be suppressed does not hold true everywhere and never has. Poor countries have neither the means nor the motivation to end piracy. Corporations who benefit from the lax laws for registering ships in countries like Panama and Liberia, who can rely on states to cover the costs of maritime defence and who sometimes benefit by hiring pirates to 'retire' outdated ships, likewise have little motivation to see piracy end.[36] Piracy has always been with us. It will always be with us. The most we can hope for is to manage the risk – to maintain piracy within tolerable limits.[37]

As you read the following documents, consider the following questions:

1   What is the emphasis of the protective measures suggested in the Best Management Practices (BMP) document? Why might this be the focus of their approach?

2   Why doesn't the BMP document recommend the use of armed violence against pirates?

3   How do the recommendations change depending on which stage of attack the crew faces?

4   Do the trends noted in the IMB report for 2017 suggest any shifts in pirate tactics and/or any change in the regions likely to be hot spots for pirate activity in the future?

5   What role did pirate suppression play in the creation of modern nation states?

6   Have the conditions that foster piracy changed in the last century? Why or why not?

7   How did economic transformations contribute to the reduction in piracy in the Atlantic and the Mediterranean?

8   How has your perception of pirates changed as a result of studying pirates in their historical context? Why?

9   Which type of piracy do you find most common in your study of global piracy?

10 Are you willing to accept piracy as a normal part of global maritime trade? Why or why not?

11 How do you think modern states should approach the challenge of piracy?

12 Now that you have studied piracy as a global phenomenon, would you change the definition of piracy proposed in this text? How and why?

'Best Management Practices for Protection against Somalia Based Piracy', 4th edition (Edinburgh: Witherby Publishing Group, 2011), 23–48. Used with permission.

Ship Protection Measures: ...

Providing additional lookouts for each watch:

Additional lookouts should be fully briefed. Considering a shorter rotation of the Watch period in order to maximise alertness of the lookouts.

Ensuring that there are sufficient binoculars for the enhanced Bridge Team, preferably anti-glare.

Considering use of night vision optics.

Maintaining a careful Radar Watch.

Well-constructed dummies placed at strategic locations around the vessel can give an impression of greater numbers of people on watch. A proper lookout is the single most effective method of ship protection where early warning of a suspicious approach or attack is assured, and where defences can be readily deployed

Enhanced Bridge Protection:

The bridge is usually the focus for any pirate attack. In the initial part of the attack, pirates direct weapons fire at the bridge to try to coerce the ship to stop. If they are able to board the vessel, the pirates usually try to make for the bridge to enable them to take control. The following further protection enhancements might be considered:

Kevlar jackets and helmets available for the bridge team to provide a level of protection for those on the bridge during an attack. (If possible, jackets and helmets should be in a nonmilitary colour).

While most bridge windows are laminated, further protection against flying glass can be provided by the application of security glass film, often called Blast Resistant Film.

Fabricated metal (steel/aluminium) plates for the side and rear bridge windows and the bridge wing door windows, which may be rapidly secured in place in the event of an attack.

The after part of both bridge wings (often open) can be protected by a wall of sandbags.

The sides and rear of the bridge, and the bridge wings, may be protected with a double layer of chain link fence, which has been shown to reduce the effect of an RPG round. Proprietary anti-RPG screens are also available.

Control of Access to Bridge:

... It is very important to control access routes to deter or delay pirates who have managed to board a vessel and are trying to enter accommodation or machinery spaces. It is very important to recognise that if pirates do gain access to the upper deck of a vessel they will be tenacious in their efforts to gain access to the accommodation section and, in particular, the bridge. It is strongly recommended that significant effort is expended prior to entry to the High-Risk Area to deny the pirates access to the accommodation and the bridge. ...

Consideration should be given to blocking or lifting external ladders on the accommodation block to prevent their use, and to restrict external access to the bridge.

... Pirates have been known to gain access through portholes and windows. The fitting of steel bars to windows will prevent this even if they manage to shatter the window. ...

Physical Barriers:

Pirates typically use long lightweight hooked ladders, grappling hooks with rope attached and long hooked poles with a climbing rope attached to board vessels underway. Physical barriers should be used to make it as difficult as possible to gain access to vessels by increasing the height and difficulty of any climb for an attacking pirate.

Before constructing any physical barriers, it is recommended that a thorough survey is conducted to identify areas vulnerable to pirates trying to gain access.

Razor Wire Razor wire (also known as barbed tape) creates an effective barrier but only when carefully deployed. The barbs on the wire are designed to have a piercing and gripping action. ...

A robust razor wire barrier is particularly effective if it is: Constructed outboard of the ship's structure (i.e. overhanging) to make it more difficult for pirates to hook on their boarding ladder/grappling hooks to the ship's structure. ...

Electrified barriers are not recommended for hydrocarbon-carrying vessels but, following a full risk assessment, can be appropriate and effective for some other types of vessel ....

Water Spray and Foam Monitors:

The use of water spray and/or foam monitors has been found to be effective in deterring or delaying pirates attempting to board a vessel. The use of water can make it difficult for a pirate skiff to remain alongside and makes it significantly more difficult for a pirate to try to climb on board. Options include: Fire hoses and foam monitors ... Water cannons ... Ballast pumps ... Steam ... Water spray rails ... Foam can be used, but it must be in addition to a vessel's standard Fire Fighting Equipment (FFE) stock. Foam is effective as it is disorientating and very slippery, making it difficult to climb through. ...

Alarms:

Sounding the ship's alarms/whistle serves to inform the vessel's crew that a piracy attack has commenced and, importantly, demonstrates to any potential attacker that the ship is aware of the attack and is reacting to it. ...

Manoeuvring Practice:
Practising manoeuvring the vessel prior to entry into the High-Risk Area will be very beneficial and will ensure familiarity with the ship's handling characteristics and how to effect anti-piracy manoeuvres whilst maintaining the best possible speed. (Waiting until the ship is attacked before practicing, is too late!) Where navigationally safe to do so, Masters are encouraged to practise manoeuvring their ships to establish which series of helm orders produce the most difficult sea conditions for pirate skiffs trying to attack, without causing a significant reduction in the ship's speed.

Closed Circuit Television (CCTV):
Once an attack is underway and pirates are firing weaponry at the vessel, it is difficult and dangerous to observe whether the pirates have managed to gain access. The use of CCTV coverage allows a degree of monitoring of the progress of the attack from a less exposed position: ...

Upper Deck Lighting: ...
Search lights for immediate use when required. ... Navigation lights should not be switched off at night.

Deny Use of Ship's Tools and Equipment:
Pirates generally board vessels with little in the way of equipment other than personal weaponry. It is important to try to deny pirates the use of ship's tools or equipment that may be used to gain entry into the vessel. Tools and equipment that may be of use to the pirates should be stored in a secure location. ...

Safe Muster Points/Citadels:
... Consideration should be given to establishing a Safe Muster Point or secure Citadel: ... The whole concept of the Citadel approach is lost if any crew member is left outside before it is secured.

It is important to note that Naval/Military forces will apply the following criteria before a boarding to release those in a Citadel can be considered: 100% of the crew must be secured in the Citadel. The crew of the ship must have self-contained, independent, reliable 2-way external communications (sole reliance on VHF communications is not sufficient). The pirates must be denied access to ship propulsion ....

Unarmed Private Maritime Security Contractors:
The use of unarmed Private Maritime Security Contractors is a matter for individual ship operators following their own voyage risk assessment. The deployment on board is subject to the national laws of the Flag State. The use of experienced and competent unarmed Private Maritime Security Contractors can be a valuable addition to BMP.

Armed Private Maritime Security Contractors:

The use, or not, of armed Private Maritime Security Contractors on board merchant vessels is a matter for individual ship operators to decide following their own voyage risk assessment and approval of respective Flag States. This advice does not constitute a recommendation or an endorsement of the general use of armed Private Maritime Security Contractors. Subject to risk analysis, careful planning and agreements the provision of Military Vessel Protection Detachments (VPDs) deployed to protect vulnerable shipping is the recommended option when considering armed guards ....

[Response to an Attack:]

If the crew of a vessel suspects that it is coming under a pirate attack there are specific actions that are recommended to be taken during the approach stage and the attack stage. It should be noted that the pirates generally do not use weapons until they are within two cables of a vessel, therefore any period up until this stage can be considered as 'approach', and gives a vessel valuable time in which to activate her defences and make it clear to pirates that they have been seen and the vessel is prepared and will resist.

Approach Stage:

If not already at full speed, increase to maximum to open the CPA. Try to steer a straight course to maintain a maximum speed. Initiate the ship's pre-prepared emergency procedures. Activate the Emergency Communication Plan. Sound the emergency alarm and make a 'Pirate Attack' announcement in accordance with the Ship's Emergency Plan. Report the attack immediately to UKMTO. ... Activate the Ship Security Alert System (SSAS), which will alert your Company Security Officer and Flag State. Make a 'Mayday' call on VHF Ch. 16 (and backup Ch. 08, which is monitored by naval units). Send a distress message via the Digital Selective Calling system (DSC) and Inmarsat-C, as applicable.

Ensure that the Automatic Identification System (AIS) is switched ON. All crew, except those required on the bridge or in the engine room, should muster at the Safe Muster Point or Citadel if constructed, so that the crew are given as much ballistic protection as possible should the pirates get close enough to use weapons. Where possible, alter course away from the approaching skiffs and/or Motherships. When sea conditions allow, consider altering course to increase an approaching skiff's exposure to wind/waves. Activate water spray and other appropriate self-defensive measures. Ensure that all external doors and, where possible, internal public rooms and cabins, are fully secured. In addition to the emergency alarms and announcements for the benefit of the vessel's crew sound the ship's whistle/foghorn continuously to demonstrate to any potential attacker that the ship is aware of the attack and is reacting to it.

Attack stage:
Reconfirm that all ship's personnel are in a position of safety. As the pirates close in on the vessel, Masters should commence small alterations of helm whilst maintaining speed to deter skiffs from lying alongside the vessel in preparation for a boarding attempt. These manoeuvres will create additional wash to impede the operation of the skiffs. Substantial amounts of helm are not recommended, as these are likely to significantly reduce a vessel's speed.

Try to remain calm:
… Offer no resistance to the pirates once they reach the bridge. Once on the bridge, the pirates are likely to be aggressive, highly agitated, and possibly under the influence of drugs (including khat, an amphetamine-like stimulant), so remaining calm and cooperating fully will greatly reduce the risk of harm.

If the bridge/engine room is to be evacuated, the main engine should be stopped … (if navigationally safe to do so). All remaining crew members should proceed to the designated Safe Muster Point with their hands visible ….

If the Pirates take Control:
In the event that Naval/Military forces take action on board the ship, all personnel should keep low to the deck and cover their head with both hands, with hands visible. On no account should personnel make movements, which could be misinterpreted as being aggressive. Do not use flash photography. Be prepared to be challenged on your identity. Brief and prepare ship's personnel to expect this and to cooperate fully during any Naval/Military action on board.

Be aware that English is not the working language of all Naval/Military forces in the region. Naval/Military forces will endeavour to respond rapidly to ongoing acts of piracy. However, because of the very large distances across the High-Risk Area, a Naval/Military response may not be possible.

Piracy and Armed Robbery against Ships: Report for the Period 1 January–31 December 2017 (London: ICC International Maritime Bureau, 2018), 30. Used with Permission.

Trends:
A total of 180 incidents of piracy and armed robbery against ships have been reported to the IMB PRC in 2017. This is the lowest number since 1995 when 188 reports were received.

In 2017, 136 vessels were boarded, there were 22 attempted attacks, 16 vessels fired upon and six vessels hijacked. Whilst the continued decline in overall numbers is welcome, the effects on crew and their safety continues to be a cause for concern. Ninety-one crew were taken hostage in 15 separate incidents and 75 crew kidnapped from their vessels in 13 separate events. Three kidnapping incidents were recorded for Q4 [fourth quarter] – all off Nigeria with 26 crew kidnapped. Three crew were killed in 2017 with one fatality from an Iranian dhow reported in Q4.

Nigeria recorded 33 reports with no vessels hijacked. There were however ten kidnapping incidents involving 65 crew. Of the 16 vessels reported being fired upon globally, seven occurred in Nigeria – further evidencing the levels of violence and threats to seafarers in these waters.

Nine incidents were recorded off Somalia in 2017. This includes a container ship fired upon by armed pirates approximately 280 NM east of Mogadishu in November. Ladders were sighted on the attack skiff – a clear indication of piratical intent. Six pirates were subsequently detained by EU NAVFOR, transferred to Seychelles and charged with 'committing an act of piracy' and 'attempting an act of piracy'. If convicted, the pirates face up to 30 years' imprisonment. This incident alone demonstrates that Somali pirates still have the capability and intent to launch attacks hundreds of miles from the coastline ....

Indonesia recorded 43 reports – almost all mainly low-level incidents – and a continued year on year decrease. The patrols by the Indonesia Marine Police also show a modest yet continued decreased in incidents at the ten designated anchorages. A tug and barge were also hijacked in November although no cargo was reported missing and all crew reported safe.

There has been a notable increase in the Philippines – up from 10 in 2016 to 22 in 2017. The majority are low level incidents against anchored vessels mainly at Manila and Batangas. Vessels underway have also been targeted with ten crew kidnapped from three separate vessels in the first quarter of 2017. In the Sulu/Celebes Sea areas. Since then alerts provided by the Philippine authorities to the PRC and broadcast on their behalf to ships have helped to avoid further successful attacks.

Notes

1   Little, *Pirate Hunting*, 286.

2   Chet, *The Ocean Is a Wilderness*, 92–94.

3   Rediker, *Between the Devil*, 256–285; Rediker, *Villains of All Nations*, 127–144; Ritchie, *Captain Kidd*, vi, 235–236; Lane, *Pillaging the Empire*, 165–191; Little, *Sea Rover's Practice*, 15–16; Marx, *Pirates and Privateers of the Caribbean*, 8–9.

4   Earle, *The Pirate Wars*.

5   Chet, *The Ocean Is a Wilderness*, 96.

6   Chet, *The Ocean Is a Wilderness*, 14–25.

7   Little, *Pirate Hunting*, 229–234.

8   Lambert, 'The Limits of Naval Power', 173–188; Pennell, 'The Geography of Piracy', 55–66.

9   Chet, *The Ocean Is a Wilderness*, 95.

10 Chet, *The Ocean Is a Wilderness*, 94–99.

11 Chet, *The Ocean Is a Wilderness*, 93–94, quote from page 68; Hanna, *Pirate Nests*, 365–415.

12 Hanna, *Pirate Nests*, 421.

13 Thomson, *Mercenaries*, 97–102.

14 Thomson, *Mercenaries*, 70.

15 Thomson, *Mercenaries*, 71; Little, *Pirate Hunting*, 228.

16 Jamieson, *Lords of the Sea*, 191–192, 212, 221.

17 Warren, *Iranun and Balangingi*, 384.

18 Boot, 'Pirates, Then and Now', 103.

19 See United Nations Security Council Resolution 2383 (2017). Adopted by the Security Council at its 8088th meeting, on 7 November 2017.

20 Pryce, 'Libya: The Next Pirate Haven?'

21 *Piracy and Armed Robbery*, 2018, 6.

22 *Piracy and Armed Robbery*, 2018, 6.

23 Eklöf, *Pirates in Paradise*, 145–146.

24 Hansen, 'Piracy, Security and State-Formation', 175.

25 Boot, 'Pirates, Then and Now', 103; *Oceans beyond Piracy*, http://oceansbeyondpiracy.org/reports/sop

26 Rosenberg, 'The Political Economy of Piracy in the South China Sea', 91.

27 Bateman, 'Confronting Maritime Crime', 145–151.

28 Eichstaedt, *Pirate State*, 181–182.

29 Hansen, 'Piracy, Security and State-Formation', 178.

30 Eichstaedt, *Pirate State*, 182; Eklöf, *Pirates in Paradise*, 158.

31 Hansen, 'Piracy, Security and State-Formation', 177.

32 Little, *Pirate Hunting*, 277–282.

33 Hutchins, 'Structuring a Sustainable Letters of Marque Regime', 819–884; Boot, 'Pirates, Then and Now', 104.

34 Scahill, *Blackwater*; Coito, 'Pirate vs. Private Security', 188–195.

35 Reid, 'Violence at Sea', 20–26.

36 Reid, 'Violence at Sea', 26.

37 Hansen, 'Piracy, Security and State-Formation', 175.

GLOSSARY

aft—The back or stern of a ship.

alcalde mayor—Head of an administrative district smaller than an *audiencia* with judicial and military authority.

Algerine—A pirate or corsair from Algeria.

amidship—Centre of a ship.

Armada de la Carrera de las Índias—Spanish treasure fleet.

armada—A fleet of warships.

articles of confederation—A contract signed by pirates before joining a crew. The articles listed the rules of discipline, settlement of quarrels and the division of booty.

asiento—A commercial contract used by the Spanish to acquire loans and to supply slaves to their colonies in America. The *asiento* for the slave trade was given to the Dutch, French and English at different times.

audiencia—Spanish administrative district in colonial America with jurisdiction over criminal and civil cases.

avería—Spanish tax on goods shipped between Spain and the American colonies to pay for the defence against pirates.

barca—Usually a small oared vessel with square-rigged sails.

bark—A single-decked, round-sterned ship of 10–100 tonnes with one to two masts usually used by coastal traders.

barque—In the West Indies, this term referred to a single-mast sloop.

barque longo—A general term for any long, narrow vessel outfitted for oars and sails. It can have one or two masts and may or may not have decks.

benzoin—Balsamic resin used to make incense, medicine and perfumes.

bey—Ottoman governors over north African territories with ties to corsairing.

bilander—A small two-masted merchant ship.

bits—Belaying posts attached to the deck.

bloody flag—A red flag that signalled that no quarter would be given to the enemy.

boatswain/bosun—Responsible for caring for the rigging and boats and for disciplining the crew.

booty—Prize or cargo of a captured ship.

boucan—A native Taino method of barbeque used by renegades on Hispaniola and Tortuga.

bow—Front part of a ship or vessel.

bowsprit—A spar that extends beyond the bow of the ship which anchors the forestays.

brigantine—Favoured vessels of buccaneers. A long, shallow draft, two-masted ship with square sails used for sea roving. It can be sailed in both shallow waters close to coastlines and on the open sea.

broadside—Simultaneous firing of cannons from one side of a ship into an enemy vessel.

buccaneer/*boucanier*—Sea rovers of the Caribbean originated on Hispaniola in the seventeenth century who preyed primarily on the Spanish.

bullion—Gold and silver treasure in bars, ingots or coin.

bunkering—Siphoning oil from pipelines and ships into pirate vessels for selling on the black market.

cake—Nigerian term for government-controlled jobs, construction projects, university access, state and national budgets, foreign business deals and oil money that can be funnelled into foreign banks.

canoe/dugout—Native American craft hollowed from a single tree. Used by buccaneers to sneak up on and outmanoeuvre prey.

captain-general—A high-ranking military officer.

caravel—A small, fast, lateen-rigged ship commonly used by the Spanish and Portuguese into the seventeenth century.

careen—Hauling a ship out of the water onto its side for cleaning and repair.

carpenter—A workman responsible for repairing wooden parts of a boat and for plugging cannon ball holes during battle.

***carreira da India*—**The sea route from Lisbon to ports in India, such as Cochin and Goa.

***cartaz* system—**The Portuguese system that forced ships in the Indian Ocean to carry passes or be subject to attack and confiscation by patrolling Portuguese fleets. The intent of the *cartaz* system was to force passing ships into Portuguese-controlled ports where they would have to pay customs duties.

***casado*—**Married settlers in the Portuguese Empire, usually in the Estado da Índia (State of India).

***cimarrón/marrón*—**A runaway African slave living in independent slave communities.

closed-quarters—Reinforced bulkhead with gunports to allow defence against boarders.

commission—Either a letter of reprisal or marque issued by a monarch or their representative to engage in maritime predation.

***corsair/corsario/corso*—**Comes from the Latin word *cursu*, which means to run, track, pursue or course. Hence, the name corsair for those who pursued or 'coursed' at sea. The term is used specifically for Mediterranean pirates from north Africa and generally for any raider sanctioned by some governmental authority.

creole—A person of mixed European and African ancestry.

***daimyo*—**A Japanese feudal lord.

***datu*—**A chief or aristocrat in Southeast Asia.

death by slicing—A Chinese method of execution in which the victim's body would be slowly carved up into 24, 36, 72 or 120 pieces.

***dey*—**Local North African mispronunciation of the Ottoman term bey. The title given to the Ottoman governors of the north African regencies after 1671.

doubloon—A gold Spanish coin.

drumler—A small, fast transport ship favoured by Dutch pirates.

East Indiaman—A large, well-armed merchant ship trading with the East Indies.

fathom—Six feet measured on the length of a weighted cord used to measure the depth of water.

***feitoria* (factory)—**Official overseas Portuguese trading station.

***felucca*—**A small sailing vessel powered by oars or one or two lateen sails that was traditionally used in the Red Sea, the Nile and the eastern Mediterranean.

filibuster/*flibustier*—French sea rovers of the West Indies, often used for nineteenth-century American adventurers who raided in Latin America and sometimes attempted to overthrow Latin American states.

flota—Fleet.

France Antarctique—French settlement at modern Rio de Janeiro from 1555 to 1567 created by the French vice-admiral Nicolas Durand de Villegaignon (1510–1575). It became a haven for Huguenot refugees from France until it was destroyed by the Portuguese.

freebooter—A rover who fights for booty and lives by plunder, direct translation of Dutch term *vryjbuiter* used to refer to the sea bandits who moved between licit and illicit activities.

frigate—A light man-of-war with forecastle and quarterdeck designed for cruising.

galleon—A large oceangoing warship with square-rigging and three or more decks and masts used especially by Spain from the fifteenth to the seventeenth centuries.

galley—A long, low, flat ship with lateen sails and oars used for warfare, trade and piracy in the Mediterranean.

galliots—A single-masted Dutch cargo boat favoured by pirates because it was small and fast.

gallivant—A 40- to 70-tonne, one-sail ship manned by twenty to forty rowers used by Malabar pirates.

***garay*—**A light raiding vessel with oar and sails preferred by the Balangingi in the nineteenth century.

grab—A 150- to 300-tonne, two-masted, shallow draft, and fast sailing ship used by Malabar pirates.

grapeshot—A mass of small round balls, slugs or pieces of metal fired out of a cannon to shred sails and to clear decks of combatants. The effects of grapeshot are much like a modern shotgun, though much more devastating.

grenade—Hollow, round cast-iron ball filled with powder and lit with a fuse used to clear decks of defenders before pirates boarded a vessel.

gunner—A petty officer responsible for maintaining a ship's guns and ammunition.

Hanseatic League—A confederation of north German merchant guilds and towns that dominated the Baltic trade between the late twelfth century and the late sixteenth century.

hardtack—A simple biscuit made of flour and salt used a staple food for sailors.

harquebus—An early matchlock firearm that was inaccurate and dangerous to use.

***hostis humani generi*—**'Enemies of all mankind', used by the Romans and later European jurists to justify violent repression of pirates.

hounds—Wooden projections fitted to the masthead that supported the rigging.

Internationally Recognized Transit Corridor—Established in 2009 in the Gulf of Aden, created by the international coalition tasked with fighting Somali pirates. International naval vessels patrolled the corridor to protect ships from attack.

Iranun/Illanun/Lanun/Illano—Maritime peoples originally from Mindanao who worked as raiders for the Sulu Sultanate.

***jarl*—**Scandinavian term for chief.

***joanga*—**A raiding vessel used by the Iranun for long-distance raids. It measured about 24–27 metres in length.

Jolly Roger—Not used until the eighteenth century, this was a black flag with a grinning skull and cross bones.

jumper—A Somali term for first pirate to board a vessel. His job is to intimidate the crew while the rest of the pirates board.

junk—A Chinese ship of various sizes, very seaworthy with high prows and several sails.

kakap/salisipan/baroto/vinta—A canoe with an outrigger used for inshore raiding in Southeast Asia.

karim—An organization of Jewish merchants in the Red Sea in the thirteenth century who banded together for protection against pirates.

kata-pontistes—A Greek phrase meaning one who throws into the sea.

keelhauling—A common form of torture in which the victim was dragged underneath the ship from side to side.

Kora-Kora—A Moluccan vessel with a high prow and stern, a large deckhouse and outriggers that is sailed and rowed.

koursa—A raid sponsored by Muslim caliphs in the Mediterranean.

kris—A Malaysian and Indonesian short sword or dagger with a heavy wavy-edged blade.

ladrone—English version of the Spanish word *ladrón,* which means thief or robber. Europeans used the term to refer to Chinese pirates in the early nineteenth century.

lanong—A heavily armed vessel with oars and sails preferred by Iranun sea raiders.

larboard—Port or left side of a ship.

lateen sail—A triangular sail.

leeward—Opposite of the direction the wind is blowing.

leistes—Greek word referring to plunder or booty.

letter of marque—A commission granted by a state, usually during wartime, to prey upon enemy shipping and commercial resources.

letter of reprisal—A commission from a state allowing individuals to recover the value of property lost to foreign raiders by raiding ships from the same nation.

lubber—A person not accustomed to life at sea.

mandarin—Technically a Chinese scholar, but the Europeans in China in the nineteenth century used the term to refer to the Chinese state and its officials.

man-of-war—A powerful warship or frigate heavily armed with cannon and propelled by sails but no oars.

Marabouts—Muslim religious leaders in the north African Barbary states.

maroon—A person deliberately or accidentally left on an isolated island or shore.

mast head—The highest part of a ship's mast.

master—Under the captain's direction, the master is responsible for handling and navigating the ship.

mate—An assistant to the master or any other petty officer on board a ship.

merchantman—A trading vessel.

mestizo—A mixed race offspring of American Indian and European parents.

matelotage—A same-sex alliance or marriage between men on Hispaniola either for business or sexual purposes. They often named each other as their heirs in case of death.

mizzen-mast—The mast astern of the main mast.

Morisco—The Spanish term for Muslims who converted to Christianity.

moro—The Spanish term for Muslims.

mother ship—Somali practice of using a larger vessel to tow speedboats out to the target area with two week's worth of supplies. The mother ship becomes the base from which the pirates scout for prey.

mulatto/mulatta—A person of mixed European and African ancestry.

musket—A long-barrelled, smoothbore, muzzle-loading firearm fired from the shoulder.

nao—A three-masted ship.

nira—Nigerian currency equal to about 32¢ in US currency.

Orang-Laut—Malaysian sea peoples and occasional raiders.

panglima—Chief of Balangingi pirate fleets.

paráos—Small, oared ships used by Malabar pirates.

pax romana—Roman peace, refers to the relative stability in the Mediterranean between 27 BCE and 100 CE.

peirates—A Greek pejorative term for raider or plunderer.

penteconter—A Mediterranean vessel with fifty oars, a ram and a deck. Over time, these ships grew larger with greater numbers of oarsmen for ramming power.

phantom ships—Hijacked ships that are repainted, renamed and given false registrations so they can be resold or used to smuggle drugs or illegal immigrants.

pickling—A torture technique often applied after sweating in which the victim was stuffed into a barrel filled with cockroaches and left to 'pickle' in the hot tropical sun.

piece of eight—Spanish silver coin worth eight *reales*.

pilot—Someone who is familiar with local sailing conditions who navigates the ship through shoals, sandbars, etc.

pinnace—A light man-of-war usually with a round belly and square stern that was used for scouting and coastal forays.

piracy—Seaborne banditry that can manifest itself as parasitic, episodic,

intrinsic or some combination of the above, given the specific historical and cultural context in which it was practised.

piragua—A galley-like boat made from an extra wide dugout canoe used by buccaneers in the Caribbean, often fitted with a mast.

pirata—A Latin word referring to maritime plunderers from which our modern term pirate descends.

port—A hole in the side of the ship where the guns were pushed out when ready to fire.

praedo—A Latin word meaning either bandit or pirate.

prahu—A Malaysian word for a sailing craft.

prao, proe, prow—A Malaysian boat with sharp bow and stern and a triangular sail.

privateer—A legally sanctioned sea rover who operated with a licence or commission from a government. The term first emerged to justify the English acquisition of Jamaica and became an official term in 1671.

prize—A captured vessel.

quartermaster—On a pirate ship, the quartermaster oversaw food and clothing disbursement, but was also supposed to represent the interests of the crew.

Raja—A Hindu term for ruler.

recoes—A mule train.

renegade/renegado—A deserter who switches sides and serves against the former side.

rōnin—An unattached Japanese samurai who has no lord or master.

roundshot—A cannon ball.

saligis—A sharpened wooden or bamboo spear used by raiders in Southeast Asia.

salisipan—A canoe-like craft with outriggers used for coastal raiding in Southeast Asia.

Saxon Shore System—Third-century series of Roman forts along both sides of the English Channel to suppress Saxon and Frankish pirates.

schooner—A two-masted ship with square sails of the eighteenth century.

sea dog—Used to refer to English sea bandits of the Elizabethan era.

shallop—A large, strong utility ship with one or more masts that could carry cannon.

shopping—A method used by pirates in the Straits of Malacca in which the pirates board ships, seize the crew's pay and other valuables until each one of them acquired a predetermined amount of cash.

skiff—A light ship's boat propelled by oars.

sloop—A swift and manoeuvrable single-masted ship with fore and aft rigged sails.

square-rigged—Sails set at right angles from horizontal yard arms attached to the masts of a ship.

starboard—The right side of a ship.

stern—The rear of the ship.

storax—Resin from the oriental sweetgum tree used as a fragrance.

swashbuckler—A rascal, bully or ruffian, usually armed with a sword, who is given to swaggering and boasting.

sweating—A torture technique in which the victim was forced to run naked through a gauntlet of the crew who stabbed him with sharp objects until he 'sweats' blood.

swivel guns—Usually a small gun or cannon mounted on a forked stand that allows it to move freely, giving it a much greater range of motion than fixed cannon.

tacking—Sailing ships cannot sail into the wind, but they can sail in that direction by sailing at an angle to the wind in a zig-zag fashion.

tael—A measure of weight in China and Southeast Asia roughly equal to 40 grams.

taïfa al-raïs—Joint-stock companies organized by Muslim corsairs of north African city-states that drew investors from every level of society.

Tierra Firme, province of—Referred to Spain's mainland colonies along the north coast of South America.

tomin—A Spanish silver coin worth one-eighth of a *castellano*.

Treaty of Alcáçovas—A treaty of 1479 between Spain and Portugal in which Spain received sole control over the conquest and colonization of the Canary Islands and Portugal received exclusive rights to exploit the coasts of Africa.

Treaty of Cateau-Cambrésis—A treaty of 1559 between France and Spain that created the practice of 'no peace beyond the line' west of the prime meridian and south of the Tropic of Cancer. The agreement allowed them carry on low-level warfare in the Caribbean without starting wars in Europe.

Treaty of Tordesillas—An agreement of 1494 that drew a line in the Atlantic about 2,000 kilometres west of the Cape Verde Islands. Portugal retained rights to exploit the non-European regions east of the line and Spain everything west of it.

tripang—A Malay word for sea cucumber.

turn Turk—A Christian phrase for Christians who abandoned Christianity to join Islam. Usually applied to Christian renegades in north Africa.

VHF radio—A short range ship-to-ship or ship-to-shore radio with a range of about 20 miles.

Victual Brothers—A guild of privateers who raided the Hanseatic shipping in the North Sea and the Baltic in the late fourteenth century.

waegu—rioters, a Korean term for Japanese pirates.

weather-gauge—In a sea battle a ship that is upwind of another ship is said to have the weather gauge because it can manoeuvre freely towards a ship that is downwind of it.

windward—The direction from which the wind is blowing, or facing the wind.

wokou—A Chinese term that combines characters for dwarf, a pejorative term for the Japanese and one for bandit. It became a catchall term used by the educated land-based elite to describe non-Chinese barbarians. Though the term referred to Japanese pirates, they were mostly Chinese.

woolding—A form of torture using a rope tied around the head that was twisted with a stick to cause unbearable suffering that might even force the eyeballs to bulge from their sockets.

SELECTED
BIBLIOGRAPHY AND
FURTHER READING

Abu-Lughod, Janel L. *Before European Hegemony: The World-System, A.D. 1250–1350*. New York: Oxford University Press, 1989.

Amirell, Stefan Eklöf and Leos Müller, eds. *Persistent Piracy: Maritime Violence and State-Formation in Global Historical Perspective*. New York: Palgrave, 2014.

Amirell, Stefan Eklöf and Leos Müller. 'Introduction: Persistent Piracy in World History'. In *Persistent Piracy: Maritime Violence and State-Formation in Global Historical Perspective*, edited by Stefan Eklöf Amirell and Leos Müller, 1–23. New York: Palgrave, 2014.

Anderson, John L. 'Piracy and World History: An Economic Perspective on Maritime Predation'. *Journal of World History* 6, no. 2 (1995): 175–199.

Anderson, John L. 'Piracy in the Eastern Seas, 1750–1850: Some Economic Implications'. In *Pirates and Privateers: New Perspectives on the War on Trade in the Eighteenth and Nineteenth Centuries*, edited by David J. Starkey, et al., 87–105. Exeter: University of Exeter Press, 1997.

Andrade, Tonio. 'The Company's Chinese Pirates: How the Dutch East India Company Tried to Lead a Coalition of Pirates to War against China, 1621–1662'. *Journal of World History* 15, no. 4 (December 2004): 415–444.

Andrade, Tonio and Xing Hang. 'Introduction: The East Asian Maritime Realm in Global History, 1500–1700'. In *Sea Rovers, Silver, and Samurai: Maritime East Asia in Global History, 1550–1700*, edited by Tonio Andrade and Xing Hang, 1–27. Honolulu: University of Hawai'i Press, 2016.

Andrade, Tonio and Xing Hang. *Sea Rovers, Silver, and Samurai: Maritime East Asia in Global History, 1550–1700*. Honolulu: University of Hawai'i Press, 2016.

Andrews, George Reid. *Afro-Latin America, 1800–2000*. Oxford: Oxford University Press, 2004.

Andrews, Kenneth R. *Elizabethan Privateering: English Privateering during the Spanish War 1585–1603*. Cambridge: University of Cambridge Press, 1964.

Antony, Robert J. ed. *Elusive Pirates, Pervasive Smugglers: Violence and Clandestine Trade in the Greater China Sea*. Hong Kong: Hong Kong University Press, 2010.

Antony, Robert J. 'Introduction: The Shadowy World of the Greater China Seas'. In *Elusive Pirates, Pervasive Smugglers: Violence and Clandestine Trade in the Greater China Sea*, edited by Robert J. Antony, 1–14. Hong Kong: Hong Kong University Press, 2010.

Antony, Robert J. *Like Froth Floating on the Sea: The World of Pirates and Seafarers in Late Imperial South China*. Berkeley: University of California Press, 2003.

Antony, Robert J. 'Maritime Violence and State Formation in Vietnam: Piracy and the Tay Son Rebellion, 1771–1802'. In *Persistent Piracy: Maritime Violence and State-Formation in Global Historical Perspective*, edited by Stefan Eklöf Amirell and Leos Müller, 113–130. New York: Palgrave Macmillan, 2014.

Antony, Robert J. 'Peasants, Heroes, and Brigands: The Problems of Social Banditry in Early Nineteenth-Century South China'. *Modern China* 15, no. 2 (April 1989): 123–148.

Antony, Robert J. 'Piracy and the Shadow Economy in the South China Sea, 1780–1810'. In *Elusive Pirates, Pervasive Smugglers: Violence and Clandestine Trade in the Greater China Sea*, edited by Robert J. Antony, 99–114. Hong Kong: Hong Kong University Press, 2010.

Antony, Robert J. 'Piracy on the South China Coast through Modern Times'. In *Piracy and Maritime Crime: Historical and Modern Case Studies*, edited by Bruce A. Elleman, et al., 35–50. Newport, RI: Naval War College Press, 2010.

Antony, Robert J. *Pirates in the Age of Sail*. New York: W. W. Norton & Co., Inc., 2007.

Antony, Robert J. 'Trade, Piracy, and Resistance in the Gulf of Tonkin in the Seventeenth Century'. In *Sea Rovers, Silver, and Samurai: Maritime East Asia in Global History, 1550–1700*, edited by Tonio Andrade and Xing Hang, 312–334. Honolulu: University of Hawai'i Press, 2016.

Appleby, John C. 'Women and Piracy in Ireland: From Gráinne O'Malley to Anne Bonny'. In *Bandits at Sea: A Pirates Reader*, edited by C.R. Pennell, 283–298. New York: New York University Press, 2001.

Atsushi, Ota. '"Pirates or Entrepreneurs?" The Migration and Trade of Sea People in Southwest Kalimatan, c. 1770–1820'. *Indonesia*, no. 90 (2010): 67–95.

Atsushi, Ota. 'The Business of Violence: Piracy Around Riau, Lingga, and Singapore, 1820–1840'. In *Elusive Pirates, Pervasive Smugglers: Violence and Clandestine Trade in the Greater China Seas*, edited by Robert J. Antony, 127–142. Hong Kong: Hong Kong University Press, 2010.

Babits, Lawrence E., et al. 'Pirate Imagery'. In *X Marks the Spot: The Archaeology of Piracy*, edited by Russell K. Showronek and Charles R. Ewen, 271–281. Gainesville: University Press of Florida, 2006.

Batchelor, Robert. 'Maps, Calendars, and Diagrams: Space and Time in Seventeenth-Century Maritime East Asia'. In *Sea Rovers, Silver, and Samurai: Maritime East Asia in Global History, 1550–1700*, edited by Tonio Andrade and Xing Hang, 86–113. Honolulu: University of Hawai'i Press, 2016.

Bateman, Sam. 'Confronting Maritime Crime in Southeast Asian Waters: Reexamining "Piracy" in the Twenty-First Century'. In *Piracy and Maritime Crime: Historical and Modern Case Studies*, edited by Bruce A. Elleman, et al., 137–156. Newport, RI: Naval War College Press, 2010.

Bateman, Sam. 'The Threat of Maritime Terrorism and Piracy Is Exaggerated'. In *Piracy on the High Seas*, edited by Noah Berlatsy, 95–107. Detroit, MI: Greenhaven, 2010.

Beal, Clifford. *Quelch's Gold: Piracy, Greed, and Betrayal in Colonial New England*. London: Praeger, 2007.

Bialuschewski, Arne. 'Pirates, Slavers, and the Indigenous Population of Madagascar, c. 1690–1715'. *The International Journal of African Historical Studies* 38, no. 3 (2005): 401–425.

Biddle, M. and B. Kjølby-Biddle. 'Repton and the Vikings'. *Antiquity* 66 (1992): 36–51.

Bjork, David K. 'Piracy in the Baltic, 1375–1398'. *Speculum* 18, no. 1 (January 1943): 39–68.

Boot, Max. 'Pirates, Then and Now: How Piracy Was Defeated in the Past and Can Be Again'. *Foreign Affairs* 88, no. 4 (July/August 2009): 94–107.

Boxer, C.R. *The Dutch Seaborne Empire, 1600–1800*. Middlesex: Penguin Books, 1965.

Bracewell, Wendy. 'Women among the Uskoks of Senj: Literary Images and Reality'. In *Bandits at Sea: A Pirates Reader*, edited by C.R. Pennell, 321–334. New York: New York University Press, 2001.

Braudel, Fernand. *The Mediterranean and the Mediterranean World in the Age of Phillip II*. Translated by Siân Reynolds. Berkeley: University of California Press, 1995.

Bromley, J.S. 'Outlaws at Sea, 1660–1720: Liberty, Equality, and Fraternity among the Caribbean Freebooters'. In *Bandits at Sea: A Pirates Reader*, edited by C.R. Pennell, 169–194. New York: New York University Press, 2001.

Brooks, E.W. 'The Arabs in Asia Minor (641–750), from Arabic Sources'. *The Journal of Hellenic Studies* 18 (1898): 182–208.

Brooks, George E. and Norman Bennet, eds. *New England Merchants in Africa: A History through Documents, 1802–1865*. Brookline, MA: Boston University Press, 1965.

Bruce, T. 'Piracy as Statecraft: The Mediterranean Policies of the Fifth/Eleventh-Century Taifa of Denia'. *Al-Masāq* 22, no. 3 (2010): 235–248.

Brunn, Per. 'The Viking Ship'. *Journal of Coastal Research* 13, no. 4 (Autumn 1997): 1282–1289.

Bueger, Christian. 'Practice, Pirates and Coast Guards: The Grand Narrative of Somali Piracy'. *Third World Quarterly* 34, no. 10 (2013): 1811–1827.

Burg, Barry Richard. *Sodomy and the Perception of Evil: English Sea Rovers in the Seventeenth-Century Caribbean*. New York: New York University Press, 1983.

Burg, Barry Richard. *Sodomy and the Pirate Tradition: English Sea Rovers in the Seventeenth-Century Caribbean*. New York: New York University Press, 1995.

Burg, Barry Richard. 'The Buccaneer Community'. In *Bandits at Sea: A Pirates Reader*, edited by C.R. Pennell, 211–243. New York: New York University Press, 2001.

Burgess, Douglas R., Jr. 'Piracy in the Public Sphere: The Henry Every Trails and the Battle for Meaning in Seventeenth-Century Print Culture'. *Journal of British Studies* 48, no. 4 (October 2009): 887–913.

Burgess, Douglas R., Jr. *The Pirate's Pact: The Secret Alliances between History's Most Notorious Buccaneers and Colonial America*. New York: McGraw Hill, 2008.

Burgess, Douglas R., Jr. *The Politics of Piracy: Crime and Civil Disobedience in Colonial America*. Lebanon, New Hampshire: University Press of New England, 2014.

Burgess, Douglas R., Jr. *The World for Ransom: Piracy Is Terrorism, Terrorism Is Piracy*. Amherst, NY: Prometheus Books, 2010.

Burnett, John S. *Dangerous Waters: Modern Piracy and Terror on the High Seas*. New York: Penguin Group, 2002.

Calanca, Paola. 'Piracy and Coastal Security in Southeastern China, 1600–1780'. In *Elusive Pirates, Pervasive Smugglers: Violence and Clandestine Trade in the Greater China Seas*, edited by Robert J. Antony, 85–98. Hong Kong: Hong Kong University Press, 2010.

Campbell, Penny. 'A Modern History of the International Legal Definition of Piracy'. In *Piracy and Maritime Crime: Historical and Modern Case Studies*, edited by Bruce A. Elleman, et al., 19–34. Newport, RI: Naval War College Press, 2010.

Canfora, Luciano. *Julius Caesar: The Life and Times of the People's Dictator*. Translated by Marian Hill and Kevin Windle. Berkeley: University of California Press, 1999.

Chambers, Anne. *Ireland's Pirate Queen: The True Story of Grace O'Malley*. New York: MJF Books, 2003.

Chaudhuri, K.N. *Trade and Civilisation in the Indian Ocean: An Economic History from the Rise of Islam to 1750*. Cambridge: Cambridge University Press, 1985.

Chakravarti, Ranabir. 'Horse Trade and Piracy at Tana (Thana, Maharashtra, India): Gleanings from Marco Polo'. *Journal of the Economic and Social History of the Orient* 34, no. 3 (1991): 159–182.

Chet, Guy. *The Ocean Is a Wilderness: Atlantic Piracy and the Limits of State Authority, 1688–1856*. Amherst: University of Massachusetts, 2014.

Chin, James K. 'A Hokkien Maritime Empire in the East and South China Seas, 1620–1680'. In *Persistent Piracy: Maritime Violence and State-Formation in Global Historical Perspective*, edited by Stefan Eklöf Amirell and Los Müller, 93–112. New York: Palgrave Macmillan, 2014.

Chin, James K. 'Merchants, Smugglers, and Pirates: Multinational Clandestine Trade on the South China Coast, 1520–1550'. In *Elusive Pirates, Pervasive Smugglers: Violence and Clandestine Trade in the Greater China Seas*, edited by Robert J. Antony, 43–58. Hong Kong: Hong Kong University Press, 2010.

Christensen, Arne Emil. 'Ships and Navigation'. In *Vikings: The North Atlantic Saga*, edited by William W. Fitzhugh and Elisabeth I. Ward, 86–97. Washington, DC: Smithsonian Books, 2000.

Clarke, H.B. 'The Vikings'. In *Medieval Warfare: A History*, edited by Maurice Keen, 36–58. Oxford: Oxford University Press, 1999.

Clulow, Adam. 'Determining the Law of the Sea: The Long History of the Breukelen Cast, 1657–1662'. In *Sea Rovers, Silver, and Samurai: Maritime East Asia in Global History, 1550–1700*, edited by Tonio Andrade and Xing Hang, 181–201. Honolulu: University of Hawai'i Press, 2016.

Clulow, Adam. 'Like Lambs in Japan and Devils Outside Their Land: Diplomacy, Violence, and Japanese Merchants in Southeast Asia'. *Journal of World History* 24, no. 2 (June 2013): 335–358.

Coito, Joel Christopher. 'Pirate vs. Private Security: Commercial Shipping, the Montreux Document, and the Battle for the Gulf of Aden'. *California Law Review* 101, no. 1 (February 2013): 173–226.

Cook, Judith. *Pirate Queen: The Life of Grace O'Malley, 1530–1603*. Cork: Mercier Press, 2004.

Cordingly, David. *Under the Black Flat: The Romance and the Reality of Life among the Pirates*. New York: Random House, 1995.

Cowley, Malcolm. 'The Sea Jacobins'. *New Republic* (1 February 1933): 327–329.

Cunliffe, Barry. *Europe between the Oceans: Themes and Variations, 9000 BC–AD 1000*. New Haven, CT: Yale University Press, 2008.

Daniels, Christopher L. *Somali Piracy and Terrorism in the Horn of Africa*. Lanham, MD: Scarecrow Press, 2012.

Davies, Charles E. *Blood-Red Arab Flag: An Investigation into Qasimi Piracy, 1797–1820*. Exeter: University of Exeter Press, 1997.

Davisson, William I. 'Essex County Price Trends: Money and Markets in 17th Century Massachusetts'. *Essex Institute Historical Collections* 103, no. 2 (April 1967): 144–185.

Dell, Harry J. 'The Origin and Nature of Illyrian Piracy'. *Historia: Zeitschrift für Alte Geschichte*, Bd. 16, H. 3 (July 1967): 344–358.

Disney, A.R. *A History of Portugal and the Portuguese Empire: The Portuguese Empire*, 2 vols. Cambridge: Cambridge University Press, 2009.

Dow, George Francis and John Henry Edmonds. *The Pirates of the New England Coast, 1630–1730*. New York: Dover Publications, Inc., 1996.

Drake, Francis. *Sir Francis Drake Revised: Calling upon This Dull or Effeminate Age, to Follow His Noble Steps for Gold and Silver*. London: Nicholas Bourne, 1653.

Druett, Joan. *She Captains: Heroines and Hellions of the Sea*. New York: Simon & Schuster Touchstone, 2000.

Dutton, George. *The Tay Son Uprising: Society and Rebellion in Eighteenth-Century Vietnam*. Honolulu: University of Hawai'i Press, 2006.

Earle, Peter. *The Pirate Wars*. New York: Thomas Dunne Books, 2003.

Eichstaedt, Peter. *Pirate State: Inside Somalia's Terrorism at Sea*. Chicago, IL: Lawrence Hill Books, 2010.

Eklöf, Stefan. *Pirates in Paradise: A Modern History of Southeast Asia's Maritime Marauders*. Leifsgade: NIAS Press, 2006.

Elleman, Bruce A. 'The Looting and Rape of Vietnamese Boat People'. In *Piracy and Maritime Crime: Historical and Modern Case Studies*, edited by Bruce A. Elleman, et al., 97–108. Newport, RI: Naval War College Press, 2010.

Elleman, Bruce A. 'The Taiping Rebellion, Piracy, and the Arrow War'. In *Piracy and Maritime Crime: Historical and Modern Case Studies*, edited by Bruce A. Elleman, et al., 51–63. Newport, RI: Naval War College Press, 2010.

Elleman, Bruce A. et al. 'Introduction'. In *Piracy and Maritime Crime: Historical and Modern Case Studies* edited by Bruce A. Elleman, et al., 1–18. Newport, RI: Naval War College Press, 2010.

Elleman, Bruce A., et al., eds. *Piracy and Maritime Crime: Historical and Modern Case Studies*. Newport, RI: Naval War College Press, 2010.

'Ending Piracy in Nigerian Waters'. *This Day Live* (5 January 2018).

'Excerpts from an Islamic History of the Maldives, Early Eighteenth Century'. In *Portuguese Encounters with Sri Lanka and the Maldives*, edited by Chandra R. de Silva. Burlington, MA: Ashgate Publishing Company, 2009.

Foucault, Michel. *Discipline and Punish: The Birth of the Prison*. New York: Vintage Book, 1977.

Fuchs, Barbara. 'Faithless Empires: Pirates, Renegadoes, and the English Nation'. *ELH* 67, no. 1 (Spring, 2000): 45–69.

Gabbert, Janice J. 'Piracy in the Early Hellenistic Period: A Career Open to Talents'. *Greece & Rome* 33, no. 2 (October 1986): 156–163.

Gaffey, Conor. 'Pirate Attacks on the Rise in West Africa as Nigerian Militants Take to the Seas', *Newsweek* (2 May 2017) http://www.newsweek.com/nigeria-piracy-somali-pirates-592976

Gaynor, Jennifer L. 'Piracy in the Offing: The Law of Lands and the Limits of Sovereignty at Sea'. *Anthropological Quarterly* 85, no. 3 (Summer 2012): 817–857.

Greene, Molly. *Catholic Pirates and Greek Merchants: A Maritime History of the Mediterranean*. Princeton, NJ: Princeton University Press, 2010.

Guerreiro, Luis R. *O Grande Livro da Pirataria e do Corso*. Lisbon: Círculo de Leitores, 1996.

Hampden, John, ed. *Francis Drake, Privateer: Contemporary Narratives and Documents*. Tuscaloosa: University of Alabama Press, 1972.

Hanna, Mark G. *Pirate Nests and the Rise of the British Empire, 1570–1740*. Chapel Hill: University of North Carolina Press, 2015.

Hansen, Stig Jarle. 'Piracy, Security and State-Formation in the Early Twenty-First Century'. In *Persistent Piracy: Maritime Violence and State-Formation in Global Historical Perspective*, edited by Stefan Eklöf Amirell and Leos Müller, 175–188. New York: Palgrave, 2014.

Healey, Christopher J. 'Tribes and States in "Pre-Colonial" Borneo: Structural Contradictions and the Generation of Piracy'. *Social Analysis: The International Journal of Social and Cultural Practice*, no. 18 (December 1985): 3–39.

Hedeager, Lotte. 'From Warrior to Trade Economy'. In *Vikings: The North Atlantic Saga*, edited by William W. Fitzhugh and Elisabeth I. Ward, 84–85. Washington, DC: Smithsonian Books, 2000.

Heller-Roazen, Daniel. *The Enemy of All: Piracy and the Law of Nations*. New York: Zone Books, 2009.

Hellyer, Robert. 'Poor but Not Pirates: The Tsushima Domain and Foreign Relations in Early Modern Japan'. In *Elusive Pirates, Pervasive Smugglers: Violence and Clandestine Trade in the Greater China Seas*, edited by Robert J. Antony, 115–126. Hong Kong: Hong Kong University Press, 2010.

Ho, Dahpon David. 'The Burning Shore: Fujian and the Coastal Depopulation, 1661–1683'. In *Sea Rovers, Silver, and Samurai: Maritime East Asia in Global History, 1550–1700*, edited by Tonio Andrade and Xing Hang, 260–289. Honolulu: University of Hawai'i Press, 2016.

Hobsbawm, Eric. *Bandits*. New York: Delacorte Press, 1969.

Hooper, Jane. 'Pirates and Kings: Power on the Shores of Early Modern Madagascar and the Indian Ocean'. *Journal of World History* 22, no. 2 (June 2011): 215–242.

Hourani, George F. *Arab Navigation in the Indian Ocean in Ancient and Early Medieval Times*. Revised and expanded by John Carswell. Princeton, NY: Princeton University Press, 1995.

http://beaufortpiratesrevenge.com/index.html

http://circleten.org/sites/circle10.org/files/captains_cove_element.pdf

http://www.dnaindia.com/entertainment/report-pirates-were-rock-stars-of-the-18th-century-1100331

Hutchins, Todd Emerson. 'Structuring a Sustainable Letters of Marque Regime: How Commissioning Privateers Can Defeat the Somali Pirates'. *California Law Review* 99, no. 3 (June 2011): 819–884.

Isorena, Efren B. 'The Visayan Raiders of the China Coast, 1174–1190 A.D'. *Philippine Quarterly of Culture and Society* 32, no. 2 (June 2004): 73–95.

Jamieson, Alan G. *Lords of the Sea: A History of the Barbary Corsairs*. London: Reaktion Books, 2012.

Jesch, Judith. *Women in the Viking Age*. Woodbrigde: The Boydell Press, 1991.

Johnson, Charles. *A General History of the Robberies and Murders of the Most Notorious Pyrates*. London: C. Rivington, J. Lacy, 1724.

Johnson, Lyman L. and Sonya Lipsett-Rivera, eds. *The Faces of Honor: Sex, Shame, and Violence in Colonial Latin America*. Albuquerque: University of New Mexico Press, 1998.

Kaiser, Wolfgang and Guillaume Calafat. 'Violence, Protection and Commerce: Corsairing and *ars piratica* in the Early Modern Mediterranean'. In *Persistent Piracy: Maritime Violence and State-Formation in Global Historical Perspective*, edited by Stefan Eklöf Amirell and Leos Müller, 69–92. New York: Palgrave, 2014.

Kelsey, Harry. *Sir Francis Drake: The Queen's Pirate*. New Haven, CT: Yale University Press, 1998.

Kenji, Igawa. 'At the Crossroads: Limahon and Wakō in the Sixteenth-Century Philippines'. In *Elusive Pirates, Pervasive Smugglers: Violence and Clandestine Trade in the Greater China Seas*, edited by Robert J. Antony, 73–84. Hong Kong: Hong Kong University Press, 2010.

Kennedy, Hugh. *Mongols, Huns and Vikings: Nomads of War*. London: Cassell & Co., 2002.

Kert, Faye. 'Cruising Colonial Waters: The Organization of North American Privateering in the War of 1812'. In *Pirates and Privateers: New Perspectives on the War on Trade in the Eighteenth and Nineteenth Centuries*, edited by David J. Starkey, et al., 141–154. Exeter: University of Exeter Press, 1997.

Kinkor, Kenneth J. 'Black Men under the Black Flag'. In *Bandits at Sea: A Pirates Reader*, edited by C.R. Pennell, 195–210. New York: New York University Press, 2001.

Koburger, Charles W., Jr. 'Selamat Datang, Kapitan: Post-World War II Piracy in the South China Sea'. In *Piracy and Maritime Crime: Historical and Modern Case Studies*, edited by Bruce A. Elleman, et al., 65–77. Newport, RI: Naval War College Press, 2010.

Kooistra, Paul. 'Criminals as Heroes: Linking Symbol to Structure'. *Symbolic Interaction* 13, no. 2 (Fall 1990): 217–239.

Kurrild-Klitgaard, Peter and Gert Tinggaard Svendsen. 'Rational Bandits: Plunder, Public Goods, and the Vikings'. *Public Choice* 117, no. 3/4 (December 2003): 255–272.

Lambert, Andrew. 'The Limits of Naval Power: The Merchant Brig *Three Sisters*, Riff Pirates, and British Battleship'. In *Piracy and Maritime Crime: Historical and Modern Case Studies*, edited by Bruce A. Elleman, et al., 173–190. Newport, RI: Naval War College Press, 2010.

Leeson, Peter T. 'An-*arrgh*-chy: The Law and Economics of Pirate Organization'. *Journal of Political Economy* 115, no. 6 (December 2007): 1049–1094.

Lehr, Peter. *Violence at Sea: Piracy in the Age of Global Terrorism*. New York: Routledge, 2007.

Levathes, Louise. *When China Ruled the Seas: The Treasure Fleet of the Dragon Throne*. New York: Oxford University Press, 1994.

Linebaugh, Peter and Marcus Rediker. *The Many-Headed Hydra: Sailors, Slaves, Commoners, and the Hidden History of the Revolutionary Atlantic*. Boston, MA: Beacon Press, 2000.

Lis, Carolin. 'Maritime Piracy in Southeast Asia'. *Southeast Asian Affairs* (2003): 62–68.

Little, Benerson. *Pirate Hunting: The Fight against Pirates, Privateers, and Sea Raiders from Antiquity to the Present*. Washington, DC: Potomac Books, Inc., 2010.

Little, Benerson. *The Sea Rover's Practice: Pirate Tactics and Techniques, 1630–1730*. Washington, DC: Potomac Books, Inc., 2005.

Loyré, Ghislaine. 'Living and Working Conditions in Philippine Pirate Communities, 1750–1850'. In *Pirates and Privateers: New Perspectives on the War on Trade in the Eighteenth and Nineteenth Centuries*, edited by David J. Starkey, et al., 69–86. Exeter: University of Exeter Press, 1997.

Lunsford, Virginia West. *Piracy and Privateering in the Golden Age Netherlands*. New York: Palgrave Macmillan, 2005.

MacKay, Joseph. 'Pirate Nations: Maritime Pirates as Escape Societies in Late Imperial China'. *Social Science History* 37, no. 4 (Winter 2013): 551–573.

Malekandathil, Pius. 'From Merchant Capitalists to Corsairs: The Response of the Muslim Merchants of Malabar to the Portuguese Commercial Expansion (1498-1600)'. *Portuguese Studies Review* 12, no. 2 (2004): 75–96.

Mallari, Francisco and Francisco Malari. 'Camarines Towns: Defenses against Moro Pirates'. *Philippine Quarterly of Culture and Society* 17, no. 1 (March 1989): 41–66.

Matthew, David. 'The Cornish and Welsh Pirates in the Reign of Elizabeth'. *English Historical Review* 39, no. 155 (July 1924): 337–348.

Mayor, Adrienne. *Greek Fire, Poison Arrows and Scorpion Bombs: Biological and Chemical Warfare in the Ancient World*. New York: Overlook Press, 2003.

McDonald, Kevin P. *Pirates, Merchants, Settlers and Slaves: Colonial America and the Indo-Atlantic World*. Oakland: University of California Press, 2015.

'Memorandum on the Maldives Islands, 1645'. In *Portuguese Encounters with Sri Lanka and the Maldives*, edited by Chandra R. de Silva, 217–221. Burlington, MA: Ashgate Publishing Company, 2009.

Murray, Dian H. 'Cheng I Sao in Fact and Fiction'. In *Bandits at Sea: A Pirates Reader*, edited by C.R. Pennell, 253–282. New York: New York University Press, 2001.

Murray, Dian H. 'Living and Working Conditions in Chinese Pirate Communities, 1750–1850'. In *Pirates and Privateers: New Perspectives on the War on Trade in the Eighteenth and Nineteenth Centuries*, edited by David J. Starkey, et al., 47–68. Exeter: University of Exeter Press, 1997.

Murray, Dian H. *Pirates of the South China Coast, 1790-1810*. Stanford, CA: Stanford University Press, 1987.

Murray, Dian H. 'The Practice of Homosexuality among the Pirates of Late Eighteenth-and Early Nineteenth-Century China'. In *Bandits at Sea: A Pirates Reader*, edited by C.R. Pennell, 244–252. New York: New York University Press, 2001.

Nadal, Gonçal López. 'Corsairing as a Commercial System: The Edges of Legitimate Trade'. In *Bandits at Sea: A Pirates Reader*, 125–138. New York: New York University Press, 2001.

Nadal, Gonçal López. 'Mediterranean Privateering between the Treaties of Utrecht and Paris, 1715–1856: First Reflections'. In *Pirates and Privateers: New Perspectives on the War on Trade in the Eighteenth and Nineteenth Centuries*, edited by David J. Starkey, et al., 106–125. Exeter: University of Exeter Press, 1997.

'Nigerians living in poverty rise to nearly 61%'. *BBC News* (13 February 2012). http://www.bbc.com/news/world-africa-17015873

Nodland, Arild. 'Guns, Oil, and "Cake": Maritime Security in the Gulf of Guinea'. In *Piracy and Maritime Crime: Historical and Modern Case Studies*, edited by Bruce A. Elleman, et al., 191–206. Newport, RI: Naval War College Press, 2010.

Noonan, Thomas S. 'Why the Vikings First Came to Russia'. *Jahrbücher für Geschichte Osteuropas, Neue Folge*, Bd. 34, H. 3 (1986): 321–348.

Nutting, P. Bradley. 'The Madagascar Connection: Parliament and Piracy, 1690–1701'. *The American Journal of Legal History* 22, no. 3 (July 1978): 202–215.

Obi, Cyril I. 'Enter the Dragon?: Chinese Oil Companies and Resistance in the Niger Delta'. *Review of African Political Economy* 35, no. 117 (September 2008): 417–434.

Oceans beyond Piracy 2016 Report. http://oceansbeyondpiracy.org/reports/sop/east-africa

Oceans beyond Piracy. http://oceansbeyondpiracy.org/reports/sop

Ormerod, Henry A. *Piracy in the Ancient World*. Liverpool: University of Liverpool Press, 1924.

Osinowo, Adeniyi. 'Combating Piracy in the Gulf of Guinea'. *Africa Security Brief: A Publication of the Africa Center for Strategic Studies*, no. 30 (February 2015): 1–8.

Paine, Lincoln. *The Sea and Civilization: A Maritime History of the World*. New York: Alfred A. Knopf, 2013.

Panikkar, Kavalam Madhava. *India and the Indian Ocean: An Essay on the Influence of Sea Power on Indian History*. London: Allen and Unwin, 1945.

Parry, J.H. *The Spanish Seaborne Empire*. New York: Alfred A. Knopf, 1969.

Patton, Robert H. *Patriot Pirates: The Privateer War for Freedom and Fortune in the American Revolution*. New York: Vintage Books, 2008.

Pearson, Andrew. 'Piracy in Late Roman Britain: A Perspective from the Viking Age'. *Britannia* 37 (2006): 337–353.

Pearson, M.N. *The Portuguese in India*. Cambridge: Cambridge University Press, 1990.

Pennell, C.R. 'The Geography of Piracy: Northern Morocco in the Mid-Nineteenth Century'. In *Bandits at Sea: A Pirates Reader*, edited by C.R. Pennell, 55–68. New York: New York University Press, 2001.

Pennell, C.R., ed. *Bandits at Sea: A Pirates Reader*. New York: New York University Press, 2001.

Pérez-Mallaína, Pablo E. *Spain's Men of the Sea: Daily Life on the Indies Fleets in the Sixteenth Century*. Translated by Carla Rahn Phillips. Baltimore, MD: The Johns Hopkins University Press, 1998.

Pérotin-Dumon, Anne. 'The Pirate and the Emperor: Power and the Law on the Seas, 1450–1850'. In *Bandits at Sea: A Pirates Reader*, edited by C.R. Pennell, 25–54. New York: New York University Press, 2001.

Peters, Edward. *Torture*. New York: Basil Blackwell, Inc., 1985.

Petrucci, Maria Gracia. 'Pirates, Gunpowder and Christianity in Late Sixteenth-Century Japan'. In *Elusive Pirates, Pervasive Smugglers: Violence and Clandestine Trade in the Greater China Seas*, edited by Robert J. Antony, 59–72. Hong Kong: Hong Kong University Press, 2010.

Piracy and Armed Robbery against Ships: Report for the Period 1 January–31 December 2016. London: ICC International Maritime Bureau, 2017.

Piracy and Armed Robbery against Ships: Report for the Period 1 January–31 December 2017. London: ICC International Maritime Bureau, 2018.

Pistono, Stephen P. 'Henry IV and the English Privateers'. *The English Historical Review* 90, no. 355 (April 1975): 322–330.

Platt, Virginia Bever. 'The East India Company and the Madagascar Slave Trade'. *The William and Mary Quarterly* 26, no. 4 (October 1969): 548–577.

Powers, James F. *A Society Organized for War: The Iberian Municipal Militias in the Central Middle Ages.* Berkeley: University of California Press, 1987.

Prange, Sebastian R. 'A Trade of No Dishonor: Piracy, Commerce and Community in the Western Indian Ocean Twelfth to Sixteenth Century'. *The American Historical Review* 116, no. 5 (December 2011): 1269–1293.

Prange, Sebastian R. 'The Contested Sea: Regimes of Maritime Violence in the Pre-Modern Indian Ocean'. *Journal of Early Modern History* 17 (2013): 9–33.

Price, Neil S. 'Belief and Ritual'. In *Vikings*, edited by G. Williams, et al., 164–195. Copenhagen: National Museum of Denmark, 2013.

Price, Neil S. '"Laid Waste, Plundered, and Burned": Vikings in Frankia'. In *Vikings: The North Atlantic Saga*, edited by William W. Fitzhugh and Elisabeth I. Ward, 116–126. Washington, DC: Smithsonian Books, 2000.

Price, Neil S. 'Ship-Men and Slaughter-Wolves: Pirate Polities in the Viking Age'. In *Persistent Piracy: Maritime Violence and State-Formation in Global Historical Perspective*, edited by Stefan Eklöf Amirell and Leos Müller, 51–68. New York: Palgrave, 2014.

Price, Neil S. 'The Scandinavian Landscape: People and Environment'. In *Vikings: The North Atlantic Saga*, edited by William W. Fitzhugh and Elisabeth I. Ward, 31–41. Washington, DC: Smithsonian Books, 2000.

Pryce, Paul. 'Libya: The Next Pirate Haven?' *Offiziere.ch* (16 June 2016). https://www.offiziere.ch/?p=28054

Ravina, Mark. 'Japan in the Chinese Tribute System'. In *Sea Rovers, Silver, and Samurai: Maritime East Asia in Global History, 1550–1700*, edited by Tonio Andrade and Xing Hang, 353–363. Honolulu: University of Hawai'i Press, 2016.

Raymond, Catherine Zara. 'Piracy and Armed Robbery in the Malacca Strait: A Problem Solved?' In *Piracy and Maritime Crime: Historical and Modern Case Studies*, edited by Bruce A. Elleman, et al., 109–120. Newport, RI: Naval War College Press, 2010.

Rediker, Marcus. *Between the Devil and the Deep Blue Sea: Merchant Seamen, Pirates, and the Anglo-American Maritime World, 1700–1750.* Cambridge: Cambridge University Press, 1987.

Rediker, Marcus. 'Hydrarchy and Libertalia: The Utopian Dimensions of Atlantic Piracy in the Early Eighteenth Century'. In *Pirates and Privateers: New Perspectives on the War on Trade in the Eighteenth and Nineteenth Centuries*, edited by David J. Starkey, et al., 29–46. Exeter: University of Exeter Press, 1997.

Rediker, Marcus. 'Liberty beneath the Jolly Roger: The Lives of Anne Bonny and Mary Read, Pirates'. In *Bandits at Sea: A Pirates Reader*, edited by C.R. Pennell, 299–320. New York: New York University Press, 2001.

Rediker, Marcus. 'The Seaman as Pirate: Plunder and Social Banditry at Sea'. In *Bandits at Sea: A Pirates Reader*, edited by C.R. Pennell, 139–168. New York: New York University Press, 2001.

Rediker, Marcus. *Villains of All Nations: Atlantic Pirates in the Golden Age.* Boston, MA: Beacon Press, 2004.

Reid, Anthony. 'Violence at Sea: Unpacking "Piracy" in the Claims of States over Asian Seas'. In *Elusive Pirates, Pervasive Smugglers: Violence and Clandestine Trade in the Greater China Seas*, edited by Robert J. Antony, 15–26. Hong Kong: Hong Kong University Press, 2010.

Risso, Patricia. 'Cross-Cultural Perceptions of Piracy: Maritime Violence in the Western Indian Ocean and Persian Gulf Region during a Long Eighteenth Century'. *Journal of World History* 12, no. 2 (Fall 2001): 293–319.

Ritchie, Robert C. *Captain Kidd and the War against the Pirates.* Cambridge, MA: Harvard University Press, 1986.

Ritchie, Robert C. 'Government Measures against Piracy and Privateering in the Atlantic Area, 1750–1850'. In *Pirates and Privateers: New Perspectives on the War on Trade in the Eighteenth and Nineteenth Centuries*, edited by David J. Starkey, et al., 10–28. Exeter: University of Exeter Press, 1997.

Robinson, Kenneth R. 'Centering the King of Chosŏn: Aspects of Korean Maritime Diplomacy, 1392–1592'. *The Journal of Asian* Studies 59, no. 1 (February 2000): 109–125.

Rodger, N.A.M. 'The Law and Language of Private Naval Warfare'. *The Mariner's Mirror* 100, no. 1 (February 2014): 5–16.

Rosengberg, David. 'The Political Economy of Piracy in the South China Sea'. In *Piracy and Maritime Crime: Historical and Modern Case Studies*, edited by Bruce A. Elleman, et al., 79–96. Newport, RI: Naval War College Press, 2010.

Rugua, Zhao. *Chau Ju-Kua: His Work on the Chinese and Arab Trade in the Twelfth and Thirteenth Centuries (Chu-fan-chi).* Translated by Friedrich Hirth and William Woodville Rockhill. Saint Petersburg: Printing Office of the Imperial Academy of Sciences, 1911.

Russell, Peter. *Prince Henry 'the Navigator': A Life.* New Haven, CT: Yale University Press, 2000.

Saletore, R.N. *Indian Pirates: From the Earliest Times to the Present Day.* Delhi: Concept Publishing Co., 1978.

Samatar, Adbi Ismail, Mark Lindberg, and Basil Mahayni. 'The Dialectics of Piracy in Somalia: The Rich versus the Poor'. *The Third Quarterly* 31, no. 8 (2010): 1377–1394.

Sawyer, Peter H. 'Scandinavia in the Viking Age'. In *Vikings: The North Atlantic Saga*, edited by William W. Fitzhugh and Elisabeth I. Ward, 27–30. Washington, DC: Smithsonian Books, 2000.

Scahill, Jeremy. *Blackwater: The Rise of the World's Most Powerful Mercenary Army.* New York: Nation Books, 2007.

Sen, Tansen. 'The Formation of Chinese Maritime Networks to Southern Asia, 1200–1450'. In *Journal of the Economic and Social History of the Orient* 49, no. 4 (2006): 421–453.

Senior, C.M. *A Nation of Pirates: English Piracy in Its Heyday.* New York: Crane, Russak & Company, Inc., 1976.

Shaffer, Lynda. 'Southernization'. *Journal of World History* 5, no. 1 (Spring 1994): 1–21.

Shapinsky, Peter D. 'Envoys and Escorts: Representation and Performance among Kozinga's Japanese Pirate Ancestors'. In *Sea Rovers, Silver, and Samurai:*

Maritime East Asia in Global History, 1550–1700, edited by Tonio Andrade and Xing Hang, 38–64. Honolulu: University of Hawai'i Press, 2016.

Shapinsky, Peter D. 'From Sea Bandits to Sea Lords: Nonstate Violence and Pirate Identities in Fifteenth-and Sixteenth-Century Japan'. In *Elusive Pirates, Pervasive Smugglers: Violence and Clandestine Trade in the Greater China Seas,* edited by Robert J. Antony, 27–42. Hong Kong: Hong Kong University Press, 2010.

Shapinsky, Peter D. 'Predators, and Purveyors: Pirates and Commerce in Late Medieval Japan'. *Monumenta Nipponica* 64, no. 2 (Autumn 2009): 273–313.

Shortland, Anja. 'Can We Stop Talking about Somali Piracy Now? A Personal Review of Somali Piracy Studies'. *Peace Econ. Peace Sci. Pub. Pol* 21, no. 4 (2015): 419–431.

Showronek, Russell K. 'X Marks the Spot—Or Does It?: Anthropological Insights into the Origins and Continuity of Fiction and Fact in the Study of Piracy'. In *X Marks the Spot: The Archaeology of Piracy,* edited by Russell K. Showronek and Charles R. Ewen, 282–298. Gainesville: University Press of Florida, 2006.

Showronek, Russell K. and Charles R. Ewen, eds. *X Marks the Spot: The Archaeology of Piracy.* Gainseville: University Press of Florida, 2006.

Shuho, Zuikei and Charlotte von Verschuer. 'Japan's Foreign Relations 1200 to 1392 A.D.: A Translation from "Zenrin Kokuhōki"'. *Monumenta Nipponica* 57, no. 4 (Winter 2002): 413–445.

Singleton, Peter. 'Defining Piracy: The Chung Tam Kwong Case and British Piracy Suppression in China in the Early 1930s'. *The Great Circle* 5, no. 1 (April 1983): 48–63.

Skidmore, Thomas E. *Black into White: Race and Nationality in Brazilian Thought.* London: Duke University Press, 1993.

So, Kwan-wai. *Japanese Piracy in Ming China during the 16th Century.* East Lansing: Michigan State University press, 1975.

Sopher, David E. *The Sea Nomads: A Study Based on the Literature of the Maritime Boat People of Southeast Asia.* Washington, DC: Memoirs of the National Museum, 1965.

Souza, Philip de. 'Piracy in Classical Antiquity: The Origins and Evolution of the Concept'. In *Persistent Piracy: Maritime Violence and State-Formation in Global Historical Perspective,* edited by Stefan Eklöf Amirell and Leos Müller, 24–50. New York: Palgrave, 2014.

Souza, Philip de. *Piracy in the Graeco-Roman World.* Cambridge: Cambridge University Press, 1999.

Souza, Philip de. 'Rome's Contribution to the Development of Piracy'. *Memoirs of the American Academy in Rome* 6 (2008): 71–96.

Stanley, Jo, ed. *Bold in Her Britches: Women Pirates across the Ages.* San Francisco, CA: Pandora, 1995.

Starkey, David J. 'A Restless Spirit: British Privateering Enterprise, 1739–1815'. In *Pirates and Privateers: New Perspectives on the War on Trade in the Eighteenth and Nineteenth Centuries,* edited by David J. Starkey, et al., 126–140. Exeter: University of Exeter Press, 1997.

Starkey, David J. 'Pirates and Markets'. In *Bandits at Sea: A Pirates Reader,* edited by C.R. Pennell, 107–124. New York: New York University Press, 2001.

Starkey, David J. 'The Origins and Regulation of Eighteenth-Century British Privateering'. In *Bandits at Sea: A Pirates Reader,* edited by C.R. Pennell, 69–81. New York: New York University Press, 2001.

Starkey, David J. and Matthew McCarthy. 'A Persistent Phenomenon: Private
Prize-Taking in the British Atlantic World, c. 1540–1856'. In *Persistent Piracy:
Maritime Violence and State-Formation in Global Historical Perspective*, edited
by Stefan Eklöf Amirell and Leos Müller, 131–151. New York: Palgrave, 2014.

Starkey, David J., et al. *Pirates and Privateers: New Perspectives on the War on
Trade in the Eighteenth and Nineteenth Centuries*. Exeter: University of Exeter
Press, 1997.

Subramanian, Lakshmi. *The Sovereign and the Pirate: Ordering Maritime Subjects
in India's Western Littoral*. Oxford: Oxford University Press, 2016.

Swanson, Carl E. 'American Privateering and Imperial Warfare, 1739–1748'. *The
William and Mary Quarterly* 42, no. 3 (July 1985): 357–382.

Thomas, James H. 'Merchants and Maritime Marauders: The East India Company
and the Problem of Piracy in the Eighteenth Century'. *The Great Circle* 36, no.1
(2014): 83–107.

Thomson, Janice E. *Mercenaries, Pirates, and Sovereigns: State-Building and
Extraterritorial Violence in Early Modern Europe*. Princeton, NJ: Princeton
University Press, 1996.

Toussaint, Aguste. 'La course et la Pirateria dans L'Ocean Indien'. In *Course et piraterie:
etudes présentées à la Comission Internationale d'Histoire Maritime à l'occasion
de son XV3 colloque internationale pendent le XIVe Congrès International des
Sciences historiques*, 703–743. Paris: Institut de Recherche et D'Histoire de Textes
Editions du Centre National de la Recherche Scientifique, 1975.

Tröster, Manuel. 'Roman Hegemony and Non-State Violence: A Fresh Look at
Pompey's Campaign against the Pirates'. *Greece & Rome* Series 2 56, no. 1
(April 2009): 14–33.

Turley, Hans. *Rum, Sodomy, and the Lash: Piracy, Sexuality and Masculine
Identity*. New York: New York University Press, 1999.

Turner, Robert F. 'President Thomas Jefferson and the Barbary Pirates'. In *Piracy
and Maritime Crime: Historical and Modern Case Studies*, edited by Bruce A.
Elleman, et al., 157–171. Newport, RI: Naval War College Press, 2010.

Uche, Chibuike. 'Oil, British Interests and the Nigerian Civil War'. *The Journal of
African History* 49, no. 1 (2008): 111–135.

Ulrike, Klausmann, et al. *Women Pirates and the Politics of the Jolly Roger*.
Translated by Nicholas Levis. Montreal: Black Rose Books, 1997.

Vainfas, Ronaldo, ed. *Dicionário do Brasil Colonial, 1500–1808*. Rio de Janeiro:
Editora Objetiva, 2000.

Vidal, John. 'Nigeria's Agony Dwarfs the Gulf Oil Spill. The US and Europe Ignore
It'. *The Observer* (30 May 2010).

Wadsworth, James E. *Agents of Orthodoxy: Honor, Status, and the Inquisition in
Colonial Pernambuco, Brazil*. Lanham, MD: Rowman & Littlefield, 2007.

Wagner, Kim A. 'Thuggee and Social Banditry Reconsidered'. *The Historical
Journal* 50, no. 2 (June 2007): 353–576.

Ward, Allen M. 'Caesar and the Pirates'. *Classical Philology* 70, no. 4 (October
1975): 267–268.

Ward, Ralph T. *Pirates in History*. Baltimore, MD: York Press, Inc., 1974.

Warren, James Francis. *Iranun and Balangingi: Globalization, Maritime Raiding
and the Birth of Ethnicity*. Singapore: Singapore University Press, 2002.

Warren, James Francis. *Pirates and Prostitutes and Pullers: Explorations in the
Ethno-and Social History of Southeast Asia*. Crawley, Western Australia:
University of Western Australia Press, 2008.

Warren, James Francis. 'Slave Markets and Exchange in the Malay World: The Sulu Sultanate, 1770–1878'. *Journal of Southeast Asian Studies* 8, no. 2 (September 1977): 162–175.

Warren, James Francis. 'The Balangingi Samal: "Pirate Wars", Dislocation and Diasporic Identities'. *The Great Circle* 33, no. 2 (2011): 43–65.

Warren, James Francis. *The Sulu Zone, 1768–1898: The Dynamics of External Trade, Slavery, and Ethnicity in the Transformation of a Southeast Asian Maritime State*. Singapore: National University of Singapore, 1981.

Warren, James Francis. 'Trade for Bullion to Trade for Commodities and "Piracy": China, The West and the Sulu Zone, 1768–1898'. In *Persistent Piracy: Maritime Violence and State-Formation in Global Historical Perspective*, edited by Stefan Eklöf Amirell and Leos Müller, 152–174. New York: Palgrave, 2014.

Warren, James Francis. 'Who Were the Balangingi Samal? Slave Raiding and Ethnogenesis in Nineteenth-Century Sulu'. *The Journal of Asia Studies* 37, no. 3 (May 1978): 477–490.

Watts, Michael. 'Imperial Oil: The Anatomy of a Nigerian Oil Insurgency'. *Erdkunde* 62, no. 1 (2008): 27–39.

Weir, Gary E. 'Fish, Family and Profit: Piracy and the Horn of Africa'. In *Piracy and Maritime Crime: Historical and Modern Case Studies*, edited by Bruce A. Elleman, et al., 207–222. Newport, RI: Naval War College Press, 2010.

Wheatley, Paul. *The Golden Khersonese: Studies in the Historical Geography of the Malay Peninsula Before A.D. 1500*. Kuala Lampur: University of Malaya Press, 1961.

Willis, Clive. *China and Macau*. Burlington, MA: Ashgate Publishing Co., 2002.

Yikona, Stuart, et al. *Pirate Trails: Tracking the Illicit Financial Flows from Pirate Activities off the Horn of Africa*. Washington, DC: International Bank for Reconstruction and Development: The World Bank, 2013.

Young, Adam J. and Mark J. Valencia. 'Conflation of Piracy and Terrorism in Southeast Asia: Rectitude and Utility'. *Contemporary Southeast Asia* 25, no. 2 (August 2003): 269–283.

INDEX

Page numbers in **bold** refer to tables; page numbers in *italics* refer to figures; 'n' after a page number indicates the endnote number.